Black British Feminism

Black British Feminism: A Reader is an outstanding collection of classic key texts and new black feminist scholarship. Tracing the crucial developments and debates of the last twenty years, this volume is the first to be entirely dedicated to the writings of black women in a British context.

The essays in this collection bring new critical insights to bear upon analyses of gendered and racialized exclusion, 'black' identity, and social and cultural difference. The specific topics discussed range across 'white feminism'; religious fundamentalism; 'mixed-race' identity; sexuality; cultural hybridity and postcolonial space; educational achievement; autobiography and oral tradition.

This timely and important book is essential reading for students and scholars of cultural studies, women's studies, sociology, literature and postcolonial studies.

Heidi Safia Mirza is Reader in Sociology at South Bank University, London. She is author of *Young, Female and Black* (Routledge 1992).

Black British Feminism

A reader

Edited by Heidi Safia Mirza

London and New York

First published 1997
by Routledge
11 New Fetter Lane, London EC4P 4EE

Simultaneously published in the USA and Canada
by Routledge
29 West 35th Street, New York, NY 10001

Typeset in Palatino by
Ponting–Green Publishing Services, Chesham,
Buckinghamshire
Printed and bound in Great Britain by
TJ International Ltd, Padstow, Cornwall

British Library Cataloguing in Publication Data
A catalogue record for this book is available from the
British Library

Library of Congress Cataloguing in Publication Data
A catalogue record for this book has been requested

ISBN   0–415–15288–7 (hbk)
ISBN   0–415–15289–5 (pbk)

For Asha

who has just learned to count potatoes
and sings in her sleep

and

Hanā

whose journey into happiness
has just begun

Throughout this book the variable presentation of the term Black, black and 'black' is in keeping with the preferred use of the individual authors.

Contents

Contributors

Only contributors of new and commissioned chapters are listed

Sara Ahmed is Lecturer in Women's Studies at Lancaster University. She undertook her doctoral studies at the Centre for Critical Cultural Theory, University of Wales, College of Cardiff from 1991–1994. She is currently working on converting her doctorate into a book, provisionally entitled *Feminist Theory and Postmodernism* (Cambridge University Press, 1998). She has also begun work on another book entitled *Strange Encounters: Embodied Others in Post-Coloniality.*

Magdalene Ang-Lygate's first career was as a computer systems analyst. After obtaining her MLitt in Women's Studies from the University of Strathclyde she has taught Women's Studies and Computing and is currently completing a Ph.D in Sociology. She is co-editor (with Chris Corrin and Millsom Henry) of *Desperately Seeking Sisterhood: Still Challenging and Building* (Taylor & Francis, 1997). Her research interests and publications are about the application of feminist postcolonial theories to empirical sociological research. She is also active as an Executive Member of the Women's Studies Network (UK) Association.

Bibi Bakare-Yusuf has an MA in Women's Studies from the University of Warwick, where she is now working on her Ph.D. Her academic research interests are subcultures, corporeal memory, black women's sexuality and violent eroticism. She has worked for BBC Radio 4 as a researcher and writes poetry and short stories. She dreams of living near the sea.

Gargi Bhattacharyya lives in Birmingham where she teaches Cultural Studies at the oh-so-highbrow University of Birmingham. Cancer, monkey, mammoth meat eater. Bigger than the tallest mountain, faster than the shortest skirts. Looking for justice in unlikely places. Looking for fun in the same. She likes bodies, dinners, dances, cups of tea – and she is trying to wriggle giggle jiggle her way towards a tastier high-tan future.

The shape of **Helen (charles)**'s name is a reflection of the fact that the 'family' names of many black people originate in the nomenclature of slave-owners. Her publications include: 'Whiteness – The Relevance of Politically Colouring the "Non"', in H. Hinds *et al.* (eds) *Working Out: New Directions for Women's Studies* (Falmer, 1992), 'Queer Nigger: Theorizing "White" Activism' in J. Bristow and A. R. Wilson (eds) *Activating Theory: Lesbian, Gay, Bisexual Politics* (Lawrence & Wishart, 1993), '(Not) Compromising: Inter-Skin Colour Relations' in L. Pearce and J. Stacey (eds) *Romance Revisited* (Lawrence & Wishart, 1995), and '"White" Skins, Straight Masks' in D. Jarrett-Macauley (ed.) *Reconstructing Womanhood, Reconstructing Feminism* (Routledge, 1996).

Jayne O. Ifekwunigwe is a Nigerian-Irish-English-Guyanese anthropologist by training and a self-taught visual artist. At the moment she is lecturing in Sociology and Anthropology at the University of East London. She is also working on book length manuscript of her Ph.D thesis, entitled *Scattered Be-longings: The Cultural Paradoxes of 'Race', Gender, Nation* (Routledge, forthcoming). Her future research involves transformations of 'Coloured' identities in post-apartheid South Africa.

Heidi Safia Mirza is Reader in Sociology at South Bank University, London, where she is also Head of Sociology. Her academic career includes teaching Afro-American Studies at Brown University USA, and research on race and gender issues in the Caribbean and Britain. She is the author of *Young, Female and Black* (Routledge, 1992). Her current research is on black women in higher education.

Felly Nkweto Simmonds is Senior Lecturer in Sociology at the University of Northumbria, Newcastle-Upon-Tyne. She has taught on issues of gender and development in Zambia, Tanzania and Sierra Leone, as well as for OXFAM (UK). Her publications include: 'Difference, Power and Knowledge: Black Women in Academia' in H. Hinds *et al.* (eds) *Working Out: New Directions for Women's Studies* (Falmer, 1992); 'Naming and Identity' in D. Jarrett-Macauley (ed.) *Reconstructing Womanhood, Reconstructing Feminism* (Routledge, 1996). She has also written on her experience of breast cancer in 'A Remembering' in P. Duncker and V. Wilson (eds) *Cancer Through the Eyes of Ten Women* (Pandora, 1996).

Pragna Patel is a long serving member of Southall Black Sisters (SBS), actively involved in the group since 1982, and responsible for founding the first black women's centre in West London. Pragna is also a founding member of Women Against Fundamentalism (WAF). She has contributed articles on issues arising out of her work in various publications, including in *Against the Grain* (SBS 1990). She is at present studying law.

Nalini Persram is a postdoctoral fellow at the University of Essex. Her research interests and publications engage in issues of feminism, colonial history, postcolonial theory, Caribbean Studies, international relations and music. She is currently preparing her doctoral thesis, *Nationalist Thought and the Caribbean World: Difference, Deference and Deferral In Guyana*, and the co-edited collection (with Jenny Edkins and Véronique Pin-Fat) *Sovereignty and Subjectivity* for publication.

Naz Rassool is Lecturer in Education in the Department of Education Studies and Management at the University of Reading. She has published in the field of the sociology of technology in education, women's studies, language and cultural pluralism in the UK, and the politics of literacy.

Tracey Reynolds, previously a student at Goldsmiths' College, University of London, is currently working on her Ph.D at South Bank University. Her doctorate focuses on issues concerning African Caribbean women and mothering in Britain.

Consuelo Rivera Fuentes' many selves and subjectivities move between doing research (on her Ph.D), writing poetry *with, about* and *for* women; teaching Women's Studies and Culture and Communication, as well as Spanish at Lancaster University. She has published several poetry books including, with Lancaster Women Writers Group, *Women's Words* (1995). Her other publications include 'Todas Locas, Todas Vivas, Todas Libres: Chilean Lesbians: 1980–1995' in M. Reinfelder (ed.) *Amazon to Zami: Towards a Global Lesbian Feminism* (Cassell, 1996), and '"They do not dance alone": The women's movement in Latin America' in T. Cosslett *et al.* (eds) *Women, Power and Resistance: An Introduction to Women's Studies* (Open University Press, 1996).

Debbie Weekes is Research Fellow at the Nottingham Trent University and is currently completing her Ph.D on the racial and gendered identities of Black adolescent women. Her additional research interests are in 'race' and education, Black cultural production, and the changing nature of Black masculinities and femininities.

Acknowledgements

There are five people without whom this book would not have been possible. Talia Rodgers conceived of the book and gave me the time, space and encouragement to do it. Karen Fletcher-Peters, cool, calm, supersonic technical superstar, whose expertise and creative insights anchored me, and helped me to pull the book together. Stewart Phillips and Aliya Mirza, my two 'homeys' who looked after me and brought me cups of tea and much love. Diane Reay, my intellectual 'soulmate' who has opened me up to new possibilities and ways of knowing within the feminist project.

Black British feminism is an ever changing, ever growing project, far greater than a limited literary mapping can imagine. Time and space constraints meant that there were more manuscripts and possible contributors than I was able to include. For all those women – Jilma Luckiby, Claudette Williams, Anita Franklin, Jan Shinebourne, Millsom Henry, Kadiatu Kanneh, Maher Anjum, Sharon Beishon, Nyarai Humba, Beverley Prevatt Goldstein, Valerie Mason-John, Kay Bhopal, Annecka Marshall, and Lola Young – an exceptional 'thank you'. We need a second volume!

Special thanks to Bev Skeggs, Jackie Stacey, Stevi Jackson, Carole Boyce Davis and Jill LeBihan for excellent advice and support in times of need. The patient and professional production team at Routledge – Sophie Powell, Diane Stafford, Tim Weiss, Sally Close, Leigh Hurlock and Jason Arthur – turned production into a pleasure. A word to my sisters in struggle, the members of the Black Women's Sub-Committee of the British Sociological Association – Rosemarie Mallett, Maud Blair, Shirin Housee, Uvanney Maylor, Shaminder Takhar and Millsom Henry – your powerful sisterhood from which academic black female collective action has been realized, has been a guiding force behind this project. I always enjoyed the generous support and academic encouragement of my students and colleagues at South Bank University – in particular Jeffrey Weeks, Stina Lyon, Miriam David and Beverley Goring. Thanks also to Siân Thomas for sharing her imaginative ideas.

Black British Feminism: A Reader has been a project two years in the making. Babies have been born, Ph.Ds achieved and lives forever changed.

It has been filled with heartache and pleasure, trials and tribulations and surprising revelations. But it was necessary, and what I have taken away with me from this place of change and newness are lasting friendships from a community of warm and generous women.

Permissions given by the following copyright holders and authors are gratefully acknowledged.

Wilson, A. (1978) *Finding a Voice: Asian Women in Britain*, London: Virago Press, pp. 48–71. Copyright A. Wilson (USA) and Little Brown (UK). Reproduced with kind permission from the author and Little Brown.

Bryan, B., Dadzie, S., and Scafe, S. (1985) *Heart of the Race: Black Women's Lives in Britain*, London: Virago Press, pp. 164–181. Copyright Bryan, B., Dadzie, S., and Scafe, S. Reproduced with kind permission from the authors and Little Brown.

Carby, H. (1982) 'White Woman Listen! Black Feminism and the Boundaries of Sisterhood' in CCCS (eds) *The Empire Strikes Back: Race and Racism in 70s Britain*, London: Routledge, pp. 212–35. Reproduced with kind permission from Routledge.

Amos, V. and Parmar, P. (1984) 'Challenging Imperial Feminism' in *Feminist Review* no.17, July pp. 3–19. Reproduced with kind permission of P. Parmar.

Phoenix, A. (1987) 'Theories of Gender and Black Families' in G. Weiner and M. Arnot (eds) *Gender Under Scrutiny*, London: Hutchinson in assoc. with OU, London, pp. 50–63. Reproduced with kind permission from Routledge.

Mama, A. (1984) 'Black Women, the Economic Crisis and the British State' in *Feminist Review* no. 17, July, pp. 22–34. Copyright A. Mama – reproduced with kind permission of the author.

Bhavnani, K. and Coulson, M. (1986) 'Transforming Socialist Feminism: The Challenge of Racism' in *Feminist Review* no. 23, June, pp. 81–92. Copyright K. Bhavnani and M. Coulson – reproduced with kind permission of K. Bhavnani.

Aziz, R. (1992) 'Feminism and the Challenge of Racism: Deviance or Difference?' in H. Crowley and S. Himmelweit (eds) *Knowing Women*, Cambridge: Polity Press, OU and Oxford: Blackwell, pp. 291–305. Reproduced with kind permission from Open University Press and the author.

Parmar, P. (1989) 'Other kinds of Dreams' in *Feminist Review* no. 31, Spring, pp. 55–65. Copyright P. Parmar – reproduced with kind permission from the author.

Kay, J. (1985) 'So You Think I'm a Mule' in B. Burford, G. Pearce, G. Nichols and J. Kay *A Dangerous Knowing: Four Black Women Poets*, London: Sheba Press, pp. 53–4. Coyright J. Kay. Reproduced with the kind permission of the Peters Fraser & Dunlop Group Ltd.

The illustration *Untitled* is reproduced with kind permission of the artist: Folake Shoga (copyright). Originally commissioned and reproduced as a book cover for Zoe Wicomb (1987) *You Can't Get Lost in Cape Town*, London: Virago.

Every effort has been made to trace all the copyright holders, but if any have been inadvertantly overlooked the publishers will be pleased to make the necessary arrangement at the first opportunity.

Introduction

Mapping a genealogy of Black British feminism

Heidi Safia Mirza

So you think I'm a mule?

'Where do you come from?'
'I'm from Glasgow.'
'Glasgow?'
'Uh huh. Glasgow.'
The white face hesitates
the eyebrows raise
the mouth opens
then snaps shut
incredulous
yet too polite to say outright
liar
she tries another manoeuvre
'And your parents?'
'Glasgow and Fife.'
'Oh?'
'Yes. Oh.'
Snookered she wonders where she should go
from here –
'Ah, but you're not pure?'
'Pure? Pure what
Pure white? Ugh. What a plight
Pure, Sure I'm pure
I'm rare . . .'
'Well, that's not exactly what I mean,
I mean . . . you're a mulatto, just look at . . .'
'Listen. My original father was Nigerian
to help with your confusion
But hold on right there
If you Dare mutter mulatto
hover around hybrid

hobble on half-caste
and intellectualize on the
"Mixed race problem",
I have to tell you:
take your beady eyes offa my skin;
don't concern yourself with
the "dialectics of mixtures";
don't pull that strange blood crap
on me Great White Mother.
Say I'm no mating of a she-ass and a stallion
no half of this and half of that
to put it plainly purely
I am black
My blood flows evenly, powerfully
and when they shout "Nigger"
and you shout "Shame"
ain't nobody debating my blackness.
You see that fine African nose of mine,
my lips, my hair. You see lady
I'm not mixed up about it.
So take your questions, your interest,
your patronage. Run along.
Just leave me.
I'm going to my Black sisters
to women who nourish each other
on belonging
There's a lot of us
Black women struggling to define
just who we are
where we belong
and if we know no home
we know one thing;
we are Black
we're at home with that.'
'Well, that's all very well, but . . .'
No But. Good bye.

                    Jackie Kay (1985)

In a time when your 'belonging', who you *really* are, is judged by the colour of your skin, the shape of your nose, the texture of your hair, the curve of your body – your perceived genetic and physical presence; to be black (not white), female and 'over here', in Scotland, England or Wales, is to disrupt all the safe closed categories of what it means to be British: that is to be white and British.

Black British feminism as a body of scholarship is located in that space of British whiteness, that unchallenged hegemonic patriarchal discourse of colonial and now postcolonial times which quietly embraces our common-sense and academic ways of thinking. Whiteness: that powerful place that makes invisible, or reappropriates things, people and places it does not want to see or hear, and then through misnaming, renaming or not naming at all, invents the truth – what we are told is 'normal', neutral, universal, simply becomes the way it is (Dyer 1988; (charles) 1992; Morrison 1992; Bonnett 1993b, 1996; Frankenberg 1993; Hall 1993; McLaren 1994a; Wong 1994; Hickman and Walter 1995; Fusco 1995).

To be black and British is to be unnamed in official discourse. The construction of a national British identity is built upon a notion of a racial belonging, upon a hegemonic white ethnicity that never speaks its presence. We are told that you can be either one or the other, black or British, but not both. But we live here, many are born here, all 3 million of us 'ethnic minority' people, as we are collectively called in the official Census surveys (Jones 1993; Storkey 1994; Mason 1995; Skellington and Morris 1996). What defines us as Pacific, Asian, Eastern, African, Caribbean, Latina, Native, and 'mixed race' 'others' is not our imposed 'minority' status, but our self-defining presence as people of the postcolonial diaspora. At only 5.5 per cent of the population we still stand out, we are visibly different and that is what makes us 'black'.

Thus being 'black' in Britain is about a state of 'becoming' (racialized); a process of consciousness, when colour becomes the defining factor about who you are. Located through your 'otherness' a 'conscious coalition' emerges: a self-consciously constructed space where identity is not inscribed by a natural identification but a political kinship (Sandoval 1991). Now living submerged in whiteness, physical difference becomes a defining issue, a signifier, a mark of whether or not you belong. Thus to be black in Britain is to share a common structural location; a racial location (Mercer 1990; Hall 1990, 1992).

In Britain in the 1980s, this shared sense of objectification was articulated when the racialized disempowered and fragmented sought empowerment in a gesture of politicized collective action. In naming the shared space of marginalization as 'black', postcolonial migrants of different languages, religions, cultures and classes consciously constructed a political identity shaped by the shared experience of racialization and its consequences. As a political articulation, it appeared strategic, but in terms of community and personal identity 'black' remains a contested space. Localized, personalized struggles for who could or should be named as 'black' (i.e. Asians, Chinese, 'mixed race') characterized the political terrain of multicultural Britain for over a decade. It was argued that such a reductionist notion of blackness erased religious and ethnic difference (Anthias and Yuval-Davis 1983, 1992; Modood 1994). The desire to be named according to (cultural) difference and not (racial) sameness, demonstrated the need for recognizing the meaning of hair, skin and colour, the importance of a shared history and religion, in the construction of identity and belonging. The translation of such need into fictions of essential racial and cultural origins among Britain's black and ethnic populations represented the desire for 'a place called home' (Martin and Mohanty 1988; Rutherford 1990). It is the desire for a 'place' that anchors us in the strategic battle for cultural preservation in the continuous war of hegemonic cultural reappropriation of difference (Higginbotham 1992; hooks 1992; Fusco 1995).

In this context, then, black feminism as a spontaneous yet conscious coalition is a meaningful act of identification. In this 'place called home' named black feminism, we as racialized, gendered subjects can collectively mark our presence in a world where black women have for so long been denied the privilege to speak; to have a 'valid' identity of our own, a space to 'name' ourselves. Challenging our conscious negation from discourse – what Gayatri Spivak calls 'epistemic violence' (Spivak 1988; see Young 1990) – we as black British women invoke our agency; we speak of our difference, our uniqueness, our 'otherness'. In a submerged and hidden world where there is no official language, words or narratives about that world (except those held in our hearts and minds), black women inhabit a third space (Bhabha 1990). It is a space which, because it overlaps the margins of the race, gender and class discourse and occupies the empty spaces in between, exists in a vacuum of erasure and contradiction. It is a space maintained by the polarization of the world into blacks on one side and women on the other (Higginbotham 1992; Crenshaw 1993).

The invisibility of black women speaks of the separate narrative constructions of race, gender and class: in a racial discourse, where the subject is male; in a gendered discourse, where the subject is white; and a class discourse, where race has no place. It is because of these ideological blind spots that black women occupy a most critical place – a location whose very nature resists telling. In this critical space we can imagine questions that could not have been imagined before; we can ask questions that might not have been asked before (Christian 1990; West 1990).

But this is not a claim to theoretical legitimacy through authentic voice. To simply 'have a place' in the academic discourse is not the project of Black British feminism. Black women do not want just to voice their experiences, to shout from the roof tops 'we have arrived! . . . listen to me . . . this is my story'. We do not claim to have a special knowledge, a privileged standpoint, a valorized subjectivity, a unique consciousness, borne out of our collective experience of marginalization and the mere 'living life as a black woman' (Collins 1991). Such a claim to epistemic privilege would be to assume a naive essentialist universal notion of a homogeneous black womanhood, no better in its conception of the self and the nature of power than that embodied in the authoritative discourses we seek to challenge (Bar On 1993; Gilroy 1993: 52; Suleri 1993).

We are engaged in a far more subtle project, a project in which over the last 20 years we have attempted to invoke some measure of critical race/gender reflexivity into mainstream academic thinking. In telling our different story, in exposing our personal pain and pleasures, Black British feminists reveal *other ways of knowing* that challenge the normative discourse. In our particular world shaped by processes of migration, nationalism, racism, popular culture and the media, black British women, from multiple positions of difference, reveal the distorted ways in which the dominant groups construct their assumptions. As black women we see from the sidelines, from our space of unlocation, the unfolding project of domination.

Genealogy offers us a way into revealing the project of domination. The Foucauldian method of genealogy attempts a critique of dominant discourses. It draws on knowledges and ways of thinking that are marginalized and stand outside the mainstream (Sawicki 1991: 28; Smart 1992: 57; Dean 1994: 138). The retrieval of counter memories, of subjugated knowledges, which are thought to lack a history, functions as a challenge to the taken-for-granted normative assumptions of prevailing discourses. Thus genealogies operate not so much as theories but as mechanisms for criticizing theories (Sawicki 1991: 53). For black feminists this provides a means to interrogate the discourses which embrace and so wish to structure our very being – the racial discourse, with its obsession with black (male) desire and fear (Goldberg 1990; West 1993); the discourse of gender, dominated with the (white) feminist project of truth seeking (Weedon 1987; Nicholson 1990; Barrett and Phillips 1992); and the discourse of class, that central structural discourse of our time, with its privileging of the universal, exclusion of agency and reduction of all things to the economic (Nelson and Grossberg 1988; Callinicos 1989; see Hall and Jacques 1989).

It could be argued that mapping the counter history of Black feminism can be no more than a mapping of the history of the objectively assigned and dialectically constructed subject positions as written and spoken for black women by others. True, if the black woman is traced in history what we see is how she is permitted to appear. We see glimpses of her as she is produced and created for the sustenance of the patriarchal, colonial and now postcolonial discourse (Spivak 1988; Mani 1992; Hawley 1994; Ching-Laing Low 1995; McClintock 1995; Parry 1995; Jayawardena 1996). She appears and disappears as she is needed, as the dutiful wife and daughter, the hard (but happy and grateful!) worker, the sexually available exotic other, the controlling asexual mother, or simply homogenized as the 'third world' woman (Mohanty 1988). In her representation she is without agency, without self-determination, a passive victim, waiting to be in-scribed with meaning from those who wish to gaze upon her and name her. She is an object, not the subject of her story. However, the project of black feminism asserts and reclaims our agency in the telling of who we are. Our voice, our being and our very presence within the patriarchal imperial project of sexualized racialization is to actively contest the system of which we form a part.

However, if genealogies span centuries, can we undertake a genealogy of Black British feminism when the immediate history of concerted black feminist activity in Britain reaches back only over the last 50 years, over the relatively short time of postcolonial migration and settlement here? West (1993) talks of a micro-institutional or localized analysis, which is part of a bigger genealogical, macro-institutional, materialist inquiry of racism. Black British feminism with its location – and with its critical project to reveal the mechanisms that promote, contest, and resist racist logics and practices in the everyday lives of black people – can be seen as such a micro-institutional genealogical project; it is to the mapping of this project that I now turn:

PART I SHAPING THE DEBATE

Migration

Using a broad notion of the project of Black British feminism as a critical social force, it could be argued that a genealogy of black British feminism as a theoretical and intellectual movement has its genesis over 50 years ago in the activism and struggles of black women migrants from the postcolonial Caribbean, Africa and the Indian sub-continent.

Official statistics and texts written about and documenting the main period of postcolonial migration from the 1940s to 1960s writes out the female story of postcolonial migration. What remains for us to gather are the snippets of black women's stories as they emerge to challenge their negation and disrupt the neat telling of those times. The narratives of black women soldiers in the Second World War (Bousquet and Douglas 1991); the writing and campaigns of Una Marson for the League of Coloured People in the 1940s; the internationally recognized political activism of Claudia Jones in the 1950s; and the sustained collective organizing of Olive Morris in the 1970s, have been kept alive by black women writers and narrators (Prescod-Roberts and Steele 1980; Dodgson 1984; Bryan, Dadzie and Scafe 1985; Jarrett-Macauley 1996).

But these stories of black female activism and engagement are in contrast to the picture that is commonly painted of black women in Britain. In the British Government's conscious drive to recruit cheap labour from the newly independent colonies in the early 1950s, it was simply assumed, that migrant workers, like their own workers, are always male. The colonial violence of enslavement and economic plunder that structured black female work as a necessity was, of course, unenunciated in the assumption, erased from official logic. Women in the colonial patriarchal discourse were invisible non-entities. Immigration law and welfare policy reinforced this assumption. Women, it was believed, came as either wives or children, dependants on the man. However, the majority of Caribbean women came independently and in almost equal numbers to men (Foner 1979; Fryer 1984) – a fact erased from the telling (Mirza 1988). Migrant women could only claim rights on the grounds of marriage: that is, through their association with men. Women emerged in the official patriarchal, neo-imperialist discourse only as subjects for sexual and racist humiliation. In the construction of women as objects of male ownership the British Government invoked a twisted cultural legitimacy to harass and deter male migrants. They used the ultimate transgression of power, the forcible and violent entering and defiling of the bodies of the invisible. Unbelievably, they tested Asian women to see if they were bonefide 'virgin' wives (Parmar 1982: 245; Brah 1992a: 70; Mama 1992: 88). Crude, overt racist brutality has been the hallmark of immigration and asylum policies in the declining embattled British state (James and Harris 1993; Solomos 1993).

Work

The pervasive image of the invisible or passive black woman was rudely interrupted by the labour struggles that exploded in the 1970s, exposing the British sweat shops (Parmar 1982). In the first chapter of this collection, Amrit Wilson in 'Finding a voice: Asian women in Britain' gives a first person account of the conditions and struggles of Asian women workers. The narrative speaks of the agency of these women in their sustained, organized class struggles in the workplace. The women themselves tell of the historically specific nature of their class and cultural consciousness which was embedded in the material relations of capitalist production. On one hand, the women were positioned in a cultural context as Asian women and were exploited and harassed on those grounds. On the other hand, the women's socio-awareness of their objective class status meant they sought collective action and trade union affiliation; a strategy that ultimately led to their defeat. The complex cultural identities and social subject positioning that were manifest in the struggle for social justice are articulated by the women themselves in their narratives of everyday life on the picket line.

While Asian women were largely located in the private sector in factory and production, Caribbean and African women were situated in the public service and caring industries. Amina Mama's chapter 'Black women, the economic crisis and the British state' maps the clear-sighted, lucid project of a restructuring of the postcolonial capitalist state; rationalizing its logic through the active production of a disenfranchised and thus contingent and disposable workforce. Black women, in large numbers compared to the white female population, were (and are) disproportionately employed in low paid, low status work (Breugel 1989; Lewis 1993; Bhavnani 1994; Owen 1994). The insidious erosion of rights emphasizes black women's shared social and material conditions in a highly-structured, gendered and racialized labour market. Race, in the context of the globalization of capital, places gender at the centre of the new working class (Ong 1987; Brewer 1993).

Identity politics

In the early 1980s black women organized not only to protect their rights in the workplace, but also to engage with the sustained fascist and racist onslaughts of white British politicians, their vanguards, the police and their lackeys, the white street mobs which inhabited (and still do) the heightened sensitized place that is the national racialized terrain of late twentieth-century Britain (Hall 1975; Gilroy 1987; Solomos 1988; Keith 1993, 1995). In this context, Bryan, Dadzie and Scafe reveal the political agency of black women in their chapter 'The heart of the race: Black women's lives in Britain'. The story of OWAAD (the Organization of Women of African and Asian Descent), which is the story of the coming together of black women in 1978, challenges the official racial discourse where black men are the valorized racialized agents, named and feared through their visible acts of riots and rebellion. Women, permitted to appear in the racial discourse (if at all) only as mothers of sons and carers of husbands, demonstrated their collective politics of engagement and subversion. The call to Afro-Asian unity by OWAAD demonstrates the emergence of an organic racialized consciousness from which evolved the conscious naming of ourselves as 'black'. It was an empowering act in an empowering time, but one that did not last (Lewis and Parmar 1983a; Brah 1992b; Williams 1993).

Ironically the legacy of that reductionist naming of 'blackness' was to shift the racial discourse onto new ground, away from confrontational struggle in the political and economic domain towards the struggle to be heard among ourselves in the social and cultural domain. OWAAD folded under the pressure from within to assert heterogenous identities. The desire for visibility through celebrating cultural, religious and sexual difference characterized the struggle for a claim on the racialized terrain in the 1980s. Seduced by this opening, a space to express our hidden subjugated selves, identity politics superficially appeared to empower marginal groups.

Identity politics, a political ideology that consumed the 1980s, was based on the premise that the more marginal the group the more complete the knowledge. In a literal appropriation of standpoint theory, the claim to authenticity through oppressive subjecthood produced a simplistic hierarchy of oppression. The outcome was the cliché-ridden discourse which embodied the holy trinity of 'race, class, and gender' (Appiah and Gates 1995), within which black women, being the victims of 'triple oppression', were the keepers of the holy grail.

The solution within this conceptualization of oppression was to change personal behaviour rather than challenge wider structures. In a time when what should be done was replaced by who we are (Bourne 1987: 1), the freedom to have was replaced by the freedom to be (Melucci 1989: 177). Identity politics offered no radical way forward in the critical project of revealing how we come to be located in the racialized and sexualized space where we reside. Whiteness, that silent pervasive patriarchal discourse, the father of identity politics, with its complementary discourse on anti-racism and new-right anti-anti-racism, was never named (see Gilroy 1990; Bonnett 1993a, 1996; Dunant 1994; Gillborn 1995, 1996).

Imperial feminism

Just as the political arena witnessed a backlash to the reductionism of identity politics, so too was there a reaction to the reductionism inherent within white feminist theory in the 1980s. The desire for equality, the struggle for social justice, and the vision of universal sisterhood was the consuming unidirectional project of white (socialist) feminism throughout the 1970s and early 1980s. Patriarchal power, its manifestation in terms of female invisibility, and the inevitable psychic social and economic oppression it engendered across the globe, was the central logic driving the feminist discourse. However, racial power within the white feminist production of knowledge about gender relations was never problematized. Whiteness was a 'given' social position. Ironically it meant that an epistemology that rests on inclusion and equality was itself excluding and unequitable. The explanation as to why feminism should be locked into such an untenable position lay in revealing the foundations of a feminist epistemology which was embedded in the project of modernity, its premise being rational universal humanism (Weedon 1987; Barrett and Phillips 1992; Harding 1992; Yeatman 1994; Alway 1995; Charles 1996).

In feminist theory, knowledge about social relations was experiential. The central drive of the feminist project was to reveal hitherto obscured realities, other worlds – the 'woman's' world, a world silenced by the privileging of masculinity. But if the 'woman's' standpoint was embedded in that given, unproblematized space of whiteness – and it was – then how could feminism claim universal legitimacy? Black women's experience was invisible, or if made visible spoken for and constructed through the authoritative, imperial voice of whiteness (Mohanty 1988, 1992; Ramazanoglu 1989; Ware 1992). The call to recognize difference and diversity in the feminist project was incompatible with the notion of an essential, universal 'woman' subject.

The struggle of black women to claim a space within the modernist feminist discourse, and at the same time to engender critical racial reflexivity among white feminists, consumed the black feminist project for more than a decade. The writings of Hazel Carby, Valerie Amos and Pratibha Parmar exemplify the height of this critical time. Hazel Carby's chapter, 'White woman listen! Black feminism and the boundaries of sisterhood', embodies the classic Black British feminist response to exclusion and white feminist authority. Centring her argument around the key areas of feminist discourse – the family, patriarchy and reproduction – she interrogates the contradiction of the white feminist theoretical claim to universal womanhood on the one hand, but the practice of exclusion of women who are different on the other. Similarly Valerie Amos and Pratibha Parmar in 'Challenging imperial feminism' focus on white feminism's subversion of the discourse around the family, sexuality and the peace movement in its unconscious attempt to valorize and represent nothing more than white women's own cultural experience as global.

White feminists were reluctant to relinquish the authority to name the social reality of the gendered subject, a reluctance manifest in a particular white feminist appropriation of the black feminist critique. While black feminists called for the recognition of racism in white feminist theorizing, white socialist feminists strategically responded with a recognition of their ethnocentrism (the valorizing of the white cultural perspective). In an article in *Feminist Review*, Barrett and McIntosh (1985) suggested the solution to the problem of black female invisibility was to simply insert an appreciation of black cultural difference into the analysis of the family, work and reproduction. Racism, the acknowledgement of which is central to developing a truly critical position in relation to the discourse on whiteness, was not up for debate in the work of white feminists, as Kum-Kum Bhavnani and Margaret Coulson in their chapter, 'Transforming socialist feminism: The challenge of racism' point out. This article, when originally published in 1986, opened out a heated but necessary and productive debate between black and white feminists. The focus on the centrality of an open reflexive appreciation of racism in the production of an ethical feminist discourse, was continued and kept alive in the constructive dialogue between black feminists (Kazi 1986; Mirza 1986) and white feminists (Lees 1986; Ramazanoglu 1986) in a special section in the journal *Feminist Review* entitled 'Feedback: Feminism and Racism'.

Throughout the 1980s black feminists in Britain responded and resisted the overarching imperial mission of white feminism by refusing to be 'named'. They invoked their agency by challenging stereotypical images of black women as passive victims through studies, research, and writing that revealed the hidden world of migrant and black British women. In that world, women were brave, proud and strong. They wrote of Asian girls' resistance in schools (Parmar and Mirza 1981; Brah and Minhas 1985) and at work (Parmar 1982; Brah 1992a); they told of the African Caribbean experience of schooling (Carby 1982b; Stone 1985; Wright 1987); they revealed black women's struggle against domestic violence (Mama 1989, 1993a) and immigration (James 1985) and the police (Mama 1993b). They engaged in black lesbian activism (see Lewis 1990); and spoke of enriching, empowering but complex alternative family forms and other ways of living and being (Lewis and Parmar 1983b; Bryan, Dadzie and Scafe 1985; Visram 1986; Bhachu 1988; Phoenix 1988, 1991).

Postmodern difference

By the end of the 1980s, the black feminist critical project to excavate the dynamics of racial power and the silences it produces within white feminist discourse left black feminists exhausted and in need for self recovery. The flattening out and reduction of difference and diversity which had been assigned to interrogate whiteness within the feminist movement had outlived its purpose. The homogenizing of black women, that empowering act of collectivity rooted in racism, began to erode black feminist theoretical legitimacy. Black feminism, it was now being said, was a politically limited project. It undermined its own position as a critical discourse by exclusionary practices which did not recognize the ethnic, religious, political and class differences among women (Anthias and Yuval-Davis 1983, 1992; Brah 1994). Now the call was for black feminists to enter into the diversionary discourse of anti-racism. Anti-racism appeared to offer a form of inclusive, strategic, engaged political activism which, (superficially at least) could cut across difference by initiating black/white or local alliances articulated around the unified struggle against the racist practices of the state (Bourne 1983; Tang Nain 1991; Knowles and Mercer 1992). The emphasis on the manifestation of racism(s) and not the deeper underlying structures of what constitutes 'race' in the British context meant that anti-racism, as a political ideology could only ever put a 'coat of paint' on the problem of black inequality (Gilroy 1990).

Sensitive to the limitations of reductionism, and with a desire to explore our difference, the black feminist theorists turned to locating black female identity at the centre of their analysis. By opening up a critical inquiry into theories of social reproduction and class inequality, black feminists de-centred the authority of such established theories to speak of and on behalf of all marginalized groups (see Mirza 1992). Ann Phoenix, in her chapter 'Theories of gender and black families', articulates the complex levels of gender difference from a race and class position. Gender is not experienced in the same way when you are positioned as working class or black, or both. Children learn these differences and reproduce them in their knowledge about the social world. Ann Phoenix shows that speci-ficity and difference is important.

A sense of reflexivity and re-negotiation within the black feminist critical space is articulated by Pratibha Parmar in her chapter 'Other kinds of dreams'. Autobiographical reflections of black women emerge in this time that speak of a desire to claim a space and so enable the healing processes of self-discovery necessary after the long journeys through migration, work, identity politics, racism and feminist exclusion of the 1980s (see Grewal *et al.* 1988). The explosion of black women's literature and poetry also makes possible new contexts for creativity. Sharing their pain and pleasures, these black women writers living in Britain give strength and wisdom to others (see Burford *et al.* 1985; Cobham and Collins 1987; Ngcobo 1988; *Wasafiri* 1988; Nasta 1991; Boyce Davis 1994). Photo-graphy, art, film and performance produce images and acts that, in celebrating diversity, reflect, deflect and destabilize the white gaze (see Rasheed 1989; Parmar 1990; Sutler 1990; *Ten.8* 1992; Fusco 1995; Ugwu 1995; Boyce and Diawara 1996; Tawadros 1996; Young 1996). Black women gained a space to write about the body and mind in terms of colonial appropriation (Kanneh 1995; Mama 1995) and in terms of disability and exclusion (Begum 1992). They explored possibilities of new social move-ments in Europe (*Feminist Review* 1993) and social change in the UK (Jayaweera 1993). They organized against religious fundamentalism (Sahgal and Yuval-Davis 1992), and campaigned for lesbian sexual politics (Mason-John 1995).

Even though black women demonstrate their undeniable presence, the theoretical inclusion of their difference still appears elusive. Whereas 1970s and 1980s feminism centred its struggle on 'the right to be equal', postmodern feminism in 1990s turned to a celebration for the 'right to be different'. The black feminist critique makes visible the inherent contra-diction of such relative pluralism. As black women we ask: is it possible to achieve equality within difference? As the concept of difference is analytically weak and ill-defined, the discursive terrain is unsure. Are we talking about difference in relation to sexual difference (men/women); difference in relation to 'race' (black/white); or difference in relation to subjectivities (between women – class/ethnicity/age/religion, etc.) (Barrett 1987; Di Stefano 1990; Scott 1990; Barrett and Phillips 1992; Brah 1992b; Farganis 1994; Maynard 1994; Charles 1996; Williams 1996).

However it is defined, difference is plagued by some central philosophical problems. First, it could be argued that celebrating and valorizing difference of any sort depoliticizes feminism. It effectively dissipates the basis for collective activism as we look inward to the self with claims to relatively oppressed status, deflecting attention away from power which is still materially located (Bourne 1987; Bordo 1990). Thus, ironically, the discourse on difference obscures how we come to give meanings to our differences. Second, the discourse on difference privileges whiteness (Spelman 1990). Razia Aziz takes up this point in her chapter 'Feminism and the challenge of racism: Deviance or difference?' The very notion of difference is relational; you are always positioned in relation to the norm, which is whiteness. In such a politicized construction, other differences of class, age, ethnicity, religion have been subdued in the selective valorizing of black/white difference. A postmodern black feminist identity, Aziz suggests, is not just based on racism and oppression but on recognizing the fluidity and fragmented nature of racialized and gendered identities. In this sense we can reclaim subjectivity from the cul de sac of identity politics and reinstate it in terms of a powerful, conscious form of political agency. This is the task facing black feminism now.

PART II DEFINING OUR SPACE

In the space opened up by the discourse on difference, black women continue the critical task of genealogical enquiry: to excavate and so reveal the seemingly imperceptible, the smallest of the small ways in which we are absorbed into the resistance of that which we are expected to be, while we live trying to be what we want to be. Oriented around issues of difference, essentialism, representation, and cultural hybridity the collective project of black feminism is now, in the late 1990s, concerned with mapping our experience. But this is not a simple mapping of experience to uncover the 'truth', but rather an engagement with experience; a placing of the self in theory so as to understand the constructions and manifestations of power in relation to the self (Essed 1994; Griffin 1996). A critical black feminist theory is grounded in relation to practice, it cannot be not separate: praxis is central to our survival (Christian 1994, 1995).

Challenging essentialized images

For a black woman to be different is to be what she is not expected to be. To be different, as Bibi Bakare-Yusuf reveals in her chapter 'Raregrooves and raregroovers: a matter of taste, difference and identity', is to subvert the restricted codes of a narrowly defined racialized essence and acceptable feminity. If young black women do not behave as 'black' in the narrow cultural sense of Jamaican underclass, then does that mean they are not 'black'? The raregroove scene is a space of re-invention, where young women appropriate black female identity; rescue it from fixed essentialized constructions of the way they 'should be'. Aspirational, middle-class young women express difference in terms of their taste and style, choice of leisure and pleasure. They are engaged in the risky business of strategic tactical cultural re-inscription which makes the hegemonic discourse of race, class and gender imperceptible.

It is argued that the new cultural racism that marks this postmodern era is legitimated thorough dominant regimes of representation (Hall 1992; Giroux 1994; McLaren 1994b). But are we what we are expected to be or are we much more? In her chapter '(Mis)representing the black (super)-woman', Tracey Reynolds takes on the unchallenged discourse of the black superwoman; that powerful, indomitable work horse; that matriarchal giant that pushes aside men and climbs on up the career ladder; that single minded calculating woman who has babies alone; that untrustworthy woman who even consorts with white men when she achieves. Does she really exist beyond representation? Whatever the evidence – and Tracey Reynolds shows there is very little in terms of substantive research on motherhood, work and education – everyone still believes she does exist. She is valorized and reproduced in white academic and social policy discourse. Reinforced in the black press, the superwoman has even become a celebrated empowering notion among black women themselves. The call is to refuse voyeuristic reception of the 'other' and to imagine the self differently in order to act otherwise.

Racialized, sexualized meanings seem to have engulfed our very ways of thinking and knowing ourselves. Debbie Weekes, in her chapter 'Shades of Blackness: Young Black Female Constructions of Beauty', explores black female assertions of black female identity through the lived reality of fixed biologically verifiable notions of blackness. Black women erect boundaries of what counts as blackness based on skin colour and hair texture which they then police. This is how identity is experienced – on the streets, on the bus, in the classroom, at home. That is how young black women talk, think and walk. High brow cultural theorists would wish to wish away such ugly, 'racist' unpleasantries in effort to cool out what does not fit (Gilroy 1987; Hall 1992; Weeks 1995). But such essentializing is not a 'fiction', an imagining, a misinformed unsound politically-incorrect, false consciousness. It *is* these young women's reality. If it is ugly, then it is only as ugly as the racial discourse from which it is honed. Lived, essentialized blackness is a mirror of pervasive unenunciated whiteness – the 'Thing'. The perverse nature of this re-inscription of power and agency through becoming a self-defined, essential racial subject needs to be understood not dismissed (hooks 1991, 1992).

Erasure: finding the spaces in between

The pervasive use of essentialist definitions of blackness has a price. In the racialized terrain, dominated by fixed racialized beliefs, those who are defined as neither black nor white carry the pain of erasure. In her chapter 'Diaspora's daughters, Africa's orphans?: On lineage, authenticity and "mixed race" identity', Jayne Ifekwunigwe reveals the lives of the *métisse*, those who are neither considered black or white, those who exist everywhere but belong nowhere. Through their construction of self, *métisse* women illuminate the contradictions and logic of an impoverished racialized discourse, a discourse grounded in crude culturalist notions of 'race', nation and culture. The *métisse* are thus the product of racialized discourse. They occupy a critical position, an orphan consciousness, creating their own space in the recalling of their English-African-Diasporic histories. By assuming visibility in their role as *griotte* (storytellers), these *métisse* narrate what is 'real' (as lived) and fictitious (as constructed) in racial discourse.

The critical place that *métisse* women occupy is interrogated by Sara Ahmed in her chapter '"It's a sun-tan, isn't it?": Auto-biography as an identificatory practice'. Memories and reflections, which are always selective, can only tell us about the way you are seen, and hence addressed, within the dominant categories of the social world. When asked, with a wink, if her colour was just a sun-tan by predatory white police, multiple levels of identification and dis-identification in the incident illuminate the instability, temporality and negotiation of racialized, gendered, classed meaning. The incident shows the impossibility of being fixed by a single name or gaze in the process of identification, when you are a racially-marked, gendered subject. Modes of address that attempt to fix the subject are riddled with contradictions and social antagonisms. The process of identifying with the collective term 'black women' makes visible the clash between two regimes of identification: gender and race. By invoking the generalizable category 'black woman', Sara Ahmed shows the impossibility yet necessity of the politically-affirming gesture of naming the self as 'black woman'.

But is the notion of a 'black woman' a viable concept? Identity politics, that ideological policing of who counts as 'black', Black or black, that has invaded our thinking and being, has without doubt, closed down our possibilities for self-definition and political engagement. Magdalene Ang-Lygate in her chapter 'Charting the spaces of (un)location: On theorizing diaspora' explores, through the invisibility of Filipina and Chinese women living in Britain, the enclosures and erasure inherent in the racialized discourse of identity politics. The political concept of blackness does not convey belonging and community, but instils a false sense of national identity that sets those with dark black skin colour apart, while silencing those who are lighter than black. It consorts with the colonialist imperialist categorization of immigrant as outsiders, alien, different. Constructions of unidimentional black identity can only reinforce white supremacy by the logics of duality. To refuse such limited racialized constructions and create over and over again our difference is to disrupt and so subvert neo-colonialist paradigms.

Moving: new identities, new meanings

Naz Rassool in her chapter 'Fractured or flexible identities? Life histories of "black" diasporic women in Britain', explores how a conscious black identity evolves among women coming from very different socio-economic, historical and geographical places now living in Britain. Life histories of women as diverse as African-Caribbean, Iraqi-Kurd, black South African and African-Indian Kenyan, reveal the organic, complex interweaving of past-present experience in the recovery of diasporic subjectivity. In the search for the self in traces of memory, what may seem on the outside as the fragmented and alienating social experience of migration and dislocation has an inner coherence and continuity. Cultural hybridity, the fusion of cultures and coming together of difference, the 'border crossing' that marks diasporic survival, signifies change, hope of newness, and space for creativity. But in the search for rootedness – a 'place called home' – these women, in the process of self-identification, dis-identify with an excluding, racist British colonizing culture. They articulate instead a multi-faceted discontinuous black identity that marks their difference.

The desire to belong, the search for a 'place called home' is interrogated by Nalini Persram in her chapter 'In my father's house are many mansions: The nation and postcolonial desire'. Through a personal narrative she takes us on a journey of unbelonging, of changing colour codings and shifting gender roles. She unmasks the hegemonic masculinist discourse of national identity that structures and informs our search for who we are. The search for our authentic self rooted in a time, a place, with a history and a culture, is reproduced in the diasporic, migrant counter-discourse on 'home'. The compensatory narrative of 'home' – 'that there is a *there* there' – with its myth of unitary origin, is produced through the masculinist discourse of 'lack'. If you lack a nation, as diasporic travellers do, then how do you celebrate who you *are*? Re-knowing identity is to remake a space that valorizes movement not location, that is determined by migrancy and not being a migrant. It is a personal journey toward belonging (see Hesse 1993).

Re-claiming and re-centring our bodies

To take the inner journey to 'self' reveals different ways of knowing. In

'Two stories, three lovers and the creation of meaning in a Black Lesbian autobiography: A diary', Consuelo Rivera Fuentes transforms herself into a site of resistance. In her reading of Audre Lorde's *Zami* she creates and re-creates her identity in and out of the text. In her diary she shares with us Lorde's bodily geographical journey towards self-construction which changes reality from within. Consuelo reveals a place inside which plays with language and makes love to poetry. It is a sensual inner space that is not determined by the dominant discourse of being black and lesbian. In this place, her many selves – the writer, the reader, the autobiographer – passionately engage with each other, until the boundaries between each identity disappears. In the end no one knows where one identity starts and where another one finishes. It is possible to create an identity with new layers of meanings, to have multiple subjectivities without separating the self into different speaking subjects: to be one with many parts. Identity is a living process; though it is temporal, spatial and shifting, it can be transformative through risk, desire, decision and struggle.

There is an assumption that theories (and hence facts) come from our heads and feelings (and hence fictions) come from our bodies. In 'My body, myself: How does a Black woman do sociology?', Felly Nkweto Simmonds makes the point that sociology labours under the fiction that social reality has nothing to do with the body. However, for black women, social theory has fed on their embodied experiences. Black bodies are killed, displayed, watched, analysed, stroked, desired because of their embodied 'otherness'. Anthropology's fascination for the anatomical landmarks of different races has fed the fantasies of the Western imagination which fuelled the desiring machine of capital. Black women cannot be dispassionate, disembodied theorists. Their social reality, their habitus, is to be black, gendered subjects in a white world. For Felly cancer gave her a new relationship with her body which allowed her to rethink her place in the social. For the black woman, revealing certain 'private information' is necessary in order to understand how others see her and her experience as a 'curiosity'.

The one thing we do know as black women, is that our eroticized, exoticized bodies have become objects of desire. They preoccupy and obsess the white gaze. Gargi Bhattacharyya, in her chapter 'The fabulous adventures of the mahogany princesses', weaves a tale in the oral tradition of her parents, and parents' parents. It is a tale that tells of the violence of colonial exploitation which has reduced us all to looking at skin colour as a way of being, defining and living. Locked into a racialized, sexualized discourse, represented as exotic others, we have forgotten other ways of imagining who we are. Gargi's folk narrative enables the reader/listener to find wisdom and meaning in sagas made up of endless episodes without having to hear the whole thing. The unfolding narrative's central logic asks: does studying our representation in pictures, books and films reveal how gender and race really work? The postmodern preoccupation of studying the effects – our action and reaction to how we are pictured – has locked us into a distracting cycle of reflecting on how we are perceived, and then believing how we are perceived is who we are. What we see as mahogany princesses does not come into it at all. The story of the mahogany princesses is part dream fantasy, part bedtime story, and part twelve-step self-help programme, which is disciplined in another way – other than what is expected in 'power tripping, name dropping' academia. It can allow us to escape our mental confines, use our knowledge, and think differently about who we are.

PART III CHANGING THE FUTURE

For black feminists, a politics of difference is a politics of engagement, which operates from a site of critical location (hooks 1991). As 'critical organic catalysts' (West 1990) we desire neither acceptance, transgression nor transcendence with regard to the mainstream. What we are involved in is active insurgency through conscious alliances, critical dialogue and intellectual rigor in our task to reveal the operations of power in which we are implicated. Our hope is, if we change the way we think and speak about things, then we might change the way we live.

Pragna Patel, in her chapter 'Third wave feminism and Black women's activism', tells of the struggle of Southall Black Sisters (SBS) and Women Against Fundamentalism (WAF) to uphold women's status through legal rights. SBS and WAF struggle in the twilight zone of the dominant patriarchal discourses of anti-racism, multiculturalism, and religious fundamentalism. Cases of domestic violence, sexual abuse and forced marriage illuminate the alliances between the state and patriarchal authority by legitimating the rhetoric of Asian male community leaders who seek to maintain the sanctity of the family for ideological empowerment. SBS and WAF are involved in campaigns to redefine the relationship of women to the criminal justice system. In so doing they work to change the language and so meaning of the law to embrace an understanding of transgressions against women (such as rape) as violations of human rights.

The sites of engagement, the locations for our insurgency are not always in the political domain where they are expected. In 'Black women in education: A collective movement for social change', I ask the question: is the desire to do well and succeed in education a subversive act? The positive orientation of black women to education is significant. They may appear on the surface to be engaged in instrumental, seemingly conservative acts of buying into the system, but this is an illusion. Black women, without access to power and privilege, redefine what education is for. The analysis of female collective action offers a new direction for thinking about new social movements, challenging masculine assumptions of social change through confrontation. Ultimately, to do well in a racist society is a radical act. Given the parameters of the world we live in, we must think about transformative struggle through inclusive acts.

Coming full circle, this collection of Black British feminist writers ends on a note of hope, for an inclusive feminism that can embrace our class, race, sexual, and (dis)ability differences. Terminology constructs boundaries and meaning. If excluded from meaning, as black women were from the meaning associated with feminism, then they become invisible. Helen (charles), in 'The language of womanism: Rethinking difference', asks if an inclusive universal feminism is both possible and desirable. The organic nature of terming means that a word must come from its value to those who use it. 'Womanism' as a self-conscious, black-based term stopped short of popular appeal. Naming the self as 'black feminist' comes from a demand to be recognized by those in power. But to focus on terminology rather than a critique of the race-sexism of white feminism leads to no change. The black feminist critique engendered a guilty paralysis among white feminists for over twenty years, and this needs to be intercepted if feminism is to move forward. Feminism as a term, and as a movement, is not static, it is not impervious to change. If feminism changes to embrace differences, rather than to be preoccupied with difference, then its meaning will change and strengthen black and white feminist activism through a unified cohesive and strategic identity.

CONCLUSION

Postmodern theory has allowed the celebration of difference, the recognition of otherness, the presence of multiple and changeable subjectivities. Black women, previously negated and rendered invisible by the inherent universalizing tendency of modernity, finally have a voice. We appear to have 'arrived'. Here we are, afforded the status of *Black British Feminism*.

Postmodernity has opened up the possibility of a new 'feminism of difference'. Such a feminism now allows black women the legitimation to do what we have been doing for long time, in our own way; we have now been afforded an intellectual space to valorize our agency, redefine our place on the margins.

But in a genealogy of Black British feminism, we need to ask how do we appear in the emerging postmodern discourse on difference? How are we being produced, and implicated in that production? The answer is, through ourselves. In writing about our world, our place on the margin, black feminists take the risk of what happens when we expose ourselves as objects of study. Laid bare by our unveiling, our inner-most life stories become objects for public gaze; our resistance is known. We engage in naming our subjectivity, telling our story. We undertake journeys of self-discovery, which are then appropriated and recorded as objective knowledge, 'original context', and 'specificities'. The dominant culture achieves hegemony precisely by its capacity to convert and recode for the authoritive other (Chow 1993; Grossberg 1996).

In this so called fragmented, dislocated, experiential reality that is postmodern Britain, the celebration and voicing of our otherness has been appropriated by the masculinist postmodern discourse, which now seeks a new legitimation through 'owning' our 'marginal' experience. In the vacuum produced through abstract theorizing, bourgeois social theorists search for a role in relation to the 'social' they deconstruct (Skeggs 1991; Jackson 1992). In their postmodern malaise, the privileged and elite wish to enter and share our third space, our place on the margin, which has now become 'trendy' to occupy. Once our problem was invisibility in white feminism now its recognition in the white male academy!

But what is this 'third space', the place of 'hybridity and translation' which privileges those who claim to be oppressed? 'Becoming marginal' appears to be a place everyone seemingly wants to occupy, to lay claim to, no matter how elite, privileged or empowered by their class (Jacoby 1995; Sivanandan 1990). The work of some male academics, both black and white, articulates a new 'imperialism of oppression' as they enter the (counter-hegemonic) space of the *truly* dispossessed and seek, through a perverse legitimacy of their 'displacement' or search for 'new knowledge', to know it better than we know it ourselves (see for example Soja and Hooper 1993; Scheurich and Young 1996; Bhabha 1990, 1996; Hall 1990, 1996).

It could be argued that we should be glad that black feminism is getting this sort of air play. After all, is this not what we have struggled to achieve: visibility and legitimation? But black feminists must be conscious of this subtle and seductive space that has opened up for us in the postmodern project of knowledge production. Black women's agency in the context of this intangible, dangerous discursive terrain means being ever 'sociologically vigilant' (Bourdieu and Wacquant 1992: 209).

To valorize our 'different' experience means we have to locate that experience in materiality. Holding on to the struggle against inequality and for social justice anchors the black feminist project. For it seems whatever the project of postmodern theorizing, black women remain subject to discrimination and exclusion. Black women remain preoccupied with their struggles against low pay, ill health and incarceration, and for access to care, welfare and education. Inspite of postmodernism, little has changed for the majority of black women, globally and nationally. For them power is not diffuse, localized and particular. Power is as centralized and secure as it always has been, excluding, defining and self-legitimating (Callinicos 1989).

In this book, we speak of black feminism, not black feminism(s). This is because the political project has a single purpose: to excavate the silences and pathological appearances of a collectivity of women assigned as the 'other' and produced in a gendered, sexualized, wholly racialized discourse. Black feminism has many ways of doing this. Over the past 20 years, as has been revealed in this genealogy, there have been many sites of struggle: migration, work, white feminist theory, and now identity and difference. Strategic multiplicity and contingency is a hallmark of Black British feminism. If anything, what our struggles demonstrate is that you can have difference (polyvocality) within a conscious construction of sameness (i.e. black feminism).

As long as there is exclusion, both in academic discourse and in materiality, there will be a black feminism. It is in this sense contingent. As long as such exclusion is produced spatially in regions, nations, and places, there will be a Black *British* feminism.

REFERENCES

Amos, V. and Parmar, P. (1984) 'Challenging Imperial Feminism' *Feminist Review* Special Issue, 'Many Voices one Chant', no.17, July, pp. 3–19.

Anthias, F. and Yuval-Davis, N. (1983) 'Contextualising Feminism: Gender, Ethnic and Class Divisions' *Feminist Review*, no. 15, November, pp. 62–75.

Anthias, F. and Yuval-Davis, N. (1992) *Racialized Boundaries: Race, Gender, Colour and the Anti-Racist Struggle*, London: Routledge.

Alway, J. (1995) 'The Trouble with Gender: Tales of the Still-Missing Feminist Revolution in Sociological Theory' *Sociological Theory*, no. 13; 3 November, pp. 209–28

Appiah, K. W. and Gates, H. L. (1995) 'Editors's Introduction: Multiplying Identities' in K. W. Appiah and H. L. Gates (eds) *Identities*, Chicago: University of Chicago Press.

Aziz, R. (1992) 'Feminism and The Challenge of Racism: Deviance or Difference?' in H. Crowley and S. Himmelweit (eds) *Knowing Women: Feminism and Knowledge*, Cambridge: Polity Press.

Bar On, B. (1993) 'Marginality and Epistemic Privilege' in L. Alcoff and E. Potter *Feminist Epistomologies*, London: Routledge.

Barrett, M. (1987) 'The Concept of "Difference"' *Feminist Review*, no. 26, July, pp. 29–41.

Barrett, M. and McIntosh, M. (1985) 'Ethnocentrism and Socialist Feminist Theory' *Feminist Review*, no. 20, June, pp. 23–47.

Barrett, M. and Phillips, A. (1992) 'Introduction' in M. Barrett and A. Phillips *Destabilising Theory: Contemporary Feminist Debates*, Cambridge: Polity Press.

Begum, N. (1992) 'Disabled Women and the Feminist Agenda' in H. Hinds, A. Phoenix and J. Stacey (eds) *Working Out: New Directions for Women's Studies*, London: Falmer Press.

Bhabha, H. (1990) (in Interview with Rutherford) 'The Third Space' in J. Rutherford (ed.) *Identity, Community, Culture, Difference*, London: Lawrence and Wishart.

Bhabha, H. (1996) 'Culture's In-Between' in S. Hall and P. duGray (eds) *Questions Of Cultural Identity*, London: Sage.

Bhachu, P (1988) '*Apni Marzi Kardhi*. Home and Work: Sikh Women in Britain' in S. Westwood and P. Bhachu (eds) *Enterprising Women: Ethnicity, Economy and Gender Relations*, London: Routledge.

Bhavnani, R. (1994) *Black Women in the Labour Market: A Research Review*, Research Series, Manchester, Equal Opportunities Commission.

Bhavnani, K. and Coulson, M. (1986) 'Transforming Socialist Feminism: The Challenge of Racism' *Feminist Review*, no. 23, June, pp. 81–92.

Bonnett, A. (1993a) *Radicalism, Anti-Racism and Representation*, London: Routledge.

Bonnett, A. (1993b) 'Forever "White"? Challenges and Alternatives to a "Racial" Monolith' *New Community* vol. 20, no. 1, pp. 173–80.

Bonnett, A. (1996) 'Anti-racism and the Critique of "White" Identities' *New Community*, vol. 22, no. 1.

Bordo, S. (1990) 'Feminism, Postmodernism, and Gender-Sceptism' in L. Nicholson (ed.) *Feminism/Postmodernism*, London: Routledge.

Bourdieu, P. and Wacquant, L. (1992) *An Invitation to Reflexive Sociology*, Cambridge: Polity Press.

Bourne, J. (1983) 'Towards an Anti-Racist Feminism' *Race and Class*, vol. 25, no. 1.

Bourne, J. (1987) 'Homelands of the Mind: Jewish Feminism and Identity Politics', *Race and Class*, vol. 29, no. 1, Summer, pp. 1–24.

Bousquet, B. and Douglas, C. (1991) *West Indian Women at War*, London: Lawrence and Wishart.

Boyce Davis, C. (1994) *Black Women, Writing and Identity: Migrations of the Subject*, London: Routledge.

Boyce, S. and Diawara, M. (1996) 'The Art of Identity: A Conversation' in H. Baker, M. Diawara, R. Lindborg (eds) *Black British Cultural Studies: A Reader*, Chicago: University of Chicago Press.

Brah, A. (1992a) 'Women of South Asian Origin in Britain: Issues and Concerns' in P. Braham, A. Rattansi and R. Skellington (eds) *Race and Antiracism: Inequalities, Opportunities and Policies*, London: Sage/OU Press (reproduced from *South Asia Research* vol. 7, no. 1, May, 1987).

Brah, A. (1992b) 'Difference, Diversity and Differentiation' in J. Donald and A. Rattansi (eds) *'Race', Culture and Difference*, London: Sage/OU Press.

Brah, (1994) 'Review Essay: Time, Place and Others: Discourses of Race, Nation and Ethnicity' *Sociology* vol. 28. no. 3, pp. 805–13.

Brah, A. and Minhas, R. (1985) 'Structural Racism or Cultural Difference: Schooling for Asian Girls' in G. Weiner (ed.) *Just a Bunch of Girls*, Milton Keynes: Open University Press.

Brewer, M. R. (1993) 'Theorising Race, Class and Gender: The New Scholarship of Black Feminist Intellectuals and Black Women's Labour' in S.M. James and A.P. Busia (eds) *Theorizing Black Feminisms: The Visionary Pragmatism of Black Women*, London: Routledge.

Breugel, I. (1989) 'Sex and Race in the Labour Market' *Feminist Review* no. 32, Summer.

Bryan, B., Dadzie, S., and Scafe, S. (1985) *The Heart of the Race: Black Women's Lives in Britain*, London: Virago.

Burford, B., Pearce, G., Nichols, G. and Kay, J. (1985) (eds) *A Dangerous Knowing: Four Black Women Poets*, London: Sheba Press.

Callinicos, A. (1989) *Against Postmodernism: A Marxist Critique*, Cambridge: Polity.

Carby, H. (1982a) 'White Woman Listen! Black Feminism and The Boundaries of Sisterhood' in The Centre for Contemporary Cultural Studies (eds) *The Empire Strikes Back: Race and Racism in 70s Britain*, London: Hutchinson.

Carby, H. (1982b) 'Schooling in Babylon' in The Centre for Contemporary Cultural Studies (eds) *The Empire Strikes Back: Race and Racism in 70s Britain*, London: Hutchinson.

(charles), H. (1992) 'Whiteness – The Relevance of Politically Colouring the "Non"' in H. Hinds, A. Phoenix and J. Stacey (eds) *Working Out: new directions for women's studies*, London: Falmer Press.

Charles, N. (1996) 'Feminist Practices: Identity, Difference and Power' in N. Charles and F. Hughes-Freeland *Practising Feminism: Identity Difference and Power*, London: Routledge.

Ching-Laing Low (1995) *White Skins/Black Masks: Representation and Colonialism*, London: Routledge.

Chow, R. (1993) *Writing Diaspora: Tactics of Intervention in Contemporary Cultural Studies*, Bloomington: Indiana University Press.

Christian, B. (1990) 'But What do We Think We are Doing Anyway: The State of Black Feminist Criticism(s) Or My Version of a Little Bit Of History' in C.A. Wall (ed.) *Changing Our Own Words: Essays On Criticism, Theory and Writing by Black Women*, London: Routledge.

Christian, B. (1994) 'Diminishing Returns: Can Black Feminism(s) Survive the Academy?' in D. T. Goldberg (ed.) *Multiculturalism: A Critical Reader*, Oxford: Blackwell.

Christian, B. (1995) 'The Race for Theory' in B. Ashcroft, G. Griffiths, H. Tiffin *The Post Colonial Studies Reader*, London: Routledge.

Cobham, R. and Collins, M. (1987) (eds) *Watchers and Seekers: Creative Women's Writing by Black Women in Britain*, London: The Women's Press.

Collins, P. H. (1991) *Black Feminist Thought: Knowledge Consciousness and the Politics of Empowerment*, London: Routledge.

Crenshaw, K. (1993) 'Whose Story is it Anyway? Feminist Anti-racist Appropriations of Anita Hill' in T. Morrisson (ed.) *Rac-ing Justice, En-Gendering Power: Essays on Anita Hill, Clarence Thomas and the Construction of Social Reality*, London: Chatto and Windus.

Dean, M. (1994) *Critical and Effective Histories: Foucault's Methods and Historical Sociology*, London: Routledge.

Di Stefano, C. (1990) 'Dilemmas of Difference: Feminism, Modernity, and Post-modernism' in L. Nicholson (ed.) *Feminism/Postmodernism*, London: Routledge.

Dogson, E. (1984) *Motherlands: West Indian Women in Britain in the 1950s*, Oxford: Heinemann.

Dunant, S. (ed.) (1994) *The War of the Words: The Political Correctness Debate*, London: Virago.

Dyer, R. (1988) 'White' *Screen: The Last 'Special Issue' on Race?* vol. 29, no. 4, Autumn, pp. 44–65.

Essed, P. (1994) 'Contradictory Positions, Ambivalent Perceptions: A Case Study of a Black Woman Entrepreneur' in K. Bhavnani and A. Phoenix (eds) *Shifting Identities, Shifting Racisms*, London: Sage.

Farganis, S. (1994) *Situating Feminism: From Thought to Action*, London: Sage.

Feminist Review (1993) Special Issue 'Thinking Through Ethnicities' vol. 45, Autumn.

Foner, N. (1979) *Jamaica Farewell: Jamaican Migrants in London*, London: Routledge & Kegan Paul.

Frankenberg, R. (1993) *The Social Construction of Whiteness; White Women, Race Matters*, London: Routledge.

Fryer, P. (1984) *Staying Power: The History of Black People in Britain*, London: Pluto.

Fusco, C. (1995) *English is Broken Here: Notes on Cultural Fusion in the Americas*, New York: The New Press.

Goldberg, T. (ed.) (1990) *Anatomy of Racism*, Minneapolis: University of Minnesota Press.

Gillborn, D. (1995) *Racism and Antiracism in Real Schools*, Buckingham: Open University Press.

Gillborn, D. (1996) 'Student Roles and Perspectives in Antiracist Education: A Crisis of White Ethnicity?' *British Educational Research Journal* vol. 22, no. 2, pp. 165–79.

Gilroy, P. (1987) *There Ain't No Black in the Union Jack*, London: Hutchinson.

Gilroy, P. (1990) 'The End of Anti-racism' *New Community* vol. 17, no. 1, October.

Gilroy, P. (1993) *The Black Atlantic: Modernity and Double Consciousness*, London: Verso.

Giroux, H. (1994) 'Living Dangerously: Identity Politics and the New Cultural Racism' in H. Giroux and P. McLaren (eds) *Between the Borders: Pedagogy and the Politics of Cultural Change*, London: Routledge.

Grewal, S., Kay, J., Landor, L., Lewis, G., Parmar, P. (1988) *Charting the Journey: Writings by Black and Third World Women*, London: Sheba Press.

Griffin, C. (1996) 'Experiencing Power: Dimensions of Gender "Race" and Class' in N. Charles and F. Hughes-Freeland *Practising Feminism: Identity Difference and Power*, London: Routledge.

Grossberg, L. (1996) 'Identity and Cultural Studies – Is That All There Is?' in S. Hall and P. duGray (ed.) *Questions Of Cultural Identity*, London: Sage.

Hall, C. (1993) *White, Middle Class and Male: Explorations in Feminism and History*, Cambridge: Polity Press.

Hall, S. (1975) 'Racism and Reaction' in Commission for Racial Equality (eds) *Five Views of Multi-Racial Britain*, London: CRE.

Hall, S. (1990) 'Cultural Identity and Diaspora' in J. Rutherford (ed.) *Identity, Community, Culture, Difference*, London: Lawrence and Wishart.

Hall, S. (1992) 'New Ethnicities' in J. Donald and A. Rattansi (eds) *'Race', Culture and Difference*, London: Sage/OU.

Hall, S. (1996) 'Introduction: Who needs "Identity"?' in S. Hall and P. duGray (eds) *Questions Of Cultural Identity*, London: Sage.

Hall, S. and Jacques, M. (eds) (1989) *New Times: The Changing Face of Politics in the 1990s*, London: Lawrence and Wishart.

Harding, S. (1992) 'The Instability of the Analytical Categories of Feminist Theory' in H. Crowley and S. Himmelweit (eds) *Knowing Women: Feminism and Knowledge*, Cambridge: Polity Press.

Hawley, Stratton J. (ed.) (1994) *Sati, the Blessing and the Curse: The Burning of Wives in India*, New York: Oxford University Press.

Hesse, B. (1993) 'Black to Front and Black Again: Racialisation Through Contested Spaces' in M. Keith and S. Pile (eds) *Place and the Politics of Identity*, London: Routledge.

Hickman, M. J. and Walter, B. (1995) 'Deconstructing Whiteness: Irish Women in Britain' *Feminist Review* no. 50, Summer, pp. 5–19.

Higginbotham, E. (1992) 'African-American Women's History and the Meta-language of Race' *Signs* vol. 17, no. 2, Winter, pp. 251–74.

hooks, b. (1991) *Yearnings: Race, Gender and Cultural Politics*, Boston: South End Press.

hooks, b. (1992) *Black Looks: Race and Representation*, London: Turnaround.

Jacoby, R. (1995) 'Marginal Returns: the Trouble with Post-Colonial Theory' *Lingua Franca* September/October, pp. 30–7.

Jackson, S. (1992) 'The Amazing Deconstructing Woman' *Trouble and Strife* no. 25, Winter, pp. 25–31.

James, S. (ed.) (1985) *Strangers and Sisters: Women, Race and Immigration*, London: Falling Wall Press.

James, W. and Harris, C. (1993) *Inside Babylon: The Caribbean Diaspora in Britain*, London: Verso.

Jarrett-Macauley, D. (1996) 'Exemplary Women' in D. Jarrett Macauley (ed.) *Reconstructing Womanhood, Reconstructing Feminism: Writings on Black Women*, London: Routledge.

Jayawardena, K. (ed.) (1996) *Embodied Violence: Communalising Female Sexuality in South Asia*, London: Zed.

Jayaweera, H. (1993) 'Racial Disadvantage and Ethnic Identity: The Experiences of

Afro-Caribbean Women in a British City' *New Community* vol. 19, no. 3, April.

Jones, T. (1993) *Britain's Ethnic Minorities*, London: PSI.

Kanneh, K. (1995) 'Feminism and the Colonial Body' in B. Ashcroft, G. Griffiths, H. Tiffin (eds) *The Post Colonial Studies Reader*, London: Routledge.

Kay, J. (1985) 'So you Think I'm a Mule?' in B. Burford, G. Pearce, G. Nichols and J. Kay (eds) *A Dangerous Knowing: Four Black Women Poets*, London: Sheba Press.

Kazi, H. (1986) 'The Beginning of a Debate Long Over Due: Some Observations on 'Ethnocentrism and Socialist Feminist Theory' *Feminist Review* 'Feedback: Feminism and Racism', no. 22, Spring, pp. 87–91.

Keith, M. (1993) *Race, Riots and Policing: Lore and Disorder in a Multiracist Society*, London: UCL Press.

Keith, M. (1995) 'Shouts of the Street: Identity and Spaces of Authenticity' *Social Identities* vol. 1, no. 2, August, pp. 297–315.

Knowles, C. and Mercer, S. (1992) 'Feminism and Antiracism: An Exploration of Political Possibilities' in J. Donald and A.Rattansi *'Race', Culture and Difference*, London: Sage/OU.

Lees, S. (1986) 'Sex, Race and Culture: Feminism and the Limits of Cultural Pluralism' *Feminist Review* 'Feedback: Feminism and Racism' no. 22, Spring, pp. 92–101.

Lewis, G. (1990) 'Audre Lorde: Vignettes and Mental Conversations' *Feminist Review* no. 34, Spring, pp. 100–14

Lewis, G. (1993) 'Black Women's Employment and the British Economy' in W. James and C. Harris *Inside Babylon: The Caribbean Diaspora in Britain*, London: Verso.

Lewis, G. and Parmar, P. (1983a) 'Black Feminism: Shared Oppression, New Expression' *City Limits* 4–10 March.

Lewis, G and Parmar, P. (1983b) 'Review Article: Black Women's Writing' *Race and Class* vol. 25, no. 2.

McClintock, A. (1995) *Imperial Leather: Race, Gender and Sexuality in the Colonial Contest*, New York: Routledge.

McLaren, P. (1994a) 'White Terror and Oppositional Agency: Towards a Critical Multiculturalism' in D. T. Goldberg (ed.) *Multiculturalism: A Critical Reader*, Oxford: Blackwell.

McLaren, M (1994b) 'Multiculturalism and the Postmodern Critique: Toward a Pedagogy of Resistance and Transformation' in H. Giroux and P. McLaren (eds) *Between the Borders: Pedagogy and the Politics of Cultural Change*, London: Routledge.

Mama, A. (1984) 'Black Women, The Economic Crisis and the British State' *Feminist Review* Special Issue, 'Many Voices one Chant', no. 17, July, pp. 3–19.

Mama, A. (1989) 'Violence Against Black Women: Gender, Race and State Responses' *Feminist Review* no. 32, Summer, pp. 30–48.

Mama, A. (1992) 'Black Women and the British State: Race Class and Gender Analysis for the 1990s' in P. Braham, A. Rattansi and R. Skellington (eds) *Racism and Antiracism: Inequalities, Opportunities and Policies*, London: Sage/OU.

Mama, A. (1993a) 'Woman Abuse in London's Black Communities' in W. James and C. Harris (eds) *Inside Babylon: The Caribbean Diaspora in Britain*, London: Verso.

Mama, A. (1993b) 'Black Women and the Police: A Place Where the law is Not Upheld' in W. James and C. Harris (eds) *Inside Babylon: The Caribbean Diaspora in Britain*, London: Verso.

Mama, A. (1995) *Beyond the Masks: Race, Gender and Subjectivity*, London: Routledge.

Mani, L. (1992) 'Multiple Mediations: Feminist Scholarship in the age of Multi-national Reception' in H. Crowley and S. Himmelweit *Knowing Women: Feminism and Knowledge*, Cambridge: Polity Press/OU.

Martin, B. and Mohanty, C.T. (1988) 'Feminist politics: what's home got to do with it' in T. de Lauretis (ed.) *Feminist Studies/Critical Studies*, Basingstoke: Macmillan.

Mason, D. (1995) *Race and Ethnicity in Modern Britain*, Oxford: Oxford University Press.

Mason-John, V. (ed.) (1995) *Talking Black: Lesbians of African and Asian Descent Speak Out*, London: Cassell.

Maynard, M. (1994) '"Race", Gender and the concept of "Difference in Feminist Thought"' in H. Afshar and M. Maynard (eds) *The Dynamics of 'Race' and Gender: Some Feminist Interventions*, London: Taylor and Francis.

Melucci, A. (1989) *Nomads of the Present: Social Movements and Individual Needs in Contemporary Society*, London: Radius.

Mercer, K. (1990) 'Welcome to the Jungle: Identity and Diversity in Postmodern Politics' in J. Rutherford (ed.) *Identity, Community, Culture, Difference*, London: Lawrence and Wishart.

Mirza, H.S. (1986) 'The Dilemma of Socialist Feminism: A Case for Black Feminism' *Feminist Review* 'Feedback: Feminism and Racism' no. 22, Spring 1986.

Mirza, H.S. (1988) 'The Career Aspirations and Expectations of Young Black Women: The Maintenance of Inequality' unpublished Ph.D., University of London, Goldsmiths' College.

Mirza, H.S. (1992) *Young, Female and Black*, London: Routledge.

Mirza, H.S. (1995) 'Black Women in Higher Education: Defining a Space/Finding a Place' in L. Morley and V. Walsh (eds) *Feminist Academics: Creative Agents For Change*, London: Taylor and Francis.

Modood, T. (1994) 'Political Blackness and British Asians' *Sociology* vol. 28, no. 4 November, pp. 859–76

Mohanty, C.T. (1988) 'Under Western Eyes: Feminist Scholarship and Colonial Discourses' *Feminist Review* no. 30, Autumn, pp. 65–88.

Mohanty, C.T. (1992) 'Feminist Encounters: Locating The Politics of Experience' in M. Barrett and A. Phillips (eds) *Destabilising Theory: Contemporary Feminist Debates*, Cambridge: Polity Press.

Morrison, T. (1992) *Playing in the Dark: Whiteness and the Literary Imagination*, Cambridge, Massachusetts: Harvard University Press.

Nasta, S. (ed.) (1991) *Motherlands: Black Women's Writing from Africa, The Caribbean and South Asia*, London: The Woman's Press.

Nelson C. and Grossberg L. (eds) (1988) *Marxism and the Interpretation of Culture*, London: Macmillan.

Ngcobo, L. (ed.) (1988) *Let it be Told: Black Women Writers in Britain*, London: Virago.

Nicholson, L. (ed.) (1990) *Feminism/Postmodernism*, London: Routledge.

Ong, A. (1987) *Spirits of Resistance and Capitalist Discipline: Factory Women in Malaysia*, Albany, New York: State University of New York Press.

Owen, D. (1994) *Ethnic Minority Women and the Labour Market: Analysis of the 1991 Census*, Manchester: Equal Opportunities Commission.

Parmar, P. (1982) 'Gender, Race and Class: Asian Women's Resistance' in Centre for Cultural Studies (eds) *The Empire Strikes Back: Race and Racism in 70s Britain*, London: Hutchinson.

Parmar, P. (1989) 'Other Kinds of Dreams' *Feminist Review* Special Issue 'The Past is Before Us: Twenty Years of Feminism' no. 31, Spring, pp. 55–65.

Parmar, P.(1990) 'Black Feminism and the Politics of Articulation' in J. Rutherford (ed.) *Identity: Community, Culture, Difference*, London: Lawrence and Wishart.

Parmar, P. and Mirza, N. (1981) 'Growing Angry: Growing Strong' *Spare Rib*, no. 111.

Parry, B. (1995) 'Problems in Current Theories of Colonial Discourse' in B. Ashcroft, G. Griffiths and H. Tiffin (eds) *The Post-Colonial Studies Reader*, London: Routledge.

Phoenix, A. (1987) 'Theories of Gender and Black Families' in G. Weiner and M. Arnot *Gender Under Scrutiny*, London: Hutchinson/OU.

Phoenix, A. (1988) 'Narrow Definitions of Culture: The Case of Early Motherhood' in S. Westwood and P. Bhachu (eds) *Enterprising Women: Ethnicity, Economy and Gender Relations*, London: Routledge.

Phoenix, A. (1991) *Young Mothers?*, London: Polity Press.

Prescod-Roberts M. and Steele, N. (eds) (1980) *Bringing it All Back Home*, Bristol: Falling Wall Press.

Ramazanoglu, C. (1986) 'Ethnocentrism and Socialist-Feminist Theory: A Response to Barrett and McIntosh' *Feminist Review* 'Feedback: Feminism and Racism' no. 22, Spring 1986.

Ramazanoglu, C. (1989) *Feminism and the Contradictions of Oppression*, London: Routledge.

Rasheed, A. (1989) *The Other Story*, Exhibition Catalogue, London: Hayward Gallery.

Rutherford, J. (1990) 'A Place Called Home: Identity and the Cultural Politics of Difference' in J. Rutherford (ed.) *Identity, Community, Culture, Difference*, London: Lawrence and Wishart.

Sahgal, G. and Yuval-Davis, N. (eds) (1992) *Refusing Holy Orders*, London: Virago.

Sandoval, C. (1991) 'US Third World Feminism: The Theory and Method of Oppositional Consciousness in the Post Modern World' *Genders* no. 10, pp. 1–24.

Sawicki, J. (1991) *Disciplining Foucault: Feminism Power and Body*, London: Routledge.

Scheurich, J. and Young, M. (1996) 'Colouring Epistomologies: Are Our Research Epistomologies Racially Biased?' Paper from research at University of Texas at Austin: USA, given at Sociology of Education Seminar, King's College University of London, January.

Scott, J.W.(1990) 'Deconstructing Equality-Versus-Difference: Or the Uses of Poststructuralist Theory for Feminism' in M. Hirsch and E. Fox-Keller *Conflicts in Feminism*, New York: Routledge.

Soja, E. and Hooper, B. (1993) 'The Spaces that Difference Makes: Some Notes on the Geographical Margins of the New Cultural Politics' in M. Keith and S. Pile (eds) *Place and the Politics of Identity*, London: Routledge.

Sivanandan, A. (1990) 'All That Melts into Air is Solid: The Hokum of New Times' *Race and Class* vol. 31, no. 3.

Skeggs, B.(1991) 'Postmodernism: What is All the Fuss About?' *British Journal of Sociology of Education* vol. 12, no. 2, pp. 255–67.

Skellington, R. with P. Morris (1996) '*Race' in Britain Today*, 2nd edn, London: Sage/OU Press.

Smart, B. (1992) *Modern Condition, Postmodern Controversies*, London: Routledge.

Solomos, J. (1988) *Black Youth, Racism and the State*, Cambridge: Cambridge University Press.

Solomos, J. (1993) *Race and Racism in Britain*, 2nd edn, London: Macmillan.

Spelman, E. (1990) *Inessential Woman: Problems of Exclusion in Feminist Thought*, London: Women's Press.

Spivak, G. (1988) 'Can the Subaltan Speak?' in C. Nelson and L. Grossberg (eds) *Marxism and the Interpretation of Culture*, London: Macmillan.

Stone, M. (1985) *The Education of the Black Child: The Myth of Multiracial Education*, 2nd edn, London: Fontana.

Storkey, M. (1994) *London's Ethnic Minorities, One City Many Communities: An Analysis of 1991 Census Results*, London: London Research Centre.

Suleri, S. (1993) 'Woman Skin Deep: Feminism and the Postcolonial Condition' in

P. Williamsz and L. Chrisman (eds) *Colonial Discourse and Post-Colonial Theory: A Reader*, Hemel Hempstead: Harvester Wheatsheaf.

Sutler, M. (ed.) (1990) *Passion: Discourses on Black Women's Creativity*, Hebden Bridge, West Yorkshire: Urban Fox Press.

Tang Nain, G. (1991) 'Black Women, Sexism and Racism: Black or Antiracist Feminism?' *Feminist Review* no. 37, Spring, pp. 1–22.

Ten.8 (1992) 'Critical Decade: Black British Photography in the 80s' vol. 2, no. 3, Spring 1992.

Tawadros, G. (1996) 'Beyond the Boundary: The Work of Three Black Women Artists in Britian' in H. Baker, M. Diawara and R. Lindeborg (eds) *Black British Cultural Studies: A Reader*, Chicago: University of Chicago Press.

Ugwu, C. (ed.) (1995) *Let's Get it On: The Politics of Black Performance*, London: ICA.

Visram, R. (1986) *Ayahs, Lascars and Princes: Indians in Britain 1700–1947*, London: Pluto.

Ware, V. (1992) *Beyond the Pale: White Women, Racism and History*, London: Verso.

Wasafiri (1988) 'Focus on Women' Special Issue no. 8, Spring, Canterbury.

Weedon, C. (1987) *Feminist Practice and Poststructuralist Theory*, Oxford: Blackwell.

Weeks, J. (1995) *Invented Moralities: Sexual Values in an Age of Uncertainty*, Cambridge: Polity Press.

West, C. (1990) 'The New Cultural Politics of Difference' in R. Ferguson, M. Gever, T. Minh-ha and C. West (eds) *Out There: Marginalisation and Contemporary Cultures*, New York: New Museum of Contemporary Art.

West, C. (1993) *Keeping the Faith: Philosophy and Race in America*, London: Routledge.

Williams, C. (1993) 'We are a Natural Part of Many Different Struggles: Black Women Organising' in W. James and C. Harris (eds) *Inside Babylon: The Caribbean Diaspora in Britain*, London: Verso.

Williams, F. (1996) 'Postmodernism, Feminism and the Question of Difference' in N. Parton (ed.) *Social Theory, Social Change and Social Work*, London: Routledge.

Wilson, A. (1978) *Finding a Voice: Asian Women in Britain*, London: Virago.

Wong, L. Mun (1994) 'Di(s)-secting and Dis(s)-closing "Whiteness": Two Tales about Psychology', in K. Bhavnani and A. Phoenix (eds) *Shifting Identities, Shifting Racisms: A Feminism and Psychology Reader*, London: Sage.

Wright, C. (1987) 'Relations Between Teachers and Afro-Caribbean Pupils: Observing Multi-Racial Classrooms' in G. Weiner and M. Arnot (eds) *Gender Under Scrutiny*, London: Hutchinson/OU.

Yeatman, A. (1994) 'Postmodern Epistemological Politics and Social Science' in K. Lennon and M. Whitford (eds) *Knowing the Difference: Feminist Perspectives in Epistemology*, London: Routledge.

Young, L. (1996) *Fear of the Dark: Race, Gender and Sexuality in the Cinema*, London: Routledge.

Young, R. (1990) *White Mythologies: Writing History and the West*, London: Routledge.

Part I

Shaping the debate

This section explores the early direction of the black feminist debate in Britain. Over twenty years ago black British women begun to document their work experiences and political struggles through the narrative accounts and testimonies of black women migrants. By the early 1980s, Black British feminists, conscious of their inability to articulate these experiences within the framework of feminist theory, began a critical dialogue with mainstream white feminism. As the key classic texts collected together in this section show, it was the charge of exclusion and ethnocentricity within white feminist scholarship that galvanized black female scholars to make visible the social and political conditions of black women in Britain. The debate took shape around a critical exchange on the centrality of the family and the definition of patriarchy in other cultural contexts. Primarily a critique of white feminism, this important but essentially reactive perspective of Black British feminism reached an impasse by the early 1990s. The white feminist discourse, unable to embrace black feminist demands for equality within the confines of its modernist logics of universalism, shifted to postmodern concerns of 'difference'.

Chapter 1

Finding a voice

Asian women in Britain*

Amrit Wilson

WORK OUTSIDE THE HOME

'Next time I won't cry, I'll make you cry'

No one, least of all Asian women workers themselves, would claim that they are highly militant or strong. What they have been in the past, in the face of their grim working lives, is resilient. They have refused to despair, accepting quite stoically what they have been given. Now this stoicism is changing. Partly it is changing because women are getting more familiar with the industrial scene and partly because of the tremendous impact and influence of the strike at Grunwick Photoprocessing. That strike has proved for always that Asian women workers can be strong, resourceful and courageous, that they can stand up, face the world and demand their rights.

In Britain there has for many years been a sub-proletariat, a sub-class of the working class who are far worse off than the main body, consisting of sweat-shop workers and homeworkers, people who are treated by employers as though they have no rights at all. Before Asian immigrants came to Britain, these jobs were done by previous waves of immigrants in certain areas (like the East End of London). But elsewhere in the country in general they were usually done by indigenous working-class women whose mothers often had similar jobs before them. Now that Asian women have taken over their positions, they move upwards, even though only slightly upwards, in the labour hierarchy. But this means more than just one group replacing another. The change is a tremendous one. At the bottom of the hierarchy of the production structure, where spirits are assumed to be crushed, have come a new army of workers – fresh, vivacious and increasingly angry. Their expectations are high because many of them have, until recently, had a middle-class life and outlook (i.e. the East African Asians) and because, unlike the British working class, they have not been ground

*Extract from Wilson, A. (1978) *Finding a Voice – Asian Women in Britain*, Virago Press, London, pp. 48–71.

down and prepared for their jobs by the British education system. Apart from this, their race, and often their language, gives them a solidarity which white workers can only rarely achieve. If they can win their battles, as one trade union organizer put it (while describing Grunwick), 'it will be a new dimension in trade union activity'. In other words it would mean that battles could be won which people have previously thought could not even be fought . . .

The strike at Grunwick Photoprocessing is exceptional in many ways. Not only are the men and women involved people of remarkable courage and strength, but unlike Imperial Typewriters or Spiralynx it is a strike of black workers in an area well known for its tradition of left-wing trade union organization . . .

However, even in this atmosphere of working-class confidence there are a number of factories and work-places where working conditions are utterly degrading. Grunwick Photoprocessing could be any factory employing Asians in any part of Britain. It is not in the mainstream of capitalist enterprise. In 1976, 80 per cent of the 440 workers were Asians, in fact it seemed that management deliberately set out to employ Asians since employment application forms asked for passport numbers and dates of arrival in the UK. Jayaben Desai, perhaps Britain's best known Asian trade unionist, described to me in the early days of the strike what it had been like working at Grunwick:

> At the Dollis Hill factory the conditions were the same as elsewhere in Grunwick, the aim was to employ our people and from them to take as much as possible, for as little as possible. At Dollis Hill they had developed their own system. On two sides there are glass cabins for the management so that they can watch you as well. He is English. He moves around and keeps an eye. You have to put up your hand and ask even to go to the toilet. If someone is sick, say a woman has a period or something, they wouldn't allow her home without a doctor's certificate, and if someone's child was sick and they had to take it to the clinic or hospital they would say 'Why are you going, ask someone else from your family to go.' Perhaps they thought that having a day off would be a chance of getting another job and breaking their hold on us.
>
> Even pregnant women who wanted to go to the clinic were told 'You must arrange to go at the weekend.' On the rare occasions when a woman did go during working hours she would be warned that that was the last time. Everyone would be paid a different wage so no one knew what anyone else was getting. And to force people to work they would make them fill in a job sheet saying how many films they had booked in. If someone did a large number they would bring the job sheet around and show the others and say 'She has done so many, you also must.' Not that they were paid more! . . .

Then one day the foreman came and said 'Mrs Desai, why have you packed up?' I said 'Why not?' . . . I went out where the rest of the staff were working and I told them 'I am leaving. You all know very well what the management are doing. This has happened to me today, it will happen to you tomorrow. You have to wake up.' Why aren't they employing white people in this factory? Because the white workers would teach them how to treat them. We are not teaching them, that is why they are treating us like this . . . I walked out and my son Sunil was behind me – he walked out too . . .

I suggested forming a union. They asked me, how? I said I didn't know either but between us all we could find out. We all agreed on that.

It was Friday, 20 August 1976. On Monday we arrived at the factory with placards we had made demanding a union. We thought, specially the boys, that placards and a demonstration were important. We stood outside the factory and asked workers entering to sign a petition demanding a union. Then we went to the Citizen's Advice Bureau (CAB) at Wembley, as my husband had suggested, and asked them for information about how to join a union. It was soon after that that we contacted APEX and the Willesden Law Centre, and got in touch with Jack Dromey . . .

But taking this stand was not easy, particularly for the women. There were at Grunwick a group of exceptional women, women of great dignity and strength of personality like Jayaben Desai and Kalaben Patel who although in no sense 'westernized' had rejected traditional attitudes that women should be submissive and passive. It was they who formed the core of the strikers, persuading and supporting other weaker women. They visited the homes of these women, talked to husbands, fathers and fathers-in-law who did not want them to take part in any struggle, and they urged the women themselves to assert themselves. This was a tremendous task . . .

The management at Grunwick had always made use of the poverty of Asians: they had preferred them to English workers to the extent that white women applying for jobs there would actually be turned away. As the Grunwick men and women frequently commented, 'Imagine how humiliating it was for us, particularly for older women, to be working and to overhear the employer saying to a young English girl "you don't want to come and work here, love, we won't be able to pay the sort of wages that'll keep you here" – while we had to work there because we were trapped.' But the directors of the company were also aware of the position of Asian women in their community and they tried to use it when they came out on strike. George Ward, the owner of Grunwick, is an Anglo-Indian. Jayaben said:

> He would come to the picket line and try to mock us and insult us. One day he said 'Mrs Desai, you can't win in a sari, I want to see you in a mini'. I said 'Mrs Gandhi, she wears a sari and she is ruling a vast country.' I spat at him 'I have my husband behind me and I'll wear what he wants me to.' He was very angry and he started referring to me as big mouth. On my second encounter with Ward he said 'Mrs Desai, I'll tell the whole Patel community that you are a loose woman.' I said 'I am here with this placard! Look! I am showing all England that you are a bad man. You are going to tell only the Patel community but I am going to tell all of England.' Then he realized that I would not weaken and he tried to get at the younger girls. About one girl he started spreading the story that she had come out only to join her boyfriend. He did this because he knew that if it got to her parents they would force her to go back in. You see he knows about Indian society and he is using it. Even for those inside he has found for each one an individual weakness, to frighten some and to shame others. He knows that Indian women are often easily shamed.

But the women were changing as well. As Mahmood, the secretary of the strike committee, put it in the tenth month of the strike: 'When the women first joined Grunwick they were just like ordinary Indian women. But now many of them can stand up in front of the gate and talk back to the managing director. If he swears, swear back at him. They can face it, which they wouldn't do before' . . .

In June 1977 the Strike Committee had finally had enough of these bureaucratic manipulations forced on them by APEX. They decided to call upon the support of the rank and file of the labour movement. A week of action began on 13 June with a mass picket at which 84 people were arrested and there was large scale police violence. In the next few weeks the size of the picket increased reaching 2,500 on 23 June. Police injuries, 243 in August 1977 (according to Merlyn Rees, Home Secretary), continually made the headlines but in fact about three times as many pickets were injured. According to a Willesden doctor quoted in *Time Out* (August 12–18): 'Two types of injury are particularly common: the first is a result of testicles being grabbed by the police. The second is a result of women having their breasts grabbed.' These injuries went in general unreported in the media . . .

On the 22 November four members of the strike committee (among them two women, Jayaben Desai and Yasu Patel) went on hunger strike outside the headquarters of the Trade Union Congress in London. They were immediately suspended from APEX and had their strike pay taken away . . .

At Grunwick the unity of the working class was achieved. Hundreds of trade unionists came day after day to support the Grunwick strikers on the picket line. But in the end it wasn't enough because they hadn't the courage to confront and defy the handful of men who control the trade union bureaucracy.

Chapter 2

Black women, the economic crisis and the British state*

Amina Mama

BLACK WOMEN AND THE ECONOMY

The relationship between the various organs of this state and its Black citizens have been discussed along with some of its many ramifications in the context of the economic crisis (Gutzmore 1975, 1983, Hall *et al.* 1978, Sivanandan 1976, Solomos *et al.* 1982). The effects of this crisis on Black women at the levels of state and economy, and effects of the strategies of Britain's ruling class for dealing with the crisis on us, have rarely been discussed. These are addressed here. Throughout it is recognized that both the crisis and the strategies have political, ideological and economic manifestations, and that these amount to a regrouping, reformulation and restructuring by forces that have a history of domestic and international exploitation in the interests of capital.

Our relations to the economy are discussed here primarily with reference to the NHS and office work, and as such focus on African and Caribbean Black women, unless specified otherwise. It is argued that these relations are constructed along the dimensions of race and gender, to the detriment of Black women, and that the contemporary situation is one in which these divisions are being upheld and accentuated by the present government's strategies for dealing with the economic crisis, and by its policies and legislation in general.

The relations of Black women to the British economy should be considered in the context of Black people, but must in addition be analysed in terms of gender. This is because they are not equatable with or reducible to those of Black men, or subsumable to those of the Black community. It is not simply a matter of going into detail about Black women as a subgroup. There are qualitative differences along the dimension of gender and its meaning in British society which have implications for Black women, and have textured the economic relations of Black people in

*This chapter is a series of excerpts from Mama, A. (1984) *Feminist Review*, Special issue, 'Many Voices, One Chant', no. 17, July 1984, pp. 22–34.

general. We have played a specific role in the rationalization processes of British capitalism.

Studies of the post-war period are often discussions of 'immigrants', and therefore collapse all of us into a single, and by implication recently arrived, generation. A second deficiency is that little of this material is gender-differentiated although there are a few recent publications on female immigrant labour (Foner 1976, Phizacklea 1983). Peach (1969) in *West Indian Migration to Britain* presumed female migration to have been a passive following of menfolk. He put the proportion of 'women and children' at over 40 per cent of the total between 1955 and 1964 (p. 45). A substantial proportion of the women are likely to have been single, since women were specifically recruited. Regardless of marital status, the vast majority of these middle-generation Caribbean women came to this country as workers. Concerning recruitment, the National Health Service and the then Ministry of Labour were in consultation with the Colonial Office as early as 1944, and the local selection committees constituting a centralized recruiting system had been set up in sixteen countries (including Nigeria, Sierra Leone, British Guiana, Trinidad, Mauritius and Jamaica) by 1948. Doctors and dentists were recruited primarily from the Indian subcontinent. It is notable that restrictive immigration did not hinder recruitment, since quota systems allowed the NHS to continue importing unskilled labour for ancillary jobs, and skilled labour was not restricted (Doyal *et al.* 1981).

The 1981 Labour Force Survey shows 47.2 per cent of white women to be economically active, as compared to 67.6 per cent of 'West Indian or Guyanese', 48.1 per cent of Indian women, 40.5 per cent of African women and 15.5 per cent of Pakistani or Bangladeshi women. This gives Black women an officially higher rate of 49.4 per cent. The location of Black women in the labour market reflects and compounds the dimensions of inequality intrinsic to British society. In accordance with racial differentiation, we are to be found in the lower echelons of all the institutions where we are employed (this in itself reflecting the patterns of a segmented labour market), where the work is often physically heavy (in the factories and mills no less than in the caring professions), the pay is lowest, and the hours are longest and most anti-social (night shifts, for example).

In accordance with gender divisions, Black women tend to be employed in particular industries (clothing and food manufacture, catering, transport and cleaning, nursing and hospital ancillary work). Jobs in the 'caring' professions (nursing, teaching, community and social work) exploit oppressive notions of 'femininity', and yet actually involve heavy labour as in the case of nurses, ancillary workers and cleaners (see Unit for Manpower Studies 1976).

The National Health Service

The NHS is a major component of Britain's Welfare State, which has been developed since the last war. Its birth was fundamentally a fruit of wartime class collaboration and social democratic consensus, and financed by the post-war boom. This was also a time when workers, like soldiers before them, were recruited from the colonies to staff the boom and facilitate white upward (and outward) mobility, while keeping wages to a minimum that would have been unacceptable to the increasingly unionized white working class. Black labour was allocated by the market to specific purposes as we have seen.

Nursing is where professional Black women are employed in the NHS, usually as State Enrolled Nurses (SENs) rather than as State Registered Nurses (SRNs), despite the fact that the lower status SEN qualification is unrecognized in many of our countries of origin. National data on overseas nurses in the NHS are not available, and the studies that have been done reveal a large and fluctuating proportion that have been recruited from Ireland, Malaysia and the Philippines. In the hospitals they studied Doyal *et al.* (1981) found 81 per cent of the qualified nursing workforce to be from overseas (within this, Irish and Malaysians were more often SRNs, ward sisters and nursing officers, while Afro-Caribbean and Filipino women more often SENs or nursing auxiliaries).

With regard to ancillary and maintenance workers the same study found that 78 per cent of ancillary workers, and within this 84 per cent of domestic and catering workers, were from overseas. The proportion of female overseas ancillaries was more than double the number of males, and within that 78 per cent of domestic and 55 per cent of catering workers.

For more detailed exposure of the stratification within nursing and the role of Black labour in facilitating the rationalization of the labour process both within the NHS and industry, the reader is referred to Doyal *et al.* (1981). They argue that, in general, migrant labour has been used to enable changes in the organic composition of capital on terms more favourable to capital accumulation. In the case of the NHS immigrants are seen as having provided a crucial source of cheap labour, enabling the NHS to meet the demands of Britain's changing demography. The ever-increasing numbers of geriatric and chronically mentally and/or physically handicapped people has resulted in a growing demand for long-term care in unpopular areas; migrant labour has been used to facilitate caring for these people without dramatically increasing costs.

The economic crisis and its attendant legislative and political changes have affected Black workers disproportionately across the board. 'Restructuring' involves closing down old, declining areas in favour of new expanding ones. It so happens that because of the historical role Black labour has played, it is exactly those sectors of the market that have employed Black people that are now closing down, while persisting discrimination ensures racist recruitment patterns in those areas being expanded and developed, which are exacerbated by unemployment. Racist redundancy policies must also be taken into account. While the NHS cannot close down overnight, as we have seen recently, it has been a focus of Tory cutbacks. The government strategy is to whittle away as much as possible while privatizing, and it is the areas where Black women work (ancillary services) that are going first. For workers, privatization means an intensified exploitation; longer hours, less bargaining power, lower wages and fewer people employed on these inferior terms. The laying-off and sacking has already provoked protest from Black women workers (see, for example, *Caribbean Times*, no. 158, March 1984).

The recent 'fish raids' and deportation of Filipino nurses are evidence that the state is using immigration legislation to regulate Black women workers according to demand, much as the Ministry of Labour and the Colonial Office acted together in earlier recruitment strategies. The current context of high unemployment means that inferior jobs are becoming attractive to white British workers who previously enjoyed the luxury of regarding these as 'below' them.

Offices

Seventy per cent of all jobs in the GLC are office jobs and 50 per cent of the Black community live in London. Recent years have seen some Black women employed in some office jobs. These have generally been low-skilled ones, in local government and welfare offices. Offices have been at the heart of the so-called 'technological revolution'. Emma Bird had this to say about it:

> women are disproportionately affected by the introduction of new technology. Not only are they more likely to lose their jobs, but they are also more likely to find that the quality of work has deteriorated in the jobs that remain.
>
> (Bird 1980)

Her estimates are comparatively low; 2 per cent (21,000) office job loss by 1985, rising to 17 per cent by 1990. In 1979, APEX predicted a quarter of a million job loss by 1983. Assessment of actual job loss is complicated by the fact that many are lost by 'natural wastage'. The West Yorkshire trade union case study concluded amongst other things that new technology leads to job losses in all the areas of women's employment, that new jobs in scientific and technical areas will favour men, that there are disturbing increases in stress and new health hazards are evident (100 per cent increase in headaches, 77 per cent increase in eye troubles and 69 per cent increase in tiredness are reported) after the introduction of new technology. As in industry, restructuring has had the effect of decreasing certain areas while increasing new ones. Predictably by now, it is the less skilled secretarial jobs, where Black women tend to be employed, that are most affected. The areas currently expanding (banking, finance and tele-communications) are not those which have tended to employ Black women, and racist recruitment and selection for training in the new skills required is preventing proportionate representation of Black women in these areas. In short, what is bad for women is worse for Black women.

To conclude this section, it needs to be pointed out that the Black woman's status as a worker is particularly important because we are more often heads of families, and have more dependants than our white counterparts. Black women are also more likely to have unemployed menfolk, and when this is not the case, Black male wage levels are low. The Black woman's wage is therefore crucial to our communities, and changes to it affect all Black people.

We can conclude that the sexist and racist devaluation of Black female labour in Britain is not only historical but also a contemporary fact and that the situation, far from improving, appears to be deteriorating. In addition to this we have particular relations to the British state, firstly as workers to capital's needs, and secondly to the legislative apparatus, particularly through immigration legislation which is used to mediate this relation and keep it on terms that do not include our interests as workers. Finally, the present strategies for coping with economic decline/crisis are particularly detrimental to Black women workers, in the NHS and offices, and presumably in the areas not covered here.

REFERENCES

Bird, E. (1980) *Information Technology in the Office: The Impact on Women's Jobs*, Equal Opportunities Commission.

Doyal, L. *et al.* (1981) 'Your Life in Their Hands: Migrant Workers in the National Health Service', *Critical Social Policy*, vol. 1, no. 2.

Foner, N. (1976) 'Women, Work and Migration: Jamaicans in London', *New Community*, vol. 5, 1–2.

Gutzmore, C. (1975) 'Imperialism and Racism: the Crisis of the British Capitalist Economy and the Black Masses in Britain', *The Black Liberator*, vol. 2, no. 4.

Gutzmore, C. (1983) 'Capital, "Black Youth" and Crime', *Race and Class*, vol. 25, no. 2.

Hall, S., Critcher, C., Jefferson, T., Clarke, J. and Roberts, B. (1978) *Policing the Crisis*, London: Macmillan.

Labour Force Survey (1981) London: OPCS/HMSO.

Peach, C. (1969) *West Indian Migration to Britain*, Oxford: Institute of Race Relations.

Phizacklea, A. (ed.) (1983) *One Way Ticket: Migration and Female Labour*, London: Routledge and Kegan Paul.

Sivanandan, A. (1976) 'Race, Class and the State: the Black Experience in Britain', *Race and Class*, vol. 17, no. 4.

Solomos, J., Findlay, B., Jones, S. and Gilroy, P. (1982) *The Organic Crisis of British*

Capitalism and Race: The Experience of the 70s, The Centre for Contemporary Cultural Studies, Race and Politics Group.

Unit for Manpower Studies (1976) *The Role of Immigrants in the Labour Market*, London: Department of Employment.

Chapter 3

The heart of the race

Black women's lives in Britain*

Beverley Bryan, Stella Dadzie and Suzanne Scafe

CHAIN REACTIONS: BLACK WOMEN ORGANIZING

The Organization of Women of Asian and African Descent, or OWAAD as it came to be known, was undoubtedly one of the most decisive influences on Black women's politics in this country. As the first national network of its kind, it brought Black women together from all parts of Britain.

OWAAD's lifetime spanned only five years, from its foundation in 1978 to its demise in 1983. During this time, it captured the imagination of many Black women and succeeded in bringing a new women's dimension to the Black struggles of the 1980s. Its national conferences, held annually from 1979 to 1982, along with its day-schools, special project committees and its newsletter, FOWAAD, served as essential points of communication for Black women, presenting us with our first opportunity to meet as women on a national scale, to exchange ideas and lend each other mutual support.

Three hundred Black women attended the first OWAAD conference in March 1979, and its effects were to ripple through the community for several years to come. The variety of women who participated in terms of age, background and politics ensured that the mood would be conveyed back into our communities at every level.

Many women were inspired to go home and set about the task of forming local Black women's groups, some of which were to outlive OWAAD by several years.

Above all, we strove to develop an internal organizational structure which was non-hierarchical, enabling Black women to determine their own priorities and the level at which they would pitch their contribution. By devising a system of rotational representation, to take account of childcare demands and other commitments, it was possible for women to choose whether and when to participate in the overall running of the

*This chapter is a series of excerpts from Bryan, B., Dadzie, S., and Scafe, S. (1985) *The Heart of the Race – Black Women's Lives in Britain*, Virago Press, London, pp. 164–181.

organization. Although the system was by no means flawless, it represented a new and self-determined approach to political organization which remained unhampered by leaders or appointed spokeswomen.

The fact that we were active and involved was not, in itself, unprecedented. What was unprecedented was that Black women had begun to articulate demands *as an organized body*, with the assurance which could only come from a strong sense of self-knowledge and mutual solidarity:

> Our group organizes on the basis of Afro-Asian unity, and although that principle is maintained, we don't deal with it by avoiding the problems this might present, but by having on-going discussions.

> When we use the term 'Black', we use it as a political term. It doesn't describe skin colour, it defines our situation here in Britain. We're here as a result of British imperialism, and our continued oppression in Britain is the result of British racism.

> Obviously we have to take into account our cultural differences, and that has affected the way we are able to organize . . . if we're involved in a Black feminist group and we take ourselves seriously, that means questioning and sometimes rejecting aspects of our culture which oppress us, and that includes marriage and the family. We don't actually take that position as a group, though. We accept that individual Black women have to work out that contradiction for themselves and as far as we're concerned, we're there to support them, not to tell them to get in line.

As the Black women's movement took shape and form, the relevance of feminism to our struggles became an increasingly contentious issue. OWAAD was built on the long-standing tradition among Black women of organizing together within our community. The basis of that organization, however, was not necessarily a feminist one, and some Black women have always rejected the term outright:

> We're not feminists – we reject that label because we feel that it represents a white ideology. In our culture the term is associated with an ideology and practice which is anti-men. Our group in not anti-men at all. We have what I'd describe as a 'controlled' relationship with them. When we have study sessions on Black history and culture, men come along. Other meetings however are exclusively women's meetings. . . . We don't alienate men because they put down Black women, because we recognize that the source of that is white imperialist culture.

The belief that feminism is 'anti-men' and therefore divisive and counterproductive is not the only reason why Black women have traditionally organized outside the women's movement. The failure of white feminists seriously to address women's issues which are to do with race and class has been a barrier which relatively few Black women have been prepared to cross:

> I think if you're a Black woman, you've got to begin with racism. It's not a choice, it's a necessity. There are few Black women around now, who don't want to deal with that reality and prefer sitting around talking about their sexual preferences or concentrating on strictly women's issues like male violence. But the majority of Black women would see those kinds of things as 'luxury' issues. What's the point of taking on male violence if you haven't dealt with state violence? Or rape, when you can see Black people's bodies and lands being raped everyday by the system?

Despite such scepticism, not all Black women have chosen to reject feminism as a basis upon which to organize. Recognizing how sexism and reactionary male attitudes towards women have worked to keep us down, we have set about the task of redefining the term and claiming it for ourselves. This has meant developing a way of organizing which not only takes account of our race and our class, but also makes our struggles against women's oppression central to our practice.

Chapter 4

White woman listen!

Black feminism and the boundaries of sisterhood*

Hazel V. Carby

The black women's critique of *his*tory has not only involved us in coming to terms with 'absences'; we have also been outraged by the ways in which it has made us visible, when it has chosen to see us. *His*tory has constructed our sexuality and our femininity as deviating from those qualities with which white women, as the prize objects of the Western world, have been endowed. We have also been defined in less than human terms.[1] We cannot hope to constitute ourselves in all our absences, or to rectify the ill-conceived presences that invade herstory from *his*tory, but we do wish to bear witness to our own herstories. The connections between these and the herstories of white women will be made and remade in struggle. Black women have come from Africa, Asia and the Caribbean and we cannot do justice to all their herstories in a single chapter. Neither can we represent the voices of all black women in Britain, our herstories are too numerous and too varied. What we will do is to offer ways in which the 'triple' oppression of gender, race and class can be understood, in their specificity, and also as they determine the lives of black women.

Much contemporary debate has posed the question of the relation between race and gender, in terms which attempt to parallel race and gender divisions. It can be argued that as processes, racism and sexism are similar. Ideologically for example, they both construct common sense through reference to 'natural' and 'biological' differences. It has also been argued that the categories of race and gender are both socially constructed and that, therefore, they have little internal coherence as concepts. Furthermore, it is possible to parallel racialized and gendered divisions in the sense that the possibilities of amelioration through legislation appear to be equally ineffectual in both cases. Michèle Barrett, however, has pointed out that it is not possible to argue for parallels because as soon as historical analysis is made, it becomes obvious that the institutions which have to be analysed are different, as are the forms of analysis needed.[2] We would

*This chapter is a series of excerpts from The Centre for Contemporary Cultural Studies (eds) (1982) *The Empire Strikes Back: Race and Racism in 70s Britain*, Hutchinson, London, pp. 212–35.

agree that the construction of such parallels is fruitless and often proves to be little more than a mere academic exercise; but there are other reasons for our dismissal of these kinds of debate. The experience of black women does not enter the parameters of parallelism. The fact that black women are subject to the *simultaneous* oppression of patriarchy, class and 'race' is the prime reason for not employing parallels that render their position and experience not only marginal but also invisible.

We can point to no single source for our oppression. When white feminists emphasize patriarchy alone, we want to redefine the term and make it a more complex concept. Racism ensures that black men do not have the same relations to patriarchal/capitalist hierarchies as white men.

It is only in the writings by black feminists that we can find attempts to theorize the interconnection of class, gender and race as it occurs in our lives and it has only been in the autonomous organizations of black women that we have been able to express and act upon the experiences consequent upon these determinants. . . . Black feminists have been, and are still, demanding that the existence of racism must be acknowledged as a structuring feature of our relationships with white women. Both white feminist theory and practice have to recognize that white women stand in a power relation as oppressors of black women. This compromises any feminist theory and practice founded on the notion of simple equality.

Three concepts which are central to feminist theory become problematic in their application to black women's lives: 'the family', 'patriarchy' and 'reproduction'. When used they are placed in a context of the herstory of white (frequently middle-class) women and become contradictory when applied to the lives and experiences of black women. In a recent comprehensive survey of contemporary feminist theory, *Women's Oppression Today*, Michèle Barrett sees the contemporary family (effectively the family under capitalism) as the source of oppression of women.

We would not wish to deny that the family can be a source of oppression for us but we also wish to examine how the black family has functioned as a prime source of resistance to oppression. We need to recognize that during slavery, periods of colonialism and under the present authoritarian state, the black family has been a site of political and cultural resistance to racism. Furthermore, we cannot easily separate the two forms of oppression because racist theory and practice is frequently gender-specific. Ideologies of black female sexuality do not stem primarily from the black family. The way the gender of black women is constructed differs from constructions of white femininity because it is also subject to racism.

Black women are constantly challenging these ideologies in their day-to-day struggles. Asian girls in schools, for example, are fighting back to destroy the racist myth of their femininity. As Pratibha Parmar has pointed out, careers officers do not offer them the same interviews and job opportunities as white girls. This is because they believe that Asian girls will be forced into marriage immediately after leaving school.

The use of the concept of 'dependency' is also a problem for black feminists. It has been argued that this concept provides the link between the 'material organization of the household, and the ideology of feminin-ity'. How then can we account for situations in which black women may be heads of households, or where, because of an economic system which structures high black male unemployment, they are not financially de-pendent upon a black man? This condition exists in both colonial and metropolitan situations. Ideologies of black female domesticity and motherhood have been constructed, through their employment (or chattel position) as domestics and surrogate mothers to white families rather than in relation to their own families. West Indian women still migrate to the United States and Canada as domestics and in Britain are seen to be suitable as office cleaners, National Health Service domestics, etc. In colonial situations Asian women have frequently been forced into prostitu-tion to sexually service the white male invaders, whether in the form of armies of occupation or employees and guests of multinational cor-porations. How then, in view of all this, can it be argued that black male dominance exists in the same forms as white male dominance? Systems of slavery, colonialism, imperialism, have systematically denied positions in the white male hierarchy to black men and have used specific forms of terror to oppress them.

Black family structures have been seen as pathological by the state and are in the process of being constructed as pathological within white feminist theory. Here, ironically, the Western nuclear family structure and related ideologies of 'romantic love' formed under capitalism, are seen as more 'progressive' than black family structures. An unquestioned common-sense racism constructs Asian girls and women as having absolutely no freedom, whereas English girls are thought to be in a more 'liberated' society and culture.

The media's 'horror stories' about Asian girls and arranged marriages bear very little relation to their experience. The 'feminist' version of this ideology presents Asian women as being in need of liberation, not in terms of their own herstory and needs, but *into* the 'progressive' social mores and customs of the metropolitan West.

Too often concepts of historical progress are invoked by the left and feminists alike, to create a sliding scale of 'civilized liberties'. When barbarous sexual practices are to be described the 'Third World' is placed on display and compared to the 'First World' which is seen as more 'enlightened' or 'progressive'.

For example, in an article comparing socialist societies, Maxine Molyneux falls straight into this trap of 'Third Worldism' as 'backward-ness'.[3] Molyneux implies that since 'Third World' women are outside of capitalist relations of production, entering capitalist relations is, necessarily, an emancipating move. This view of imperialism will be addressed in more detail later in the chapter. At this point we wish to indicate that the use of such theories reinforces the view that when black women enter Britain they are moving into a more liberated or enlightened or emancipated society than the one from which they have come.

If we take patriarchy and apply it to various colonial situations it is equally unsatisfactory because it is unable to explain why black males have not enjoyed the benefits of white patriarchy. There are very obvious power structures in both colonial and slave social formations and they are predominantly patriarchal. However, the historically specific forms of racism force us to modify or alter the application of the term 'patriarchy' to black men. Black women have been dominated 'patriarchally' in different ways by men of different 'colours'.

In questioning the application of the concepts of 'the family' and 'patriarchy' we also need to problematize the use of the concept of 'reproduction'. In using this concept in relation to the domestic labour of black women we find that in spite of its apparent simplicity it must be dismantled. What does the concept of reproduction mean in a situation where black women have done domestic labour outside of their own homes in the servicing of white families? In this example they lie outside of the industrial wage relation but in a situation where they are providing for the reproduction of black labour in their own domestic sphere, simultaneously ensuring the reproduction of white labour power in the 'white' household. The concept, in fact, is unable to explain exactly what the relations are that need to be revealed. What needs to be understood is, first, precisely *how* the black woman's role in a rural, industrial or domestic labour force affects the construction of ideologies of black female sexuality; and second, how this role relates to the black woman's struggle for control over her own sexuality.

If we examine the recent herstory of women in post-war Britain we can see the ways in which the inclusion of black women creates problems for hasty generalization. In pointing to the contradiction between 'home-making as a career' and the campaign to recruit women into the labour force during post-war reconstruction, Elizabeth Wilson[4] fails to perceive migration of black women to Britain as the solution to these contradictory needs.

Black women were recruited more heavily into some of these areas than others. Afro-Caribbean women, for example, were encouraged and chose to come to Britain precisely to work. Ideologically they were seen as 'naturally' suitable for the lowest paid, most menial jobs. Elizabeth Wilson goes on to explain that 'work and marriage were still understood as alternatives ... two kinds of women ... a wife and a mother or a single career woman'.[5] Yet black women bridged this division. They were viewed simultaneously as workers and as wives and mothers. Elizabeth Wilson stresses that the post-war debate over the entry of women into the labour force occurred within the parameters of the question of possible effects on family life. She argues that 'wives and mothers were granted entry into paid work only so long as this did not harm the family'. Yet women from Britain's reserve army of labour in the colonies were recruited into the labour force far beyond any such considerations. Rather than a concern to protect or preserve the black family in Britain, the state reproduced common-sense notions of its inherent pathology: black women were seen to fail as mothers precisely because of their position as workers.

One important struggle, rooted in these different ideological mechanisms, which determine racially differentiated representations of gender, has been the black woman's battle to gain control over her own sexuality in the face of racist experimentation with the contraceptive Depo-Provera and enforced sterilizations.[6]

It is not just our herstory before we came to Britain that has been ignored by white feminists, our experiences and struggles here have also been ignored. These struggles and experiences, because they have been structured by racism, have been different to those of white women. Black feminists decry the non-recognition of the specificities of black women's sexuality and femininity, both in the ways these are constructed and also as they are addressed through practices which oppress black women in a gender-specific but none the less racist way.

Black feminists in the US have complained of the ignorance, in the white women's movement, of black women's lives. In Britain too it is as if we don't exist. The accusation that racism in the women's movement acted so as to exclude the participation of black women, has led to an explosion of debate in the USA.

US black feminist criticism has been no more listened to than indigenous black feminist criticism. Yet, bell hooks's[7] powerful critique has considerable relevance to British feminists. White women in the British WLM are extraordinarily reluctant to see themselves in the situation of being oppressors, as they feel that this will be at the expense of concentrating upon being oppressed. Consequently the involvement of British women in imperialism and colonialism is repressed and the benefits that they – as whites – gained from the oppression of black people ignored. Forms of imperialism are simply identified as aspects of an all embracing patriarchy rather than as sets of social relations in which white women hold positions of power by virtue of their 'race'.

The benefits of a white skin did not just apply to a handful of cotton, tea or sugar plantation mistresses; all women in Britain benefited – in varying degrees – from the economic exploitation of the colonies. The pro-imperialist attitudes of many nineteenth- and early-twentieth-century feminists and suffragists have yet to be acknowledged for their racist implications. However, apart from this herstorical work, the exploration of contemporary racism within the white feminist movement in Britain has yet to begin.

Feminist theory in Britain is almost wholly Eurocentric and, when it is not ignoring the experience of black women 'at home', it is trundling 'Third World women' onto the stage only to perform as victims of 'barbarous', 'primitive' practices in 'barbarous', 'primitive' societies.

It should be noted that much feminist work suffers from the assumption that it is only through the development of a Western-style industrial capitalism and the resultant entry of women into waged labour that the potential for the liberation of women can increase. For example, foot-binding, clitoridectomy, female 'circumcision' and other forms of mutilation of the female body have been described as 'feudal residues', existing in economically 'backward' or 'underdeveloped' nations (i.e. not the industrialized West). Arranged marriages, polygamy and these forms of mutilation are linked in reductionist ways to a lack of technological development.

However, theories of 'feudal residues' or of 'traditionalism' cannot explain the appearance of female 'circumcision' and clitoridectomy in the United States at the same moment as the growth and expansion of industrial capital. Between the establishment of industrial capitalism and the transformation to monopoly capitalism, the United States, under the influence of English biological science, saw the control of medical practice shift from the hands of women into the hands of men. This is normally regarded as a 'progressive' technological advance, though this newly established medical science was founded on the control and manipulation of the female body. This was the period in which links were formed between hysteria and hysterectomy in the rationalization of the 'psychology of the ovary'.[8]

These operations are hardly rituals left over from a pre-capitalist mode of production. On the contrary, they have to be seen as part of the 'technological' advance in what is now commonly regarded as the most 'advanced' capitalist economy in the world. Both in the USA and in Britain, black women still have a 'role' – as in the use of Depo-Provera on them – in medical experimentation. Outside of the metropoles, black women are at the mercy of the multinational drug companies, whose quest for profit is second only to the cause of 'advancing' Western science and medical knowledge.

The herstory of black women is interwoven with that of white women but this does not mean that they are the same story. Nor do we need white feminists to write our herstory for us, we can and are doing that for ourselves. However, when they write their herstory and call it the story of women but ignore our lives and deny their relation to us, that is the moment in which they are acting within the relations of racism and writing *his*tory.

CONSTRUCTING ALTERNATIVES

Concepts which allow for specificity, whilst at the same time providing cross-cultural reference points – not based in assumptions of inferiority – are urgently needed in feminist work. The work of Gayle Rubin[9] and her use of discrete 'sex/gender systems' appears to provide such a potential, particularly in the possibility of applying the concept within as well as between societies.

This concept of sex/gender systems offers the opportunity to be historically and culturally specific but also points to the position of relative autonomy of the sexual realm. It enables the subordination of women to be seen as a 'product of the relationships by which sex and gender are organized and produced'. Thus, in order to account for the development of specific forms of sex/gender systems, reference must be made not only to the mode of production but also to the complex totality of specific social formations within which each system develops.

What are commonly referred to as 'arranged marriages' can, then, be viewed as the way in which a particular sex/gender system organizes the 'exchange of women'. Similarly, transformations of sex/gender systems brought about by colonial oppression, and the changes in kinship patterns which result from migration, must be assessed on their own terms, not just in comparative relation to other sex/gender systems. In this way patterns of subordination of women can be understood historically, rather than being dismissed as the inevitable product of pathological family structures.

At this point we can begin to make concrete the black feminist plea to white feminists to begin with our different herstories. Contact with white societies has not generally led to a more 'progressive' change in African and Asian sex/gender systems. Colonialism attempted to destroy kinship patterns that were not modelled on nuclear family structures, disrupting, in the process, female organizations that were based upon kinship systems which allowed more power and autonomy to women than those of the colonizing nation.

In concentrating solely upon the isolated position of white women in the Western nuclear family structure, feminist theory has necessarily neglected the very strong female support networks that exist in many black sex/gender systems. These have often been transformed by the march of technological 'progress' intended to relieve black women from aspects of their labour.

In contrast to feminist work that focuses upon the lack of technology and household mechanical aids in the lives of these women, Leghorn and Parker[10] concentrate upon the aspects of labour that bring women together. It is important not to romanticize the existence of such female support networks but they do provide a startling contrast to the isolated position of women in the Euro-American nuclear family structure.

In Britain, strong female support networks continue in both West Indian and Asian sex/gender systems, though these are ignored by sociological studies of migrant black women. This is not to say that these systems remain unchanged with migration. New circumstances require adaptation and new survival strategies have to be found. However, the transformations that occur are not merely adaptive, neither is the black family destroyed in the process of change. Female networks mean that black women are key figures in the development of survival strategies, both in the past, through periods of slavery and colonialism, and now, facing a racist and authoritarian state.

Families do not simply accept the isolation, loss of status, and cultural devaluation involved in the migration. Networks are re-formed, if need be with non-kin or on the basis of an extended definition of kinship, by strong, active, and resourceful women. Cultures of resistance are not simple adaptive mechanisms; they embody important alternative ways of organizing production and reproduction and value systems critical of the oppressor. Recognition of the special position of families in these cultures and social structures can lead to new forms of struggle, new goals.[11]

In arguing that feminism must take account of the lives, herstories and experiences of black women we are not advocating that teams of white feminists should descend upon Brixton, Southall, Bristol or Liverpool to take black women as objects of study in modes of resistance. We don't need that kind of intrusion on top of all the other information-gathering forces that the state has mobilized in the interest of 'race relations'. White women have been used against black women in this way before and feminists must learn from history. The WLM, however, does need to listen to the work of black feminists and to take account of autonomous organizations like OWAAD (Organization of Women of Asian and African Descent) who are helping to articulate the ways in which we are oppressed as black women.

Black women do not want to be grafted onto 'feminism' in a tokenistic manner as colourful diversions to 'real' problems. Feminism has to be transformed if it is to address us. Neither do we wish our words to be misused in generalities as if what each one of us utters represents the total experience of all black women . . .

In other words, of white feminists we must ask, what exactly do you mean when you say 'WE'??

NOTES

1 W. Jordan, *White Over Black*, London, Penguin, 1969, pp. 238, 495, 500.
2 My thanks to Michèle Barrett who, in a talk given at the Social Science Research Council's Unit on Ethnic Relations, helped to clarify many of these attempted parallels.
3 M. Molyneux 'Socialist Societies Old and New: Progress Towards Women's Emancipation?' in *Feminist Review*, no. 8, Summer, p. 3.
4 E. Wilson, *Only Halfway to Paradise: Women in Postwar Britain 1945–1968*, London, Tavistock, 1980.
5 Ibid., pp. 43–4.
6 OWAAD, *Fowaad*, no. 2, 1979.
7 b. hooks, *Ain't I a Woman*, Boston, Mass., South End Press, 1981, p.138.
8 B. Erenreich and D. English, *For Her Own Good*, New York, Doubleday Anchor, 1979.
9 G. Rubin, 'The Traffic in Women: Notes on the Political Economy of Sex' in R.R. Reiter (ed.) *Towards an Anthropology of Women*, New York, Monthly Review Press, p. 167.
10 L. Leghorn and K. Parker, *Women's Worth, Sexual Economics and the World of Women*, London, Routledge and Kegan Paul, 1981, p. 44.
11 M. Davis Caufield, 'Cultures of Resistance' in *Socialist Revolution*, vol. 4, no. 2, October 1974, pp. 81, 84.

Chapter 5

Challenging imperial feminism*

Valerie Amos and Pratibha Parmar

It is our aim in this article to critically examine some of the key theoretical concepts in white feminist literature, and discuss their relevance or otherwise for a discussion and development of Black feminist theory. However, our concern here is to show that white, mainstream feminist theory, be it from the socialist feminist or radical feminist perspective, does not speak to the experiences of Black women and where it attempts to do so it is often from a racist perspective and reasoning.

Our starting point is the oppressive nature of the women's movement in Britain both in terms of its practice and the theories which have sought to explain the nature of women's oppression and legitimize the political practices which have developed out of those analyses. In describing the women's movement as oppressive we refer to the experience of Black and working-class women of the movement and the inability of feminist theory to speak to their experience in any meaningful way.

Few white feminists in Britain and elsewhere have elevated the question of racism to the level of primacy, within their practical political activities or in their intellectual work. The women's movement has unquestioningly been premised on a celebration of 'sisterhood' with its implicit assumption that women qua women have a necessary basis for unity and solidarity; a sentiment reflected in academic feminist writing which is inevitably influenced by the women's movement and incorporates some of its assumptions.

While one tendency has been for Black women to have either remained invisible within feminist scholarship or to have been treated purely as women without any significance attached to our colour and race, another tendency has been the idealization and culturalism of anthropological works. Often we have appeared in cross-cultural studies which under the guise of feminist and progressive anthropology, renders us as 'subjects' for 'interesting' and 'exotic' comparison. For instance, the book *Women*

*This chapter is a series of excerpts from (1984) *Feminist Review*, Special issue, 'Many Voices, One Chant', no. 17, July 1984, pp. 3–19.

United Women Divided (Bujra and Caplan 1978) looked at women's solidarity in cross-cultural perspectives and 'discovered' that solidarity was no unitary concept. The authors defined feminist consciousness and then proceeded to judge other cultural situations to see if they are feminist or not. While acknowledging that there are problems about uncritically accepting women as a universal category, this is purely on the basis of differential relations in class and status hierarchies as well as factors such as age and kinship affiliation. There is no apology for, no awareness, even, of the contradictions of white feminists as anthropologists studying village women in India, Africa, China for evidence of feminist consciousness and female solidarity.

The failure of academic feminists to recognize difference as a crucial strength is a failure to reach beyond the first patriarchal lesson. Divide and conquer in our world must become define and empower.

Many white feminists' failure to acknowledge the differences between themselves and Black and Third World women has contributed to the predominantly Eurocentric and ethnocentric theories of women's oppression.

We now turn to look at three critical areas in which Black women's experience is very different from that of white women. White women have benefited fundamentally from the oppression of Black women and before any kind of collective action takes place it is necessary to reassess the basis on which we ally ourselves to the white feminist movement. The three areas we have chosen as illustrations of our thesis are the family, sexuality and the women's peace movement. Each of these areas, in very different ways, points to the 'imperial' nature of feminist thought and practice.

FAMILY

The socialist feminist view of the Black family in Britain relates strongly to the politics of the British left, and their perception of colonial, neo-colonial and imperialist relations. Within this framework the Black family is seen as a problem in terms of its ability to adapt to advanced capitalist life – it is seen as a force prohibiting 'development' – and this view has been informed by the broader political and social analysis of our countries of origin as backward, needing to emerge into the full force of capitalist expansion before overcoming their economic, social, political and cultural 'underdevelopment'.

Black women cannot just throw away their experiences of living in certain types of household organization; they want to use that experience to transform familial relationships. Stereotypes about the Black family have been used by the state to justify particular forms of oppression. The issue of fostering and adoption of Black kids is current: Black families are seen as being 'unfit' for fostering and adoption. Racist immigration legislation has had the effect of separating family members, particularly of the Asian community, but no longer is that legislation made legitimate just by appeals to racist ideologies contained in notions of 'swamping'. Attempts have actually been made by some feminists to justify such legislative practices on the basis of protecting Asian girls from the 'horrors' of the arranged marriage system.

SEXUALITY

The struggle for independence and self-determination and against imperialism has meant that for Black and Third World women in Britain and internationally, sexuality as an issue has often taken a secondary role and at times has not been considered at all.

As we have increasingly grown confident in our feminism, some of us have begun to look at the area of sexuality in ways that are relevant to us as Black women. The absence of publicly overt debates on and around sexuality by Black women does not mean that such discussions have not been taking place.

Black women's continued challenges to the question of forced sterilization and the use of the contraceptive drug Depo Provera has meant that such campaigns as the National Abortion Campaign have been forced to reassess the relevance of their single issue focus for the majority of working-class Black women, and to change the orientation of their campaigns and actions.

It is worthwhile at this point to look back at history and highlight the fact that some of the unquestioned assumptions inherent in contemporary feminist demands have remained the same as those of the nineteenth- and early twentieth-century feminists who in the main were pro-imperialist.

Women were being defined as the breeders of the race, bearing and rearing the next generation of soldiers and workers of the imperial race. Within this context developed a new definition of women's role and the pressures which led to the formation of an ideology of motherhood.

White feminists have attacked this for its oppressiveness to them but not on the grounds of race and anti-imperialism. Such a development of women as mothers duty bound to reproduce for the race went alongside the development of an imagery of them as vulnerable creatures who needed protection not only at home but also in the colonies.

There are historical counterparts of contemporary white male use of the image of vulnerable and defenceless white women being raped and mugged by Black men, images which are reinforced by racist ideologies of Black sexuality. Also in responding to the use of physical violence to control white women's sexuality, white feminists have singularly failed to see how physical violence to control the sexuality of Black men is a feature of our history (e.g. lynching). This has implications for analyses and campaigning around sexual violence.

The racist ideology that Black and immigrant men are the chief perpetrators of violent crimes against women permeates not only the racist media fed regularly by police 'revelations' of 'racial' crime statistics, as in 1982, but also sections of the white women's liberation movement as illustrated by their actions and sometimes their non-action.

NUCLEAR POWER ON THE NORTH LONDON LINE

With the setting up of the Greenham Common Women's Peace camp in 1981, world attention has focused on the women's peace movement in Britain.

The women's peace movement is and continues to remain largely white and middle-class because yet again their actions and demands have excluded any understanding or sensitivity to Black and Third World women's situations.

Internationally, while Black and Third World women are fighting daily battles for survival, for food, land and water, western white women's cries of anguish for concern about preserving the standards of life for their children and preserving the planet for future generations sound hollow. Whose standards of life are they fighting to preserve? White, middle-class standards undoubtedly. Recently, Madhu Kishwar, an Indian feminist came to speak to the Women For Life on Earth and she stressed that what is needed is a realization that:

> A movement for disarmament begins with a movement against the use of guns, the everyday weapons. Here (in Britain) you may have a fear of nuclear holocaust and death and destruction – in India millions die of water pollution – that is a more deadly weapon for women in India. I think it is very important that nuclear piles be made targets for political action, but we have to begin with confronting the guns and the dandas (sticks) that is disarmament for us.
>
> (Kishwar 1984)

Many women at Greenham have begun to experience for the first time the brutality of the British police and some are slowly realizing why many Black women are not willing to deliberately expose themselves to it when it is an everyday occurrence for them, anyway. Black women are up against the state everyday of our lives, and the terror of a coercive police force, a highly trained military and the multifarious arms of the 'welfare' state are familiar ground to us.

The choice to demonstrate 'peacefully' or take non-direct action has never been available to us. When thousands of Black people marched against the National Front racists in Southall, in Lewisham, police were ready to do battle with their truncheons, riot shields and horses. Self-defence in such instances has been the only option and the armoury available to us has consisted of bricks, dustbin lids, chilli bombs and petrol bombs. The question of deliberating over how best to fight our oppressor is not an abstract one for us nor for people involved in national liberation struggles around the world.

CONCLUSION

For us the way forward lies in defining a feminism which is significantly different to the dominant trends in the women's liberation movement. We have sought to define the boundaries of our sisterhood with white feminists and in so doing have been critical not only of their theories but also of their practice. True feminist theory and practice entails an under-standing of imperialism and a critical engagement with challenging racism – elements which the current women's movement significantly lacks, but which are intrinsic to Black feminism. We are creating our own forms and content. As Black women we have to look at our history and at our experiences at the hands of a racist British state. We have to look at the crucial question of how we organize in order that we address ourselves to the totality of our oppression. For us there is no choice. We cannot simply prioritize one aspect of our oppression to the exclusion of others, as the realities of our day-to-day lives make it imperative for us to consider the simultaneous nature of our oppression and exploitation. Only a synthesis of class, race, gender and sexuality can lead us forward, as these form the matrix of Black women's lives.

Black feminism as a distinct body of theory and practice is in the process of development and debate both here in Britain and internationally and has begun to make a significant contribution to other movements of liberation, as well as challenging the oppression and exploitation of Black women.

REFERENCES

Bourne, J. (1983) 'Towards an Anti-Racist Feminism' *Race and Class*, vol. 25, Summer 1983, no. 1, pp. 1–22.
Bujra, J. and Caplan, P. (eds) (1978) *Women United, Women Divided, Cross Cultural Perspectives on Female Solidarity*, Tavistock, London.
Kishwar, M. (1984) Interview in *Outwrite*, no. 22, February 1984.

Chapter 6

Transforming socialist feminism*

The challenge of racism

Kum-Kum Bhavnani and Margaret Coulson

In their article 'Ethnocentrism and Socialist-Feminist Theory' in *Feminist Review* no. 20, Michèle Barrett and Mary McIntosh promise a re-examination of their own work in the light of criticisms raised by black women, and they do summarize some of the criticisms which have been made (Barrett and McIntosh, 1985: 41–2). They state that they endeavour to identify 'elements of ethnocentrism in our previous work, and [we] have pointed to important issues where the analysis we have presented has been seriously marred by the failure to consider ethnicity and racism' (1985: 44).

Although Michèle and Mary present an important and interesting contribution, it fails to open up the kind of area of discussion which is needed. This is because they lose sight of the central issue in the challenge which has been made – which is racism. By bringing another issue, namely ethnocentrism, into the foreground, they end up with their own previous conceptual categories intact.

The challenge of racism can often be avoided, particularly in quasi-academic discussions. In calling their article, 'Ethnocentrism and Socialist-Feminist Theory', Michèle and Mary suggest that ethnocentrism is the central problem for socialist-feminism. To us, the central problem for socialist-feminist theory is racism, of which ethnocentrism may be a consequence. As far as we can see, the role of the state and international capital in creating and perpetuating inequalities between black people and white people is lost through the use of a term such as ethnocentrism. Further, the word and indeed the concept seem to imply that the problem is one of cultural bias, supported by ignorance. It then follows that, if more sociological information is presented, the problem can be overcome. We are arguing, however, that to consider racism as the central issue involves a fundamental and radical *transformation* of socialist-feminism.

Despite their intentions, Michèle and Mary's method of re-examination denies the possibility of a radical transformation of their own previous

*Extract from (1986) *Feminist Review*, no. 23, June 1986, pp. 81–92.

analysis. The conceptual framework of *The Anti-Social Family* (Barrett and McIntosh, 1982) provides the fixed reference point from which modifications and additions are considered in the light of more information about black women. 'Woman' continues to be defined as a universal category and the oppressive and anti-social character of 'the family' is reasserted. Many feminists have been justifiably angered when (male) socialists have used this method in response to feminist critiques of socialist theories and practices. We do not dismiss the significance of the analysis of family/household forms and ideologies. However, we think that if we are to change the conceptual framework we have to begin by asking different questions. When we try to understand the condition of women we ask, what is it that oppresses women? What shapes the lives and identities of women? What shapes the lives and identities of black women? One way into the last question is through an examination of the political dynamic. If we consider what issues black people have been struggling over during the past five or ten years in Britain, we see that these struggles have revolved around challenging racism, specifically in relation to the state: over deportation and anti-deportation campaigns, and the police. From asking these questions and reviewing these struggles we are drawn to the need for fresh analysis of the relationship between the state and 'the family' and of how this differs for black and white people. This may lead us to an analysis, and some understanding, that the state may have different strategies for each group.

In resisting the pressure to review their conceptual framework/ categories, Michèle and Mary let go of the possibility of developing a new and challenging discursive space. In reinstating 'the family' as a key concept and as a key site for the oppression of women, the only concession they appear to make to the charge of racism is in acknowledging culturally different household forms. Because they recast this charge of racism into ethnocentrism, they only identify cultural differences; 'race' drops out of focus and ethnicity comes to the fore and this is reflected in the title of their article. By treating racism as almost synonymous with ethnocentrism, they obscure, and thus avoid examining, how *racism* relates to black families.

The analysis of *The Anti-Social Family* cannot be stretched to cover the situation of black women in Britain. In many circumstances 'the family' is not socially privileged and protected in respect of black people; indeed, it is often under attack from the state and from individual racialists. In the context of racist oppression, black families are often not 'anti-social' in the sense used by Michèle and Mary but can become not only a base for solidarity but also for struggle against racism. Not only is there a basis for solidarity within black households, but that can also lead to very real material distinction between black women and white women. For instance, as we have noted elsewhere, black and white mothers may have completely different experiences and perceptions of the oppressive nature of the state. The worries black mothers may have about children being late home from school can be as much to do with fears of police harassment as with fears of sexual assault. To carry this discussion further requires a fuller analysis of the relationship between 'the family' upheld by the state, in dominant ideology and social practice, and black families, within the overall context of a racist society.

The first point we would wish to make is that through arguing that an analysis of racism must be central to socialist-feminism, we do not claim to be presenting 'an answer'. We would, however, see that an analysis which we all, as socialist-feminists, need to develop is based on the idea of a racially structured, patriarchal capitalism (excuse the mouthful!). This leads us to examine how 'race', class and gender are structured in relation to one another. How do they combine with and/or cut across one another? How does racism divide gender identity and experience? How is gender experienced through racism? How is class shaped by gender and 'race'? To take these questions on does require a fundamental redrawing of the conceptual categories of socialist-feminism, and it may help us to develop a more adequate politics.

To have placed 'ethnic difference [as] necessarily . . . as important a consideration as racism itself' (Barret and McIntosh, 1985: 28) is, at best, to forget the substantial critiques of the concepts of 'multi-culturalism' and 'ethnicity' and the ways in which these can be used to bolster and legitimate racism (e.g. Carby, 1979). Thus, Michèle and Mary's conclusion (1985: 44) can appear rather dishonest. They summarize their article but do not explicitly state that they have, in effect, *rejected* the criticisms of Hazel Carby and the editors of 'Many Voices, One Chant' (Amos *et al.* 1984). These critiques, amongst many others, have jettisoned ethnicity and ethnic disadvantage as analytical concepts, but Michèle and Mary do not take up and challenge these arguments; they reject them by ignoring them. As we have tried to show, one consequence of not understanding the centrality of racism and its challenge is that socialist-feminism becomes distanced from the political dynamic. The danger of this distancing can be seen in the language used: Michèle and Mary's use of 'disabling' ('[we have] to recognize this disability in ourselves' (1985: 24)) is inappropriate and offensive. Offensive because it ignores the movement of women with disabilities and the criticisms they have made about disabilist assumptions. Inappropriate because when feminists have ignored and refused to see or hear black women, this has not been due to a 'disability'. White academic women, especially, are not so powerless; they have some responsibility for the political and academic choices which they have made. In the instance of Michèle and Mary's piece, they have *chosen* to highlight ethnicity as an analytic concept rather than racism. Thus, they are not 'disabled', they are mistaken.

The importance of this is in relation to political action. Many feminists employed as academics and teachers have been struggling within their educational institutions for greater equality of opportunities for women through challenging conditions of service, employment practices, gendered segregation in jobs and education, and so on. Rarely do these same women, if white, challenge the racism of such institutions with the same clarity and energy. Indeed, sometimes they see anti-racism as competing with anti-sexism for resources and support – for example, in recruitment of staff or students – thus operating on an assumption that anti-sexism concerns white women and anti-racism concerns black people.

The final point of our conclusion is to repeat that an assumption of automatic sisterhood from white women towards black women is ill-founded. Sisterhood can only be nurtured and developed when white women acknowledge the complex power relationships between white women and white men in relation to black women and black men. This needs to be done not only through acknowledgement, but also through re-examining feminist practices.

REFERENCES

Amos, V., Lewis, G., Mama, A. and Parmar, P. (eds) (1984) 'Many Voices, One Chant: Black Feminist Perspectives' *Feminist Review*, no. 17.
Barrett, M. and McIntosh, M. (1982) *The Anti-Social Family*, Verso, London.
Barrett, M. and McIntosh, M. (1985) 'Ethnocentrism and Socialist-Feminist Theory' *Feminist Review*, no. 20.
Carby, H. (1979) 'Multicultural Fictions', Stencilled Paper Series Birmingham: The Centre for Contemporary Cultural Studies, University of Birmingham.
Carby, H. (1982) 'White Woman Listen! Black Feminism and the Boundaries of Sisterhood' in The Centre for Contemporary Cultural Studies (eds) *The Empire Strikes Back: Race and Racism in 70s Britain*, Hutchinson, London.

Chapter 7

Theories of gender and black families*

Ann Phoenix

While different processes for the acquisition of gender have been theorized, the structure that facilitates those processes (that is, the nuclear family) is ... usually implicitly assumed. In a similar way the content that is to be processed is presumed to be obvious and commonly shared. However, societal divisions of race and class mean not only that the process of gender development is different for different groups of people, but also that gender is differently experienced by black people and white people, by working-class people and middle-class people.

Comparing differences between any two groups tends to polarize them and minimize their similarities. A secondary effect of this is that the two polarized groups appear internally homogeneous. However, there are important within-group differences between women and between men which have relevance for theories of gender development. The effects of racism and what this means for the class position of black people means that black children grow up knowing that black women and black men are in a qualitatively different position from white women and white men.

Since stereotypes usually have political implications and can provide a window on how different groups are perceived in a society, it is useful to consider how women and men are commonly stereotyped. Women are stereotyped as being the complementary opposite of men. They are supposed to be nurturant, passive, weak and non-competitive, while men are supposed to be aggressive, active, powerful and competitive – qualities which have frequently been used to justify male dominance of society. This is allegedly the content that girls and boys learn in the process of becoming gendered.

Black children's acquisition of gender identity is therefore qualitatively different from that of white children. Contact with the media and with other societal institutions means that black children cannot help but learn that black people and white people occupy different structural positions.

*Extract from Weiner, G. and Arnot, M. (eds) (1987) *Gender Under Scrutiny*, Hutchinson in assoc. with the OU, London, pp. 50–63.

They learn that their parents, and hence they, are excluded from positions of power within society. Black children simultaneously learn that black people are stereotyped in different ways to those in which white people are stereotyped. From this they learn that gender differences between black males and black females are qualitatively different from white female–male differences. Hence black children learn about racism as well as about gender differentiation.

However, in contrast with what they learn from the wider society, black children learn more positive gender models from their own social networks. Black women's participation in the labour market means that black children grow up accepting that mothers can also be employed. The fact that black children are more likely than white children to live with other relatives as well as their parent(s) means that they have a wider variety of people to interact with and with whom to develop close relationships.

While there are undoubtedly gender differences between black women and black men (see Hull *et al.*, 1982), the denial of power to black people that results from racism, and the fact that black women and black men occupy different gender positions from white women and white men, mean that the 'dominant/subordinate model' of sexual power relationships is not applicable to black people in the same way it is to white people (Lorde, 1984).

This does not mean that black people automatically reject the dominant ideological stereotypes of gender roles. Being subject to the same ideological forces as white people means that many black people accept dominant ideologies of gender (see Staples, 1985). This probably occurs for three reasons. First, because being relatively powerless makes people desire the positions, and so espouse the attitudes of those who are perceived to be more powerful (see Fanon, 1952; and Henriques *et al.*, 1984). Second, because being at variance with accepted societal practice means that individuals are subject to stigmatization. Avowed acceptance of dominant ideology may well be (in Goffman's (1963) terms) in compensation for the stigma that attaches to individuals who do not fit societal norms. An effort is thus made to reduce the social distance between stigmatized individuals and the rest of society, and hence to remove stigma. The third reason is because the pervasiveness of patriarchal structures means that individual subjectivity cannot help but be affected by them (Thompson, 1977).

It is important to recognize that individuals can simultaneously accept dominant gender stereotypes and actively resist racism because they disagree with the basis on which black people and white people come to occupy different societal positions. It is because black women and white women occupy different structural positions that many young black women actively resist the gender stereotypes that are constructed as 'normal' femininity. So, for example, the passivity and weakness that is meant to elicit a powerful male's protection is redundant for black women (and white working-class women) whose fathers and male peers do not occupy positions of power. It is not surprising then that black female school students and white working-class school students are reported to be more boisterous at school than their white middle-class counterparts, and should be sceptical about the benefits of marriage for them (Sharpe, 1976; Bryan *et al.*, 1985; Lees, 1986).

Because racism operates structurally to maintain black people in a state of relative powerlessness in comparison with white people, most black people are working class. Black children and white working-class children therefore have some common experiences of what it means to be gendered – in particular learning what it means to be excluded from and different from mainstream society. To be a black child, to be a working-class child, or to be a white, working-class child is to occupy qualitatively different societal positions from white, middle-class children.

However, racism does not only differentiate between black women and white women. It also differentiates the working class in such a way that in a public context white working-class women are advantaged over black working-class women and over black working-class men. This is graphically illustrated in the following quote from Gail Lewis's description of relationships between her black father and white mother.

> Another thing was my Mum's contempt for my Dad because of his humble demeanour in the face of white authority. Throughout their marriage it was agreed that Mum would deal with any authorities that had to be faced. . . . And since they both believed that by 'rights' the man should do this kind of stuff, then it only served to reinforce their shared belief in my Dad's inadequacy. Which led to him having to 'prove' himself by reasserting his dominance over her as a man. It was a situation that was fed by racism and their attempt at overcoming it.
>
> (Lewis 1985, p. 232)

CONCLUSIONS

By ignoring issues of race and class, current theories of gender, and the research on which these are based, actually address the development of gender identity in the white middle classes. This means that black children (and white working-class children) are rendered invisible in the processes of normal gender development, but visible in pathological categories like 'father-absent' households.

Theories of gender will become ecologically valid (Bronfenbrenner, 1977) if they take account of household organizations other than the nuclear family, and the different experiences of people of different classes and colours. This must not, however, be an adding-on of an account of black gender development to an unchanged account of white middle-class development, since this would still result in black people appearing pathological by comparison with the familiar account of white gender development.

Instead, theoretical accounts of gender development must centrally include structural factors like participation in the employment market, household structure, the operation of class and of racism. Gender development is therefore much more complex than current theories recognize. To concentrate solely on race would obscure the fact that shared class means that black working-class people and white working-class people have common exclusions from sources of societal power. However, the fact of racism means that there are experiences which are exclusive to black people. Structural relations and emotional relations need to be related together so that we gain insights into the psychic development of black children and white working-class children.

REFERENCES

Bronfenbrenner, U. (1977) 'Towards an Experimental Ecology of Human Development', *American Psychologist*, no. 23, pp. 513–31.

Bryan, B., Dadzie, S., and Scafe, S. (1985) *The Heart of the Race: Black Women's Lives in Britain*, Virago, London.

Fanon, F. (1952) *Black Skins, White Masks*, Pluto Press, London.

Goffman, E. (1963) *Stigma*, Penguin, Harmondsworth.

Henriques, J., Hollway, W., Urwin, C., Venn, C., and Walkerdine, V. (1984) *Changing The Subject*, Methuen, London.

Hull, G. T., Scott, P. B. and Smith, B. (eds) (1982) *All the Women are White, all the Blacks are Men, but Some of us are Brave*, The Feminist Press, New York.

Lees, S. (1986) *Losing Out: Sexuality and Adolescent Girls*, Hutchinson, London.

Lewis, G. (1985) 'From Deepest Kilburn', in L. Heron (ed.) *Truth, Dare or Promise: Girls Growing up in the Fifties*, Virago, London.

Lorde, A. (1984) 'Scratching the Surface: Some Notes to Barriers to Women and Loving' in *The Best of the Black Scholar: The Black Woman II*, special edn of the *Black Scholar*.

Sharpe, S. (1976) *Just Like a Girl: How Girls Learn to be Women*, Penguin, Harmondsworth.

Staples, R. (1985) 'Changes in Black Family Structure: the Conflict Between Family Ideology and Structural Conditions', *Journal of Marriage and the Family*, no. 47, pp. 1005–13.

Thompson, E. P. (1977) 'Happy Families', *New Society*, 8 September 1977, pp. 499–501.

Chapter 8

Other kinds of dreams*

Pratibha Parmar

In 1984 a group of us who guest edited a special issue of *Feminist Review* entitled 'Many Voices, One Chant: Black Feminist Perspectives' stated in our editorial: 'We have attempted to provide a collection of perspectives which are in the process of continual development, refinement and growth. It [the issue] also indicated some of the diversities within Black feminism, a diversity from which we draw strength' (Amos *et al.*, 1984: 2).

Rereading that issue now, four years later, it seems difficult to fathom where the optimism and stridency which many of us had who were active in the black women's movement has gone, and why. Where are the diverse black feminist perspectives which we felt were in the process of growth? And where indeed is the movement itself? In moments of despair one wonders if those years were merely imagined.

There is no doubt about the dynamic effects that the black women's movement and black feminism has had, not only on the lives of black women but also on the Women's Liberation Movement and on other progressive movements. One of the challenges that black feminism posed was to the Eurocentric theories and practices of white feminism. The take-up of this challenge was very slow, indeed sometimes defensive and racist.

For me, while there are several problems with some of the critiques and responses that have emerged in recent years to this debate on the challenge of black feminism to white feminist theories, the most important point has been that at least and at last white socialist-feminists are beginning to rethink their positions. But it is not only white socialist-feminists who are rethinking.

Critical self-evaluation is a necessary prerequisite for *all of us* engaged in political struggle if there is to be any movement away from intransigent political positions to tentative new formulations. And such self-evaluation has already begun amongst some black women. In the preface to *Charting the Journey*, the editors ask:

> For where are we at present? Instead of at least the semblance of a Black

*Extract from (1989) *Feminist Review*, Special issue, 'The Past Before Us: Twenty Years of Feminism', no. 31, Spring 1989, pp. 55–65.

women's movement, the futile 'politics' of victim and guilt tripping runs rampant and is used to justify actions that any self-respect would deem impossible. Or there is the tendency towards the collective adornment of moral and political superiority which is supposed to derive from the mere fact of being a Black woman. That this is so gives rise at least to a wistful sigh and more often to a scream from the far reaches of the soul – the only way to express one's disbelief and bewilderment that we could have got here from there.

(Grewal *et al.* 1988: 3)

What follows is a number of initial and exploratory thoughts which have emerged out of discussions with friends and fellow activists; discussions which have focused on how to move out of the political and theoretical paralysis that seems to prevail.

IDENTITY POLITICS

In these post-modernist times the question of identity has taken on colossal weight particularly for those of us who are post-colonial migrants inhabiting histories of diaspora. Being cast into the role of the Other, marginalized, discriminated against, and too often invisible, not only within everyday discourses of affirmation but also within the 'grand narratives' of European thought, black women in particular have fought to assert privately and publicly our sense of self: a self that is rooted in particular histories, cultures and languages. Black feminism has provided a space and a framework for the articulation of our diverse identities as black women from different ethnicities, classes and sexualities, even though at times that space had to be fought for and negotiated.

To assert an individual and collective identity as a black women has been a necessary historical process, both empowering and strengthening. To organize self-consciously as black women was and continues to be important; that form of organization is not arbitrary, but is based on a political analysis of our common economic, social and cultural oppressions. It is also based on an assumption of shared subjectivities, of the ways in which our experiences of the world 'out there' are shaped by common objective factors such as racism and sexual exploitation.

However, these assumptions have led to a political practice which employs a language of 'authentic subjective experience'. The implications of such a practice are multifold. It has given rise to a self-righteous assertion that if one inhabits a certain identity this gives one the legitimate and moral right to guilt trip others into particular ways of behaving. The women's movement in general has become dominated by such tendencies. There has been an emphasis on accumulating a collection of oppressed identities which in turn have given rise to a hierarchy of oppression. Such scaling has not only been destructive, but divisive and immobilizing. Unwilling to work across all our differences, many women have retreated into ghettoized lifestyle 'politics' and find themselves unable to move beyond personal and individual experience.

Identity politics or a political practice which takes as its starting point only the personal and experiential modes of being has led to a closure which is both retrogressive and sometimes spine chilling. Take for instance, the example of an article that appeared in *Spare Rib* entitled 'Ten Points for White Women to Feel Guilty About'. The title alone made some of us cringe in despair and consternation. There is an inherent essentialism in such articulations which has become pervasive within the women's movement in general and has led to political fragmentation. Lynne Segal has convincingly critiqued the biologistic and essentialist thinking which has begun to dominate much feminist analysis and practice in the 1980s and I would agree with her conclusion that 'Whereas the problem for women's liberation was once how to assert personal issues as political, the problem has now reversed to one where feminists need to argue that the political does not reduce to the personal' (Segal, 1987: 243).

REFERENCES

Amos, V., Lewis, G., Mama, A. and Parmar, P. (eds) (1984) 'Many Voices, One Chant: Black Feminist Perspectives' *Feminist Review*, no. 17.

Grewal, S., Kay, J., Landor, L., Lewis, G. and Parmar, P. (1988) *Charting the Journey: Writings by Black and Third World Women*, Sheba, London.

Parmar, P. (1987) 'Other Kinds of Dreams: An Interview with June Jordan' *Spare Rib*, October 1987.

Segal, L. (1987) *Is the Future Female? Troubled Thoughts on Contemporary Feminism*, Virago Press, London.

Chapter 9

Feminism and the challenge of racism
Deviance or difference?*

Razia Aziz

THE PROBLEM OF DIFFERENCE

Black women bring to feminism lived realities of a racism that has marginalized and victim-ized them in the wider world. In their writings the bid for a feminism that 'sees' agency and struggle in black women's lives is explicit. This involves giving black women centre-stage, and refusing consignment to the role of exotic sideshow.

In attempting to shift the ground of feminist discourse, the adversary has at times appeared to be *white feminists* but is in fact, I would venture, white feminism – by which I expressly do *not* mean any feminism espoused by white feminists. I refer, rather, to any feminism which comes from a white perspective, *and* universalizes it.

I do not propose that white feminism is a clearly defined, coherent and internally consistent body of thought that feeds off conscious racist intentions. It is, rather, a way of seeing which, however inadvertent, leaves identifiable traces. It subsists through a failure to consider both the wider social and political context of power in which feminist utterances and actions take place, and the ability of feminism to influence that context.

Much of the black women's critique has highlighted the suppression within feminism of black/white *difference*. This can happen in one of two ways: the first is the denial of difference which is implicit in the assumption that all women have certain interests (rather than others) in common. On closer inspection, supposedly universal interests turn out to be those of a particular group of women. For instance, the pro-abortion feminist stance of the 1970s did not take into account the fact that many black women's reproductive struggles were around the right to keep and realize their fertility. For these women abortions, sterilizations and Depo Provera[1] were all-too-easily available, and were often administered without adequate consultation and/or under the shadow of poverty. These are not experiences restricted to black women, but it was the intervention of black

*Extract from Crowley, H. and Himmelweit, S. (eds) (1992) *Knowing Women: Feminism and Knowledge*, Polity Press, OU and Blackwell, Cambridge, pp. 291–305.

women which exposed the in fact narrow base of what seemed to some to be a universal demand, and transformed the campaign – which now focuses on choice and reproductive rights.

The second way in which it was claimed black/white difference has been suppressed in feminism is through its re-presentation as black deviance. The issue is that black women have been marginalized in feminist discourses, so that when they are depicted, it is as the exception. This problematizes the ways in which black women differ from white feminism's standard of woman, rather than the general applicability of this standard.

To address this problem requires the prior recognition that black women's historical position as peripheral to the grand workings of power in society has precluded them hiding behind a mask of generality: too often the exception, the special case, the puzzling, more-oppressed or exotic anomaly (even within feminism), they have been largely denied the voice of authority by which white women appear to speak on behalf of the female sex as a whole. Black women's particularity is transparent because of racism; any failure of white women to recognize *their* own particularity continues that racism.

THE INSEPARABILITY OF BLACK AND WHITE EXPERIENCE

In keeping with the politics of black resistance, an appropriation of imperialist history has been integral to black women's political practice. In this way they have forged an identity deeply imbued with temporal and spatial solidarities: with their political and familial predecessors on the one hand, and with Third World liberation movements on the other. It is not my view that black women have a monopoly on internationalism, *or* that black women – in the First World – have an identity of interests with Third World women. Nevertheless, black women have frequently been left 'holding' the argument for the simultaneous consideration of class, 'race', imperialism and gender. This is not because only they can see it, but because they live it in a particularly acute way.

White women are as much part of social relations as black women are. Therefore, they must be as knowledgeable about the interactions of these structures of domination, albeit from a very different position. Racism, however, relies on a perspective of deviance which obscures white particularity. This masks the fact that white-ness is every bit as implicated as black-ness in the workings of racism. Thus, whether or not they are aware of it, *racism affects white women constantly.*

In articulating black women's experiences of the British state, the labour market, their families and their sexualities, black feminist writers have emphasized black/white difference (sometimes at the expense of other issues). However, it is important to note that theirs are not stories parallel to those of white women, but intricately intertwined with them. Black women cannot – even if they wanted to – speak of their struggles outside of the context of racism and resistance (if only because their colour is never 'invisible'); white feminists, on the other hand, can speak – and many do – as if that context did not exist.

The point is not, I would argue, that white women experience the state (to take one example) as patriarchal, whereas black women experience the state as racist *and* patriarchal: if the state is racist, it is racist to everyone; it is merely more difficult for white people to see this, because part of the racism of the state is to treat and promote white-ness as the norm.

BEYOND THE DEBATE

I (wish to) make a point which is conceptually simple, but politically complex: namely that the energetic assertion of black/white (or any other) difference tends to create fixed and oppositional categories which can result in another version of the suppression of difference. Differences *within* categories – here black and white – are underplayed in order to establish it *between* them. Consequently, each category takes on a deceptive air of internal coherence, and similarities between women in the different categories are thus suppressed.[2]

These effects are not deliberate: in fact the writers I have drawn upon all note the heterogeneity of black women as a group. Having done so, however, they tend to leave this fact untheorized. The heterogeneity of *white* women as a group, on the other hand, goes almost unacknowledged. Here I concur with Martin and Mohanty's observation that critics of white (or Western) feminism have concentrated on its inadequacy in dealing with black women, but have left virtually unexamined the implicit assumption that it is '*adequate* to the task of articulating the situation of white women' (Martin and Mohanty, 1986, p. 193).

In order to unravel the issues raised by stressing black/white difference, I will focus first on how issues of *class* are raised or ignored in order to emphasize that difference. I will then offer some comments on the strategy of black-ness as it relates to the problem of *culture* and identity.

THE PROBLEM OF CLASS

There has been some acknowledgement by black women that white working-class women have also been marginalized in the feminist move-ment. Take, for instance, Amos and Parmar:

In describing the women's movement as oppressive we refer to the experiences of Black and working-class women of the movement and the inability of feminist theory to speak to their experience in any meaningful way.

(Amos and Parmar 1984, p. 4)

However, this observation drops out of their argument. They were not alone in failing to engage with white working-class (or Irish) women's struggles, and – crucially – *how the existence of these struggles affects black/white difference and potential black/white solidarity.* Class often disappears in the desire to make a point against white feminism; for instance when Carby states that, 'Black people ... have a solidarity around the fact of race, which white women of course do not need to have with white men' (1982, p. 213), she is clearly not thinking of white working-class struggles such as the 1984–5 miners' strike.

It is of course not only class, but also ethnic, religious and even imperialist differences among white women that are implicitly denied here. In the attempt to deliver a jolt to white feminist complacency, certain issues of political significance are neglected, with the effect of homogenizing white women. The significance of such omissions is that they de-emphasize the oppression of *white* women by other white women, leaving black women *apparently* the sole aspirants to that dubious accolade.

A different problem arises when we consider the *self-preservation* of black women. Here class has been used selectively in a way that seems to deny the diversity of black women. The most common manifestation of this is the majoritarian approach: since *most* black people are working class, it is okay to behave as if they *all* are. I am not attacking analyses of the exploitation of black people and the role of capitalism in producing it, only noting a tendency to *class*-ify black people – a social group that displays class diversity *and* mobility.

This tendency inadvertently supports the unexamined position demonstrated in the following quotes:

All black people are subordinated by racial oppression, women are subordinated by sexual domination, and *black women are subordinated by both as well as class.*

(Foster-Carter 1987, p. 46; *emphasis added*)

Black women are subjected to the *simultaneous* oppression of patriarchy, class and 'race'.

(Carby 1982, p. 213)

The effect of this is to represent black women as *homogeneously oppressed in almost every politically significant way.* In bringing this argument, I could (as a black middle-class woman) be accused of special pleading; which is precisely my point: unless black identity *is* class identity, black middle-class people cannot be considered a 'special', or deviant, case.

Black people are an extremely heterogeneous group, and racism does not affect them all in the same ways. Some of us – thanks to factors such as a university education – manage to publish articles and speak, in spite, and because,[3] of racism, with the voice of authority afforded by class privilege! Many black struggles have focused on the issue of survival with dignity in the face of violence, poverty and humiliation, but black identity is not built on that alone.

THE PROBLEM OF CULTURE AND IDENTITY

The tendency to homogenize the oppression of black people comes from an understandable desire to find common ground and to resist the power of racism to divide black people from one another. However, it remains the case that perhaps more than half the people who may be labelled 'black' do not identify as such: I refer, of course, to the majority of British people of South Asian descent.

In spite of the criticisms of the 'ethnicity' approach there is a real political and experiential issue to be answered which is not just about divisive strategies of *racism* but about actual historical differences in the nature of colonialism, imperialism, racism and representation – and how these are appropriated.

The growth of anti-Muslim racism and the Islamization of Muslim communities in Britain during and since the Rushdie Affair is only one particularly acute example of why cultural *identity* matters. This example is of interest to all black women because of the profound consequences for Muslim *women* (many of whom identify with Islam) of the move towards fundamentalism (which is, of course, not confined to Muslim communities). The strategy of underplaying inter-black difference has never been equal to this challenge of *subjectivity*: at a time like this, it can appear at best politically naive, and at worst irresponsible.

Any line of argument chosen to emphasize black/white difference will tend to deny the complexity of both black and white experience. This may be unavoidable, but unless it is explicitly acknowledged a racial essentialism can emerge through the back door of fixed and oppositional identities. If alliances are seriously sought, the strategy of stressing one difference is limited. The dilemma is clear, even if its solution is not: in order for difference to be taken seriously it has to be established in debate and action; but it is important to take a broad view of the political consequences of this process, otherwise there is a risk of again detaching difference from history.

The issue of identity is one which best crystallizes this dilemma. Rooted as it is in complex layers of struggles and contexts, identity is not neat and coherent, but fluid and fragmented. Yet attempts to assert it seem to undermine potential solidarities between specific groups of women. In the final section, I address the question of identity more directly. I ask what post-modernist thinking can offer feminists seeking to progress on the issues raised by racism. In doing so, I attempt to locate a space in which a feminism of difference might take root.

LOCATING A FEMINISM OF DIFFERENCE

Recent years have seen the demise of grand (or modernist) theories; namely those which claim to establish *a fundamental determinant* of history (such as class or patriarchy). This demise is very closely related to the inability of such theories to respond to the complexities of difference and power. Socialist-feminists have attempted to juggle the grand structures of 'race', class and gender without giving one of them overall primacy. This strategy has not, however, been totally successful. It has become increasingly apparent that the attempt to combine (and so 'democratize') grand theories of 'race', class and gender may be unworkable. The endeavour tends to produce and multiply unwieldy and static categories without much analytical power (such as 'the white, middle-class male') as the list of oppressions becomes as long as the range of political struggles is multitudinous.

This 'democratization' of oppressions can be seen in retrospect as an attempt to push grand theory to its limits. It was accompanied by the growth of a phenomenon often labelled 'identity politics'. Oppressions tended to be increasingly regarded as 'relative', with attached identities that tended to be elevated above criticism. This can lead to an inward-looking identity politics where oppressions are added and subtracted. The capacity to analyse the *interrelations* between identities and social relations, and to establish political priorities, is thereby seriously weakened.

Identity politics ceases to be progressive when it sees the assertion of identity *as an end in itself.* Jenny Bourne (1983) urges us to ask what identity *does* in relation to the politics of resistance. Does identity politics promote or does it divert resistance, providing a sanctuary for people who do not want to acknowledge that they are oppressors? Bourne laments the analytical and political loss of privilege of the *material* (particularly the economic) as a determining factor separate from and somehow more real than language, culture and representation. Yet this dethroning need not take the ahistorical route Bourne criticizes. The view that language is constitutive of reality can, instead, open the field for historically aware analyses of the relationship between, for example, 'race', class and culture.

A focus on representation as a social *act* allows us to understand the ways in which the historical, the biological and the material are given a reality and meaning through language. It offers us a more complex conception of power as exercised in all manner of social interactions. Crucially, it allows us to see competing discourses – for instance those of dominant racism, of ethnicity and of black resistance – as *intrinsic* to the exercise of power in society.

This paradigmatic shift is rightly labelled *post-modernist* as it is a response to – and an attempt to move beyond – the weaknesses of grand theory. At its heart is an entirely different treatment of *subjectivity* – or the way in which people live and understand their selves and identities.

Post-modernism is *deconstructive*: it sees subjectivity as a *product* of power rather than its author; and agency as power's way of acting through the individual. Power, in this understanding, is exercised in historically specific discourses (or ideologies) and practices: in contrast to the modernist conception, it is not unitary and zero-sum, but diffuse, constantly changing and plural. Post-modernism is therefore antithetical to essentialism of any kind – racial, sexual or human.[4] It proposes that the selves we think are fixed and unitary are actually unstable, fragmented and contradictory. It can thus potentially help us look at changes and tensions (such as that of oppressor/oppressed) in who we understand ourselves as being.

Such a perspective can save identity from 'mummifying' by challenging us self-consciously to deconstruct our identities. This act of deconstruction is *political*, as it exposes the intricate operations of power that constitute subjectivity. Thus the particular deconstruction of the identity 'woman' that black women have achieved can be seen as exposing the link between racism at large and its subjective articulation. Nor is black identity somehow privileged (as I have tried to show): the cost of a 'home' in any identity is the exercise of a power to include the chosen and exclude the Other.

I may appear at this point to be espousing contradictory positions – am I *for* or *against* the assertion of identity? – in response to which I simply re-state the question: 'What is identity for?'

In providing us with self-presentations of black women as subjects of history, black women have established their identity as an influential political fact. An anti-humanist insistence on always *de*-constructing subjectivity ignores political context and the importance of identity in resistance. The assertion of identity is a process people can relate to because it reclaims agency and makes them feel power-ful. The importance of this cannot be underestimated. Furthermore, any focus on language and subjectivity which divorces them from material forces (such as the current crisis and restructuring of capitalism) also divorces theory from some of the things that affect people most severely.

Post-modernism does not immunize us from the responsibility to locate ourselves relative to the political movements of our time: as a discourse, it is part of – and is implicated in – the very power relations in society that we analyse and aim to change. If a feminism of difference is to compete with reactionary forces for the spaces caused by political schisms, it needs to incorporate *both* the deconstruction of subjectivity *and* the political necessity of asserting identity. Additionally, its recognition of the fact that language and culture constitute reality needs to coexist with a recognition of the unmitigated realities of violence, economic exploitation and poverty. For a feminism of difference, these questions need to be answered in relation to the imperatives of each historical moment. This requires a degree of self-consciousness and responsibility of thought, utterance and action from our oppressed and oppressor selves alike, which is nowhere near prevalent as yet. But the potential for alliance between and among black and white women depends upon it.

NOTES

1 A long-acting, injectable contraceptive banned in the United States because of disturbing side-effects.
2 See Phoenix (1988) for a good, short study which challenges this tendency.
3 By this I mean that being black made it far more likely that I would be asked to write this kind of article.
4 In other words it is anti-*humanist*, rejecting the idea of an essential humanness shared by all human individuals.

REFERENCES

Amos, V. and Parmar, P. (1984) 'Challenging Imperial Feminism', *Feminist Review*, no. 17, pp. 3–20.
Bourne, J. (1983) 'Towards an anti-racist feminism', *Race and Class*, vol. XXV, no. 1.
Carby, H. V. (1982) 'White women listen! Black feminism and the boundaries of sisterhood', in The Centre for Contemporary Cultural Studies (eds) *The Empire Strikes Back: Race and Racism in 70s Britain*, London, Hutchinson.
Foster-Carter, O. (1987) 'Ethnicity: the fourth burden of Black women – political action', *Critical Social Policy*, no. 20, pp. 46–56.
Martin, B. and Mohanty, C. T. (1986) 'Feminist politics: what's home got to do with it?', pp. 191–212 in T. de Lauretis (ed.) *Feminist Studies/Critical Studies*, Bloomington, IN, Indiana University Press.
Phoenix, A. (1988) 'Narrow definitions of culture: the case of early motherhood', in S. Westwood and P. Bhachu (eds) *Enterprising Women: Ethnicity, Economy and Gender Relations*, London, Routledge.

Part II

Defining our space

The new and original chapters gathered together in this section demon-strate that while black British feminism now in the late 1990s is still concerned with the specific task of challenging cultural imperialism in its many forms (including white feminism), black feminists have also had to shift their focus to a new project – that of interrogating intellectual possibilities. Questioning the postmodern preoccupation with 'difference', identity, subjectivity and essentialism, black feminist scholars in this section explore issues as diverse as 'mixed race' identity, lone motherhood, popular culture and media representations. They challenge theories of racism and nationalism, re-think definitions of blackness and re-define black female sexuality. Revealing their world through the oral traditions of story telling, life histories and autobiography, and reworking soci-ological and psychological theory, black British feminists demonstrate that they are now not only engaged in the process of claiming a space within their disciplines, but also exploring the power of their diversity and difference. Examining the critical creativity of the 'marginal' space they occupy, black British feminism, though positioned 'on the margins', can no longer be considered marginal scholarship.

Chapter 10

Raregrooves and raregroovers

A matter of taste, difference and identity

Bibi Bakare-Yusuf

INTRODUCTION

In contemporary Britain, black women[1] have access to a wide range of black and non-black expressive cultural practices that they can and do participate in. However, there is a tendency for the cultural practices of one particular black national group to appear as the essence of all black cultural practice. The patterns of migration and the timing of various waves of immigration into Britain have resulted in a hegemony of Caribbean culture in general, and Jamaican culture in particular. It is the under-class and working-class Jamaican cultural practices which are called upon to speak for and represent the cultural taste of all Britain's blacks. For example, Rastafarianism, blues parties, reggae and Ragga music, shebeens, the use of ganja, etc., have become synonymous with black everyday life and expressive cultures. This is also the case in both black and white youth cultural practices, 'yoof'-media discourse, and also in cultural studies.

Constructing a notion of a collective black community as though untouched by difference or internal contradiction has the effect of homogenizing the expressive cultures of the various black groups in Britain. This kind of homogenizing reflects the power of racism on the one hand, and on the other, a refusal by white mainstream culture to come to terms with difference among black settlers in Britain, who may have originated from Africa, Asia or the Caribbean. Stuart Hall has argued that because the political and the cultural struggle of black Britons has constituted an attempt to stave off invisibility in the white mainstream discourse, this has resulted in the construction of a singular, unified black community (Hall 1992). Difference within black communities, however, almost always threatens to disrupt any effort to construct a notion of 'the black community' or a uniformed 'black experience'. These differences are important and refuse to be contained by what Hortense Spillers (1987) has refered to as 'the ruling episteme' that tries to contain all difference. Baldwin (1985), Gilroy (1987), Bhabha (1984) and, from a feminist perspective bell hooks

(Childers and hooks 1990), have pointed out that ignoring difference among black people has had the disastrous effect of disregarding the different cultures, histories, customs, gender, sexual practices and the economic reality that operates in the formation of diasporic experience and post-colonial 'identity'.

The invocation of a unified experience may serve the purpose of providing black communities with an 'organising category of a new politics of resistance' (Hall 1992: 252). This is especially the case for a group who have experienced the violence of mainstream exclusionary practices. Appeal to a common experience is often invoked as a kind of harmonious entity that will liberate and offer protection from 'racial capitalism' (Hill Collins 1990; Benhabib 1986). Iris Marion Young has argued that the appeal of communitarian ideals in feminist politics and in social relations generates exclusions which helps reproduce homogeneity (1990: 301). I would suggest therefore that once the aims of coming together have been achieved, any notion of communitarian ideals or shared experiences should be abandoned and new alliances should be formed. Failure to do so only serves to show our own complicity in a racist discourse which tries to lock black communities in the fixity of its own construction. It also obscures the way appeals to communitarian ideals or shared experiences can potentially oppress and exclude the very same people it seeks to liberate.

Over-emphasis on black commonalities, at least in the political and to an extent, cultural fields, neglects intra-racial differences which constitute the complex nature of post-colonial black British experience. Points of connection, disconnection, cross-connections among black people get subsumed under the limited code of 'race', which impedes critical reflection. Reasons for this are touched upon by Audre Lorde who observed that, 'within Black communities where racism is a living reality, differences among us often seem dangerous and suspect. The need for unity is often misnamed for homogeneity' (1984: 119).

This homogenizing tendency to perceive the diversity of a heterogeneous collective sets in place strategies which police deviation. Black women who find themselves deviating from the norm impose measures of auto-correction by adopting habits, linguistic patterns, style, attitude, taste and aspirations of the dominant black culture to the neglect of their own culture and social origins. An example of this would be second generation Africans who wear dreadlocks[2] and listen to Reggae, and also those who adopt Jamaican patois. Alternatively, black women might reject the norm and select from the full range of black expressive cultures. These rich wells of black cultural expression affirm and validate their own experience of being black and female in Britain. I am in no way positing a kind of ethnic or cultural exclusivity; the expressive culture of the black diaspora, as Gilroy has usefully shown, has been one of borrowing and cultural inter-mixture (Gilroy 1987). On the contrary, I am inviting us to recognize that Britain's blacks are not only from the Caribbean, but from Africa and Asia. As Hall points out:

> What is at issue is the recognition of the extraordinary diversity of subjective positions, social experiences and cultural identities which compose the category 'black'; that is, the recognition that 'black' is essentially a politically and culturally constructed category, which cannot be grounded in a set of fixed trans-cultural or transcendental racial categories and which therefore has no guarantee in Nature.
>
> (Hall 1992: 254)

This chapter then is a tentative exploration into the notion of taste, in order to understand the way black women in Britain struggle to articulate the plurality of their identities, cultural ethnicity, cultural capital and experience, against the backdrop of some 'essentializing past', which attempts to homogenize the (re)presentation and experience of the black (female) subject. I do this by examining how their identity is expressed through the choices they make in the pursuit of pleasure and/or leisure. This will be placed within the context of the 'raregroove' scene in London in the mid-1980s which attracted specific groups of black and white youth. The popularity of raregroove music and raregroove dance space, I will argue, is important to the theorization of youth subcultures and the rethinking of black identity. Questions of race, gender, education, cultural ethnicity, region and economic capital as aspects of black identity – that are often elided in mainstream (black and white) discourse – are reflected in the raregroove scene. It problematizes the idea (perhaps more appropriately the 'ideal') of an unworked theory of 'the black community' by attending to diversity and internal contradictions; and simultaneously it attempts to problematize the notion of an homogeneous 'authentic' black female experience.

RAREGROOVE AS A SUBCULTURE

Although the raregroove scene is primarily dominated by black men and white women, I am interested in the ways in which black women who are visibly present use this 'anti-aesthetic cult' (Gilroy 1993a: 40) to re-draw their characteristic positionings. This is a novel development because the shared racial and cultural values which usually inform the theoritical construction of black female identity are displaced by diversity. Furthermore, the presence of black women in the raregroove subculture is a challenge to their exclusion from writing and research on youth subculture.

Much of the work on youth subcultures which developed in the early days of CCCS (1982) had very little to say about the activities of women in general and black women in particular. In her early critique of subcultural theory, Angela McRobbie (1991) bemoans the marginalization of young woman from subcultural theory. The absence of women, McRobbie argues, has to do with the narrow preoccupation of the theorists involved. Until very recently subcultural theory has been concerned with the activities of working-class white male youth; especially when they showed signs of resistance from official culture (Hall and Jefferson 1976; Hebdige 1979; Willis 1978). In general subcultural theory exhibited a romanticized reverence for youth culture as expressed in street culture, as opposed to the night-club culture, and made a distinction between youth culture and consumer culture. Because it upheld the concept of youth culture as being totally autonomous and opposed to the vagaries of capitalist seduction, youth cultures were viewed as authentic, capable of exerting changes in the social structure from below.

Recent works on youth cultures have shown that far from being distinct, consumer and youth culture have always 'merged, involved in an ongoing relationship' (McRobbie 1994: 156). The narrow preoccupation of sub-cultural work with the activities of white working-class boys necessarily excluded the activities of women in general and black women in particular because they do not fit so neatly into an analysis which fundamentally draws on a class analysis (Mirza 1992). More recent critiques suggest that youth cultures are an effect of various factors which do not solely rely on class antagonism. We can now explore the way class, gender, sexual and racial meanings affect and inform the performance of youth cultures. To this end I will attempt to analyse the activity of black women in one youthful arena – raregroove – by locating their activities within the context of the work of Pierre Bourdieu and Donna Haraway.

The raregroove scene developed in London in the early 1980s at ware-house parties and on pirate soul radio stations. DJs from pirate radio stations pursued the Pandora's box of the past, revitalizing forgotten and unknown soul tracks as a reaction to the commercialization and in-corporation of black expressive music into a bland 'format' – such as pop soul – which is served up for the white mainstream. Raregroove music then, is an eclectic mix of black musical genres which 'placed a special premium on politically articulate American dance-funk recordings from the Black Power period' (Gilroy 1993a: 40). There are several defining characteristics of 'raregroove' as a musical aesthetic: funk and early rap, which reflected urban experiences, issues and black consciousness with its funky, chunky, bassy and dance vibe. Most importantly, 'raregroove' according to Judge Jules 'is a testimony to the power of the DJs' (Jules 1986: 6). Songs like Lyn Collins' 'Think', Black Bird's 'Rock Creek Park', Hank Ballard's 'How You Gonna Get Respect? You Haven't Cut Your Process Yet', Maceo and the Macks' 'Cross the Track' and The Equals' 'Funky Like a Train', together with tracks by The JBs, James Brown and early Roy Ayers are the quintessential anthems of raregroove. The 'conscious rap' prior to 1987 – such as NWA's 'Express Yourself', Public Enemy's 'Bring the Noise' or 'Rebel Without a

Pause', and Eric B and Rakim's hip hop rendition of Bobby Bryd's 'I Know You Got Soul' – are some of the few contemporary tracks that were popular in London's black night clubs in the mid- to late 1980s.

With this rediscovery, DJs brought together in their warehouse parties 'groups that hadn't previously been under one roof together: yardies, trendies, yuppies, punks, sloanes, soul boys and girls' (Jules 1986: 6). As the warehouse faded due to over-zealous police tactics, the scene became fragmented, re-emerging in West End night clubs. The social mixture that had existed within the context of the warehouse parties became more diffused. Now the sloanes, yuppies, trendies and soul boys and soul girls that remained made connections with each other, and with a much maligned era, expressing their dissatisfaction with mainstream culture through their music and fashion.

The predominately male DJs expressed their dissatisfaction with the musical taste of mainstream culture through their control over the music deck. Women voiced their dissatisfaction by speaking through the body, especially as expressed in the arena of dance and fashion. Fashion was used to express their discontent and total indifference to the conformity and uniformity of the dominant culture and the safeness of 1980s mix 'n' match fashion. They turned their attention back to the 1970s fashion with its tacky masquerade of provocative hot pants brazenly worn with crocodile skin knee-high platform boots, garishly coloured turtle neck sweaters, yellow halter tops, mohair sweatshirts and flares, all paraded in a carnivalesque performance of grotesquerie. The 1980s revitalization of this fashion moment recovered the dissident spirit of the 70s. It also introduced that motif of 1980s youth, the flagrant display of youthful flesh in coquettishly ripped Levi 501s. This fashion bricolage represents the way these women have read society.

Night clubs such as Carwash, Raw at the YMCA on Tottenham Court Road, Babylon at Heaven, Dance Wicked under the Arches, Soul 2 Soul at the Africa Centre and Delirium at The Astoria served as outlets to express allegiance to 1970s music and fashion motifs. They paid homage to the Black Power and Civil Rights movements which gave rise to much of the music we now call raregroove (Gilroy 1987; Brown 1994). Past associations, however, were severed so as to express and encapsulate the cultural and racial mix of these integrated London clubs and parties in the 1980s. The nostalgia for this era is imbued with an authenticity which is absent compared to the ephemerality of 1980s music and style.

RAREGROOVE AS A SOCIAL AND CULTURAL EXPRESSION

When these women's activities are placed within the context of Pierre Bourdieu's work on the 'judgement of taste' it illuminates that process which he terms distinction (Bourdieu 1992). It allows us to understand how the articulation of similarity and difference among raregroovers and non-raregroovers is negotiated. According to Bourdieu, cultural preferences such as the choice of clothing, leisure activities, food, entertainment and all matters of taste are, 'the production of upbringing and education' (ibid.: 1).

The legitimacy we impart to our own aesthetic choices are bound up in dominant regimes of cultural representation. These aesthetic choices and cultural performances, he argues, are invariably social. For Bourdieu, the aesthetic and cultural choices being made by people function to indicate their social position in a field composed of different classes. The making of these choices is the process by which the field of difference is constituted. The process of distinction Bourdieu proposes, has the effect of:

> being the product of the conditionings associated with a particular class of conditions of existence, it unites all those who are the product of similar conditions of existence while distinguishing them from all others.

> (ibid.: 56)

If distinction is a process by which a class of people unite and separate, then the aesthetic choices people make, 'are the practical affirmation of an inevitable difference' (ibid.: 56). For black female raregroovers steeped in the 'conditionings' of a black community with its own internal contradictions and differences, black women raregroovers' choice of a particular leisure activity which is not normally considered characteristic is an attempt to make a separation from the lived reality of a shared history of white domination. Not only is this act a separation from white expectation, but it is also an attempt to foreground their material existence in a way which separates them from other black women. Therefore, the invention and enactment of a black expressive culture – such as the raregroove scene – is an occasion wherein they can position themselves in a social world that is not predicated solely on the expectation of racial homogeneity, but which acknowledges other factors which affect black people in Britain such as education, parental nationality, career aspirations, regional upbringing, family history of migration, etc. Matters of taste, such as in music, the arts, fashion, furniture, even friends, are shaped by the social environment. As Bourdieu explains, 'One would have to analyse fully the social uses, legitimate or illegitimate, to which each of the arts, genres, works or institutions considered lends itself' (ibid.: 18). Furthermore Bourdieu contends that objects which serve the social purpose of distinction the most, are those considered legitimate as works worthy of veneration, or those about to be legitimized, such as jazz, photography and cinema. These matters of taste, 'enable the production of distinctions ad infinitum by playing on divisions and sub-divisions into genres periods, styles, authors etc.' (ibid.: 16). Thus, distinction becomes a tool for the basis of social judgements.

An understanding of raregroove music, dance and lifestyle, developed within this paradigm of consumer choice, provides an entry into this musical pseudo-genre. This permits us to address the multiplicity and diversity of black women's positioning within discourses of race, gender, sexuality, class, ethnicity, region and leisure. It also enables us to recognize the different ways black women negotiate, construct and deconstruct their parental culture, other black cultures, and dominant white mainstream culture. Because black women are variously positioned within regimes of black and white discourses, the raregroove scene is a liberatory space used for the re-articulation of an individual self; which becomes one identity in a range of social groups which now constitute British post-colonial nationality and experience.

In this context then, the participation of black women in the raregroove scene can be seen as a subversive response to a totalizing definition of black female identity. In this definition, black women are always presented as one homogeneous mass perpetually acted upon by a coercive power in which they have no way of 'talking back'. But what we see in their participation in the raregroove scene is an attempt to challenge this totalizing definition through their musical taste and its visual corollary in dress and life-style. 'Nothing more clearly affirms one's "class", nothing more infallibly classifies, than tastes in music,' writes Bourdieu (1992: 19).

For Bourdieu, music classifies one's class position because music, in the bourgeois world, is perceived to be the most spiritual of the arts and thus a love of music is seen as a guarantee of spirituality. This is so because

> Music is bound up with 'interiority' ('inner music') of the deepest sort ... [and] for a bourgeois world which conceives its relation to the populace in terms of the relationship to the body, 'insensitivity to music' doubtless represents a particularly unavowable form of materialist coarseness.
>
> (ibid.: 19)

This dialectic between the coarse and the refined is precisely what the raregroove DJs are responding to. This is reflected in their strategy of recovery, retrieval and repackaging of music in which the political spirit of the various moments of black struggle through the 1960s and 1970s are reflected.

A significant number of songs subjected to the labelling effort of DJs were previously unreleased B-sides or had failed to gain acceptance when they were first released in the US. DJs on pirate radios sought to give this music a new lease of life. The rarity of some of these records accord them a legitimate aesthetic appreciation which was absent in their original formulation. Bourdieu explained that the social use that is made of a product is part of the process of making distinction:

> Nothing is more distinctive, more distinguished, then the capacity to confer aesthetic status on objects that are banal or even 'common' (because the 'common' people make them their own, especially for aesthetic purposes), or the ability to apply the principles of a 'pure' aesthetic to the most everyday choices of everyday life.
>
> (ibid.: 5)

For example, Tom Brown's 'Funkin' for Jamaica' was an ordinary 'common' soul track, it was undifferentiated from other soul tracks of the period, readily available from any car-boot sale for about 50 pence. However, once subjected to the 'labelling effect' of DJs like Norman Jay ('Godfather of raregroove'), the music ceased to be 'common' and accessible. The value of the music is radically altered in relation to 'the social marks attached to them at any given moment' (ibid.: 86). Music labelled as such is infused with a 'symbolic capital' not accorded to more popular forms of black music. A hierarchy of taste is immediately constructed in the process of distinction-making. This process Bourdieu terms 'the principle of hierarachization' (1993).

Because raregroove is a reaction against a popularized aesthetic, music included under the term is inflected with a 'symbolic capital' that only those with relevant 'cultural accumulation' and a certain image of 'cultural competence' are deemed able to decode in the way raregroove DJs have encoded it. For example, whereas a song may have originally been a celebration of black self-love and pride, black power, autonomy and unity, in the new context of raregroove it was appropriated, becoming an expression of individual autonomy and representing a utopian ideal. Expressed in collective pleasure, unrestricted by fixed racial boundaries, gender codes, or ideals of cultural homogeneity, the music changes meanings. This suggests that the consumption of music and the production of musical meaning are deeply interdependent. Consumers construct new meaning out of existing meaning to express their own specific social, historical and economic position.

Raregroove music then, exhibits instances when cultural competence and social positioning are used profitably in the market-place. This reinforces the cultural product, and induces new investments, as well as reassuring the legitimacy of the cultural product (Bourdieu 1992). Raised from its semi-existence, music labelled as raregroove acquires a symbolic meaning which reinstates and redefines it as, 'sets of stylistic possibilities', from which raregroove DJs and raregroovers, 'can select the system of stylistic features consisting of lifestyles' (ibid.: 230). We can observe this in their adaptation of 70s music and fashion motifs combined with a utopian element, whose aim, according to Gilroy, is to 'defend and extend spaces for social autonomy and meets the oppressive power of racial capitalism' (1993a: 41–2). We can note this in the cultural and racial mix of the scene.

THE CHALLENGE OF RECOGNIZING DIFFERENCE

The multi-racial character of the raregroove scene attracted black women who felt confined by ideas of black and female activities and roles. As black women we occupy a place in which tensions exist in both our relationships amongst ourselves, and also in the wider black communities. Black women's participation in this scene highlights difference, what Bourdieu would call 'conditionings associated with a particular class' (1992: 56). As I suggested earlier, black communities are modulated by factors such as education and material privilege. These differences makes alliances predicated solely on race almost impossible. Our identities as black people have always to be contested and negotiated along multiple axes. Gilroy makes the point that we must engage in

> rethinking the question of racial identity, secure in the knowledge that people inhabit highly differentiated and complex, even decentred, identities. Race carries with it no fixed corona of absolute meanings. Thus, gender, class, culture and even locality may become more significant determinants of identity than either biological phenotype or the supposed cultural essences of what are now known as ethnic groups
>
> (Gilroy 1993a: 109)

I suggest, therefore, that the imperative for participation in the raregroove scene is pleasure, coupled with a secret desire to address the different ways black women occupy, in Audre Lorde's term, a 'house of difference':

> Being women together was not enough. We were different. Being gay-girls together was not enough. We were different. Being Black together was not enough. We were different. Being Black women together was not enough. We were different. Being Black dykes together was not enough. We were different[. . . .] It was a while before we came to realise that our place was the very house of difference rather than the security of any one particular difference.
>
> (Lorde 1982: 226)

This concept of difference provides a language with which we can begin to address the different ways we are oppressed as blacks, as women, as lesbians and all the other 'others', and the different ways we might be privileged. The diverse experience of black women in Britain cannot be theorized as a seamless list of oppressions.

It is often the case that when the emphasis is placed on the way particular groups are oppressed, the tendency is to overlook how they might be privileged in other arenas. We need to develop a language which will take into account our different positioning in the social world. In particular, we need to acknowledge the way a privileged black woman can make choices that are out of the reach of her non-privileged sister. For example, the fact that I have made the choice not to work and devote a whole year to writing has to be located in my own position as a privileged woman with a family willing to support me in my choice. My own choice and individual history cannot be compared with other black women for whom the reality of poverty or the threat of poverty is a hindrance to even dreaming of writing. Therefore, as bell hooks reminds us, it is important not to allow our desire to share in the collective reality of 'black women' stop us from recognizing the difference in our social circumstances (hooks in Childers and hooks 1990). These differences are real enough for us not to assume that all black women experience oppression in the same way. bell hooks has called for the need 'to make a distinction between what it means to be from an oppressed group and yet be privileged – while still sharing in the collective reality of black women' (ibid.: 75).

It is no longer viable nor useful to reduce black women's reality to the taxonomy of oppression. As Donna Haraway suggests, focusing on 'victimhood as the only ground for insight, has done enough damage' (1990: 199). It does not allow us to recognize the profound, pleasurable differences between us, particularly those of sexuality, economic position, aspiration, politics and desire. I am in no way attempting to negate or discount the reality that black women are affected by various oppressive regimes, but in looking at black women's involvement in the raregroove scene, I emphasize the way the black female body becomes 'both a locus of action and a target of power' (Crossley 1995: 60).

The black women who participated in the raregroove scene cannot easily be compared to black women in such subcultures as reggae or hip-hop and more recently ragga (Rose 1990; Skeggs 1994). Raregroovers are a group whose specific 'conditionings', which are reflected in their consumer choices and access to either/or both 'economic' and 'educational capital', separates them out as relatively priveleged. Women in the raregroove scene have access to skills and official qualifications in a way that other black women in other black subcultures do not have. Although black women in the raregroove scene are united in part because of their blackness, this shared experience of migration and post-colonial position-ing is of less significance than their shared stake in asserting a certain value system; one which situates them firmly among those with the desire for upward social mobility.

Furthermore, I suggest that cultural inter-mixturing occurs in all situations where migration informs identity. The raregroove scene is a site of this radical inter-mixturing. Black female raregroovers are interacting with a group whom by virtue of their race and class position are already in possession of racial, educational and economic capital, which is necessary to participate in the social field. Thus black women too are able to enter into a series of social networks which may procure them access to a wider social field than that which they will ordinarily have access to. This kind of amassing of social networks Bourdieu terms social capital. Citing Bourdieu, Moi describes social capital as a 'relational power' whereby a given person accumulates a number of useful cultural, economic, or political relations (Moi 1991: 102).

For aspirational black females, the interaction with people from diverse social backgrounds (that is different class, race, ethnic, geographical location and so on) provides the opportunity for social contacts, and access to future 'life-skills' in the form of work and employment (McRobbie 1994: 161). While I am aware that the exchange of any capital between and among white raregroovers will not necessarily circulate among black women in the same way, I am however, concerned to show that black women who are already consecrated (Bourdieu's term) within the field of legitimacy are able to participate in the field. Situated thus, they are in a position to amass social capital which will enable them to 'develop or increase other forms of capital and may greatly enhance [their] chances of achieving legitimacy in a given field' (Moi 1991: 103). Since capital is needed to produce more capital, those black women without the necessary capital to begin with are effectively debarred from benefiting and participating in the social web of interrelated networks that is raregroove. The fact that some black females can participate within the field of legitimacy, as Bourdieu might argue, allows the dominant culture to demontrate their libertine ideals. It is the presence of this small minority within the dominant structure that Bourdieu refers to as the 'miraculous exceptions'. The presence of this 'miraculous exception' within the dominant group always gives legitamacy to the lie that the black presence is racial and gender neutral (Moi 1991).

Interactions between any groups or individuals, especially with the dominant groups, is never treated (with good reason!) as innocent, but viewed with suspicion and ambivalence. However, as Gilroy points out, youth cultures are often sites for contesting ideas of nationalism, racial exclusivism, subjectivity and identification, precisely because they are based on a distancing from the sobriety of mainstream culture. Gilroy puts it thus:

> I think it is possible to show that youth cultures are essentially hybrid social and political forms ... their transnational and international character points to new conceptions of subjectivity and identification that articulate the local and the global in novel and exciting patterns ... the notion of any culture based primarily around age and generation contains an inherent challenge to the logic of racial and national and ethnic essentialism.
>
> (Gilroy 1993b: 6)

In the process of making distinctions between themselves as raregroovers and non-raregroovers, I suggest that black women are aware of the material reality which separates them from other black women. They recognize points of connection and similarity with other raregroovers who may be white, whilst also aware of the distance between them because they are lacking in racial capital. Thus, black female raregroovers may bond with other black women non-raregroovers on account of race, however, this bond maybe disrupted by other factors such as status, aspiration, pleasure, desire, access to a given cultural capital and so on – the absence of which may necessitate a bonding with white female raregroovers.

Read against a backdrop of economic recession, mass apathy and neo-conservative ascendancy, this kind of social contact for black women raregroovers can also serve as a future investment through the forging of strategic friendships (Moi 1991). By choosing wisely to befriend members of the dominant culture, black women demonstrate awareness of their lived reality, and the importance and relevance of 'social capital' which is necessary for them to participate, effectively in the wider social world.

TRANSGRESSING THE BOUNDARIES OF 'IDENTITY'

I suggest that Donna Haraway's cyborgian metaphor could posit another way of re-evaluating black women's participation in the raregroove scene, challenging Bourdieu's notion of distinction-making.

Haraway's use of the cyborg metaphor (1990) helps to elucidate on the multiplex possibilities and foreclosures which is characteristic of the present moment. She recognizes the rich, pregnant, and contradictory locations of our identities. Accordingly, the cyborg is a phenomenon which pleasurably violates seemingly fixed boundaries; a phenomenon which 'transgressed boundaries' – particularly those between humans and machines, animals and machine and idealism and materialism (ibid.). While a Bourdieuian notion of distinction-making enables an analysis of black women who are separate from other black women in terms of musical taste, Haraway's cyborgian metaphor facilitates the disruption of that process. That is, black women in the rargroove scene are able to cross boundaries and make connections with groups they may have no previous connection with.

The raregroove scene, then, can be read as the moment of the dissolution of old boundaries between socially disparate groups: white women and black men, black women and white men, white women and black women, Africans and Caribbeans and Asians, yuppies and trendies. Social distinctions such as gender, race and ethnicity are open to microscopic scrutiny for their validity as referential catogories in contemporary positioning and identity.

This invariably opens up new avenues and new sites for rethinking black female subjectivity, experience, pleasure and desire. The apparent fixity of the innocuous and coherent notion of identity tightly structured around the codified prison house of race, gender and class which according to Haraway has become the basis for belief in 'essential' unity is now disrupted. Furthermore as Haraway posits:

> There is nothing about being 'female' that naturally binds women. There is not even such a state as 'being' female, itself a highly complex category constructed in contested sexual scientific discourses and other social practices. Gender, race, or class consciousness is an achievement forced on us by the terrible historical experience of the contradictory social realities of patriarchy, colonialism, racism and capitalism.
>
> (ibid.: 197)

Contesting the signifier 'black', James Baldwin posed this question in the 1950s, and I quote him at length:

> Is it possible to describe as a culture what may simply be, after all a history of oppression? That is, this history and these present facts, which involve so many millions of people who are divided from each other by so many miles of the globe, which operates and has operated under such very different conditions, to such different effects, and which has produced so many sub-histories, problems, traditions, possibilities, aspirations, assumptions, languages, hybrids – is this history enough to have made of the Earth's black population anything that can legitimately be described as a culture? For what beyond the fact that all black men [and women] at one time or another left Africa or have remained there, what do they really have in common?
>
> (Baldwin 1985: 49)

As these two quotes illustrate the signifier 'black' or 'woman' becomes deeply problematic when it is called upon to stand for and address a diverse experience. The dissolution of these signifiers is inevitable. The dissolution of boundaries, even if only temporarily, Haraway suggests, facilitates the recognition of the interconnection and cross-connection of all living organisms:

> a cyborg world might be about lived social and bodily realities in which people are not afraid of their joint kinship with animals and machines, not afraid of permanently partial identities and contradictory standpoints. The political struggle is to see from both perspectives at once because each reveals both dominations and possibilities unimaginable from other vantage points.
>
> (Haraway 1990: 154)

For black women who are unhappy with what Greg Tate calls the 'romance with being black' (see Dent 1992), the raregroove scene provided them with a context in which they could give expression to the diverse ways in which black female subjectivity is lived. They can invent and reinvent themselves without adhering to the fixed racial regime. The raregroove scene offers this context precisely because it is *not* modulated entirely by ethnic, cultural or racial particularities. Rather it is an important space for the (re)negotiation of the terms by which race, ethnicity and culture are expressed, normalized and contested. The women who entered such a space were struggling, 'to remake the world in their own image' (Baldwin 1985: 50). Raregroove space enabled them to do so as they affirm their cultural identities and, if need be, relinquish the restrictive code of racial essence and acceptable femininity. Thus, women in this space could still be Swiss, Scottish, English, and still be white; Nigerian, Ghanaian, Indian, Trinidadian and still be black and British. This marks the moment which Stuart Hall describes in 'New Ethnicities' as the 'end of the innocent notion of the essential black subject' (1992: 254).

This is not to suggest that the raregroove scene is immune from the politics of race and racism, but rather to offer an example of different forces which come to bear on the 'fact of blackness' (Fanon 1993: 109), and the way it is lived in and through gender, sexuality, ethnicity, culture, aspiration and class position. In essence, what I am trying to suggest, is that it is precisely their resistance to the fixity of racial and gender identity which propelled black women into the scene. An analysis of the rare-groove scene illustrates the point at which racial homogeneity is merely a template for the more diverse and significant social conditionings which act to distinguish these black women from others.

This way of viewing black women's contradictory locations favours a more complex theorizing of black and female identity, which privileges the different facets of black female experience. We can then begin to understand how the lived reality of black women is contested and negotiated along lines structured by difference. This recognition will invariably create the condition where difference can be rethought using Bourdieu's idea of distinction-making. Similarly, assertions of homo-geneity can be disrupted and connection can be established using Haraway's cyborgian metaphor. Central to raregroove music and lifestyle is distinction-making, and the transgressing of normative expectations. Statements of difference enable black women to actively challenge the constraints of identity and identification. This facilitates a move towards a politics of affinity. In moving toward a politics of affinity, our contra-dictory perspectives as black women are revealed as we embrace our individual and collective identities, that are unique to this particular historical moment.

ACKNOWLEDGEMENTS

Grateful thanks are due to my two sisters, Bum Daramola and Ekow Essuman, and to Trevor Thomas, who helped in the preparation of this, and in particular to Jackie Stacey and Terry Lovell.

NOTES

1 The term 'black' is used to connote women with one or both parents descending from Africa, Asia and the Caribbean. It used as a political category, 'coined as a way of referencing the common experience of racism and marginalization in Britain and [it] came to provide the organizing category of a new politics of resistance, amongst groups and communities with, in fact, very different histories, traditions and ethnic identities' (Hall 1992: 252).

2 We need to understand that the context in which dreadlocks are now worn is a far cry from its early association with the religion of Rastafarianism. It has now become a sign appropriated by a variety of groups in order to articulate their subject position.

REFERENCES

Baldwin, J. (1985) 'Princes and Powers' in *The Price of the Ticket: Collected Non-Fiction 1948–1985*, London: Michael Joseph (essay originally published 1951).

Benhabib, S. (1986) 'The Generalized and Concrete Other: Toward a Feminist Critique of Substitutionalist Universalism' in *Praxis International* vol. 5, no. 4, pp. 402–24.

Bhabha, H.(1984) 'Of Mimicry and Men: The Ambivalence of Colonial Discourse' in *October* vol. 28, Spring.

Bourdieu, P. (1992) *Distinction: A Social Critique of the Judgement of Taste*, London: Routledge.

—— (1993) *The Field of Cultural Production*, London: Polity Press.

Brown, M. (1994) 'Funk Music as Genre: Black Aesthetics, Apocalyptic thinking and Urban Protest in Post-1965 African-American pop' in *Cultural Studies* vol. 8, no. 3, Oct.

Childers, M. and hooks, b. (1990) 'A Conversation about Race and Class' in M. Hirsch and E. Fox Keller (eds) *Conflicts in Feminism*, New York: Routledge.

CCCS (1982) *The Empire Strikes Back: Race and Racism in 70s Britain*, London: Hutchinson.

Crossley, N. (1995) 'Merleau-Ponty, the Elusive Body and Carnal Sociology' in *Body and Society* vol. 1, no. 1, March.

Dent, G. (1992) 'Black Pleasure, Black Joy: An Introduction' in G. Dent (ed.) *Black Popular Culture*, USA: Bay Press.

Fanon, F. (1993) *Black Skin, White Masks*, London: Pluto.

Gilroy, P. (1987) *There Ain't No Black in the Union Jack*, London: Hutchinson.

—— (1993a) *Small Acts*, London: Serpent's Tail.

—— (1993b) 'Between Afro-centrism and Euro-centrism: Youth Culture and the Problem of Hybridity' in *Young: Nordic Journal of Youth Research* vol. 1, no. 2, May.

Hall, S. (1990) 'Cultural Identity and Diaspora', in J. Rutherford (ed.) *Identity: Community, Culture and Diaspora*, London: Lawrence and Wishart.

—— (1992) 'New Ethnicities' in J. Donald and A Rattansi (eds) *'Race', Culture and Difference*, London: Sage.

Hall, S. and Jefferson, T. (eds) (1976) *Resistence Through Rituals*, London: Hutchinson.

Haraway, D. (1990) 'A Manifesto for Cyborgs: Science, Technology, and Socialist Feminism in the 1980s' in L. Nicholson (ed.) *Feminism/Postmoderism*, New York: Routledge.

Hebdige, D. (1979) *Subculture: The Meaning of Style*, London: Methuen.

Hill Collins, P. (1990) *Black Feminist Thought*, London: Routledge.

Jules, J. (1986) 'Raregroove' in *Soul Underground*, November issue.

Lorde, A.(1982) *Zami: A New Spelling of my Name*, London: Sheba.

—— (1984) 'Age, Race, Class, and Sex: Women Redefining Difference' in *Sister Outsider*, California: The Crossing Press Feminsts Series.

McRobbie, A. (1991) *Feminism and Youth Culture: From Jackie to Just Seventeen* London: Macmillan.

—— (1994) *PostModernism and Popular Culture*, London: Routledge.

Mirza, H. (1992) *Young, Female and Black*, London: Routledge.

Moi, T. (1991) 'Appropriating Bourdieu: Feminst Theory and Pierre Bourdieu's Sociology of Culture' in *New Literary History* vol. 22.

Nicholson, L. (ed.) (1990) *Feminism/Postmodernism*, New York: Routledge.

Rose, T. (1990) 'Never Trust a Big Butt and a Smile' in *Camera Obscura* vol. 123, May, pp. 110–31.

Skeggs, B. (1994) 'Refusing to be Civilized: "Race", Sexuality and Power' in A. Haleh and M. Maynard (eds) *The Dynamics of 'Race' and Gender: Some Feminist Interventions*, London: Taylor and Francis.

Spillers, H. (1987) 'Mama's Baby, Papa's Maybe: An American Grammar Book' in *Diacritics* vol. 17, Summer.

Willis, P. (1978) *Profane Culture*, London: Routledge.

Young, I.M. (1990) 'The Ideal of Community and the Politics of Difference' in L. Nicholson (ed.) *Feminism/Postmodernism*, New York: Routledge.

Chapter 11

(Mis)representing the black (super)woman

Tracey Reynolds

INTRODUCTION

In Britain during the last decade the press has been preoccupied by the 'Crisis in the Black Family',[1] (*Voice*, 28 February 1995). This 'crisis' has been constructed around the perceived degeneration of male–female relations within the African-Caribbean community. Evidence of this phenomenon has been taken to be the increasing number of black households where the female heads the family and the male is absent. Two images are employed by the press to explain the assumed breakdown in family relations. The first casts the black man, who exists on the fringes of family life, as lazy, feckless, unreliable, sexually irresponsible, and undeserving of their female counterparts. In great contrast the second image characterizes the black woman as the strong, single, and independent 'superwoman'. Acknowledged as the 'lynch pin' of black family life, she excels both in educational attainment and career success, while still finding the time to rear her children single-handedly. This image of the 'black superwoman' is clearly a celebratory one.[2] To what extent is this image an honest representation of the lives of African-Caribbean women in Britain or a mythical image fabricated by the media?

This article aims to demystify the construction of the 'black super-woman' by investigating the inconsistencies between the popular media discourse and sociological evidence. In doing so two central themes are addressed. First, how closely do black women's lives in Britain correlate with that of the 'superwoman' image? Second, to what extent is the image central to the identity of African-Caribbean women? In an effort to answer these questions, during the course of the chapter I examine the historical cultural tradition of African-Caribbean women, including the matrio-focal family structure; high black female educational and career success; the presence of economic independence and autonomy among black women, and the deteriorating nature of relationships between black men and women. My argument is that the 'superwoman' is a fiction popularized by the media which has now filtered through our common-sense discourse and influences both policy and academic discourses on African-Caribbean family life.

CONTEXTUALIZING THE 'BLACK SUPERWOMAN'

> Black women are out-performing them [black men], educationally and in the job market. These women acquire senior status at work, become part of a different culture and they move onto a world where they have few black male equals.
>
> *(Guardian,* 2 July 1994, p. 11)

> She [black woman] is more likely to work full time than other women. She [black woman] is ambitious and is more likely . . . than black men to continue her education after school leaving age. And she still has time to bring up her children single-handed.
>
> *(Guardian,* 21 March 1995, p. 3)

In investigating the social construction of this 'positive' image of the 'black superwoman' there appears to be two contradictory explanations for her origin. On the one hand she is constructed within a biological and hence essentialist paradigm. On the other, the 'superwoman' is an outcome of a narrow and reductionist account of historical struggle.

In the first emphasis there is an assumption that, in the black women's physical and genetic make up there is something that predisposes her to be naturally resilient and hard working, with the ability to survive and succeed against all odds:

> Many of them [black women] have endured incredible hardships and have children to support but they are determined. . . . They seem to be very resilient.
>
> *(Voice,* 18 June 1991, p. 13)[3]

> Black women have long been central to our community and little recognition has been given to our resourcefulness and endurance in bringing up our children alone.
>
> *(Voice,* 24 August 1993, p. 6)

Such a biological determinist standpoint as a means to define the experiences of African-Caribbean women is problematic. Firstly, it is one-dimensional, assuming the homogeneity of black women and ignoring the very real differences that exist between them. Factors such as social class, age, island of origin/descent and spatial locality inform black women's experiences of living in Britain. Ideological, social, economic, historical and political forces which are also significant in determining these experiences are therefore obscured from analysis.

By assuming a biologically defined homogeneity among black women the differential achievements and progress made by black women in the struggle against racial and sexual inequalities in society cannot be explained. Similarly, by defining the success of black women as natural gives us no explanation other than a biological one to account for black women who are deemed 'not successful'.

Recently, there has been the re-emergence of the essentialist debate which claims that black people are genetically less intelligent (see Murray and Herrnstein, 1994). Murray and Herrnstein's argument is essentially a re-working and reconfirmation of Murray's previous work (see Murray, 1983). Its central premise is grounded in the theory that there exists a fixed and immutable hierarchy of intelligence which is genetically defined and racially specific. White people, as a racial grouping, are positioned towards the top of this hierarchial strata whilst black people reside at the bottom.

Murray and Herrnstein's debate is given a powerful legitimating function by the use of statistical data, charts and other 'scientific tools' to elucidate their findings. This enables Murray and Herrnstein to move their discourse away from an emotional subjective viewpoint towards 'objective knowledge'. Discussions challenging their use of statistical data for analysis and the notion of 'objective truth' have been dealt with elsewhere (see Fraser, 1995; Fischer *et al.*, 1996). My central concern here is that Murray and Herrnstein's debate acts to throw a 'smoke screen' over wider social issues and again pathologizes black people. Murray and Herrnstein, in presenting their argument as 'objective knowledge', obscure the political agenda in their writing. The re-emergence of this discourse coincides with a period in American politics which has witnessed a backlash towards liberal policies such as affirmative action and welfare spending and programmes targetted at deprived individuals, primarily in urban city areas (ibid).

Although cultural and political differences exist between America and Britain, the Murray and Herrnstein debate has met with some support here (Thatcher, 1995). However, the black British press condemned it for the racist attitude it adopted:

> Murray and his friends should have taken a much more responsible approach while carrying out their so-called studies. . . . Any study that ignores the social, psychological and moral impact of slavery and colonialism on not just the victims but also on the perpetrators is not worth its weight in dried ink.
>
> (*Voice*, 29 November 1994, p. 6)

Ironically, the black press appear to be using the same essentialist terms of reference as Murray and Herrnstein when discussing black women.

A second emphasis in the social construction of the 'black superwoman' has been the persistence of the reductionist discourse on slavery. As Mohammed suggests:

The restrictions on marriage enforced by slave owners weakened the conjugal ties while often leaving the mother/child bond intact. This has led to the paradoxical view of Caribbean women as overburdened superwoman castrating and evicting men from the family.

(Mohammed 1988, p. 5)

For the media slavery is viewed as the primary rationalization for the experiences of black men and women in post-colonial societies:

Since slavery destroyed the traditional Black family. . . . Black men and women have been in the process of negotiating a new type of relationship, perhaps unique in the western world. This relationship has had to acknowledge the independence of the Black woman, who under slavery had already established herself as the breadwinner, and in post-slavery society, had increasingly become the matriarchal figurehead of the family.

(*Voice*, 2 August 1994, p. 12)

Although there is no doubting that the impact of slavery was significant on the development of cultural traditions, to valorize slavery as the primary determinant of the black experience in Britain today greatly underestimates the adaptive capacity of black people to cultural change. Arguments that attribute existing black family structures and familial/gender relations to slavery inadvertently portray black people as objects rather than subjects of their cultural development. The assumption is that black people allow only outside forces to structure their development. Black people have always assumed an active, participatory and progressive role in adapting and subverting their oppression. The early feminist movements in the Caribbean in the 1800s (Momsen, 1993), and in Britain during the 1970s and 1980s (Bryan *et al.*, 1985), show how black women made rational, economic, and political choices, independent of the dominant patriarchal and racist discourses.

The impact of a reductionist discourse on slavery is used to reinforce a static, culturally specific, perception of black family life. The dominant common-sense perceptions of black life as an outcome of this discourse include: the matrio-focal or female centred family; lone-motherhood; high male absenteeism from the household; black women in the dual role of domestic and economic provider; and high educational success. I now turn to an interrogation of each of these assumed phenomena in the light of sociological evidence.

INTERROGATING LONE-MOTHERHOOD

The 1991 Census recorded that 49 per cent of African-Caribbean families are headed by a lone-mother compared to 14 per cent of the general population (OPCS, 1991). Analyses which attempt to explain this phenomena, are centred within two causal explanations: firstly, the historical cultural tradition of the matrio-focal family, an outcome of slavery, (Gonzalez, 1985; Powell, 1986); secondly, the pervasive idea that black women are forced into lone-motherhood as a direct result of black men's behaviour and actions.

On the first point that the persistence of matrifocality accounts for a high percentage of lone-mothers, there is little evidence or consensus about such a familial structure. No single clear definition exists of what exactly constitutes a 'matrio-focal' family:

> Matrio-focality may imply that the women in a society have a 'rather good status' generally, or that they may have more control over income or expenditure . . . it may refer to the society where male absenteeism leads to a predominance in households headed by women.
>
> (Mohammed 1988, p. 172)

In this sociological definition 'matrio-focality' is used to embrace diversity of experiences and situations. However, the very real differences between these black women are often diluted, or at the very worst ignored in media constructions of the matrio-focal family. Here the matrio-focal family is often portrayed as fixed and immutable. In reality conjugal relationships and familial structures are not static as individuals move through a series of relationships over their lifetime.

In her analysis of family formations, Powell developed a four-part classification of conjugal unions to illustrate the diversity and fluidity of familial structures: single; visiting; common-law; and married (Powell, 1986). Powell noted that Caribbean women move in and out of these unions, spending only a brief period of time in each. Importantly, marriage and the 'traditional' nuclear family structure is still held in high esteem, and is a family model which many women, across all socio-economic groups, aspire to. This is borne out in the statistics. In Barbados, 39 per cent of the population exist within the nuclear family structure, as do 37 per cent in Antigua and 38 per cent in St Vincent (Powell, 1986). Evidence of this challenges the media assumption that the matrio-focal is the norm throughout the Caribbean and amongst African-Caribbean families.

Central to media discourse of the matrio-focal family in Britain, is the idea that black women assume household headship, power, and authority within the family. It is an oversimplification to suggest that black mothers will automatically assume household headship if there is no permanent male spouse present within the home. Other factors which may determine household headship, for example household composition (number of adults and/or presence of male figures in home), income, skills, age and status of household members, are often overlooked from analysis (Moses, 1985). Furthermore, not all households follow the same pattern of having one person at one given time assuming power and authority within them, an example being households where a number of adult members make decisions and occupy positions of power and authority in areas of specific interest to them.

On the second point – that black women are forced into lone-mothering as a result of black men's behaviour – there appears to be a social class context to the way in which this is conceptualized by the press. In debates rationalizing lone-motherhood amongst black middle-class professional women, often personified as the archetypal 'superwoman', the idea is that lone-motherhood is deliberately and rationally chosen by them. Lone-motherhood, it is argued, is the only option available to these women, as a result of a lack of available, eligible black men who can equal them educationally and professionally.[4] There is acknowledgement of a:

cry by Black women, particularly those in work or who have middle class aspirations, about the lack of eligible Black men. More and more, they are increasingly echoing their American sisters who have long bemoaned the fact that all Black men are either gay, in jail, unemployed or only interested in white women.

(*Voice*, 2 August 1994, p. 12)[5]

As a result black women are:

Fed up waiting for the right man to come along . . . [and] are increasingly deciding to have babies alone without the would-be father's knowledge. . . . It's very cool, calm, and collected. They're the type of person who is going to have a year's supply of nappies delivered.

(*Voice*, 18 April 1995, p. 19)

In contrast the working-class black lone-mother is often personified as the teenage single mother, with low income and dependent on welfare benefits. It is argued that women who belong to this social group actively choose motherhood as their only viable route into adulthood or rather naively perceive motherhood as a prime vehicle in which to exert control over their 'irresponsible', 'unreliable' and 'sexually promiscuous' male partners:

Faced with high unemployment and under-achievement at school . . . pregnancy is the best of a bad lot. . . . Frustrated by their lack of control over a man they will 'pin prick a condom'.

(*Voice*, 18 April 1995, p. 20)

Acting as a direct antithesis to the middle-class 'superwoman' image, the teenage single mother represents a potent media image of black family life in Britain. Whilst lone-motherhood amongst middle-class black women is seen as a rational, calculated ploy in response to a lack of eligible black male partners of equal social status, the treatment of lone-motherhood amongst low income black women is altogether different. It is attributed to promiscuity and desperation (and welfare greed!) rather than a preferred cultural choice.

In her study of teenage motherhood, Ann Phoenix challenged many media assumptions concerning teenage motherhood. Teenage mothers make up only 5 per cent of lone-mothers in Britain. Phoenix's findings determined that young women, both black and white, under 20 years old, become pregnant for many of the same reasons as older women. The fact that many of the young mothers in her study were welfare recipients had more to do with their socio-economic position, independent of the age they become mothers. Furthermore, the fact some of the young women in Phoenix's study were married (22 per cent), challenges the assumption that teenage motherhood equates to lone-motherhood (Phoenix, 1991). None the less, somehow one has become synonymous with the other in social policy, particular among the New Right.

Women who become lone-mothers through death or incarceration of a male spouse/partner are never given consideration in media representations of the black lone-mother. Presumably, it does not fit in with the 'superwoman' image, which highlights black men negatively. For it is black male attitudes and actions which are presented as one of the primary causes of the high incidence (relative to white women) of black lone-motherhood in Britain.

The sexual fate of the single 'black superwoman' appears to be a central preoccupation with the media. Having pathologized the black male as lazy and ineffectual, the solution appears to be inter-racial relationships. This form of media attention is certainly divisive and contentious, creating hostilities between the sexes, preventing a forum in which a progressive debate on wider issues on racism and inequality can take place:

> They [black women] have got fed up waiting for an eligible man, who has a job, has ambitions and will offer them the emotional and financial security. They are now seeking these qualities from white men.
>
> (*Voice*, 2 August 1994, p. 12)

The single status of black women is also another preoccupation of the popular press:

> One of the most shocking figures which emerged over the last few weeks was that something like 60 per cent of black women between the ages of 20–39 were single . . . amongst these women there must be a problem of appalling unhappiness and loneliness; and a terrible feeling of rejection.
>
> (*Voice*, 28 February 1995, p. 8)

Paradoxically, while singlehood is celebrated as a 'superwoman' trait, it is also perceived as psychologically damaging to black women's well-being!

Notions of black femininity appear to be constructed around the dual and often interrelated images of motherhood and the 'superwoman'.[6] Motherhood has always been a central preoccupation of theorists, attempting 'to get to the heart' of black women and their experiences. Although not exclusive, British analysis of African-Caribbean mothering preoccupies itself with an emphasis on the strong mother–daughter bond. This bond is seen as essential to an understanding of how black mothers raise their daughters to survive and succeed in the face of racial and sexual discrimination in society (see Foner, 1979; Bryan *et al.*, 1985). The construction of black motherhood also centres on the 'double burden' of having to combine both domestic and employment activities endured by the black mother.

The *Guardian* newspaper on 12 June 1991, in article entitled 'Flying Colours', reported on a meeting held by a black community organization to address the issue of black male–female relations in Britain today. One of the key speakers, Tony Sewell, implied mothering skills accounted for the difference in societal success between black men and women (see *Guardian*, 12 June 1991, p. 12). Sewell, a black journalist, trivialized his explanations of differentiated success with his suggestion that black mothers spoilt and pampered their sons whilst exposing their daughters, at an early age, to the social realities of life for black people in Britain. Not only does this article make mass generalizations from unsupported evidence about parenting behaviours of black mothers, but it ignores the significant issues at work which determine the differential male/female experience, for example, the effects of labour market patterns and institutional racism in informing differentiated gender career and educational success. Instead Sewell, like the New Right, targets and holds the black mother accountable for wider societal problems by pathologizing her behaviour.

Constructing the identity of black women around motherhood undermines the contributions made by black women outside the mothering role. Also, no rationale is provided as to how women who do not have children define their identity and gain status in society. Fundamentally, by conceptualizing black women primarily in the role of mother, racist stereotypes of black women, which attribute 'breeding' as their primary function in life, are reinforced (Murray, 1983).

EVALUATING BLACK MALE MARGINALITY

Black men are perceived as occupying a very marginal position in the lives of African-Caribbean women. Male absenteeism from the family unit is a popular focus of the media. In no other culture is the issue of male absenteeism given such dominant coverage. This makes male absenteeism appear to be culturally specific to black families of Caribbean descent, although it can be identified across different societies and cultures.

The social and economic factors which determine black male absenteeism are rarely discussed. Instead distorted generalizations concerning the black man form the basis of explanations:

> For too long black men have failed to support women and our children, a reality that all black men and women must seriously reflect upon.
>
> (*Voice*, 24 August 1993, p. 6)

> If todays black woman has brought credit to her race, the black man is a different story. Not only does he have a tendency to opt out when the patter of tiny feet comes along, he is over represented in prisons and the dole queues.
>
> (*Guardian*, 21 March 1995, section 9: p. 3)

> The 'Linford Christie syndrome' of one-parent families is now disturbingly ingrained in black society. . . . Young black males have adopted societal norms and are a lot more care-free in their responsibilities.
>
> (*Sunday Express*, 13 August 1995, p. 2)

Not only does this negative discourse reinforce racist stereotypes and assumptions but it also greatly obscures the influence and involvement black men have always possessed within the family, not just as fathers but as grandfathers, uncles, brothers and other male kin of which there is much evidence.

Mirza's study redefining the social construction of black womanhood in Britain vividly illustrates the active and influential role fathers assume towards their family. In interviews of black 16–18-year-old schoolgirls, black fathers were viewed in a positive manner by family members (Mirza, 1992):

> 'Most men do understand the problems faced by women, I think so anyway. I go to my dad whenever I have a problem.' (Laurie, aged 16, aspiration: journalist; father: telephonist)

> 'Since my mum died my dad brought us up. . . . All he cares about is seeing us do well and going to college' (April, aged 16, aspiration: art therapist; father: British Rail ticket collector).
>
> (Mirza 1992, p. 159)

Bryan *et al.* also acknowledge the significant support and contribution black men in Britain have provided towards childrearing and other domestic duties within the home. This is especially true of the early migration years. In the 1950s and 1960s, when the vast majority of black women were first generational mothers in Britain, they did not have female family members and kinship relations to depend on for support. Support from others, outside the black community, was often not forthcoming in this openly hostile and racist society (Bryan *et al.*, 1985).

From my own personal experience, as a typical second-generation, black, working-class woman growing up in South London, my father performed a very active and supportive role in the family, particularly during my formative childhood years. My father undertook a variety of domestic functions commonly regarded as 'traditional' female roles, so as to support my mother who was in full-time employment and had to commute daily to Central London. Indeed, some of my earliest memories are of my dad bathing and dressing my sisters and myself for school and later beginning preparations for dinner. There exists no evidence to suggest that my childhood experience and the vital role my father played within this is the exception to the rule rather than the norm in black family life.

In second-, third- and even fourth-generation African-Caribbean families in Britain, the majority of black women are still fairly young (of working age) and are more likely than women of other cultures to be in full-time employment (Bhavnani, 1994). As such, they are less likely to have time to provide full comprehensive female support. This challenges the popular idealized notion that female kinship networks are the primary vehicle employed by mothers to obtain childrearing and domestic support. This popular notion assumes kinship networks are cultural phenomena specific only to black communities (Stack, 1974; Collins, 1994).

Many studies inadvertently reinforce the centrality of black female kinship networks by valorizing women and marginalizing men. One such example is Pulsiphier's study on the life-cycle of Jamaican women sharing a houseyard (Pulsiphier, 1993). In the study men are identified as peripheral to the lives of these women, crucially obscuring their influence in effecting family forms. By their very absence, in effect, it is the men who maintain the persistence of female-dominated houseyards across successive generations. This reinforces an important point which often goes unaddressed: even where the male spouse is deemed absent (in a normative sense) from the household, he will still maintain a significant effect on the lives, perceptions and social realities of family members.

In the United Kingdom, the relatively high incidence of black female-headed households, 49 per cent (OPCS, 1991), does not give an accurate picture of what is occurring in reality within black families and male–female relations. In a life-cycle context, Mirza observed that although single parent black women are categorized as 'lone-mothers', a significant proportion of these women (79 per cent) actually have a male partner and exist within a stable conjugal union. As such the majority of black children, at any one given time in their life, exist within a stable traditional two-parent household. Admittedly, black women do most of the childrearing and domestic tasks, but this is by no means culturally specific to the black community and can be identified in studies of white British family lives (see Oakley, 1974; Richardson, 1994).

From media representations of black family life it could be easily assumed that the black lone-mother is an over represented group among single-families in Britain. In reality, ethnic groups including African-Caribbean people comprise only 7 per cent of single-parents in Britain (NCOPF, 1993). Despite this evidence, the dominant image of the single parent as being the black lone-mother, remains persistent among the media and hence in the public mind.

MAPPING THE ECONOMIC AND EDUCATIONAL EXPERIENCE OF BLACK WOMEN

The image of the 'black superwoman' has been sustained in part by the high levels of black female economic independence and labour market autonomy. The 1993 Labour Force survey revealed that 76 per cent of black women are economically active (*Employment Gazette*, 1993). However, it could be argued that this high incidence of black female economic activity in Britain is more a direct response to social and economic conditions in this society rather than the outcome of a cultural historical tradition where women always work. In the past, migration policies during the 1950s and 1960s encouraged both black men and women to seek employment in Britain. Today, the sex segregation of the labour market, a decline in 'traditional' male sectors of employment and the increasing 'feminization' of the labour market has resulted in more employment opportunities for black women (Bhavnani, 1994). Such economic phenomena has given fuel to the 'superwoman' image.

A popular misconception is that female economic activity equates to economic autonomy and the opportunity to freely assume responsibility over money earned. Caribbean feminist theorists persistently reinforce the image of the strong, independent and autonomous black women (see Barrow, 1986). However, at the same time they also reveal a profound sense of female powerlessness and dependency on familial relations, kinship groups, men, the Church, and the community at large for support. Despite this contradictory stance in the Caribbean theorists' work, black female independence and economic autonomy is also assumed to prevail among African-Caribbean women in Britain. As a result, high economic activity is misrepresented by the popular press, as a cultural phenomena which is passed down intergenerationally from mother to daughter. Rationalizing it in this manner ensures that the assumption of high African-Caribbean female economic activity persists despite evidence to the contrary.

The concentration of black women in specific fields of employment directly challenges recent press coverage that leads us to believe that African-Caribbean women are excelling in all occupational sectors. Black women have traditionally been concentrated in specific sectors of employment. The last twenty years has seen a shift in the areas of employment with movements away from the National Health Service, as semi-skilled and unskilled manual labour, towards clerical/administrative employment and other service industries.

A significant proportion of African-Caribbean women are now employed in public administration (40 per cent) and, to a lesser extent, retail and distribution (25 per cent) and banking and finance (12 per cent). However, it is a misconception to presume that black women are over-achieving in these areas. Often career choices and opportunities are narrowly defined so the majority of black women are concentrated in lower positions such as clerical officers, secretaries, sales assistants, etc. Moreover, a significant proportion of black women are clustered at the bottom of their respective professional and career ladders with little opportunity for promotion, often earning less than their white male and female colleagues (Breugel, 1989).

Despite a relatively high proportion of women employed by central and local government, a 'glass ceiling' is clearly in operation. Only 8 per cent of black women are found in senior and middle management positions (Jones, 1993). Furthermore they are becoming increasingly channelled into areas where there exists a high proportion of black service users (Bhavnani, 1994). Stringent government policies ensure that job security is now an issue for black women in public sector areas. Horizontal occupational mobility, often to private sector organizations, is increasingly being used as an effective strategy with which to combat and resist changes in the public sector occupational structure.

In a bid to maintain the image of the 'black superwoman', poverty and unemployment, very real issues for black women, are often obscured from media representations. Instead, poverty and unemployment are primarily analysed from a black male perspective. This contrasts with recent studies examining poverty within white communities in Britain. Increasing emphasis is now being paid to the growing visibility of white women in poverty or what is usually referred to the 'feminization of poverty' (Glendinning and Millar, 1991). So far systematic academic research into black female poverty in Britain, outside the confined area of teenage motherhood, has yet to be adequately addressed. Black male and female unemployment is rarely compared. However, comparisons measuring the extent of unemployment between black and white men, and black and white women prevail (Mirza, 1993). In reality there exists little difference in unemployment figures between black men and women: 16 per cent and 13 per cent respectively (*Employment Gazette*, 1993), which dispels media myths that black women are 'having it all' in terms of career success, and 'leaving behind' the 'lazy' and 'ineffectual black man' (*Sunday Times*, 19 February 1995, section 9: p. 8).

A similar distortion of the black female experience is apparent in the debate on the widening gap in educational attainment between black men and women. It was reported that African-Caribbean men comprise less than 1 per cent of the student population in higher education compared to 16 per cent of African-Caribbean women (*Times*, 31 March 1992). The 1991 Labour Force survey stated that 61 per cent of black women, aged 16–59, possess higher and other professional qualifications (*Employment Gazette*, 1993). These figures actively encourage the 'black superwoman' image and its oppositional counterpart, the 'ineffectual' black man. Behind the celebration of academic achievement of black women is an implicit idea that as a group black women 'naturally' possess the skills to overcome struggles which black men do not have. It is often assumed that black men see education as futile and support other short term, often illegal, means as a way to progress in society:

> The BMWs and gold chains have more of an instant attraction to the youngsters [young black men] than education and pursuing professional careers. . . . They see that educated people still come up against racism, so they decide to take what they see as an easier route to earning money.
>
> (*Voice*, 18 June 1991, p. 13)

In contrast it is argued that black women favour the meritocratic ideal which advocates education as being the prime vehicle for upward social mobility, and a means of 'getting on' in British society (*Guardian*, 21 May 1995). However, these oppressing attitudes to education are not gender specific, that is characteristic to either males or females, nor are they culturally specific to the black community. Differing attitudes among young men and women to education can be found across other cultures in Britain.[7] What determines people's attitudes to education has more to do with experiences of schooling. For example, it is well documented that due to racism and sexism black people, no matter how motivated, are often denied the opportunity of an adequate level of education (Mirza, 1992; Gillborn, 1995).

Investigating black women's experiences of higher education Mirza (1995) noted that over 90 per cent of mature black female students came from administrative and caring professions. She argued that as a result of inequalities suffered by many black women within the educational system, such careers which encouraged further training and education increased their opportunities for access to higher education. Mirza states that in effect, black women have had to use 'the long (back door) route' as the primary means with which to obtain further education. A segregated labour market, with a large proportion of black men concentrated in semi-skilled and unskilled manual occupations, ensures that this route is effectively closed for the majority of black men in Britain.

However, despite increasing numbers of black women acquiring high academic and professional qualifications, they are more likely than their white counterparts to be employed in jobs for which they are overqualified and do not reflect their academic achievements (*Employment Gazette*,

1993). Therefore, upward social mobility for black women through education and objectively defined by occupation is not as rapid a progression as the popular press would have the public believe. Nor is there much evidence to support the belief that the majority of black women are 'leaving black men behind' in terms of educational and job success:

> Black women seem to be getting on better in Britain, in terms of having good careers, than black men. . . . 'We [black women] have worked hard to get where we are and we're mixing in different social circles. . . . We've somehow outgrown the black men of our age.'
>
> (*Evening Standard*, 9 October 1994, p. 20)

CONCLUSION

The 'black superwoman' is an image fabricated by the press that has little to with the reality of black women's lives and the social realities faced by them. None the less, this image has been accepted by the public and now assumes a 'common sense' reality. Even amongst academics she is celebrated as a positive social phenomena. However, the 'black superwoman' in Britain is constructed in essentialist terms (such as in terms of her natural qualities of resilience) or through employing a reductionist historical cultural rationale (with a static and naive approach to the effects of slavery).

The detrimental consequences of the media's construction of black male and female identities can be clearly seen in the way they are narrowly defined, that is, 'the black superwoman' and 'the irresponsible feckless black man'. Both of these definitions are mythical. They have the effect of deflecting attention away from more substantive issues that concern black people such as racism, nihilism and incarceration. The never ending media debates, investigating the pros and cons of inter-racial relationships and absent fathers, prevent other issues of importance to black people from being discussed. It is only by discarding these narrow and highly contentious stereotypes of black family life and male–female relations that our energies can be channelled towards more positive and constructive discourses.

NOTES

1 For example see: 'Flying Colours', *Guardian*, 12 June 1991; 'Black Men: Losers in a One-sided Sexcess Story?', *Voice*, 18 June 1991; 'A Question of Mixed Emotions', *Evening Standard*, 9 October 1991; 'Sisters do it for Themselves', *Times*, 31 March 1991; 'Young, Single and Black', *Independent*, 2 July 1993; 'Our Families Need Fathers', *Voice*, 24 August 1993; 'The Silent Revolution – Part II', *Voice*, 2 August 1994; 'She's gotta have it all', *The Sunday Times*: section 9, 19 February 1995; 'No Finance, No Romance', *Voice*, 28 February 1995; 'The Myth and the Mister', *Guardian*, 21 March 1995; 'The Ethnic Timebomb', *Sunday Express*, 13 August 1995.

2 The popular press and black feminists alike have celebrated the 'black superwoman', the latter advocating the term as one in which to combat racist and patriarchal ideology (see Davis, 1981; Collins, 1991).

3 The *Voice* is a popular black newspaper concerned primarily with topics which specifically affect the black community. Established in 1982 the newspaper is circulated throughout the Greater London and Midlands areas of Britain. Current readership figures stand at approximately 300,000. In contrast, the *Guardian*, *Evening Standard*, *Sunday Express* and *Sunday Times* are mainstream British newspapers circulated throughout the United Kingdom.

4 The debate focusing on black middle-class lone-motherhood is an American one. It is argued that the pool of available African-American women significantly outnumber that of men, so that there today exists a widening gulf between single affluent black men and women (Chapman, 1988; McAdoo, 1988). This debate has been uncritically adopted by the British media in depicting the experiences of black men and women in Britain. In doing so, obvious cultural differences that exist between the two countries are overlooked.

5 This viewpoint is popularized in the recent film version of Terry MacMillan's book *Waiting to Exhale* (see *Guardian* 24 January 1996).

6 Although an association between femininity and motherhood is by no means restricted to analysis of black women and can be found in analysis of white women in Britain (see Richardson, 1994; Ribbens, 1994) the image of the 'superwoman' is.

7 A BBC1 television programme, *Panorama*, broadcast on Monday 16 October 1995 at 9.40 p.m. indicated that differing attitudes to education amongst white male and female teenagers in Britain may be the key reason why an increasing number of white women and a declining number of white men are entering higher education.

REFERENCES

Barrow, C. (1986) 'Finding the Support: Strategies for Survival' in J. Massiah (ed.) *Women in the Caribbean – Part I, Social Economic Studies*, Institute of Social and Economic Research: University of the West Indies.

Bhavnani, R. (1994) *Black Women in the Labour Market: A Research Review*, Research Series: Equal Opportunities Commission.

Breugel, I. (1989) 'Sex and Race in the Labour Market' in *Feminist Review*, no. 32, summer.

Bryan, B., Dadzie, S. and Scafe, S. (1985) *The Heart of the Race – Black Women's Lives in Britain*, London: Virago Press.

Chapman, A. (1988) 'Male-Female Relations: How the Past Affects the Present' in H.P. McAdoo (ed.) *Black Families*, 2nd edn, California: Sage Publications.

Collins, P.H. (1991) *Black Feminist Thought – Knowledge, Consciousness and the Politics of Empowerment*, Boston and London: Unwin Hyman.

Collins, P.H. (1994) 'Shifting the Center: Race, Class and Feminist Theorizing about Motherhood' in B. Bassin, M. Honey, and M.M. Kaplan (eds) *Presentations of Motherhood*, New Haven: Yale University Press.

Davis, A. (1981) *Women, Race and Class*, London: The Women's Press.

Employment Gazette (1993) *Ethnic Origins and the Labour Market*, London: Department of Employment (Feb.): HMSO.

Fischer, C. S., Hout, M., Jankowski, M.S., Lucas, S.R. Swidler, A., Voss, K. (1996) *Inequality by Design: Cracking the Bell Curve Myth*, New Jersey: Princeton University Press.

Foner, N. (1979) *Jamaica Farewell, Jamaica Migrants in London*, London: RKP.

Fraser, S. (ed.) (1995) *The Bell Curve Wars: Race, Intelligence and the Future of America*, New York: Basic Books.

Gillborn, D. (1995) *Race and the Anti-Racism in Real Schools*, Buckingham: Open University Press.

Glendinning, C. and Millar, J. (1991) 'Poverty: the Forgotten Englishwoman – Reconstructing Research and Policy on Poverty' in M. Maclean and D. Groves (eds) *Women's Issues in Social Policy*, London: Routledge.

Gonzalez, N. (1985) 'Household and Family in the Caribbean: Some Definitions and Concepts' in F.C. Steady (ed.) *The Black Woman Cross-Culturally*, Rochester, Vermont: Schnenkman Books, Inc.

Jones, T. (1993) *Britain's Ethnic Minorities*, London: Policy Studies Institute.

McAdoo, H. (ed.) (1988) *Black Families*, 2nd edn, California: Sage Publications.

Mirza, H. (1992) *Young, Female and Black*, London: Routledge.

Mirza, H. (1993) 'The Social Construction of Black Womanhood in British Educational Research: Towards a New Understanding' in J. Arnot and K. Weiler (eds) *Feminism and Social Justice in Education: International Perspectives*, London: The Falmer Press, Taylor and Francis Inc.

Mirza, H. (1995) 'Black Women in Higher Education: Defining a Space/Finding a Place' in L. Morley and V. Walsh, (eds) *Feminist Academics: Creative Agents for Change*, London: Taylor and Francis Inc.

Mohammed, P. (1988) *The Caribbean Family Revisited* in P. Mohammed and C. Shepherd (eds) *Gender in Caribbean Development*, Women and Development Studies Project Group, University of the West Indies.

Momsen, J. (1993) 'Development and Gender Divisions of Labour in the Rural Caribbean' in J. Momsen (ed.) *Women and Change in the Caribbean*, Bloomington: Indiana University Press.

Moses, Y. (1985) 'Female Status, The Family and Male Dominance in the West Indian Community' in F. Steady (ed.) *The Black Women Cross-Culturally*, Rochester, Vermont: Schnenkman Books, Inc.

Murray, C. (1983) *Losing Ground: American Social Policy, 1950–1980*, New York: Basic Books

Murray, C. and Herrnstein, R. (1994) *The Bell Curve – Intelligence and Class Structure in American Life*, New York: The Free Press.

National Council for One-Parent Families (1993) *Annual Report, 1992–3*, London: NCOPF.

Oakley, A. (1974) *The Sociology of Housework*, Oxford: Martin Robertson.

OPCS (1991) 'Trends in the Numbers of One-parent Families in Great Britain', *Population Trends*, no. 65, autumn 1991.

Phoenix, A. (1991) *Young Mothers?*, London: Polity Press.

Powell, D. (1986) 'Caribbean Women and Their Familial Experiences' in J. Massiah (ed.) *Women in the Caribbean – Part I, Social and Economic Research*, University of the West Indies.

Pulsiphier, L. (1993) 'Changing Roles in the Life Cycles of Women in Traditional West Indian Houseyards' in J. Momsen (ed.) *Women and Change in the Caribbean*, Bloomington: Indiana University Press.

Ribbens, J. (1994) *Mothers and Their Children – A Feminist Sociology of Childbearing*, London: Sage Publications.

Richardson, D. (1994) *Women, Motherhood and Childrearing*, London: Macmillan Press.

Stack, C. (1974) *All Our Kin: Strategies for Survival in a Black Community*, New York: Harper and Row.

Thatcher, M. (1995) *The Path to Power*, London: HarperCollins.

Chapter 12

Shades of Blackness

Young Black female constructions of beauty

Debbie Weekes

Her blackness is fine. The blackness of her skin, the blackness of her mind.
Her beauty cannot be measured with standards of a colonised mind.
(Méshell NdegeOcello 1993)

This chapter aims to explore the complex ways in which beauty is defined
by young Black women. It explores why specific physical signifiers such
as hair texture and skin colour have come to symbolize the boundaries
along which young Black women define Blackness. In my own conversations with groups of young Black women, many have spoken of their
identities in essentialist ways, in terms of fixed, natural, immutable
characteristics. In contrast, however, definitions of Black identity in the
academy and certain forms of popular culture, move away from fixed and
unitary conceptions of Blackness, towards conceptualizing it as fragmented and diverse (hooks 1991; Gilroy 1993; Mercer 1994). This chapter
will argue that the restrictive definitions of being Black for these young
women are located within ideas of Blackness which exist within their own
communities. These fixed definitions have to be understood in the context
of Black people's marginal positions within society and as such, can be
seen as 'strategic' (Spivak 1987; Fuss 1989). For these young Black women,
talking about Black identity as one-dimensional and based on specific
physical and phenotypical signifiers may serve a certain purpose for
marginalized groups – that of relative empowerment.

The ways in which Black women talk about their identities are highly
gendered. It is their use of hair texture and skin colour as specific signifiers
of Blackness that this discussion will primarily focus upon. It has been well
documented by Black feminists that Black women occupy experientially
unique spaces in relation to both Black men and White women (Carby
1982; Collins 1986). Black feminist thought has the potential to theorize
and develop an understanding of how Black women come to construct
definitions of themselves which are clearly situated in the way they
experience their social positions and hence their racial identities. Through
conducting a series of interviews with young women of African descent,

aged 14–20,[1] the tensions within essentialist definitions of Black identity are explored. Some of the women who defined themselves as Black were placed on the boundary of 'acceptable' Blackness by others who claimed racial authenticity. What became clear from this research was that the racial definitions of what constitutes 'acceptable' Blackness was framed in terms of an essentialist construction of Black womanhood. Black womanhood was signified by the length and texture of a young woman's hair, the shade of her skin, and often by the nature of her parentage.

Black popular culture's attempt to construct an image of what it means to be 'Black' through music, dress and art defines Black identity in monolithic and essentialist terms. The theoretical rejection of this popular notion has gathered momentum in the academy, especially within postmodern analyses (hooks 1991; Hall 1992; Gilroy 1993; West 1993). These analyses argue against authenticity and instead recognize that Blackness is a social, political and cultural construction. If attempts are made to proscribe what Blackness should be, this assumes the existence of an essential Black identity. As Dyson (1993) argues 'although it is undeniably rooted in pigment and physiology, racial identity transcends their boundaries' (Dyson 1993: xx). However the authenticity of a Black woman's identity can often be measured in relation to the physical signifiers of hair and skin. Criticism has been applied to Black women who have sought to alter their physical appearance and are seen as attempting to move away from their racial identity. Criticism has also been directed towards those who are constructed (by others) as closer to 'Whiteness' by virtue of such signifiers as straight hair and light skins.[2] The question then is how does the outward representation of physical features of Black women come to be aspired to or rejected?

STANDARDS OF BEAUTY

Though femininity is bound up with heterosexuality and the ability of women to appear attractive to men (Wolf 1990; Mama 1995), Black women occupy a differential racialized space within and against these constructions. The entire concept of feminine attractiveness has been heavily based upon dominant definitions of beauty which have far reaching consequences for Black women. Not only has female beauty been constructed to objectify women, the assumption of Whiteness as the norm indicates that Black and White women are objectified differently. The signifiers of hair texture, skin shade and shape of lips and noses are reacted to in terms of their approximation to Whiteness. Constructing boundaries around Blackness in relation to these signifiers illustrates a response by Black individuals that Whiteness and its associated outward signifiers have been used as a yardstick by which difference has been measured.

The issues of definitions of beauty being tied to male notions of attractiveness have been discussed in relation to body image and the negative effects of these definitions (Wolf 1990). The effects of White masculine definitions of beauty on Black women have meant racialized criteria of attractiveness are often inextricably linked to the European standard. Thus though on the whole Black women may not suffer greatly from the problems of anorexia,[3] their perceptions of body image become problematic when the health implications of bleaching creams are considered (James 1993: 238). Additionally, as one Black female respondent in Alibhai-Brown and Montague's study highlighted, some of the Black women she had seen with White partners had attempted to hide the shapes of their bodies, which were often bigger than White counterparts, in order to please and remain attractive to them (Alibhai-Brown and Montague 1992: 290).

The historical association of Whiteness as a yardstick of beauty has become internalized not just by Black women but by Black men also. This process of negating the beauty of Black textured hair and darker shades of skin has strong implications for Black women in terms of appearing attractive to males. As young women, many Black girls experienced rejection from Black males as 'in white dominated situations black and white boys alike tend to conform to the prevailing aesthetic, and fancy white (if not blonde) girls more' (Mama 1995: 103). Contemporary Black writers have explored the implications for Black women when Black men negate their physical appearances in favour of women who represent the European ideal (Morrison 1979). The construction of Black femininity as ugly and White womanhood as beautiful is highlighted by Cleaver's description of an elderly American Black man's construction of these images:

> There's a softness about a white woman, something delicate and soft inside her. But a nigger bitch seems to be full of steel, granite-hard and resisting . . . I mean I can't analyse it, but I know that the White man made the Black woman the symbol of slavery and the White woman the symbol of freedom. Every time I embrace a Black woman I'm embracing slavery, and when I put my arms around a White woman, well, I'm hugging freedom.
>
> (Cleaver 1968: 107)

James has noted that skin bleaching and hair straightening are practices carried out in the main by Black women which he directly relates to the preference of Black men for women with European-like phenotypical characteristics (1993: 282). Therefore some of the persistence which exists amongst Black women who seek to deny and reject the importance of European standards of beauty are made more urgent in view of the ways in which they are judged as beautiful or not by male peers.

Black female discourses around the issues of hair and skin illustrate the nature of the 'emotional ambiguity' which physical constructions of Black womanhood evoke for Black women (Mercer 1990). Mama's research on

Black women illustrates their ambiguous feelings about their natural hair textures and dark shades of skin. As one respondent in her study explained 'I used to press my hair with a hot comb, but I never really liked straight hair, I used to just *ease it out* so that it wasn't too tough, but *not really straighten it*' (Mama 1995: 115; italics added). Mama suggests this displays an ambivalence between wanting and yet not wanting to have hair that was straighter and not 'too tough'. Additionally, with the redefinition of Blackness in the 1960/70s, Afro hairstyles became associated with political change and Black self-knowledge. Artificial straightening of hair and bleaching of skin with creams, processors, hot combs, etc., which were equated with White definitions of womanhood were rejected. It then follows that women who continued to ascribe to these processes were perceived as victims of self-hatred. For example Bryan *et al.* have talked about the ways in which negative racialized imagery within the media and elsewhere constructed young African-Caribbean girls in the early 1980s. They describe the way young women wore school cardigans on their heads to emulate White female peers, used bleaching creams for 'uneven skin tones', processed their hair until it became damaged and suffered the pain of regular use of the hot comb (1985: 223–6). They explain these processes in terms of 'mental slavery' whereby Black women saw attributes of Whiteness as a way of escaping poverty and racism. hooks, on the other hand, has argued that though at one time Black women adopted straightened hair styles because they were easier to manage at times when they were particularly over-worked and exploited, straightened hair continues to remain a dominant form of dressing the hair when such conditions no longer exist (1993: 85). However, Mercer (1990) has argued that stressing the importance of 'natural' styles such as those exhibited in the 1970s Afro and the dreadlocks of Rastafarianism does not necessarily rectify the negation of Black beauty. Though he believes that these styles attempted to revalorize the previously negated texture of Black hair (which has been historically conceived of in similar ways to the blackness of the skin), he finds the opposition between natural and artificial problematic. The Afro and the dreadlocks were constructed as a return to nature, and rejected the European notions of 'cultivating' and taming Black hair into straightness. Black hair was politicized by positing the aesthetic of beauty. However, Mercer argues that the synonymity of Afro with natural invoked a 'dualistic logic of binary oppositionality' between that which appears natural and hence 'authentic', and that which has been cultivated (Mercer 1990: 255). Thus in view of the assumed rejection of European standards, these oppositions between that which is natural (and hence Black) and that which is not were nevertheless symptomatic of eurocentric notions of duality. Therefore he questions their very oppositionality as signifiers of Black subversion. Additionally, once the Afro was commodified through the design of wigs for White individuals, it was no longer a Black political statement. The ease with which the style was commodified illustrates for Mercer that its aesthetic value was already dictated by the White dominant culture.

THE BLACKER THE BERRY

Discourses of Black womanhood, which are played out within Black popular culture, influenced how the young women in my research constructed ideas of beauty and definitions of Blackness. The extracts below are taken from readers' letters pages in a British Black woman's magazine called *Pride*. The magazine suggests it is aimed at the 'woman of colour', and has a wide Black female readership. These extracts can be used to contextualize the young women's ideas of Blackness.

> I feel I must comment on the front cover of the [latest] issue featuring Veronica Webb. I feel insulted that you should use her picture on the front cover when two pages further in you have a selection of 10 beautiful Black women. Veronica Webb does not reflect the image of a Black woman, as she is obviously of mixed race. I actually thought she was white until I read the article. Why couldn't her picture have been on the inside? Maybe you should launch a magazine for mixed-race people. After all Black is beautiful and we should not have to apologize for our dark skin.

> I was under the impression that [this] is a magazine for Black British women, so why does the winner of [the *Face of 94*] competition resemble a white woman? No disrespect to the winner herself, but she is nearer to white than Black. I presumed the whole point of such a competition was to give Black British women a chance to portray their beauty. There are many light skinned, coolie haired women in the modelling industry already. Why wasn't a dark skinned woman given a chance?

And in response:

> Does a Black woman have to be as Black as coal with a nose spread from ear to ear before she is a true beautiful Black woman? . . . I find it very offensive that because I may not be the right shade of Black (I'm mixed race) I might not be considered a true Black woman. How many Black people can honestly claim that they are descended from a pure Black family line?

> When oh when are we going to get rid of this dark skin/light skin divide? White people must be laughing at us. They no longer need to abuse us for our skin colour because we seem to be doing a fine job all by ourselves. They hated us for being Black (no matter what the shade) and we're hating ourselves for the same thing. A fair skinned person

does not look white – he/she looks fair skinned. A dark skinned person with thin lips, a flat behind and long, flowing hair looks dark skinned. Does a fair skinned person with thick lips, short Afro hair and a big behind look more Caucasian than the person I described above? No. If you break this down to its lower common denominator, it would read 'Why are Black people like white people?' and you can't get more absurd than that.

(Extracts from the letters pages in *Pride* magazine May/June, Dec/Jan 1994, February/March 1995)

This selection of letters from *Pride* appeared in response to two separate events. The first was the placing of a mixed parentage model, Veronica Webb, on the front cover of an earlier issue, and the second relates to the selection of the winner of the 'Face of '94' modelling competition, hosted by *Pride* magazine, who was also of mixed parentage. Both women were light skinned with naturally straight hair textures. Important questions arise about the way in which the writers of these letters have erected boundaries related not only to shade of skin, but parentage. They appear to be using biological definitions of Blackness. How far does the redefinition of racial signs, such as broad noses and dark skin, become strategic in terms of embracing positive possibilities, or restrictive in becoming exclusive and closed?

One of the important ways in which such essentializing can be understood is related to the historical legacy of a preoccupation with skin shade. Colonialist ideas have fed into contemporary representations of Blackness through the legacy of 'shade prejudice'. This legacy emerged historically from slave owner preferences for mulatto slave women, and the prevalence of pigmentocracy which dominated many of the Caribbean plantation societies. Mama (1995) refers to this persistence as 'colourism' – the 'desire [of Black women] for long flowing hair, lighter skin and aquiline features' (Mama 1995: 150). Black African Caribbeans living in Britain have brought with them a conception of *Caribbean* identity which distinguishes between various shades of Black. As Lewis (1969) has argued: 'in absolute terms ... West Indian life is ... a multi-layered pigmentocracy suffering from its own private disease of subtle "shade" prejudice' (quoted in James 1993: 243). The ways in which colour coding came to signify social status in many Caribbean islands, where darker skinned individuals were located within the poorer sections of various island societies and the lighter skinned within the middle class, illustrated the pervasiveness of the links with Whiteness (Foner 1979: 32). The women who spoke ambivalently about using hot combs and lightening creams in Mama's study are situated within ideas of beauty which existed around them. What Mama defines as the 'colonial-integrationist discourse', permeates the ways in which the parents of her female participants responded negatively to their children's dark skins and 'nigger' hair (Mama 1995: 103–4). Many Black feminist writers have recalled the importance placed upon 'good hair' and 'good colouring' by parents both within the Caribbean and America (Jones 1970; Collins 1990; hooks 1993). Parents born in the Caribbean would often derogate (or have experienced criticism themselves) those in their families who had failed to marry 'light'. As Walter Rodney observed of the Caribbean:

> The language which is used by black people in describing ourselves shows how we despise our African appearance. 'Good hair' means European hair, 'good nose' means straight nose, 'good complexion' means light complexion. Everybody recognises how incongruous and ridiculous such terms are, but we continue to use them and to express our support of the assumptions that white Europeans have a monopoly on beauty, and that black is the incarnation of ugliness.
>
> (Rodney 1975: 33)

However, though the hierarchy of shades may have been undermined once migrants attempted to settle in Britain, through a subsuming of all individuals within a homogeneous racial categorization, its legacy does not go unnoticed. Despite the reclamation of Blackness on the part of the Black Power Movement, 'shade prejudice' has persisted. Thus the legacy of colonialist definitions of beauty cannot be ignored when attempting to theorize the essentialist discourse among young Black women, which in their letters clearly policed each other within a biologically reductionist definition of Black womanhood.

BRIGHT IS BEST?

Creating essentialized identities on the basis of skin colour and hair texture places many mixed parentage individuals on the boundaries of Blackness. This is relevant to the young mixed parentage women in my research. Many spoke of the preoccupations of others with *their* shades of skin. This had differing effects on the young women in terms of how they viewed Black women. Here Sandra, a young woman of mixed parentage, talks about the way she felt ostracized by other young Black women:

> At school it was really like you had a bunch of Black girls and a bunch of White girls. In my class there was a bunch of White girls with one Black girl who was really White, y'know? I went round with them. The other Black girls would always be like, oh Sandra, y'know your hair, your this. You know, they used to go on about my hair because my hair was really long but they used to make it out like you shouldn't have long hair and you shouldn't be light skinned and you shouldn't be this. They were really stupid. And I made friends with a couple of them, really

good friends and they calmed down. But it was like they were really jealous. It was more jealousy than anything. So I felt more comfortable with White girls cause they didn't go on about anything, they just took me for Sandra. It was just kid's stuff, I don't think it really meant anything.

Candice in response to similar forms of ostracism from young Black women responded differently. She continued to have Black women as friends though the majority of young women she considered to be close were also of mixed parentage. Here however her response has led to additional forms of essentializing girls of same race parentage:

Candice: 'cause they [other Black girls] say 'look at them, you mixed up bitch, she thinks she's black' and things like that. You get it all the time. Or you get called a 'no nation' . . . yeah 'cause you ain't got no White nation, no Black nation.
DW: Is it more from guys or girls?
Candice: Girls, bitchy ones . . . there's nuff Black bitches . . . they're all bitchy, they really are bitchy, you find that most Black girls are really bitchy.
DW: When does this happen . . . on the street, at school or what?
Candice: Street, when you're in a dance.
DW: And do they say it to your face?
Candice: No. You can hear em saying it . . . 'look at 'em, look at 'em, they think they're hot', you know you just hear it. You just walk by.
DW: How does it make you feel?
Candice: Good sometimes, 'cause they're just jealous.
DW: They're just jealous of you?
Candice: Yeah, they want to *be* like me . . . it's true though they're jealous, 'cause most of 'em's got no hair, when their skin's dry it's just tough and . . . they have to buy cream . . . they have to, they're jealous.

Candice felt that she was being placed on the margins, outside of the concept of Blackness as employed by young Black women. Concepts of Blackness were being defined at her expense. She thus defined her racialized identity by rejecting the definition as 'other' and placing Black females on the margins. However, the policing of Black womanhood and constructing of essentialized boundaries around racial identity has implications for both reinforcing the identities of the women who are positioned within its boundaries, and negating the identities of those it places outside.

It is the recognition of the physical signifiers of facial features and hair textures as European and a subsequent rejection of their significance, which indicates a general movement amongst racialized groups to distance themselves from Whiteness. Processes of 'distancing' involve placing specific groups on the margins of definitions of Blackness, which may include reinforcing the links which people of mixed parentage have to Whiteness. In other words this may involve reminding them that though the 'one drop' rule[4] may place them within the boundaries of the group 'Black', their White parentage problematizes how they may experience their membership:

> I mean I was in this salon one day, my friend is the manageress . . . and whenever they do new hairdo's right, they done the relaxed look and everything, she takes me in to show to the other stylists how to do the hair. So one day I was in there and there was this Black girl in there and she had short hair, I mean she was a really lovely girl, and this girl says 'oh your hair's come out really nice, you've got really nice hair' and I goes 'oh thank you', and she goes 'yeah, all half breeds have nice hair'. That was it, I just went apeshit. Because she didn't say it like, 'oh yeah all half breed' . . . I mean, if she said it in a more polite way . . . but she did say it to be offensive, she really did, and even if she didn't say it to be offensive, I'd say 'no love, I'm mixed race'.
>
> (Sandra)

Attributing the category of mixed parentage to an individual who is not of mixed parentage on the basis of shade of skin or hair texture illustrates how these signifiers are often the initial basis for categorizing individuals in racial terms. One young woman in the sample had long straightened hair and light skin which confused people who sought to categorize her:

DW: Well tell me the difference, why did you put light skinned here [on the form] and you only put Black there [on an earlier form]?

Jasmine: I dun . . . why did I put that? That's a point, I dunno. Yeah why did I put that?

DW: Do you know why?

Jasmine: Light skinned, no probably because . . . I put light skinned black 'cause everyone thinks I'm half caste, if you know what I mean?

DW: Do they?

Jasmine: Everyone sees me as half caste, and . . . I say to my dad, oh everyone thinks I'm . . . 'Oh are you mixed race or whatever?' and I says no I'm black and they go 'Oh my gosh!' and they start feeling your hair and, 'Oh I didn't know you was black.' That's why I put that, you know.

DW: Does it get on your nerves?

Jasmine: Sometimes it does, but it don't really bother me anymore. And then my dad goes 'Just tell them that you're *black* you're not half caste.'

Jasmine and her father reject the label of mixed parentage, not only because it is not a racial 'reality' for them, but also because it holds the stigma of linkage to Whiteness. In relation to the ways in which individuals seek to categorize others on the basis of specific signifiers, it is useful to examine how young Black women responded to the issues of mixed relationships and children of mixed parentage. Some of them felt that the shade of skin categorized an individual:

Naomi: Well I wouldn't go out with a White person, [must be either] half-caste or Black.

Mariah: Well what I'm saying ... right, I probably ... I would now but ... I don't think I'd like to marry [a white person] 'cause I ... wouldn't have a ...

Desiree: Three-quarter ...

Mariah: Yeah [I'd like] a dark kid.

DW: So you're saying exactly the same thing [as Naomi] Mariah?

Mariah: No, no, no ... I don't know. I says I don't want to but I would like to have a [dark] kid, but then again, I would marry one [a White person] if, it depends if it's love or whatever.

Here Mariah, the only one in the group above who is of mixed parentage is concerned about the skin shade of the child she may have if she has a relationship with a man who is White. Though she disagreed with Naomi who did not want a mixed relationship, her reason was her recognition of the way in which others may respond to a child of mixed parentage. Francine, who is of same race parentage, rejected a mixed relationship as it would call into question her and her child's racial authenticity, which would be clearly physically defined:

'Cause I want my child to be Black, don't want it to be mix up. Mind you I'd go out with a half caste person, but I s'pose they're Black really aren't they?

(Francine)

These examples show how physical characteristics (signified by skin colour) have been conflated with 'racial' authenticity.

CONCLUSION

The displays of boundary making evident within the *Pride* letters and the mixed parentage women's accounts illustrate that issues of 'colourism' and essentialism have become intricately woven. The constructions of Black womanhood in the *Pride* letters were based upon essentialist boundaries which sought to exclude lighter skinned women. The rejection of fair skinned women was in terms of their closeness to Whiteness. In contrast the women of mixed parentage in the research sample felt they had been positioned by the influence of colourism, in which closeness to Whiteness was envied and desired. These two separate issues illustrate the complexity of discussing Black female constructions of beauty. At one extreme there is a rejection of European ideas of womanhood and at the other an assumption that these qualities are desired. However what these issues also highlight is the underlying influence of Whiteness as a yardstick for beauty.[5]

The debate on defining Black womanhood illustrates the tension between essentialist and anti-essentialist ideas in the construction of racial identity. With its emphasis on deconstruction (of concepts such as Blackness and womanhood), postmodern analysis has far reaching consequences for the darker skinned women who police the boundaries of Black female identity. These women who in the letters attempted to construct an image of Black womanhood, used a specific racialized script which promoted an image of Blackness. Within postmodern frameworks such definitions are rejected because they are informed by the same biologism which constructs 'Black' as inferior. The consequences of such narrow definitions are clearly shown in the pain experienced by Black women who fail to conform to these standards by virtue of their parentage. However, attempting to understand the assertions by the dark skinned women within a historical framework has gone some way towards explaining why these attitudes persist. It also illustrates that not only are Black women attempting to reject the ways that they are considered unattractive due to length/texture of hair and shade of skin, but also in this rejection, that they wish to move away from the position of 'Other'. By exercising their ability to control their definition of womanhood, now redefined in terms of the visual and physical distance from Whiteness, Black women become 'strategically' empowered. Through this process, Black individuals who wish to redefine notions of Blackness do so from the position of subject rather than object. Black people who do so wish to redefine themselves as subject in order to exert some control over their lives (hooks 1989; Hartsock 1990). As hooks has argued:

> As subjects people have the right to define their own reality, establish their own identities, name their history ... as objects, one's reality is defined by others, one's identity created by others, one's history named only in ways that define one's relationship to those who are subject.
>
> (hooks 1989: 42)

The movement from object to subject is illustrated by the emphasis on the importance of natural (hair) styles (despite the commodification of the Afro) which shows the wish to move away from the negative associations of kinky hair with ugliness as defined by others. In similar ways the women readers who felt affronted at the image of Veronica Webb (though not, interestingly, at the image of British model Naomi Campbell who exhibits straightened hair, and quite recently was abrogated in the media for agreeing to promote a lipstick with images of her skin whitened (see Dowdney 1995: 3)) wished to move away from the negative associations of dark skin with ugliness. However, the ways that such strategic essentializing occurs creates rifts between Black women which means that essentializing on the basis of skin shade and hair texture has limited political possibilities. Brooks (1953) in her novel *Maud Martha* exemplifies the internal divisions inherent in this destructive discourse. She wrote in reference to a darker skinned woman whose husband was attracted to a lighter skinned woman, 'I could go over there and scratch her upsweep down. I could spit on her back. I could scream . . . [but] if the root was sour what business did she have up there hacking at a leaf?' (quoted in Collins 1990: 422). Similarly, Collins articulates the relationship between racial identity and racial power that informs the essentialising discourse in which young Black women are embedded in her discussion of Toni Morrison's (1979) *The Bluest Eye*:

> Frieda [is] a dark skinned 'ordinary' Black girl. . . . She wonders why adults always got so upset when she rejected the white dolls they gave her and why light-skinned Maureen Peal, a child her own age whose two braids hung like 'lynch-ropes down her back', got the love and attention of teachers, adults, and Black boys alike. Morrison explores Frieda's attempt not to blame Maureen for the benefits of her light skin and long hair afforded her as part of Frieda's growing realization that the 'Thing' to fear was not Maureen herself but the 'Thing' that made Maureen beautiful.
>
> (Collins 1990: 82)

Engaging in bitter dialogue between darker and lighter skinned women does not address the social relations which have produced this discourse. Thus it is necessary to focus upon the 'Thing' which constructs Whiteness as the yardstick by which beauty is judged. Hair and skin are used as physical signifiers for the purpose of judging how 'Black' a person is, and as one of the *Pride* letter writers suggested earlier, they are used to indicate how near or far a Black person is from Whiteness.

Theories of 'race' and womanhood have become separated from the way identity is experienced. The complex ways in which we talk about our identities at the experiential level do not always fit with those expressed at the conceptual level. The tendency toward fluid, multiple constructs of identity in anti-essentialist theory is in contrast to the fixed and narrow constructions expressed, at times strategically, by young Black women. Black feminist theory, in reinforcing the importance of Black female experience to an understanding of gender, can go some way towards bridging the gap between theory and lived reality. Though I have attempted to initiate discussion around the ways Black women position each other, one of the most important signifiers for Black women is the way we experience our Blackness, and negating this aspect of each other can only make it more difficult to challenge the 'Thing' which constructs the categories of race and gender which we inhabit.

NOTES

1 The research for this chapter constitutes part of a larger study on the identities of 31 young Black women aged 14–16, of whom 13 were of mixed parentage. It also includes conversations held between myself and an older mixed parentage woman (aged 20) on aspects of her identity. All mixed parentage women interviewed categorized themselves as such, and many of the sample considered their ancestry African.

2 The extent of media criticism which has been levelled at the music artist Michael (and his sister Latoya) Jackson over the years illustrates that these associations of physical signifiers with Whiteness are not only made within Black communities.

3 It has been suggested that issues of body image and eating disorders may not occur in the same way amongst Black women as they do with White women (see Quindlen 1994; Fine and Macpherson 1994).

4 This rule refers to the categorization of an individual as Black, by virtue of known African ancestry. Many persons of mixed parentage were historically rejected by White society on the basis of an identity created out of a taboo sexual relationship (see Tizard and Phoenix 1993; Gordon 1995).

5 This has led to the suggestion that White women, though oppressed by the 'beauty myth', are complicit in its negative effects on the bodies of Black women, because this myth is constructed around them (see Trepagnier 1994).

REFERENCES

Alibhai-Brown, Y. and Montague, A. (1992) *The Colour of Love: Mixed Race Relationships*, London: Virago.

Brooks, M. (1953) *Maud Martha*, Boston: Atlantic Press.

Bryan, B. Dadzie, S. and Scafe, S. (1985) *Heart of the Race*, London: Virago.

Carby, H. (1982) 'White Woman Listen! Black Feminism and the Boundaries of Sisterhood' in CCCS (ed.) *The Empire Strikes Back: Race and Racism in 70s Britain*, London: Hutchinson, pp. 212–35.

Cleaver, E. (1968) *Soul on Ice*, London: Cape.

Collins, P. (1986) 'Learning from the Outsider Within: The Sociological Significance of Black Feminist Thought' *Social Problems*, vol. 33, no. 6, pp. 14–32.

Collins, P. (1990) *Black Feminist Thought*, London: Harper Collins.

Dowdney, M. (1995) '£250,000 is all White for Naomi: Naomi Campbell appears to be White in new Italian Cosmetics Ad', *Daily Mirror*, 18 October, p. 3.

Dyson, M (1993) *Reflecting Black: African American Cultural Criticism*, Minneapolis: University of Minneapolis Press.

Fine, M., and Macpherson, P. (1994) 'Over Dinner: Feminism and Adolescent Female Bodies' in H. Radtke and H. Stam (eds) *Power/Gender: Social Relations in Theory and Practice*, London: Sage, pp. 219–46.

Foner, N. (1979) *Jamaican Farewell: Jamaican Migrants in London*, London: Routledge & Kegan Paul.

Fuss, D. (1989) *Essentially Speaking: Feminism, Nature and Difference*, London: Routledge.

Gilroy, P. (1993), *The Black Atlantic*, London: Verso.

Gordon, L.R. (1995) 'Critical "Mixed Race"?' *Social Identities* vol. 1, no. 2, August, pp. 381–95.

Hall, S. (1992) 'The Question of Cultural Identity' in S. Hall, D. Held and T. McGrew (eds) *Modernity and its Futures*, Cambridge: Polity Press.

Hartsock, N. (1990) 'Foucault on Power: A Theory for Women' in L. Nicholson (ed.) *Feminism/Postmodernism*, Routledge: London, pp. 157–76.

hooks, b. (1989) *Talking Back: Thinking Feminist Thinking Black*, Boston: South End Press.

hooks, b. (1991) *Yearning: Race, Gender and Cultural Politics*, London: Turnaround.

hooks, b. (1993) *Sisters of the Yam: Black Women and Self Recovery*, London: Turnaround.

James, W. (1993) 'Migration, Racism and Identity Formation: The Caribbean Experience in Britain' in W. James and C. Harris (eds) *Inside Babylon: The Caribbean Diaspora in Britain*, London: Verso, pp. 231–87.

Jones, A. (1970) 'Black Pride? Some Contradictions' in T. Cade (ed.) *The Black Woman: an Anthology*, New York: Signet.

Lewis, G. (1969) 'Race Relations in Britain: A View from the Caribbean', *Race Today*, vol. 1, no. 3.

Mama, A. (1995) *Beyond the Masks: Race, Gender and Subjectivity*, London: Routledge.

Mercer, K. (1990) 'Black hair/Style Politics' in R. Ferguson, M. Gever, T. Minh-ha and C. West (eds) *Out There: Marginalization and Contemporary Cultures*, Cambridge, Mass.: MIT Press, pp. 247–64.

Mercer, K. (1994) *Welcome to the Jungle: New Positions in Black Cultural Studies*, London: Routledge.

Morrison, T. (1979) *The Bluest Eye*, London: Chatto & Windus.

NdegeOcello, M. (1993) *Plantation Lullabies*, Maverick Recording Company.

Quindlen, A. (1994) 'Dolly Day Dreaming', *Guardian*, 15 September, p. 14.

Rodney, W. (1975) *The Groundings with my Brothers*, London: Bogle L'Ouverture.

Spivak, G. (1987) *In Other Worlds: Essays in Cultural Politics*, New York and London: Methuen.

Tizard, B. and Phoenix, A. (1993) *Black, White or Mixed Race? Race and Racism in the Lives of Young People of Mixed Parentage*, London: Routledge.

Trepagnier, B. (1994) 'The Politics of White and Black Bodies' in K. Bhavnani and A. Phoenix (eds) *Shifting Identities Shifting Racisms*, London: Sage, pp. 199–207

West, C. (1993) *Keeping the Faith: Philosophy and Race in America*, New York: Routledge.

Wolf, N. (1990) *The Beauty Myth*, London: Chatto & Windus.

Chapter 13

Diaspora's daughters, Africa's orphans?

On lineage, authenticity and 'mixed race' identity

Jayne O. Ifekwunigwe

INTRODUCTION

This chapter addresses problematic conceptions of place and belonging for individuals in Britain who are classified as neither Black nor White.[1] By virtue of lineage, those of 'mixed race', as they have come to be known, or *métis(se)*[2], as I wish to rename them, situate themselves within at least two specific and yet over-lapping historical narratives. While they can claim both indigenous and exogenous roots, this duality has implications for their constructions of identities. Stuart Hall suggests:

> Cultural Identity ... is a matter of 'becoming' as well as 'being'. It belongs to the future as much as to the past. It is not something which already exists, transcending place, time, history and culture. Cultural identities come from somewhere, have histories. But, like everything which is historical, they undergo constant transformation. Far from being eternally fixed in some essentialized past, they are subject to the continuous 'play' of history, culture and power. Far from being grounded in a mere 'recovery' of the past, which is waiting to be found, and which when found, will secure our sense of ourselves into eternity, identities are the names we give to the different ways we are positioned by and position ourselves within the narratives of the past.
>
> (1990: 225)

In gender-specific, family centred narratives of *métisse* women, the inherent tensions between being and becoming Black, being and becoming continental African or African Caribbean, and being English as opposed to British epitomize the psychosocial struggles between subjectivity and alterity. The specific lived and named realities of the *métisse* women in this study represent heightened forms of the angst facing all people in the Diaspora.[3] Their experiences of multiple identities, which are necessarily contradictory, socioculturally constructed and essentialized, demand new paradigms for looking at citizenship and belonging.

The particular focus of my study is the interrogation of postmodern

Diaspora constructions of gender, selves and communities and paradoxical representations of 'race', nation, culture, and generation. My pioneering qualitative ethnographic work with *métisse* women in Bristol between 1990 and 1992 had six purposes. First was to formulate a new lexicon which more appropriately describes individuals who by virtue of birth and 'blood' do not fit neatly into preordained sociological and anthropological categories. Second, my intention was to create non-hierarchical discourses of difference which silence colour-blind ideologies. Third, I wished to address unique psychosocial dynamics between societally deemed White mothers and their Black daughters by adding a racialized dimension to previous feminist psychoanalytic work on mother/daughter relationships.[4] Fourth, I intended to invoke the textual strategy of the *griot(te)* in order to acknowledge and work with inherent tensions in ethnography between orality and literacy. Fifth, I proposed to popularize usage of the term 'orphan consciousness' to describe the 'late modern' (Gilroy 1993b) plight of Diaspora sons and daughters. Finally, in the context of different family forms and communities, I intended to normalize the lived and complex cultural realities of *métis(se)* individuals and their families, thereby writing against previous psychopathological and monolithic interpretations of experiences.[5]

RE-NAMING AND RE-CLAIMING

At the moment, countless terms abound to describe 'mixed' people and usually reflect the prevailing political and social attitudes regarding racial and ethnic pluralism. As part of a constantly expanding inventory there are: 'mixed race', 'mixed parentage', 'mixed heritage', 'mixed blood', 'mixed racial descent', 'mixed descent', 'mixed origins', 'mixed ethnicity', 'multiethnic', 'dual heritage', 'multiracial', 'biracial', 'inter-racial', 'creole', 'mestizo' or 'mestiza' to the more derogatory and colloquial 'half caste', 'mulatto' or 'mulatta', 'half blood', 'half breed', 'hybrid', 'zebra', 'Heinz 57' and the list goes on. In England, currently the most popular terms appear to be 'mixed parentage' and 'dual heritage'. Tizard and Phoenix, the authors of *Black, White or Mixed Race?* (1993) define those of 'mixed parentage' as 'people with one White parent and one Black parent of African or Afro-Caribbean descent' (1993: 6). Although an improvement on 'mixed race' which legitimates and reifies the sociocultural construct 'race,' the term 'mixed parentage' fails in its presumption that the 'mixing' is first generation. Anthropologist Michael Banton has attempted to popularize the implicitly ambiguous 'mixed origins' which could describe any individual with a diverse background – i.e. English and Scottish – and not solely individuals who stem from a mixture of so-called different races. 'Dual heritage' pinpoints the convergence of different cultures and ethnicities; however, the fact that it is de-racialized also broadens its potential relevance.

A complicating matter is the concomitant lack of consensus in Britain over who is Black, which has become an essentialized political term lacking both dynamism and fluidity and frequently confused with nationality (Modood 1988). The Census classification system clearly embodies this rigid fixity of terminology. The first time the government Census attempted to calculate the number of non-White people in Britain was 1991. Out of a total British population of 54.9 million people, just over 3 million or 5.5 per cent were then designated as ethnic minorities. The major 'ethnic' subheadings of the Census are Black-Caribbean, African, or Other; Asian-Indian, Pakistani, Bangladeshi, or Other; Chinese; and Other. This classification system is flawed in its conflation of race, ethnicity and nationality and discriminatory in its homogenization of peoples from continental Africa and the Caribbean. This categorization scheme is most problematic when accounting for the ethnic origins of people of so-called mixed or multiple ethnicities, wherein there are two significant and interlocking factors at work. First, the prevailing and inconsistent social and political stance that anyone who does not look White is seen as Black impinges on identity construction for many multiethnic *métis(se)* people. Second, in specific temporal, spatial, and sociocultural contexts, self-identification for this group may or may not coincide with the aforementioned classification. They often negotiate several different identities depending on 'where they are' both physically and psychologically and with whom they are interacting. I will talk about the negotiation of the public and private later on. However, both Anne Wilson's study of mixed race children (1987) and my own research (Ifekwunigwe, forthcoming) on *métis(se)* adults and identity formation coincide with Okamura's notion of an ethnic identification which is by nature operationally situational (1981). In other words, on the night of the Census, for simplicity's sake, an individual may have reported themselves as Black-Caribbean (of which there are 500,000) when in fact they have one White English parent. In another context, that same individual could just as adamantly identify or be identified as *métis(se)* or at times even White.

Accordingly, presuming that individuals self-identify as 'Other' rather than as one of the eight other possible categories, this group comprises what the 1991 Census would classify as that nebulous 'Other' – Black-Other (178, 400); Asian-Other (197, 500) and more than likely, Other-Other (290, 200) (NEMDA 1991). In the county of Avon, out of a total population of 932,674, ethnic minorities make up less than 2 per cent of the population, and cumulatively the 'Others' – Black, Asian, and Other – comprise less than 1 per cent (Office of Population Censuses and Surveys 1991). In Bristol, the city where I conducted my ethnographic research, out of a total population of 376,146, ethnic minorities constitute 3.6 per cent and the 'Others' 1.4 per cent (Office of Population Censuses and Surveys 1991). Hence, a representative sample of this group is actually not a very large number. Having said that, my ethnographic project included only twenty-five women and men with British or European mothers and continental African or African Caribbean fathers. They constituted the core group of participants in my two year long Bristol-based ethnographic doctoral research.

In his essay, 'Critical "Mixed Race"?', L.R. Gordon teases out six different claims in favour of what he calls 'a critical race theory premised upon mixed race identity' (1995: 388). A 'mixed race' standpoint, he suggests, is a necessary part of a racial discourse that is based on the premise of skin colour. If 'race' means 'pure' Black or White then there must be recognition of mixtures which are neither 'pure' Black nor 'pure' White. This acknowledgement of 'other' forms of 'race' in turn debunks the notion of racial purity by suggesting 'racelessness'. Mixture thus is an enigma that some choose politically to acknowledge as a category and others not. In practical terms, Gordon argues that 'mixed race' can lead to an anti-racist strategy. By diluting identities based on racial purity and mythical filial ancestry, 'mixed race' can point to the possibility of a 'raceless' future with a new and cultivated shared existential identity and reality.

What is needed is a term that does not glorify 'race' yet acknowledges the existence of racialism while also centring the lived manifestations of the sociocultural markers of ethnicity, class, gender, and generation. Similarly, Gilroy states:

> In these circumstances, it may be easier to appreciate the utility of a response to racism that doesn't reify the concept of race, and to prize the wisdom generated by developing a series of answers to the power of ethnic absolutism that doesn't try to fix ethnicity absolutely but sees it instead as an infinite process of identity construction.
>
> (Gilroy 1993b: 223)

I introduce the terms *métissage, métisse* for females and *métis* for males. My own operationalization of these concepts emerged after much reading and research as well as the result of a series of conversations with both a Senegalese Comparative Literature scholar (Diop 1993a) and a Senegalese cultural critic (Koubaka 1993). *Métissage* is a concept which is generally associated with France and French speaking Canada, and certain Francophone African and Caribbean countries (Marquet 1983; Lionnet 1989; Burley *et al*. 1992). The English translation of *métis(se)* which appears in the second edition of the Collins French Dictionary (1987) is 'half-caste', 'half-breed' or 'mongrel'. However, it has been re-appropriated by others including myself in much the same way as 'hapa', a derogatory term with Hawaiian etymological origins and describing people who are half native Hawaiian or Asian and half White, has been reinscribed by a politicized group of students at the University of California, Berkeley who stem from the aforementioned backgrounds.

In the French African context, in its conventional masculine or feminine forms, *métis(se)* refers to someone who by virtue of parentage, embodies two or more world views, 'A Euro-African' to use Leopold Senghor's term (Marquet 1983). However, in Senegal, *métis(se)* is not exclusively a 'racial' term used to differentiate individuals with one French parent and one Senegalese parent from those who are 'pure' Senegalese. *Métis(se)* could also pertain to people with parents from different ethnic groups within a country (i.e. Yoruba and Ibo) or from different countries (i.e. Senegal and the Congo). One can go one step further with this definition to include the postmodern 'cultural' *métis(se)* or *métis(se) culturel*. This describes anyone who by virtue of travel, education, and experience represents an amalgamated 'hybrid' identity. Historian Vovelle also uses the term *métis culturel* which for him is synonymous with 'cultural broker', 'traffic officers' and 'bricoleurs' (1982). In the words of Trinh Minh-Ha, 'the place of my hybridity is also the place of my identity' (1992: 29).

On the other hand, *métissage* is a mind set or a newfangled shorthand way to talk about the now universal constructs: oscillation, contradiction, paradox, hybridity, creolization, mestizaje, 'blending and mixing', polyglot, heteroglossia, transnationalities, multiple reference points, multiculturalism, so-called multiraciality, 'belonging nowhere and everywhere,' and endogenous and exogenous roots. For me, *métissage* is also that prescriptive antidote to Diaspora angst. It is about the *process* of opening up hybrid spaces and looking at the sociocultural dynamics of 'race', gender, ethnicity, nation, class, and sexuality and their relationship to the mechanics of power. This is quite similar to Appiah's definition of postmodernism: 'Postmodernism can be seen, then as a new way of understanding the multiplication of distinctions that flow from the need to clear oneself a space; the need that drives the underlying dynamic of cultural modernity' (1992: 145). Lionnet refers to *métissage* as 'the site of undecidability and indeterminacy, where solidarity becomes the fundamental principle of political action against hegemonic languages' (1989: 6).

Métissage is a concept which at its best operates simultaneously and differentially at the level of the individual, the family, the community, and the state. *Métissage* works within the realm of what Goffman (1959) would refer to as 'front stage' and 'back stage' or at what Anzaldúa would refer to as the 'borderlands' where life exists on borders and margins with a shifting multiplicity of identities (1987). Barth (1969) would also situate *métissage* at the 'ethnic boundary' where according to Wallman (1979), one can differentiate between 'us' and 'them'. Wherever one locates *métissage*, what is most significant is that:

the notion of crossroads as a special location where unforeseen, magical things can happen might be an appropriate conceptual vehicle for re-thinking the dialectical tension between cultural roots and cultural routes, between the pace constituted through and between places and the space marked out by flows. The irreducibly diagonal concerns that grow from the desire to take diaspora interculture seriously suggest that the image of the crossroads might contribute something to rethinking the relationship between time and space in modernity and the narratives of nationality and location it generates.

(Gilroy 1993a: 193)

METHODOLOGY

I met project participants myself along the first year of my ethnographic journey, through friends, acquaintances, teachers, social workers, artists and other professionals or through other participants themselves. The small size of my sample does not make it representative in an empirical sense. However, even with just twenty-five respondents certain important themes emerged which contribute to previous, more recent important sociological, psychological, and anthropological British research by Sue Benson (1981) on mixed race families, by Anne Wilson (1987) on mixed race children, by Yasmin Alibhai-Brown and Anne Montague on mixed race relationships (1992) and by Barbara Tizard and Ann Phoenix on mixed parentage young people (1993). In addition, qualitative social scientists attempting similar naturalistic analyses can benefit from my recommendations and conclusions.[6]

I collected the original narratives in Bristol via open-ended tape-recorded interviews, between 1990 and 1992. The age of the primary participants, both men and women, ranged from 13 to 45. With the exception of two native Bristolian women, everyone I spoke with had been born and had come of age elsewhere – Jamaica, the United States, London, the north of England, Liverpool, Wales, Nigeria, Birmingham, and so on. They had found their way to Bristol either for work, education, or for personal reasons and their current subject positions can only be articulated in light of the city of Bristol's previous involvement with the slave trade. This unspoken association mirrors the uneasy relationship other English–African Diaspora constituents have with the former Empire; 'They see their place in the metropolis as the inevitable consequence of an earlier act of trespass and transgression' (Oguibe 1994: xx). Similarly:

It starts from recognition of the African diaspora's peculiar position as 'step-children' of the West and of the extent to which our imaginations are conditioned by an enduring proximity to regimes of racial terror . . .

it seeks deliberately to exploit the distinctive qualities of perception that DuBois identified long ago as 'double consciousness'.

(Gilroy 1993a: 103)

In the introduction to their book, Tizard and Phoenix report that, at present, 'nearly 30 per cent of people (27 per cent for men and 28 per cent for women) of African Caribbean origin who are under the age of thirty who are married, or cohabitating have a White partner' (1993: 1). The fact that this figure excludes continental Africans limits its utility. According to the 1991 Census, there are 212,000 continental Africans in the United Kingdom. How do their marital and co-habitation patterns compare with those in the African-Caribbean communities? Alibhai-Brown and Montague quote a 1985 figure from the last Office of Population Censuses and Labour Force Survey: '27 per cent of Black British husbands are in mixed marriages and 14 per cent of Black women' (1992: 13). However, the ambiguity of the term 'Black British' leads one to wonder whether individuals who were born either in the Caribbean or continental Africa are included in this sample. Regarding children, Coleman (1985) estimates that of all the people of mixed White and African-Caribbean origin, more than 50 per cent are under the age of 10. This figure makes the work that my colleagues and I have completed all the more significant for the mental health and well-being of future generations. One can surmise that more African-Caribbean and continental African men than women engage in mixed relationships of which children are frequently the product. Nevertheless, the number of women of continental African or African-Caribbean origin mothering children with British or European men is rising in response to shifts in social attitudes, and the economic and educational mobility of Black women among other factors.

The majority of people I spoke with were the product of a union between a White 'majority' female and a Black 'minority' male. One can explain this in terms of gender politics and economics. Historically, across cultures and classes, it was generally the man who was mobile and the woman who remained at home (Fryer 1984; Walvin 1973; Patterson 1963). Respondents' fathers came from Nigeria, Ghana, Jamaica and Tanzania or were African-American and their mothers were Irish, English, Scottish and German. Nigerian men followed by Ghanaian men fathered the most children in my particular sample. There was one woman whose mother was Trinidadian and her father White American. Her parents had met while he was stationed at an American military base outside London.[7]

Participation in this project consisted of respondents providing me with a series of tape-recorded testimonies about their childhoods, gender politics, racial and ethnic identity, class background, nationalism, family, sexuality, creativity, parenting, and racism, among a variety of topics. I acquired separate notebooks for each storyteller and I used them to record my responses to each session as well as to keep track of all the questions generated from each listening. By the time the edited testimonies appeared as text I had listened to them in full four times. The first time was immediately after each session. While their voices were still singing in my head I formulated questions that were in direct response to their testimonies. These questions would serve as a guide, not as the basis, for the next storytelling session. I repeated this approach until the participants decided that they had finished testifying and concluded that we had reached the core or the marrow – what was/is significant to each one of them in their everyday lives. I refer to this interview technique as the 'artichoke method'. The ethnographer has to peel off several layers of skin before the heart of the matter is revealed.

Upon finishing the sessions I listened to every single testimony again for insights and patterns. The third listening entailed labour-intensive transcription, which was at times encumbered by regionally specific accents. The final listening was for clarification and verification of specific segments of testimonies. It was at this final stage that I realized that I had far too much rich and evocative material to work with and that I would have to wittle my original focus down to one or more key themes. From the first to the fourth listening, I maintain that so much was lost in committing oral performance to tape and then translating the tape to text – the cadence and rhythm of the men and women's regionally specific accents, as they spoke to me, the visual beauty carved out in detail on their 'Euro-African' faces, as well as the cultural medleys manifesting themselves in both their living spaces and their sociocultural worlds.

When I began the process of writing, I confirmed for myself what I had suspected earlier – there was no way that I could adequately do justice to all twenty-five life stories. Including them all in the final 'polythesis' which ethnographic film-maker David MacDougall (1993) refers to as 'an interplay of voices' – and I add ideas – would have been a lengthy process and one that would ultimately have resulted in my truncating their experiences. I tried working with fifteen, then nine and finally six. The task of selecting the final six was not an easy one. All twenty-five were eloquent and engaging storytellers. Among a larger cast of nineteen stars, the ones I had to leave behind included Andrew, a polylingual Anglo-Ghanaian; Twilight from a multigenerational so-called multi-racial Jamaican family; Harmony, an extremely talented and wise-beyond-her-years 15-year-old Anglo-Ghanaian poet; and three very insightful women who were now social workers but as children had been adopted by White English middle-class families – Anglo-Nigerian Zaynab, Scots-Nigerian Claudia and Anglo-Ghanaian Sharon, who had grown up completely in care in a socially isolated children's home in the north of England.

In order to highlight the problematic racialized relationship between mothers and daughters, the final polythesis featured the narratives of six women – two sets of sisters and two women who had grown up in care with what I refer to as mother surrogates. Two of the women were raised in Liverpool in the midst of the then burgeoning Black Power Movement by a working-class Irish mother and without their Bajan (from Barbados) father. The other two sisters were brought up in Nigeria during the turbulent postcolonial 1960s and neocolonial 1970s by middle-class parents – in particular, a Northumberland (English) mother and a Yoruba (Nigerian) father. The other two women, one Anglo-Nigerian and the other Deutsch-Tanzanian, spent their formative years in care in middle-class, all White English or Welsh children's homes outside London and Cardiff, respectively. They were each socialized by 'mother surrogates' prior to the explosive debates about welfare policy as it pertains to transracial fosterage, placement, and adoption. As a Nigerian-Irish-English-Guyanese anthropologist, my own auto-ethnographic narrative which unfolds in Nigeria, Lancashire, and Los Angeles, California, is also interwoven with their stories to create a Baktinian 'dialogic' patchwork.[8] In so doing, I purposely challenge conventional ethnography and tackle phenomenological and epistemological concerns associated with prior conceptualizations of Diaspora, 'race,' nation, generation, and identity. Consequently, as insider and outsider, I blur the boundaries between subjective experience and objective social scientific inquiry.

INVOKING THE ORAL TRADITION: *MÉTISSE* WOMEN AS *GRIOTTES*

I argue that the ways in which the women I worked with tell their stories are as newfangled *griottes*. Their memories preserve and reinterpret senses of past cultures, while also providing scathing sociopolitical commentary and cultural critiques of contemporary English-African Diasporic life. *Griotte*, as it appears in the feminine form, is another term I have re-appropriated. It is a West African, Senegalese – that is Wolof – term which describes a traditional story-teller. However, though they may not be actually named *griots*, most African cultures have a specific term to describe someone who functions as tribal poet, story-teller, historian or genealogist and whose role is to recount culturally specific and provocative parables of daily life (Jegede 1994). Moreover, these definitions will have different operationalized meanings in different cultural contexts and more importantly at different historical moments. For example, in traditional Senegalese society these individuals, usually men, were part of a caste, were generally attached to royal families and learned the craft of story-telling or 'praise singing' on an apprenticeship basis. However, with the impact of social change the *griot's* traditional role has changed. Membership in this group no longer precludes specific training handed down from one generation to the next. There are now what one could only call *'faux griots'*. That is one can now call oneself a *griot* without having received specialized training from an elder *griot*. Upon hearing of a ceremony or public celebration taking place which will honour the members of an elite family, an enterprising individual would simply approach the head of the family and for a certain amount of money offer to sing the praises of the family in much the same manner as a court jester or entertainer (Diop 1993b). Furthermore, scholars of African popular culture – most notably music – have also broadened the usage of *griot* to describe the performance styles of artists such as the Senegalese Baaba Maal, Malian Salif Keita, or Alpha Blondie from Cote d'Ivoire. With the exception of a community of women musicians in Mali, women per-formers are generally not recognized in this genre. In light of this gendered over-sight, my research seeks to redress women's invisibility by placing women in the role of *griotte*.

WHITE EQUALS ENGLISH?: AKOUSA'S TESTIMONY

While I was in the midst of conducting the initial research between 1990–1992, there was an ad campaign for the sweets 'Smarties'. Billboards and sweet wrappers read: 'Find out the real secret to the white Smarties.' The answer was: 'They are white all the way through . . . they are made with white chocolate'. An analogous assumption would be that only people fitting the protypic phenotypic description of a White person can be English. Everyone else will have to make do with British. In addition, the former is a citizen and the latter a mere subject. For example, Oguibe states: 'That one is born in Hackney, London of parents born in Hackney, London themselves is never sufficient proof of belonging for people of African descent in Britain' (Oguibe 1994: xvii).

Akousa

Akousa is Irish-Bajan and grew up in Liverpool amid a strong African-Caribbean community and with her Irish mother and her brother and sister. She is a Rasta[9] and yet not everyone sees her as a Rasta. She sees herself as a 'light-skinned' Black woman, and yet not everyone sees her as Black. Here she describes some contradictory English attitudes towards 'race', colour and citizenship:

> I think at the end of the day, White society has never accepted me. They've seen me as a contamination to their stock. Diseased person, and even worst than havin' two Black parents, worse than even that. If you come to extermination, we would probably go first. Nazi Germany.

That's the sort of vibe I get off White people. With Black people generally, I know they have accepted me as I am. I've been part of their community. I've been raised with Caribbean culture. . . . I don't consider myself half of any ting. I cannot be half. When people call me that I say, 'Do you see Black on one side and White on the other?' If they call me 'Coloured', I say, 'You see my stripes?' Like I've been coloured in or somethin'. There was this White woman on the coach one day and she said to me, 'If you put a straight wig on you, you'd be White. You'd look White.' Friggin' hell. Man, I may be light, but you can't get away from the fact that I do have strong African features. Even if you did stick a wig on me, it surely would look strange. And what makes her think I would want to wear a wig in the first place, and that I want to look like a White person? Rather than lookin' the way I look, which I was quite happy with. You have a lot of White people tryin' to get you to change to look White. You want to get rid of this African look that you've got. I find that really weird. That was another sort of problem that I had with White people.

The other thing that they used to do to me which used to really make me cringe was they'd been on holiday to Costa del Sol and they've got their sun tans, and this was when I was workin' at Marks and Spencers. They love the scene of a light-skinned Black person so they can come up to you and say 'Look, I'm darker than you.' Then, I'd go, 'Well yours only last three weeks, mine last forever, love . . .'

Akousa's commentary brings to the forefront what I refer to as the social chameleon phenomenon: *Métis(se)* people with so-called 'ambiguous' phenotypes, i.e. very fair complexions; blue, green or hazel eyes; more 'pointed/sharp' facial features; light coloured or straight hair, who can 'change colour' from one social context to the next. Here, Akousa has described herself or has been described as *métis(se)*, White and Black.

IS IT ALL IN THE BLOOD?: RUBY'S AND YEMI'S STORIES

The founder of the American Negro Academy, Alexander Crummell, defines a 'race' as 'a compact homogeneous population of one blood ancestry and lineage' (1862). While Paul Gilroy refers to 'race' as 'kinship where . . . the family is the approved natural site where ethnicity and racial culture are reproduced . . . and in this authoritarian pastoral patri-archy, women are usually identified as the agents and means of this process of cultural reproduction' (1993a: 195–7). These two definitions serve my analytical purposes well although operationalizing them within the famil-ial contexts I researched produces a major paradox. Apparently, White English women are mothering Black British children.

Ruby

As previously mentioned, many factors influence the ways in which White women accomplish the task of bringing up so-called Black children. The circumstances surrounding the birth of the *métis(se)* child, the prevailing attitudes towards mixed relationships, the class background all affect the uniqueness of experience. Ruby is Anglo-Nigerian and was brought up in a children's home outside London until she left at age 16, even though both her birth mother and other blood relatives were alive. Their rationale for placing her there was they wanted her to 'have a proper growing up experience.' There was an overwhelming shame surrounding her birth. Her father was married and Black African, which made it impossible for both Ruby's birth mother and grandmother to fully accept her. However, like a benevolent missionary, her grandmother would visit Ruby under the guise of 'Auntie,' taking care of her material needs, buying her presents, taking her and her mates on outings and so on. However, as the following narrative reveals, this benevolence did not include acknowledging Ruby as a 'blood relative':

> So I became very adept at hiding. I was sixteeen or seventeen – quite big but I had actually lived quite a sheltered life. That period of time with my Gran brought out very much to the fore what her attitude to me was and why it was like that. It was 80 per cent because of the colour of my skin; the other 20 per cent was the fact that I was an illegitimate child. For my grandmother and her generation, that was quite a shameful thing. But had I been a White illegitimate child it would have been very different. So as I say 80 per cent because of colour – she didn't want to be associated in the blood line with a Black grand-daughter. She was ashamed of me and her neighbours didn't know that I was related to her. She never had any photographs of me or anything like that.
>
> She was selling her house at the time so there were all sorts of people coming to the house. I remember this awful period where people would come to the house and I would do crazy things: do things like hide under the bed, in the wardrobe, hide in the bushes, in the garden all the time. It was very important that they didn't see me there so they didn't ask any odd questions about who I was and therefore embarrass my grandmother. That was very odd and really sort of sharpened up the conflict that I had with my grandmother, really up until the time of her death, that in a sense never really got resolved. It became clear to me that she was ashamed of the colour of my skin more than anything else.

What Ruby clearly needed was a place to belong, not a place to hide. Her grandmother's public embracing of Ruby as a legitimate blood relative would have facilitated the process of self-incorporation that to this day Ruby has not accomplished.

Yemi

Yemi, whose mother is English and father Yoruba from Nigeria, grew up in Nigeria in a middle-class family where both her English and Nigerian relations accepted her. However, her troubled relationship with her mother drove her to attempt suicide at age 13 and transformed her kinship relationship with her father from daughter to honorary son:

> By the time I was 13, my mother and I started to have very serious head-on collisions. . . . The long and short of all this is I attempted suicide around that time. She liked to exclude me. She tried all sorts of things. She played the piano. She would be playing the piano downstairs in the living room, this musical. She had a big thick book of songs you could sing. Some were hymns; some were sea shanties. All sorts of different things we could sing. We'd come down and start singing and she'd say to me, 'Go away, you're spoiling the song with your voice.' I wouldn't be trying to spoil the song. Maybe I was singing too loud or off key. Who cares. So on a particular Saturday, I searched the whole house for what I was going to take to kill myself, because I had had enough. I felt she didn't really love me. . . . Everything I could find I took. . . . They were supposed to be out for hours. . . . When they came back I was so shocked and I thought YEEH they're back already and I'm not dead . . . I told her. 'Oh you idiot,' she said, 'Get inside the car. You're nothing but trouble you.' She put the other ones in the house. Got inside the car and drove me to our family doctor. An old man called Dr Renshewe, who had been our doctor since I was a little little girl. He took me quickly to his own bedrooom gave me an emetic to make me sick. He gave me some salt or soap. I don't even know what it was; it tasted like soap. I was sick. I told him, 'She doesn't love me. She'd be much happier if I wasn't there.'
>
> The result of this was that she had very little to do with me after that. My Dad took me every evening when he came back to my uncle's house. Every single evening. When he was going out, he didn't actually leave me with her ever again. He took me whenever he went to my uncle's. He took me when he was going to his farm. He took me when he was going to Ijebu or when he was going on one of his trips. My Dad and I became very close which was very good. My mother and I can't actually get along very well. It's now that I see her that I realize I'm not the crazy one when I was young. I was in no way disturbed. She's the nutter. She's the difficult one and picks favourites. It's not reasonable to have more than one child if you have this mentality of picking favourites and having the others as horrible. Also, because of this change with my father, I got very close to my cousins. So, I am closer to my cousins than my other sisters, very, very close. They are all boys. So, I now get to know how to speak Yoruba, Yoruba morals, the life itself better than my

sisters. Ostensibly this was because I was actually flung out by my mother, or stepped away from my mother. Then all of these things were accessible to me.

What Yemi has to say about her family of origin does not really differ from family dynamics which play themselves out in contexts which are not *métis(se)*. As such, Yemi succeeds in normalizing *métis(se)* family life and strife. However, her narrative is also in keeping with a prevailing theme which is the impress of the White English mother or the White English mother surrogate in the transmission of White English culture in all its variations. Even if the Black father is physically present, as was the case in Yemi's family, White English cultural codes are frequently reified at the expense of Black African or Caribbean referents in all their complex manifestations. From linguistic silences to dietary omissions, more often than not it is Black/African/Caribbean culture which is subverted. The privileging of White English culture in *métis(se)* households has serious dialectical implications for *métisse* identity formation since it is a racialized, essentialized and socially constructed Black/African identity that society-at-large imposes. In Yemi's case, her squabble with her mother puts her in a position wherein she now has access to Yoruba culture which had previously been perceived as male and from which she had been excluded.

ON ADDITIVE *BLACKNESS*: TESTIMONIES FROM SIMILOLA, SARAH, AND BISI

The well-intentioned political mandate encouraging *métis(se)* people to identify solely as Black renders their White parent invisible, but not forgotten. As aforementioned, until recently the White parent was the mother. The six women featured here all have White English, German, or Irish birth mothers. Akousa, Sarah, Bisi and Yemi were raised by their biological mothers. The other two women, Ruby and Similola, were raised by White English women, who were the matrons in the children's homes where they spent their formative years. Consequently, their first experiences of gender and of what it means to be a woman are witnessed through their White caretakers. Yet society tells them that they must deny this reality in the name of an ill-founded racialist system.

The push by Black and implicitly White people to encourage *métis(se)* people to identify as Black is supposed to provide what *griotte* Bisi refers to as 'protective colouration'. Actual biological origins and cultural realities have little bearing in a society that discriminates on the basis of phenotype. With the criteria for Black membership as limited as they are, society at large generally 'sees' *métis(se)* people only as Black. What one's family and life experiences have been as well as the cultural constitution of one's household account for very little in a racially confused world.

Aligning themselves with Black people can provide a cushion against the inevitable blows of racialism. However, what this recommendation ignores is the indelible impress of individual circumstance which makes the process of identifying with Blackness, Black people and Black cultures painful, mystifying and gradual for many *metis(se)* women and men. Black children, that is with two Black biological parents, who have grown up in care, in transracial adoption situations, or in predominantly White suburbs, also struggle with these issues.

For many *métis(se)* people who grow up in predominantly White English environments, this form of Black-washing also threatens to erode a substantial part of their psychosocial foundation, which at the contested time is either White or *métis(se)*. Psychologists refer to this process as 'negriscence' or coming to terms with one's Blackness or being Black (Russell *et al.* 1992). Though this model is a cumulative or developmental one, its typology of Black traits seems to suggest that there is an essential Blackness which *métis(se)* people can strive towards but never completely attain. This paradigm also does not stress the qualitative starting point of the journey. I refer to the process of coming to terms with one's Blackness as Additive Blackness. That is, the person starts with her or his foundation and builds forward, without having to sever ties with their often White English roots. From their own emblematic experiences, the *métisse griottes* I worked with speak against the generalizing and subjugating tendencies of much of the discourses on Black people in the English-African Diaspora. Their collective voices demand a revision of the British double caste system which binds Black people both economically and racially.

Similola

Similola is Deutsch-Tanzanian. She grew up in a Welsh children's home where she was made to feel that being White and Whiteness were the ideal standards by which she should measure her self-worth. In the long run, she knew she could never be completely White and being White-identified always seemed to lead to disappointment and rejection for her. Here she describes a strategy she devised for coping with her ambivalence associated with Blackness and Whiteness:

> I decided, I'm going to have a Black day or a White day. My White day I was ... I'd dress differently for starters. I'd usually wear jeans on my White days. I used to wear jeans because I thought it's more acceptable amongst White students to wear jeans. It seemed like kind of a White uniform in a way and you didn't see many Black girls wearing jeans at that time. So, I'd wear jeans, and whatever else – the bits and pieces that go with it – t-shirts, whatever. Then, on my Black days, I'd

wear flowery skirts and very bright clothes and people used to say 'God' and I actually got to quite enjoy it. It sounds very silly at that time. I'm not sure if it affected my behaviour in any way. At that phase, I was more outgoing and I tended to be a bit more – to let more of myself show, and not be so self-conscious. Because it was my Black day and I'd think: Oh, I can get away with these things in front of White people because they don't expect Black people to act like them so I can be a bit more outrageous than I normally would. In the end, I couldn't cope with both of these identities. I'd decide the night before. Not necessarily one day. . . sometimes it would be like I'd enjoy my Black day so much on one Monday and I'd think . . . it must have been all psychological, I don't think so totally, but I used to notice people treated me differently as well and they reacted towards me in a different way.

To me it was something to do with acknowledging my Blackness. To me, I thought, I can't be Black if I don't wear bright coloured clothes. I had this period of going round dressed all in black clothes and I thought if I wore black clothes all the time I wouldn't be noticed. It wasn't like now where people wear black clothes all the time. It was the time when black wasn't even vaguely fashionable. It was only worn for funerals and that was it. I got into this wearing black clothes thing thinking I'd be totally unnoticed. My whole wardrobe was full of black clothes. To me it was an even greater step to suddenly switch into really bright – 'cause I'd got so comfortable with black. Even though people do notice you it's what you yourself feel. I used to feel that when I wore black I was totally insignificant and totally unnoticed. It suited me at that time to be like that and to just fade into the background and not be noticed for any reason. The giant leap into brightness for me was so huge that I used to dare myself. I'd go into shops and buy very, very, bright coloured clothing and then dare myself in the evening to put it on the next day. I'd say, 'God, are you gonna wear that tomorrow or not?' Sometimes I would, sometimes I wouldn't. Now, I don't even, I don't want to try and dress in a Black way, just because I want to identify with being Black. 'Cause to me now that's so superficial anyway, there is so much more to it than that and I don't feel the need for that kind of thing anymore. People have to accept me for what I am and if they don't it's just tough.

The way Similola describes her Black days/White days scheme is similar to the ways in which *métis(se)* people who are 'trying on' being Black for the first time oscillate uncomfortably between the two. Clothes supposedly being an extension or reflection of one's inner self, this binary dress scheme points to the notion that one's appearances determines the way one is categorized and there are essentialized Black and White ways of dressing/being.

Sarah

Irish-Bajan Sarah is Akousa's younger sister and her recollections of her childhood and adolescence in Liverpool are remarkably different from Akousa's. Recollections of her life are interwoven with vivid descriptions of the houses she and her family lived in and they become veritable signposts along her journey. At one stage she recalls the way in which she found solidarity in difference and marginality through her friendship with two other *métisse* girls:

> My friends at school were: I had one friend who was White, and then she moved to this new housing estate that they built. I had one friend who was Indian, Esther Pamjit. She was really big, very big. She was mixed race as well. She was half Indian and half English. Her Mum was English. She had this hair that was really thick that went really down to her bum – really thick, thick, thick head of hair. She used to always have it in a thick plait going down her back. She's really big and she's quite like a tomboy. Very quite masculine; she wasn't you know like – 'Huh ha hoh' [feminine gesture] – she was very – 'Uhhh' [masculine gesture]. Then, I used to have another friend, let me see if I can remember her name . . . Her father was Nigerian and her mother was English. I can't remember her name, maybe it'll come back. I seen her when I was in Liverpool. I hadn't seen her in years. Ngozi that was it, Ngozi. She was really tall. Like somebody who's too tall for their age. Ngozi, and she was big as well. And I was the smallest one amongst them. So we used to hang around together. 'Cause we were all just – we didn't fit in. Do you know what I mean? All three of us were from mixed race families, and the three of us were all funny shapes and sizes for what little girls are supposed to be. So we used to kind of hang around and find solace with each other.

Like most of the *griottes'* identity narratives, Sarah's testimonies are framed in terms of turning points – leaving school, first love relationship, getting married, having children, etc. However, in light of what I refer to as Additive Blackness, the awakening of Black consciousness is also a milestone that each of the women reaches at different stages and in remarkably different ways. Here Sarah talks about the beginnings of her emergent Black identity:

> At home, Black Power was just comin' in and my sister went to the corner shop and seen her first Afro and came home and said, 'Oh, I've seen some Afros in the shop. Oh, they're really brilliant.' These group of women with Afros, she's sayin' how brillliant they were. At home, we were startin' this awareness of Black power and Black identity. We always related to bein' Black, because all of the signals we got from when we were growin' up, we were nothin' else. We definitely were not White.

Even when we were growin' up, my Mum would get angry with us, she always used to call us 'Black bastards'. It was always that we were 'Black' this or 'Black' that. When the Black Power started comin' along and all the positiveness that brought at that time was like brilliant. Like somethin' we could really feel good about.

Bisi

Racism is most difficult to swallow when it is dished out by members of one's own family. Here, Bisi, who is Yemi's younger sister, talks about how she coped with her own White English mother's racism:

A lot of the modern consciousness I have of being African and being Black, which is not the same thing, is probably in spite of my mother. Being Black in the sense that I feel now, that would be in spite of her. It's not something she agrees with. But you must remember that when she went to Nigeria she was in her twenties. She spent her formative years there not here. She has very little knowledge of how racism operates and how it affects people – American, Caribbean and African. The sort of feeling that there is the unity there, consciousness. One can get something from it and one owes something to it. She would say things like, 'Why do you want to put yourself on the side of those who are feeling victimized? Put yourself on the winning side.' She would stress this to us very much, that we have an English family and English roots, and some heritage from them as well which is bannered. It's funny though, when I started relaxing about it and owning that there is quite a lot of English in me, basically. When I could come up with that admission, then that's almost when I started making Mbari [an Ibo art form primarily practised in Eastern Nigeria – the artist erects shrines to placate the Earth goddess] and really finding that yes, there is a lot of English, but there is also a lot of African.

When I left Bristol in 1992, Bisi gave me an original pastels self-portrait as a going away present (illustrated here, Figure 13.1). In it her hands are each noticeably painted a different colour – one brown and the other white. Her hands are clutching at her mouth and at her eye seemingly searching for some recognition. This piece is a powerful emblem for all *métis(se)* people who try to make sense of their place in society. Here Bisi has re-framed the negativity that usually dominates most depictions of our lived experiences.

CONCLUSION

In the ethnographic contexts of families and communities, I have demon-strated the different ways in which cultural memories shape contradictory

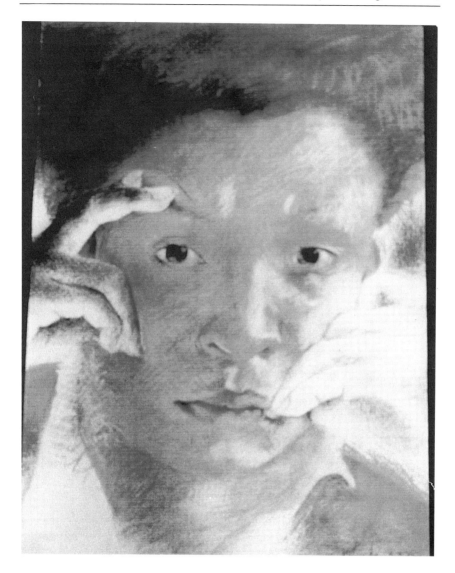

Figure 13.1 Untitled: Folake Shoga

meanings of 'race', gender, generation and cultures for women in Britain who by virtue of birth transgress multiple boundaries and challenge essentialized constructions of identities, place and belonging. Their narratives of identities demonstrate the hierarchical and at times paradoxical ranking of the essentialized constructs and concepts of Blackness, Whiteness, Englishness, Caribbeanness and Africanness in English society. Their remembered lived experiences also show us how *métis(se)* people must manage, negotiate and interpret these paradoxes in their everyday lives. Overall, the *griottes'* rememberances, located in both colonial and post-colonial contexts, shed light on the complexities of African and African-Caribbean Diasporic social and cultural life too often distorted by historians. Their transnational identities represent both their family constellations as well as their individual experiences. These transnationalities challenge the very notion of the English–African Diaspora as a static and unitary forma-tion which obviates cultural, national, ethnic, regional, and class differences, among others and, of course, ignores inter-racial collaborations.

The African Diaspora(s) in general and the English–African Diaspora in particular remain fertile ground for the cultivation of an orphan con-sciousness. An orphan consciousness emerges when one does not grow up with one's natal parents or kin – in this case 'Mama Africa'. In a metaphorical sense, one's image of that person can then only be an imaginary construction, such as the cultural imposition of an essentialized Pan-Africanism by some of Africa's displaced daughters and sons (Asante 1988). The Negritude movement, Rastafari, Garveyism and 'Americo-centrism' are particular examples of orphan consciousness in that they do not recognize the significant influences of multiple lineages and fail to differentiate between the real and the authentic. In an Amerocentric perspective: 'Contemporary Africa as I have said appears nowhere, the newly invented criteria for judging authenticity are supplied instead by a restored access to an imagined, though not imaginary, idea of African forms and codes' (Gilroy 1993a: 197).

I am contending that the six featured *métisse* women speak against an orphan consciousness. By naming their gendered, class-bound, regionally specific and generation-centred experiences as those of *métisse* women, the *griottes'* identity narratives, which are both fictitious and real (Martin, 1995), become political testimonies. The *métisse* women re-insert them-selves as active subjects, creating their own place in the re-telling of English–African Diaspora histories. A mosaic of cultures and histories is emblem-atic of their multiple reference points. This multicultural and diachronic scheme reflects the complex realities of all postcolonial, transnational people in the English–African Diaspora.[10] Appiah's description of identit-ies mirrors this perspective:

> Identities are complex and multiple and grow out of a history of changing responses to economic, political, and cultural forces, almost always in opposition to other identities ... that they flourish despite what I earlier called our 'misrecognition' of their origins; despite that is, their roots in myths and lies.
>
> (Appiah 1992: 178)

Akousa, Sarah, Ruby, Similola, Yemi, and Bisi are all products of history, the by-products of colonialism and imperialism. Their fathers are from

Nigeria, and Barbados, formerly under British colonial rule, as well as Tanzania, formerly under the auspices of Germany. Their mothers are Irish, English, and German. The unresolved postcolonial struggles between Africa and Europe, Blackness and Whiteness, Black man and White woman are all permanently inscribed on the faces of these *métisse* daughters.

In closing, I will give Anglo-Nigerian film-maker Ngozi Onwurah the final word. This is an excerpt from the autobiographical film piece 'The Body Beautiful' wherein she declares her allegiance to her White English mother. In this scene, she and her mother are lying naked in bed together, pink and brown skins mingle, youthful and aging bodies lie side by side:

> A child is made in its parents' image. But to a world that sees only in Black and White, I was made only in the image of my father. Yet, she has moulded me, created the curves and contours of my life, coloured the innermost details of my being. She has fought for me, protected me with every painful crooked bone in her body. She lives inside of me and cannot be separated. I may not be reflected in her image, but my mother is mirrored in my soul. I am my mother's daughter for the rest of my life.
>
> (Onwurah 1990)

ACKNOWLEDGEMENTS

I extend boundless gratitude to all the *griot(tes)* (men and women) who generously gave their time and retrieved painful and pleasant memories in order to make this organic project possible.

NOTES

1 In the primary text, the referents 'Black' and 'White' appear in italics to emphasize the fact that 'racial' categories are not biological concepts but rather social and cultural constructs which are frequently negotiated, re-invented, re-defined and intrinsically related to the dynamics of power and prestige. Ethnic affiliations and national identities are constructed in the same manner and are equally as problematic. However, in the interest of simplifying my argument, I have not italicized these concepts. In England, the locus of my current research, there is very little consensus as to where actual demarcations of the 'racial' (Black and White) end and the ethnic (eg. English, Jamaican, or Nigerian) and the national (eg. British, Caribbean, or African) begin. For an example of this, look at the 1991 Census categories for 'ethnicity' wherein in fact, 'race', ethnicity and nationality have been conflated. This lexical confusion makes the task of identities-construction a daunting project for *métis(se)* individuals in Britain.

2 *Métis(se)* (*métis* – masculine and *métisse* – feminine) is the French-African term I have chosen to describe project participants all of whom have British or European mothers and continental African or African Caribbean fathers. I will be discussing the genesis of this term at greater length in the primary text.

3 I write against the African Diaspora as static monolith notion propagated by so many Afrocentric/cultural nationalist scholars who situate the African Diaspora exclusively in its *locus classicus* – the transatlantic slave trade. Instead, I advocate conceptualizing the African Diaspora(s) as a dynamic, interlocking and interdependent network of specific and culture-bound geopolitical spheres, each of whose constituencies are sensitive to and impacted by the particular nation-states of which they are a part – i.e. the English–African Diaspora, the French–African Diaspora, the United States–African Diaspora, and so on. In other words, each of the African Diaspora communities has common cultural roots emanating from the African continent. However, these geographical and cultural groupings represent diverse outcomes to a common heritage of slavery, colonialism, 'neo-postcolonialism' and racism. These differences must be located in appropriate historical, social, cultural and political contexts that do not erupt simply in the either/or, margin to centre, push/pull dichotomies characterizing so much of the migration literature.

4 See Scheper-Hughes (1992), Chodorow (1978); Ruddick (1989).

5 The broad scope of the area I have carved out for myself dictates that any paper I write on my work devotes more time and space to the critique of and explicaton of terms, methodology and concepts than would ordinarily be necessary where there is both consensus and a glut of directly relevant primary and secondary source material.

6 There are qualitative and not quantitative gender differences in the degree of marginalization of people from the aforementioned backgrounds. That is, *métis* men and boys and *métisse* women and girls all seem to have the same degree of difficulty finding a niche for themselves in society. However, it is how these difficulties play themselves out differently in the lives of females and males and not the degree of difficulty. In contrast, Tizard and Phoenix's psychosocial study of the experiences of racism of mixed parentage young people found specific gender and class differences, with males and working-class young people experiencing more racist taunts than females and those from middle-class backgrounds (1993).

7 Hence, Black continental African and African-Caribbean men sailed into the ports of Liverpool and Cardiff, had relationships and sometimes fell in love and settled down with local White English and Welsh women (Little 1948; Collins 1957; Fryer 1984). In fact, in Liverpool and Cardiff, romantic liaisons and marriages between Black seamen and local White women supposedly precipitated the 1919 'race riots' in these two port cities with longstanding Black dockland settlements (Fryer 1984). Children were frequently the results of such unions and their birth brought to the forefront racist attitudes about purity, pollution and 'racial hygiene':

> Flung out into the slumland culture of the port towns, black seamen focused upon themselves considerable racial hostility as they became linked in the public mind with growing crime rates and prostitution when they co-habitated with white women and produced 'half caste' children.
>
> (Rich 1986: 121)

In 1927, the Colonial Office calculated 45 West African undergradutes; by the early 1950s the number swelled to 2,000 with 1,000 students in London alone. However, as Killingray states, in the introductory chapter to an edited collection on Africans in Britain, 'all too often written records, invariably produced by men, focus on activities dominated by men so that research on women is additionally difficult' (1994: 17). Quantifying the number of continental African women students in Britain between the turn of the century and the present is a perfect example of this dilemma. Historical research does support the fact that continental African men were sent by the colonial authorities to study in England in greater numbers than continental African women (Killingray 1994). At university, many men met their future White English wives and/or mothers of their children. Many African-American GIs stationed in Europe (England and Germany, in particular) during World War II left broken hearts and *métis(se)* children behind, (Fryer 1984; Opitz 1991).

8 Ethnographic fieldwork then becomes a series of conversations wherein according to Bakhtin, 'language lies on the borderline between oneself and the other. . . . the word in language is half someone else's' (1953: 293). Bakhtin uses the term 'heteroglossia' to describe this process (see Bakhtin 1953, 1981).

9 Rastafarians – members of a religious group (others refer to as a 'cult') which originated in Jamaica and who reject Western ideas and values ('Babylon') and regard Haile Selassie, the former emperor of Ethiopia, as divine.

10 Throughout this paper, I have neglected the other permutations and combinations of Diasporic *métis(se)* that exist in England. To put multiple and complex experiences together would have downplayed the social and cultural complexitites within and without diasporic interwoven communities. Moreover, even now, in the age of globalization and as we approach the millenium, those of us of African origin are still at once revered and feared. Despite the fact that there have been longstanding *métis(se)* communities in Liverpool, England and Cardiff, Wales since at least the end of the nineteenth century, Black African mixed with White British is still viewed by the general populus and politicians alike as problematic. The words of White English politician Enoch Powell's 1968 'Rivers of Blood' speech warning White English people of the evils and dangers of 'race mixing' ring true today and such ideas are evident in much right-wing propaganda.

REFERENCES

Alibhai-Brown, Yasmin and Montague, Anne (1992) *The Colour of Love: Mixed Race Relationships*, London: Virago Press.

Anzaldúa, Gloria (1987) *Borderlands/La Frontera: The New Mestiza*, San Francisco, CA: Spinsters, Aunt Lute.

Anzaldúa, Gloria (ed.) (1990) *Making Face, Making Soul*, San Francisco, CA: Aunt Lute.

Appiah, Kwame Anthony (1992) *In My Father's House: Africa in the Philosophy of Culture*, New York: Oxford University Press.

Asante, Molefi, Kete (1988) *Afrocentricity*, Trenton, NJ: Africa World Press.

Bakhtin, Mikhal (1953/1981) 'Discourse in the Novel ' in Michael Holquist (ed.) *The Dialogic Imagination*, Austin: University of Texas Press, pp. 259–442.

Barth, Frederik (ed.) (1969) *Ethnic Groups and Boundaries: The Social Organization of Cultural Difference*, Boston: Little, Brown.

Benson, Sue (1981) *Ambiguous Ethnicity: Inter-racial Families in London*, Cambridge: Cambridge University Press.

Berreman, Gerald (1979) *Caste and Other Inequities: Essays on Inequality*, Meerut, India: Folklore Institute.

Burley, David V. *et al.* (1992) *Structural Considerations of Metis Ethnicity: An Archaeological, Architectural, and Historical Study*, Vermillion, S.D.: University of Dakota Press.

Chodorow, Nancy (1978) *The Reproduction of Mothering: Psychoanalysis and the Sociology of Gender*, Berkeley: University of California Press.

Clarke, Edith (1966) *My Mother Who Fathered Me*, London: George Allen and Unwin.

Cohen, Robin (1995) 'Fuzzy Frontiers of Identity: The British Case', *Social Identities*, 1(1): 35–62.

Coleman, David (1985) 'Ethnic Intermarriage in Great Britain', *Population Trends*, 40 London: HMSO, pp. 4–10.

Collins, S. (1957) *Coloured Minorities in Britain*, Guildford: Lutterworth Press.

Crummell, Alexander (1862) *The Future of Africa: Being Addresses, Sermons, Etc*, Detroit: Negro Press.

Davies, Carol Boyce (1994) *Black Women, Writing and Identity*, London: Routledge.

Day, Beth (1974) *Sexual Life Between Blacks and Whites*, London: Collins.

Dent, Gina (ed.) (1992) *Black Popular Culture*, New York: Dia Center for the Arts.

Diop, Samba (1993a) Personal Communication.

Diop, Samba (1993a) *The Oral History and Literature of the Wolof People of Waalo, Northern Senegal: The Master of the Word (Griot) in the Wolof Tradition*, Lampeter, Wales: Edwin Mellen Press.

Frazier, Edward Franklin (1966) *The Negro Family in the United States*, Chicago: University of Chicago Press.

Fryer, Peter (1984) *Staying Power: The History of Black People in Britain*, London: Pluto Press.

Gilroy, Paul (1993a) *Small Acts: Thoughts on the Politics of Black Culture*, London: Serpent's Tail.

Gilroy, Paul (1993b) *The Black Atlantic: Modernity and Double Consciousness*, London: Verso.

Goffman, Erving (1959) *The Presentation of Self in Everyday Life*, New York: Doubleday.

Goffman, Erving (1963) *Stigma: Notes on the Management of Spoiled Identity*, Englewood Cliffs, N.J.: Prentice-Hall.

Gonzales, Nancie (1970) 'Toward a Definition of Matrifocality' in Norman Whitten and J. Szwed (eds) *Afro-American Anthropology*, New York: Free Press, pp. 231–244.

Gordon, L.R (1995) 'Critical "Mixed Race"?', *Social Identities*, 1(2): 381–95.

Gossett, Thomas (1965) *Race: The History of an Idea In America*, New York: Schocken Books.

Hall, Stuart (1990) 'Cultural Identity and Diaspora' in Jonathan Rutherford (ed.) *Identity, Community, Culture and Difference*, London: Lawrence and Wishart, pp. 222–37.

Head, Bessie (1990) *A Woman Alone: Autobiographical Writings*, Oxford: Heinemann.

Henriques, Fernando (1975) *Children of Conflict: A Study of Interacial Sex and Marriage*, New York: Dutton.

Herskovitz, Melville (1958) *The Myth of the Negro Past*, Boston: Beacon Press.

hooks, bell (1992) *Black Looks: Race and Representation*, London: Turnaround.

Husband, Charles (ed.) (1982) *'Race' In Britain*, 2nd edn, London: Hutchinson.

Ifekwunigwe, Jayne (forthcoming) *Scattered Be-Longings: Cultural Paradoxes of 'Race', Nation, and Generation in the English–African Diaspora*, London: Routledge.

Jegede, Tunde (1994) *African Classical Music and the Griot Tradition*, London: Goodwin Press.

Jordan, Glenn and Weedon, Chris (1995) *Cultural Politics*, Oxford: Blackwell.

Jewsiewicki, Bougumil (1995) 'The Identity of Memory and the Memory of Identity in the Age of Commodification and Democratization', *Social Identities* 1(2): 227–62.

Keith, Michael (1995) 'Shouts of the Street', *Social Identities*, 1(2): 317–32.

Killingray, David (ed.) (1994) *Africans in Britain*, Ilford, Essex: Frank Cass.

Koubaka, Henri-Pierre (1993) Personal communication.

Kureishi, Hanif (1991) *The Buddha of Suburbia*, London: Faber and Faber.

Lemelle, Sidney and Kelley, Robin D.G. (eds) (1994) *Imagining Home: Class, Culture and Nationalism in the African Diaspora*, London: Verso.

Lewis, Oscar (1966) 'The Culture of Poverty', *Scientific American*, 215 (4): 19–25.

Lionnet, Francolse (1989) *Anthropological Voices: Race, Gender and Self-Portraiture*, Ithaca, New York: Cornell University Press.

Little, Kenneth (1948) *Negroes in Britain: Racial Relations in English Society*, London: Routtedge.

MacDougall, David (1993) 'The Subjective Voice in Ethnographic Film', paper presented at University of California, Berkeley, California.

Magubane Bemard Makhosezwe (1987) *The Ties That Bind: African American Consciousness of Africa*, Trenton, NJ: Africa World Press.

Marquet, Marie-Madeleine (1983) *Le Métissage Dans La Poesie de Leopold Sedar Senghor*, Dakar: Nouvelle Editions Africaines.

Martin, Denis-Consant (1995) 'The Choices of Identity', *Social Identities* 1(1): 5–20.

Miles, Robert (1993) *Racism after 'Race Relations'*, London: Routledge.

Minh-Ha, Trinh T. (1992) *The Framer Framed*, New York: Routledge.

Modood, T. (1988) 'Black Racial Equality and Asian Identity', *New Community*, 14(3): 397–404.

Mudimbe, V. Y. (1988) *The Invention of Africa*, Bloomington, Indiana: Indiana University Press.

National Ethnic Minority Data Archive (1991) *Ethnic Minorities in Great Britain*, Coventry: University of Warwick.

Office of Population and Censuses and Surveys (1991) London: Government Statistical Service.

Oguibe, Olu (ed.) (1994) *Sojourners: New Writings By Africans in Britain*, London: African Refugee Publishing Collective.

Okamura, John (1981) 'Situational Ethnicity', *Ethnic and Racial Studies* 4(4): 452–65.

Onwurah, Ngozi (1990) *The Body Beautiful* (film), London: British Film Institute.

Opitz, May *et al.* (eds) (1991) *Showing Our Colors: Afro-German Women Speak Out*, Amherst: University of Massachusetts Press.

Patterson, Shelia (1963) *Dark Strangers*, Bloomington, Indiana: Indiana University Press.

Pieterse, Jan (1992) *White on Black: Images of Africa and Blacks in Western Popular Culture*, New Haven: Yale University Press.

Powdermaker, Hortense (1939) *After Freedom*, New York: Viking.

Pryce, Ken (1974) *Endless Pressure*, Bristol, England: Bristol Classical Press.

Rich, Paul (1986) *Race and Empire in British Politics*, Cambridge: Cambridge University Press.

Richmond, Anthony (1973) *Migration and Race Relations in an English City*, Oxford: Oxford University Press.

Rex, John (1995) *Race and Ethnicity*, Milton Keynes: Open University.

Rex, John (1995) 'Ethnic Identity and The Nation State: the Political Sociology of Multicultural Societies', *Social Identities*, (1): 21–34.

Roberts, Diane (1994) *The Myth of Aunt Jemima: Representations of Race and Region*, New York: Routledge.

Ruddick, Sara (1989) *Maternal Thinking: Towards a Politics of Peace*, Boston: Beacon Press.

Russell, Kathy, Wilson, Midge and Hall, Ronald (1992) *The Color Complex: The Politics of Skin Color Among African Americans*, New York: Anchor.

Scheper-Hughes, Nancy (1992) *Death Without Weeping: The Violence of Everday Life in Brazil*, Berkeley: University of California Press.

Shepperson, George (1968) 'The African Abroad or the African Diaspora' in T. O. Ranger (ed.) *Emerging Themes of African History*, Dar es Salaam, Tanzania: East African Publishing House, pp. 152–176.

Shyllon F. (1977) *Black People in Britain*, Oxford: Oxford University Press.

Small, Stephen (1994) *Racialized Barriers*, London: Routledge.

Smith, R. T. (1956) *The Negro Family in British Guiana*, London: Routledge.

Stack, Carol B. (1975) *All Our Kin*, New York: Harper and Row.

Thompson, Vincent Bakpetu (1987) *The Making of the African Diaspora in the Americas*, England: Longman.

Tizard, Barbara and Phoenix, Anne (1993) *Black, White or Mixed Race?*, London: Routledge.

Vovelle, M. (1982) *Ideologies et Mentalités*, Paris: Maspero.

Wallman, Sandra (1979) 'The Boundaries of Race–Processes of Ethnicity in England', *Man* (13): 200–17.

Walvin, James (1973) *Black and White: The Negro and English Society*, London: Allen Lane.

Wilson, Anne (1987) *Mixed Race Children: A Study of Identity*, London: Allen and Unwin.

Worsley, Peter (ed.) (1970) *Modern Sociology*, Harmondsworth, Middlesex: Penguin.

Zhana (ed.) (1988) *Sojourn*, London: Methuen.

Chapter 14

'It's a sun-tan, isn't it?'

Auto-biography as an identificatory practice

Sara Ahmed

How to begin a reflection on one's past? How to make the self in writing a scene on which issues of race and gender are played out? Why, and under what conditions, does that auto-biographical gesture become possible or desirable? How to perform that gesture without being implicated in a discourse of authenticity, whereby the remembering of my gendered and racialized encounters would become readable as representative?

In writing the self, one does not uncover or recover the truth of one's past experiences. This much may be clear from recent feminist inter-ventions into autobiography, whether understood as a literary genre, or as a mode of critical intervention (Friedman 1988; hooks 1989; Stanley 1992; Probyn 1993). On the contrary, writing of the self in the form of an individuated memory may serve to de-stabilize the boundary between the subject and its others, and so dramatize the inseparability of the subject from the realms of the social and the political. Auto-biography as indi-viduation – as a story of the gradual separation and perfection of the individual self – has been identified by feminists as a specifically masculine genre, as a way of writing that marks, and is marked by, privilege and social agency. As Susan Friedman puts it, 'The emphasis on individualism as the necessary pre-condition for autobiography is thus a reflection of the privilege, one that excludes from the canons of autobiography those writers that have been denied by history the illusion of individualism' (Friedman 1988: 39).

In Jenny Sharpe's *Allegories of Empire* the analysis of the exclusive nature of the auto-biographical self is taken further. In her reading of *Jane Eye*, Sharpe argues that the story of the individuation of the female narrator relies on a racializing of the authorial signature. She writes:

> One way to consider the power relations in *Jane Eyre* is to read the writing of a female self and the voicing of women's oppression as a privileged mode of address for the feminist individualist. It is a mode of address that is unavailable to the subaltern women who are repres-ented in the novel.
>
> (Sharpe 1993: 32)

The white woman gains partial access to the privilege of the authorial 'I', through the negation or exclusion of Black women. They become signs of that which she is not; of an abject and irrational embodiment which she can speak of through the discourse of enlightened authority (for example, the white woman as missionary). Her gesture of 'speaking for' the Black women presupposes their violent effacement as subjects. In this sense, autobiography as individuation functions as a racialized as well as gendered practice. I would take this point further and argue that auto-biography as individuation never quite takes place. It is precisely those marginalized and abject figures which return to haunt the authorial self and to remind her of her immersion in a violent sociality. Here, Black women are present as a trace of the impossibility of the female signature, or of any *ontologically secured* category of 'women's writing'.

So in writing auto-biographically of my experiences as a mixed race, middle-class and migrant woman I am writing against this discourse of individuation which discloses the truth of the individual subject in terms of its withdrawal from the realm of sociality. Auto-biography may become of interest to Black feminism precisely because it renders explicit the subject's immersion within the social and the political. It is a critical reflection on the self – and its history or its becoming – that may dramatize the unstable but determinate relation between the subject and its others. Auto-biography may write its subject only insofar as it renders its subject a subject, that is, an embodied and located entity which is representable only through its partial negation or loss. As a writing of the subject, auto-biography may traverse that impossible distinction between the psychic and the social.

Indeed, it may be through a discourse on the personal – on the becoming of the subject – that resistant and resisting political (dis)identifications may be rendered possible. For already the story of the individuated self is exposed as phantasy, or the story of the woman who writes simply as woman. Auto-biography forges the possibility of a collective address – where, for example, one can speak as and to (if not for) Black women, precisely by exposing the determination of an individuated story by broader structures of identification. The subject is located, divided and immersed. It is this subject that may be the subject of Black feminism. To this end, I locate myself in my analysis . . .

I was born in England in 1969 but migrated to Australia with my family in 1974. I returned to Britain in 1991 to complete my studies and I currently teach courses on gender, race and colonialism at the Centre for Women's Studies, Lancaster University. I am a product of a mixed race marriage. My father, who is from Lahore, Pakistan, lost much of his own cultural heritage when marrying my English mother: he did quite literally marry (into) the West. So although as a young person I was very aware of not being white, not being like 'the others', I was never aware of actually what I might be, never able to positively address what my difference really was. I was not simply in-between identities, for my upbringing was 'fully Western' (although infrequent trips to Pakistan did affect my own sense of another culture being there, it simply wasn't there *for me*). So as a young person I didn't positively claim an identity from an in-between-ness (I am mixed race, or I am a migrant).

More importantly, my sense of self was established precariously in terms of being inadequate to the model of appropriate (white, European) identity that I saw upheld around me. On one occasion (traumatic to recall) I tried to walk as far away as possible from my father when I saw some friends from school. I thought I could pass for white if I disassociated myself from him. But the jibes about my Asian-ness continued throughout my childhood and adolescence. At times I felt like an uncomfortable and dirty white person. It wasn't until I came to recognize the politics of racism as a form of social violence that I was able to recognize and critique my own discomfort. That ability was partly due to my access to power and knowledge determined by my middle-class upbringing. But it was also as a result of spending more time in Pakistan after my schooling. Now I remain uncertain how to name or identify myself, but take that uncertainty as empowering rather than simply risky.[1]

I re-present myself here for the purposes of defining what or whom I *cannot* speak for: I cannot speak for either white British women, or for South Asian women in Britain or, really, for any particular or clearly demarcated group of women at all. But what I want to argue is that my inability to speak on behalf of any group of women is not an *exception* of biography or place, but a *trace of a dynamic that troubles the very collision of race and gender in structures of identification*. It is this *symptomatic nature of the failure of my own personal address* that my passage into auto-biography will attempt to explore: the way in which the impossibility of adequately naming myself for the demands of representation is symptomatic of the impossibility of the racially marked and gendered subject being addressed through a singular name. So here the negation and loss of the subject that is marked out by auto-biography is predicated on the play of different names or identifications which perpetually fix and lose their subjects (for example, woman, man, Black, mixed race, Aboriginal, white, working class, middle class). The contradictions between these names – understood as relations of address – which call subjects into being are played out in the unstable trajectory of an autobiographical intervention. In other words, the autobiographical gesture is structured – either implicitly (as phantasies of individuation) or explicitly (as political strategies of (dis)identification) by the antagonism between different relations of power, such as gender, class and race, whereby the subject is assigned into different, divisive and contradictory positions. This assignment is not a fixation, but a story of loss, difference and movement.

So I write, now, as a Black feminist living in Britain, and my chapter involves remembering an event that happened to me in 1984 when I lived in Adelaide and that seemed to me to be critical in the development of my own political identifications. But between that time, and this time, I have travelled. I have not kept still. I have been to Pakistan, and I have come to Britain. The structuring of my life around a series of dis-locations is a reminder of the impossibility of 'returning' to a previous place through memory. Return is impossible. As we move, we shift; the trajectories upon which we travel emphasize the fluidity of our identifications. So this narrative is not a dialogue between two times and two places, between now and then, and here and there. The telling is more complex than this.

Such instability seems to me to be constitutive of migration and of the subject as migratory. The migratory nature of subjectivity has been well examined and, in the work of some theorists, has become a privileged metaphor for the crisis of identification peculiar to the contemporary 'postmodern' and postcolonial world (for example, Chambers 1994). But I am not speaking of migration in this sense. I am not speaking of migration if migration is to be seen as a figure for a generalizable philosophy of difference. This generalizability is predicated on a loss of recognition of the antagonism between subject positions which renders the experience of migration both gendered and racialized. In the stories I was told of both my Pakistani family's flight from India to the newly created Pakistan, and my father's migration from Pakistan to England, in my migration from England to Australia, and in my 'return' to England, my experience of dis-location has not simply been pleasurable or radical (in its performance of de-stabilization); it has been violent as well. Migration as dis-location may remind us of the impossibility of the subject as an identity in general, but it may also function as a trace of the particularity of, and antagonisms between, subject positions. We may, after all, remember the difference between migrants and refugees; we may remember that a dispro-portionately large number of the world's refugees are Black women. When remembering these issues one can recognize *the violence of the rhetorical gesture which takes 'migration' as a privileged metaphor for the disruption of identities*. What my relation to migration may reveal is the way my remembering of the event performs the logic of dis-location which the narrative is itself about.

Furthermore, if the instability of my auto-biographical gestures bears a relation to migration then it also bears a relation to mixed racial identities. Such identities are often re-inscribed in critical discourse in terms of hybridity. The mixed race subject is a hybrid subject; a subject determined by a radical mixing of different 'races'; a subject whose impurity is a sign of its inability to belong to any singular time or place. Of course, 'hybridization' has, like 'migration', been generalized as a metaphor for the radical force of cultural difference – understood in the sense of cultural untranslatability, as that which refuses the logic of identity (Bhabha 1994: 162–4). As you could imagine from my comments on migration, I see this as a potentially violent gesture in the sense that it may elide the structuring role of antagonisms between relations of address. I do see the hybridity of my mixed-race identity as exposing the 'fragility' of racial identifications (for example, by putting the system of colour coding under stress – I can 'pass' for a white woman). To this extent, I understand hybridity as having implications for the impossibility of a (pure) racial identity *per se*. But this symptomatic reading does not constitute its generalizability. For being of mixed-race identity also has a particular set of limitations and positionings – including an acute sense of being inadequate to any available cultural identity – which constitute the instability of *this* auto-biography and its trajectory of migration and loss. These positionings do not exist independently from the gendering of subjects and the different demands on women and men in relation to 'reproducing' cultural identifications (for example, the 'woman' as symbol of nation). So my narrative is *constrained* or *delimited* by the particularity of mixed-race, classed and gendered positionings. Both symptomatic and particular: what we have is the failure of my personal address as an unstable and irreducible *trace* of the violent collision between gender, class and race in structures of identification. Not being able to simply write myself in the security of names . . . this much may be clear. But what to do with that knowledge? Where do we go from here? How does this relate to the auto-biographical articulation of the Black woman as a subject position?

This question of how the 'Black woman' becomes articulated as a subject position within auto-biographical narratives requires a shift in analysis from identity to identification. That is, we no longer can assume that the subject simply 'has' an identity, in the form of a properly demarcated place of belonging. Rather, what is required is an analysis of the processes and structures of identification – both psychic and social – whereby identities *come to be seen as* such places of belonging. By shifting the analysis in this way, both race and gender can be theorized not as fixed and stable 'essences' but as construction-in-process where meanings are negotiated and re-negotiated in the form of antagonistic relations of power. Yet this begs the question: how to theorize identification? And indeed: how to theorize identification in a way which does not assume the singularity of 'the subject', regardless as to whether we understand the subject in terms of 'becoming' rather than 'being'?

The singularity of the model of identification – however much of it remains bound up with the failure of the subject – has implications for racial politics and for the relation between Black women and psychoanalysis. Psychoanalysis has provided us with a model of both identification[2] and how the subject becomes sexually differentiated. Judith Butler suggests in *Bodies that Matter* that it is the assertion of the priority of sexual difference over racial difference that has marked psychoanalytic feminism as white (Butler 1993: 181). Indeed, the use of psychoanalysis has invariably meant that other differences are explained through an act of translation back into the model which elaborates the division of subjects into sexes (the resolution of the Oedipal crisis, castration anxiety and the phallic logic of fetishism).[3] As Anne McClintock concludes:

> I do not see racial fetishism as stemming from an overdetermined relation to the castration scene. Reducing racial fetishism to the phallic drama runs the risk of flattening out the hierarchies of social difference, thereby relegating race and class to secondary status along a primarily sexual signifying chain.
>
> (McClintock 1995: 183–4)

Given this, in order that a psychoanalytic approach to identification as phantasmatic and as an impossible resolution to otherness can help elaborate an understanding of subjectivity as racialized and gendered, in a way which does not assume the ontological priority of the latter, we need to be able to theorize the division *between* (as well as within) various structures of identification. I think this can best be done if we begin to see how identifications *traverse* the distinction between the psychic and the social and hence do not function as a logic of the subject. It is through such an approach that 'Black women' as a subject position (however unstable) can be made visible. That visibility is predicated on an analysis of the *antagonistic* and *divisive* nature of identifications.

The following auto-biographical example can be read as a text which negotiates these multiple regimes of identification. This example relates back to an incident when I was 14 years old, walking around the streets of Adelaide without any shoes on (I was in a 'scruffy' phase). I was stopped and addressed by two policemen in a car. They called me over, asked me what I was doing (I said I was walking) and then asked me why I wasn't wearing shoes (I can't remember my reply, but I was indignant about my rights). The policeman closest to me asked me if I was Aboriginal. Again I was indignant, replying 'no'. The other policeman interrupted, gave me a wink, and said 'it's a sun-tan, isn't it?'. I smiled, but did not reply. They asked me where I lived and I told them, and mentioned which school I went to (a private girls' school). They said that was fine, but to wear shoes. I asked them why they had stopped me. They said there had been some break-ins in the area recently, and that they were checking it out. Needless to say, this incident ended in tears, and left me angry and resistant.

Looking back, there were a number of complex identifications and dis-identifications going on, often unconscious, in the sense of forming contexts that were not obvious at the time, or upon a literal reading of the event. It seems to me now that the policemen addressed me, in the first instance, as working class (from dress), as Aboriginal (from colour). This identification *read* me as a subject, *by rendering me a suspect*, as a danger to the Law (of property), a potential robber. Here, the absence of shoes becomes fetishized as an object which signifies not simply a lack of proper dress, but an improper status as somebody who does not belong to this middle-class and respectable suburb, somebody whose presence can only have the function and effect of a threat. Indeed, the address shifts immediately from the absence of shoes to a query about race. The address of the policemen in the first instance, their positioning of me as a suspect, somebody to be queried and interrogated, was on the mistaken assumption I was Aboriginal. Their question demanded to know the extent of my threat by demanding to know whether my racial origin was Aboriginal. In this sense, Aboriginality becomes figured as the most threatening or disruptive presence. But the error of their address gave me a space to address them, through denial and disavowal.

Through returning their address a shift occurred which forced a dis-identification from my identity as suspect. Not an Aboriginal (but perhaps only sun-tanned), not working class (in fact quite well off). My denial of being Aboriginal and my failure to name or declare my race (which of course was unnoticed or invisible to them) implicated me in their structure of address, by rendering Aboriginality something to be disavowed. The gesture of smiling can here be figured as a collusion, a desire in some sense to be figured as white, as respectable, as somebody who has a legitimate right to walk in these leafy suburbs. My disavowal thus suggests an implicit desire for 'whiteness'. That desire creates an imaginary (and impossible) conception of a purified and ideal self, as well as a coherent social order (to which I could 'fit in'), by assigning certain values to 'whiteness'. Such an assignment entails a disavowal and repudiation of the other, of 'Blackness', or Aboriginality. As such, desire itself projects an imaginary presence through a process of exclusion. The temporality of the act of disavowal stages the impossibility of desire's fulfilment generally, but also the racialist logic that demands the purification of colour, as a reminder of an-Other that refuses to inhabit these terms and returns (to walk the streets) only as a threat.

However, the explicit racial confrontation cannot suspend the gendered nature of my position. The original address was surely then an address not simply to an Aboriginal, but to an Aboriginal woman. Theorists such as Jan Pettman in *Living in the Margins* have argued the Aboriginal woman is always already sexualized in White Australian colonial narratives (Pettman 1992: 27). So if the original address (Are you an Aboriginal?) positioned my colour as a stain, as a sign of a natural criminality determined by the fact of my skin, then how does this criminalization of colour link with the gendering of the address? It may suggest that the Black woman is defined in terms of the physicality of her skin, as a stain which confirms her over-sexed being, her threat to the proper social and sexual order of the domesticated suburb. She is constructed in this sense as a social and sexual danger.

We may also consider, though, that if the address had been to an Aboriginal man the discourse may have been more confrontational, or less questioning. One can only speculate here, but perhaps the policemen's address and the way it constructed the subject (as being able to affirm or deny the question) traversed the distinction between criminality (Aboriginality) and desire (woman). In other words, the 'danger' posed by the woman when addressed as Black entails an ambivalent or contradictory positioning as somebody to be excluded *and* questioned (as a partial inclusion; an invitation to return the address). The ambivalence may be linked to the way in which the position of Aboriginal or Black woman is not explicitly named, functioning as an invisible sub-text to the encounter. That invisibility is a sign not of the *vacant* nature of the position of the Black woman, but rather of the difficulty of her being addressed through a logic of purely racialized interrogation (Are you an Aboriginal?) given her absence from *dominant* narratives of race. The way in which the gendering of the address to the Aboriginal is invisible will be taken up later on.

The disavowal of Blackness in my return of the policeman's address was also structured by a class dynamic whereby legitimacy was restored to my presence through naming my school (a private girls' school). This information was not asked for – but projected by me onto them as a sign that I was 'with them', that they were policing for me, rather than against me, as an owner rather than a taker of property. The disavowal and repudiation of Aboriginality hence structured a desire to be taken as inhabiting the policing demand, as somebody worthy of protection, as white and middle class: a tax payer not a dole bludger or a waster.

The structure of identification which involved the exchange of a wink and the quip about being sun-tanned caused me the most discomfort. Although inspired by my dis-identification as Aboriginal (which was implicated in the assigning of certain values to Aboriginality, as something to be disavowed) and my refusal to identify my race, this quip both made light of their mistake (their hailing of the wrong person, their error of reading) while positioning me as woman, a recipient of a wink (and of a gaze), and as someone who sun-bathes, who tans her body. The entrance of the body into the exchange shifted me from being suspect to object, from a threat to property, to property itself. While defining the body in terms of leisure, where colour is a sign of a 'higher' class, the quip shifted my *attention* from the social and racial relation of policeman to suspect, to the sexual relation of man to woman. Here, the gendering of the subject becomes an *explicit* aspect of the encounter. The colour of my body was evoked as an adornment rather than a stain, as 'a paying attention to the body'. Here, colour is literally a detachable signifier, inessential to the subject, and hence acceptable. By rendering colour inessential rather than essential, the exchange rendered my body something to be valued, adorned, protected. Colour becomes inscribed as a detachable signifier, positioning me as essentially white, as truly and properly white underneath the luxury of a brown veil. The white woman, by sun-tanning, may appropriate and domesticate the hyper-sexuality which is signified by Black skin, rendering the presence of colour a temporary aberration which confirms the proper sexual order based on her protection from Black men by white men. Inscribed as a white woman, I became the legitimate object of the policeman's protective gaze.

I dealt with the uncertainty and anxiety over my body and colour by addressing the policeman, in the structure of a demand: a demand that they explained their presence, their interruption of my walk. That demand gave me a point of entry into identifying them as racist (although, of course, I would not have been able to return their address in the form of a demand unless I'd already dis-identified myself as Aboriginal, as I would not have had the inscribed agency to speak lawfully, to speak with legitimacy). Their explanation linked their project (fighting street crime) to their identification of me as Aboriginal, which made me a suspect. Through identifying the racism that constituted their identification, I withdrew from the situation very angry, and ashamed that I had dis-avowed being Aboriginal, and had so been implicated in a structure of racial identification which (despite my own desire for whiteness and legitimacy) I sensed was wrong. By returning their address in the structure of a demand, I hence read the policemen and assigned them to a place in my own self-identification as not-white and not-racist.

What this example may evoke is the complexity of the identification process. The very temporality of identifications renders not only that they can miss their mark, but that they always do miss their mark, by enacting the divisions that frustrate the identification of the subject by a singular name. The over-lapping of the issues of race, class and gender in this 're-called event', suggests that the relation of power to identification is *constitutive but divisive*, where the position of the subject is perpetually assigned and threatened by their designation in related, but distinct, regimes of difference. The constant negotiation of identifications temporarily assign the subject to a fixed identity (both racial, class and gendered) which are open to contestation in the negotiation of everyday encounters with the Law, family and others.

It is here the position of Black women is rendered visible, in the very contradictions – the violent collisions – between the racialized and gendered gazes with which she is addressed and which constitute the *instability* of the encounter. For as it became clear in my account it is only through a recognition of the antagonism between relations of address that we can make explicit the positioning of Black women; the *explicit* confrontation shifted my attention from race *to* gender and hence elided the 'Black woman' as a site of contradiction and ambivalence. By rendering visible the collision between race and gender, 'the Black woman' becomes articulatable as a sign of the subject's inability to be fixed adequately by a single name or gaze in such encounters.

I have written throughout of 'the event' which has unfolded, perhaps significantly, like a kernel in a story. It has unfolded to disclose what may seem to function as a 'truth': the truth about subjectivity, the truth about 'Black women' as rendering visible the collision between regimes of identification. These may seem to be truths that I have disclosed to you as the 'author' and 'knower' of my own story. What I want to do now, by re-thinking and re-reading my interpretation, is to dislodge any such impression of knowability. Firstly, one can only begin by complicating the supposed discreteness of 'the event'. True, I have written of it as such. But it is the act of remembering, an act which is both critical, affirmative and selective, that places boundaries and edges around the story, giving it its seeming internal coherence. Through auto-biographical identification (and dis-identification), the event has functioned as a term in an argument. But this rhetorical gesture, in which memory plays a crucial part, is not exhaustive. And if I have written in a way which implies the exhaustability of the event, I have also exposed the impossibility of that exhaustion in part through the very *performative* aspect of my narrative. My story entails its own elisions, its own figuration, its own forgettings. It is the link between remembering and the loss of stability of my reading that I will now attempt to uncover; a link that may re-stage how the identification of Black women relates to the instability of social antagonisms.

How to do justice to the Black woman who has been re-claimed from this story of disavowal and repudiation? Is that reclaiming a figuring of the Black woman which loses sight of the *particularity* of her various inscriptions even as its renders visible her impossibility as a discrete identity? Returning then to this event (which I lovingly must fetishize as a lost object), we can see that the invisibility of the Black woman in the original encounter ('Are you an Aboriginal?' to 'Its a sun-tan, isn't it?') constituted a form of ambivalence in which the linear narrative (race to gender) begins to break apart. It is here that I thought I saw her (myself) struggling to get out – in the staging of a collision. But the gesture of taking the 'Black woman' as a figure for what is elided in the narrative of race to gender remains just that – a gesture. It relies on a *figuration*.

This figuring of the Black woman as a sign of an ambivalence which de-stabilizes the encounter is problematic precisely in what it cannot speak of. That is, it cannot speak of the divisions and antagonisms within the signifier 'the Black woman'. We need to ask: which Black woman? There are many possibilities that are at play – either explicitly or implicitly – in the narrative: Aboriginal woman, Asian woman, mixed-race woman. How to speak of their difference? What history the slippage from Aboriginal into a generalized category of Blackness erases is the history of racism towards Aboriginal peoples, not just from White Australia, but also from Asian immigrants. How to speak of the difference of the Aboriginal woman, even if she is only present in this narrative in the form of a misrecognition? But then, this misrecognition led to a second mis-recognition – it shifted the address to that of the (sun-tanned) white woman. Between these images the cultural and historical particularity of my racial identification (however much bound up – biographically – in phantasy) was left out. This elision of an identification that is neither Aboriginal woman or white woman was an elision that my own narrative kept in place. By focusing on the antagonism that is covered over by the signifier 'Black women', I am forced into naming myself – an identification which is temporary and partial: Mixed race; Pakistani father, English mother; hybrid woman. Inevitably this identification has the structure of a misrecognition and does not resolve the traumatic *lack of belonging* which is constitutive of the relation of address. Furthermore, the internal division within this signifier 'the Black woman' relates to class structures. It was through my self-identification as middle class rather than working class that I was able to re-negotiate my position within the encounter.[4] If I had been *already positioned* as either Aboriginal or as working class, such movement within the encounter may not have been possible.

But the signifier 'the Black woman' or 'Black women' is not made impossible by 'confessing' to the internal antagonism that divides its terms. My figuration of the Black woman did perform an injustice against the particular positionings of Black women. This injustice does not entail a simple belief in the impossibility of the category. The *gesture* of conjoin-ing Black and woman, of making that connection, still enables us to see that the instability of identifications are a result of social antagonisms, of the irreducibility of conflict and difference. But that irreducible conflict and difference is performed by the very gesture of figuring the Black woman in this way; where the conjoined signifiers get broken apart by the force of 'internal' antagonisms. The gesture undoes itself. But it still takes place. That 'taking place' has the form of the uncertain trajectory of this mixed race, middle-class and migrant woman.

CONCLUSION

The Black feminist critique of ethnocentrism in white feminist discourse was an important starting point for beginning to address the interlocking of race and gender in structures of identification (Carby 1992). No longer can we separate race and gender as separate or discrete categories but, if we are to make the experiences of Black women visible in feminist politics, then we must see them as mutually constitutive, as manifesting themselves only in relation to each other (hooks 1989; Pettman 1992; Brewer 1993). Part of the critique of ethnocentrism was hence the questioning of the foundational nature of the category of 'women' in feminist discourse. But an alternative and equally pressing question may then become: Does Black feminism rely on the foundational nature of the category of 'Black women' in its very critique of ethnocentrism? Does the very idea of rendering 'Black women' visible in feminist politics undo the critical force of the critique of foundationalism that has enabled that idea in the first place? Indeed, can we speak of 'Black woman' in the singular? How does the 'Black woman' become articulated and identified within the context of a loss of proper (or ontologically secured) notions of either 'Black' or 'woman'?

My analysis has suggested that the categories 'Black women' and 'Black woman' need not function as foundational categories and that, indeed, the act of bringing the social relations of gender and race together in the form of adjoined signifiers (Black, women, woman) operate precisely to make visible the *identificatory practices* which constitute the subject's *instability*. The non-foundational nature of these categories was made clear through auto-biography; through the rendering explicit of the determinate and yet unstable relation between the subject and its others. That instability resides in the shifts of the narrative according to the contradictions and divisions between the relations of address which attempt to fix the subject. The conjoining of 'Black' and 'woman' through the auto-biographical gesture enables us to figure how the collision between such relations of address constitutes the (seemingly individuated) realm of the subject (who writes and is written) at the same time as it constitutes the subject's impossibility. So for me, 'Black woman' and 'Black women' are impossible but necessary categories. Beyond that, they suggest trajectories of becoming rather than being. To speak of 'becoming Black woman' is not to say that the position is an empty or vacant space that can be filled by any subject. Rather, 'becoming Black woman' points to that difficult auto-biographical traject-ory in which the antagonism between relations of address – including relations of address between Black women – constitutes the instability of subjects in their encounters with others.

Given this I would argue that the difficulty of the singular and the plural – of either Black woman or Black women – cannot be understood as an indicator of degrees of essentialism (whereby the Black woman would be seen as an even more reductive phantasy of a singular identity). Both categories are identifications that position and partially fix subjects, both entail phantasy and misrecognition, and both are open to de-stabilization precisely insofar as they make visible the constitutive antagonism between relations of address. So to return to one of my questions: how does the 'Black woman' become articulated and identified within the context of a loss of proper (or ontologically secured) notions of either 'Black' or 'woman'? We can speak of the 'Black woman' insofar as the conjoining of these signifiers points to the collision between identificatory practices of race and gender that constitute the subject's migratory and hybrid passage into being. Identification practices partially fix subjects into posi-tionalities – but it is an inadequate fixation. The conjoined signifiers 'Black' and 'woman' point to this inadequacy as predicated on the violent collision between gender and race in structures of identification. To speak of the 'Black woman' is not to deny the antagonisms between Black women, but to render visible the antagonisms that structure and de-stabilize en-counters between gendered and racialized others. Moreover, as an overt political strategy, as an affirmative and auto-biographical (dis)identifica-tion, speaking as, of and to the Black woman, is to resist the dominant narratives of gender and race, whereby identifications are perceived as singular, or as divided only in relation to themselves. As a Black woman, I must remember not to forget.

NOTES

1 Although I could describe myself as mixed race I do not see that this simply constitutes a racial identity. Despite this, and for reasons that will hopefully become clearer throughout my article, I have come to identify myself as a Black woman. This identification (which is also a dis-identification from other forms of naming and evaluation) is self-consciously political and affirmative. However, it is not a confident gesture; it is not without its hesitations and uncertainties. The conjoining of two words (Black, woman) makes the identification unstable and shifting. And then there are the divisions within those words; as singular entities they may elide my specific positioning as a migrant, mixed-race woman.

2 The child's accession into the realm of subjectivity within Lacanian psycho-analysis in predicated on a structure of identification. In Lacan's 'The Mirror Stage as Formative of the Function of the I', the child sees itself in the mirror, and misrecognizes the images as itself. This act 'rebounds in the case of the child in a series of gestures in which he experiences in play the relation between the movements assumed in the image and the reflected environment – the child's own body, and the persons and things' (1977: 1). This play with an image structures the relation of the child to its body and to others, in the form of an identification, that is, in 'the transformation that takes place in the subject when he assumes an image' (1977: 2). Such an identification is imaginary and phantasmatic, projecting from the fragmentation of the bodily state a specular and Ideal-I, understood as the agency of the ego (1977: 2). I think we can establish from this the limits of identification as defined in 'the mirror phase'. For the act of the child seeing itself in the mirror and misrecognizing the image as itself is a singular process, however much that act is taken figuratively to signify that which structures the impossibility of 'becoming' a subject, in the sense of *being* an image. What is the significance of a theory which takes its *figure* of subjectivity in such a singular act? I use 'figured' here deliberately. I am not claiming that this figuring exhausts the terms of psychoanalysis (which complicates the discreteness of the subject again and again) but rather that the reliance on the 'mirror phase' and the figure of the child's encounter and

projection of an image, is over-determined by the status of the subject as *signifier*. In this sense, the narrative reliance on the figure enables the return of the letter to the subject whose singularity as signifier is already assured (the complication of identification is hence contained by the outlines established by this metaphoric reliance). That *figure* is certainly associated with the whole question of the *nature* of the subject, for the child's misrecognition of its image which comes to *stand for* 'the assumption of an alienating identity, which will mark with its rigid structure the child's entire mental development' (1977: 4). Is it this very *metaphoric reliance* that situates the psychoanalytical refusal to complicate the discreteness of the signifier 'the subject'?

3 Such a translation is even evident in the work of a theorist who occupies the terrain of the postcolonial – Homi Bhabha argues:

> For fetishism is always a 'play' or vacillation between the archaic affirmation of wholeness/ similarity – in Freud's terms: 'All men have penises'; in ours 'All men have the same skin/ race/ culture' – and the anxiety associated with lack and difference – again, for Freud 'Some do not have penises'; for us 'Some do not have the same skin/ race/ culture.'
>
> (Bhabha 1994: 74)

Here, the recognition of racial difference as constitutive of the subject is enabled only through a re-working of the Freudian logic of castration anxiety. Racial difference is hence positioned as secondary or derivative to a logic of sexual differentiation which hence *already* functions as ontological; as a self-evident way of explaining *in itself* the structuring of desire and difference *in general*.

4 Indeed, I thank Beverley Skeggs for pointing out to me in a seminar discussion that I tend to lose sight of the class issues in my reading of the event. The relation between race and class is also divisive. Remaining at an auto-biographical level, I recall that however much I appealed to my school as an indicator of class in this encounter (and hence was able to re-negotiate my position through the authority of class), my experience of that school (as one of the few non-white students) was of profound discomfort and alienation. While occupying a privileged material position, I remained at odds with the ideological make up of this middle-class school with its assumptions about Christianity and whiteness.

REFERENCES

Bhabha, Homi (1994) *The Location of Culture*, London and New York: Routledge.

Brewer, Rose M. (1993) 'Theorizing Race, Class and Gender: The New Scholarship of Black Feminist Intellectuals and Black Women's Labour' in Stanlie M. James and Abena P.A. Busia (eds), *Theorising Black Feminisms: The Visionary Pragmatism of Black Women*, London and New York: Routledge, pp. 13–30.

Butler, Judith (1993) *Bodies that Matter: On the Discursive Limits of 'Sex'*, London and New York: Routledge.

Carby, Hazel (1992) 'White Women Listen: Black Feminism and the Boundaries of Sisterhood' in The Centre for Contemporary Cultural Studies (eds) *The Empire Strikes Back: Race and Racism in 70s Britain*, London: Hutchinson, pp. 212–35.

Chambers, Iain (1994) *Migrancy, Culture and Identity*, London and New York: Routledge.

Friedman, Susan Stanford (1988) 'Women's Auto-Biographical Selves: Theory and Practice' in Shari Benstock (ed.), *The Private Self: Theory and Practice of Women's Auto-biography*, Chapel Hill: University of North Carolina Press, pp. 34–62.

hooks, bell (1989) *Talking Back: Thinking Feminist, Thinking Black*, London: Sheba Feminist Publishers.

Lacan, Jacques (1977) *Écrits: A Selection*, trans. Alan Sheridan, London: Tavistock Publications.

McClintock, Anne (1995) *Imperial Leather: Race, Gender and Sexuality in the Colonial Context*, London and New York: Routledge.

Pettman, Jan (1992) *Living in the Margins: Racism, Sexism and Feminism in Australia*, St Leonards, NSW: Allen and Unwin.

Probyn, Elspeth (1993) 'True Voices and Real People: The "Problem" of the Auto-biographical in Cultural Studies' in Valda Blundell, John Shepherd and Ian Taylor (eds), *Relocating Cultural Studies: Developments in Theory and Research*, London and New York: Routledge, pp. 105–22.

Sharpe, Jenny (1993) *Allegories of Empire: The Figure of Woman in the Colonial Text*, Minneapolis and London: University of Minnesota Press.

Spelman, Elizabeth V. (1992) *Inessential Woman: Problems of Exclusion in Feminist Thought*, London: The Women's Press.

Stanley, Liz (1992), *The Auto/biographical I: The Theory and Practice of Feminist Auto/biography*, Manchester: Manchester University Press.

Chapter 15

Charting the spaces of (un)location

On theorizing diaspora[1]

Magdalene Ang-Lygate

> The new moon, as science duly demonstrates, cannot be seen at all. To speak of the thin crescent moon as being new is to forget that only when the dark half faces the earth is the moon truly new.
>
> (Trinh T. Minh-Ha 1991: 1)

> To name ourselves rather than be named we must first see ourselves. For some of us this will not be easy. So long unmirrored, we may have forgotten how we look. Nevertheless, we can't theorise in a void; we must have evidence.
>
> (Lorraine O'Grady 1992: 14–23)

SILENT SPACES OF (UN)LOCATION

Although I was born almost exactly a year before Malaya, as it was then called, gained its independence from Britain in 1957, I have no personal memory of British rule. Yet, because of centuries of British intervention in that country, I am a child of the colonial era and I grew up influenced by powerful remnants of British empire. As Straits Chinese, my grandfathers, my parents, aunts and uncles attended English speaking schools and they worked and identified with the British administration. I did not know it then, but a postcolonial world had begun and I was part of it. The cow who jumped over the moon and the dish that ran away with the spoon had the same surreal input into my childhood as Shakespeare's *Macbeth*, stories of Christmas trees, snow and memorized lineage of the British monarchy. Although I was a daughter, I was the first in my family to go to university and because I too was English-educated, it seemed very normal for me to travel several thousands of miles to study at a university in Britain. It took me a long time to recognize this as a privilege because all my white female colleagues at university saw their financial independence, freedom to travel and access to higher education as their right, not a privilege.

However, years later, in conjunction with my awakening to feminist politics and thinking, I also became conscious that I had never really queried why it was that although I was by birth Malaysian Chinese, I was always more fluent in the English language than in Chinese or Malay. Or why it was that the name by which I was known was an Anglicized biblical one when I had a perfectly good Chinese name. Nor indeed why it was that Malaysian women and men of my generation considered it common-place to be educated in the west[2] or to have family members scattered all over the globe. At the time, these contradictions did not register nor did they seem to matter. Looking back now at this period between when I first arrived in 1975 and the time when I realized that there was such a 'thing' as feminist discourse, I am intrigued by my own lack of analysis of my positioning as an immigrant Chinese woman in postcolonial British society. However, what was worse was the gradual realization that eurocentric feminist 'knowledge' was similarly ignorant and silent about transnational diasporic experiences like mine. I was more than half way through a Women's Studies course before a chance meeting with another feminist nonya[3] alerted me to the large gaps of knowledge that feminist scholarship supposedly addressed.

In the 1980s, North American feminists bell hooks (1981), Cherrie Moraga and Gloria Anzaldúa (1983), Gloria T. Hull, Patricia Bell Scott and Barbara Smith (1981), Audre Lorde (1984), Elizabeth Spelman (1988) and others like them began to address issues related to multilayered female subjectivities. They accused white feminists of suppressing differences amongst women and insisted instead on exploding the category 'woman'. For them, being female, being Black/Jewish/Chicana/Japanese, being lesbian/heterosexual, being working/middle/upper class – being what-ever – were interconnected and inseparable from each other. Speaking from a variety of cultural backgrounds and social positions, they insisted for example that the privileging of 'race',[4] colour or descent over and above other social categories, say of nationality, class, sexuality and so on, obscured the experiences of women's complex identities. Accordingly, because different meanings reside in different combinations of time and space, the twin aspects of historical and geographical positioning that contribute to the complex realities of diasporic women must be explored in resistance to systems that seek to perpetuate ahistorical and apolitical myths of universal women's experiences.

However, unlike the North American experience, daily realities of on-going global migration and resulting transnational diasporic experiences are often neglected and insufficiently accounted for in British feminist discourse. Partly because of its particular acquaintance with anti-racist discourse and the 'race' relations industry, Black feminism as practised in Britain was dominated by 'race' politics and important issues of diversity and difference were marginalized. By prioritizing the politics of 'race' identity and the pursuit of strategies that demanded a unitary Black female identity, many women who chose not to privilege 'race' in the makeup of their complex identities became alienated and did not readily identify with such a narrow vision of Black British feminism. Subsequently, in spite of widely recognized acceptance of the need to contextualize women's experiences within given social frameworks, the hybrid influences of culture, politics, history and language that stem from postcolonial traditions are seldom acknowledged, let alone identified or analysed. In this chapter I want to explore some experiences of diaspora that I have either encountered personally or gathered during the course of my own empirical research work. The spaces of (un)location I refer to are uncharted territories where the shifting and contextual meanings of diaspora reside – caught somewhere between, and inclusive of, the more familiar experiences of (re)location and (dis)location.[5]

PROBLEMATIC LANGUAGE OF (UN)LOCATION

Most of my research work centres on the immigration[6] experiences of Chinese and Filipina women who originate from Pacific and Southeast Asian countries and who have settled in Scotland. Paying particular attention to their notions of 'home', community, sense of self and sense of belonging, I listen to the oral accounts of these women. Although I had initially expected this process to be a straight-forward study because I am an immigrant Malaysian Chinese woman myself and the women were willing to speak to me freely, one of the main problems I have encountered is in the deficiency and inadequacy of available vocabulary. I try to write about women like us and place us within a feminist/anti-racist or womanist context.[7] In writing from this perspective, I have had to use permutations, words such as 'black', black, Black, diasporic, immigrant, migrant, visible minority, ethnic, non-white, women of colour, 'Third World' women, native (female) Other – all of which are individually wanting and inaccurate. Instead of adopting longer descriptive styles like 'diasporic women of colour' or 'black and other minority ethnic', it has often been tempting to cut corners and revert to less verbose forms of description – using for example, the more familiar terms like Black, 'Third World' or ethnic minority. However, each of these terms is themselves problematic, tinged with ambiguous meanings and invested with un-examined notions of 'correctness'.[8]

Daphne Patai and Noretta Koertge (1994: 50) coined the term IDPOL to describe a currently popular game where identity politics is combined with ideological policing. They observed that in recent years, identity politics has changed from a neutral term used by social scientists to describe the various methods that social movements have employed to 'alter self-conceptions and societal conceptions of their participants' to that of attempts by particular groups 'to gain political advantage from whatever makes it identifiable as a (usually disadvantaged or oppressed) group'. In making this observation, they query the usefulness of trying to play or win such games without examining the underlying structures that permit these games to exist. For some time now, in both my research work and in my feminist activism, I have been concerned that the debates and practices surrounding 'black' issues, particularly diasporic women's experiences, which have been largely unproblematized and complicit with IDPOL. Whilst it is important to maintain academic integrity in using terms and descriptions in the proper context, it is just as important for feminist scholars to understand what is actually at stake when we neglect to see the implications of possible complicity with unproblematized and unlocated struggle. Given the legacy of white supremacy and a pathological denial of difference, it is all the more vital that the complex realities of (un)location are not silenced through a lack of suitable vocabulary.

The issue of 'black' women and the critique of 'white' feminism has gained prominence in recent years but what do we mean by 'black' and who counts as 'black'? The term 'black' has different meanings when used in different academic and cultural contexts. For example, in the USA, Black has a more specific reference to peoples of African descent with a specific history as slaves – whatever their countries of origin. Whereas in Britain, it is used more loosely as a political category that is grounded on skin colour and shared ex-colonial origins.[9] However, in recognizing that this is in fact a eurocentric Americanism that is not always claimed by peoples of African descent, I use Black (in upper case) when referring specifically to peoples of African descent who are located in Britain. Although Mirtha Quintanales (1983), a migrant to USA from Cuba, was writing about immigrant experience in the North American context, her observations about the problem of racism and the anti-racist struggle there is equally applicable to immigrant experience in Britain when she commented,

> Many African peoples are 'Black', but ask a Nigerian, an Ethiopian etc. what her identity is and she will tell you 'Nigerian' or 'Ethiopian', or whatever . . . Obviously, 'Black Culture' is an American phenomenon. Many of us don't really understand this.
>
> (Quintanales 1983: 155)

It is a mistake to fall prey to a racist/sexist mythology that insists that our experience of 'blackness' as non-Caucasian women puts us all in the same category as victims of racism, or that social inequality and injustice is ultimately reducible to 'race' or colour differences, without also drawing attention to the specific histories and experiences of racism. In rejecting notions of a coherent homogeneous 'blackness', I use the term 'black' (in quotes) reluctantly to try and communicate the problematics of using such a term and limit its use only within the context of British anti-racist political discourse, representing all peoples who suffer discrimination because of their skin colouring or racial descent.

I accept that in certain circumstances, identity politics as a political strategy has been used extensively and successfully. For example, in the anti-apartheid struggle in South Africa the category 'black' provided non-white peoples with a critical location from which to speak. Yet, the usage of the term 'black' other than with reference to specific campaigns falls into a binary opposition trap that artificially separates 'blacks' from 'whites' – as if racism is confined to these categories alone. What worries me is that when this kind of game is played, we are actually being complicit with a structure that is built on a principle of binary dualism that inevitably undoes the possibility of difference. Accordingly, the possibility of theorizing difference is confined to difference-as-opposition rather than difference-as-diversity. For example, translated into anti-racist discourse, there is no room in this particular schema for peoples of mixed parentage nor is there any space available for admitting the possibility of 'black'–'black' or 'white'–'white' racism, for example between South Asian and African-Caribbean or between English and Irish peoples. In retaining the current terminology of anti-racism in Britain that is based on this black/white rationale, the actual realities of many immigrant experiences of inter-ethnic racism is denied[10] and the structures which feminists seek to change become reproduced. In the British context, the stability of terms such as 'black' cannot be taken for granted despite the political pressure to do so.

Similarly, the term 'Third World' is problematic because the concept of one distinct 'Third World' actually describes regions and individual countries of Africa, Asia, the Caribbean, Latin America and the Middle East. Although these countries share a common predicament with respect to their economic status in a competitive world economy having suffered the after effects of colonization, the differences and variations between and within 'Third World' regions is enormous – such as in religion, political systems, culture and class structures. 'Ethnic minority' is another difficult term as it is often used as a blanket term for all peoples of colour inclusive of 'white ethnic minorities'. Apart from its eurocentric imperialist over-tones and the fact that globally, Caucasians are distinctintly in the minority, its usage also draws attention to a curious anomaly whereby we all know what we mean when we use the category 'minority' to apply to an empirical majority. More recently, in the European context, the term 'visible minority' is being used to distinguish between 'white minorities' and 'non-white minorities'. In addition, on the strange assumption that black and white are not colours, the preferred phrase in the USA for non-African, non-Caucasian peoples is 'people of colour'.

Likewise, in Britain the term Asian is used to describe peoples who

originate from the Indian subcontinent (themselves widely varied culturally) and there seems to be no distinction between Asians who are British
subjects and those who are not (Modood 1994). However, in the USA the
category Asian usually applies to peoples from the Indian subcontinents
as well as from Southeast and Pacific Asian countries such as Japan, Korea
and the Philippines. Upon obtaining citizenship, these groups of peoples
are then referred to as Asian-American, Chinese-American, Japanese-
American and so on. The status of 'immigrant' seems to be more transient
in the USA than it is in Europe. In Britain, we have no words to describe
British-born 'immigrants'. Our adoption of a British 'black' identity does
not convey notions of belonging and community. Instead, it is a sort of
enrolment into a falsely coherent alternative national identity that other-
izes us and sets us apart – dislocating emphasis on material commonalities
such as the struggle for decent housing, good jobs, secure futures for our
children. Subsequently, 'black' peoples – whatever their length of stay or
national status – are automatically viewed as permanent sojourners rather
than as active citizens who participate fully in society. The processes of
otherizing are unchecked and it is as if non-white peoples, labelled as
'Third World' and such like, only exist outside of Europe and that ethnic
minorities in the west exist only within their own ethnic ghettos.

However, everyday experiences and realities of diasporic women of
colour are not easily dissected and separated. Whilst admitting that one's
'race' is a crucial component of identity/identification, the privileging of
'race' or descent over and above other social categories and the adoption
of a 'black' identity may force such women to pretend that they do not
engage in life on multiple and sometimes conflicting levels.[11] Yet, this is
often what identity politics insists on. An unwritten assumption is made
that goes like this. If you are non-white, then you are 'black'. If you are
'black', your oppression is racial and you will lay claim to and testify of
your racial victimization. The impossibility of such simplistic rules of play
hides other processes of racialization. For instance, in a male-biased
society, the experience of racialization is different for 'black' men and
'black' women. For example, when Edward Said (1978) claimed that
'black' peoples are orientalized and demonized as 'heathens', 'pagans',
'uncivilized', 'barbaric', and so on, in eurocentric narratives of anthropology, religion and colonialism, his learned argument unfortunately failed
to include a gendered analysis. The recognition of simultaneously multiple
identities allows a more constructive argument that 'black' women are not
only racialized but also sexualized, exoticized and eroticized – all at the
same time (Fanon 1986; Kabbani 1988). Yet the use of a singular fraudu-
lently coherent category 'black' persists even though it presents a different
social division based solely on a perceived primary identity – 'race', itself
a socially constructed identity – without acknowledging that 'blackness'
is not a homogeneous experience for women and men.

IDENTITY ENCLOSURES OF (UN)LOCATION

Suniti Namjoshi (1988: 1–2) tells an amusing story about a blue donkey who lived beside a red bridge. The donkey was considered aesthetically unsuitable because the pinkness of the carrots she ate and her own blueness clashed horribly with the red bridge; the townfolk wanted her to do something about it. It seemed that a white donkey would have been more acceptable to the town councillors. The donkey's refusal to change colour or move away led to long debates over whether her blueness was inherent or intentional. In the end, most of the villagers got used to her colour and they did not notice it anymore. Some would occasionally bring her 'a bunch of blue flowers that she put in a vase'. This story appeals to me because it highlights the absurdity and arrogance of those people who go around telling others what they should be in order to fit in. Further, the blue donkey's resistance to such pressure pleases me because she refused to play that game. Not once did she suggest that the bridge be repainted blue to fit in with her. Nor did she attempt to justify the worth of blue when compared to white. If she had done this, she would have been complicit with the irrational colour-based logic that prompted the initial request. Instead, she refused to engage on the basis of colour by insisting that she was only different because she was a donkey.[12]

The influence of postmodernism on feminist scholarship has sparked significant contributions to the debates surrounding multilayered identities and subjectivities. A common consensus is that the notion of identity as a static and unitary trait is no longer viable. Instead, identities are seen as shifting, pluralistic, and dynamic aspects of all social relationships. It is not only about how we see ourselves but is also a social product that is negotiated through time and space, constructed within hierarchies of power (eg. Said 1978; Bhabha 1990; Haraway 1991; Hall 1992; Allen 1994; Bhavnani and Phoenix 1994). Women's realities encompass a whole range of different identities and subjectivities – all enmeshed, interconnected and inseparable – along shifting imaginary lines. However, postcolonial feminist theorists further assert that the agency/structure dyad through which identities are supposed to be forged and negotiated do not sufficiently account for the unequal power relations that lie not only in personal agency but also in institutionalized structures that perpetuate white male supremacy. They have repeatedly maintained that the native–woman–other identity enclosure that surrounds, in this case, the non-white ex-colonial immigrant woman, does not require her to acknowledge the imaginary spaces and meanings that have been assigned for her occupation. The seeming coherence of this enclosure – a racialized and sexualized space where a woman from Southeast Asia is homogenized mainly as an exotic/erotic sexual being, through popular stereotypes of say 'lotus blossom' or 'dragon lady' – hides the diverse structures which operate beneath these notions (Kabbani 1988; Ling 1989). This identity enclosure to which she is confined is primarily a product of dominant eurocentric–imperialist imagination to which she has little control. Through the deconstruction of western literary texts, Gayatri C. Spivak's writings (1985, 1988, 1992, 1993) explore the subject-positions of 'Third World' women caught within power structures that are not only patriarchal but also colonialist and imperialistic. Similarly, Trinh T. Minh-Ha (1987, 1989, 1991) sought to describe from her own perspective as a Vietnamese-American film-maker the meanings of 'difference' for a woman who was both perceived of as woman and as alien. Chandra T. Mohanty (1988: 61) suggested that under 'western eyes',[13] the identities of diasporic women who are seen as outsider–incomers are products of dominant–insider imagination and hence categorization. Unfortunately, social theorizing about what is material and not simply imagined or representational, has been slow to incorporate these observations. The colonialist and imperialist mentality met with little effective resistance and continues to construct enclosures – imaginary and material – within which immigrant women are racialized and sexualized.

During the course of my research work, in response to an invitation to describe their identity, all the women I interviewed insisted that while they may have assumed British identity, they were definitely Chinese or Filipina. Only one woman interviewed described herself additionally as 'black'. She had migrated from Malaysia with her family when she was a young teenager and happened to be an active anti-racist activist, highly politicized and familiar with the kinds of words she thought she should be heard using. This single occurrence raised a number of questions: Who counts as 'black'? Who identifies as 'black'? Who decides that the category 'black' should be applied?

It was unsurprising that 'black' identity did not figure in the interview narratives of most of the women I interviewed. They neither mentioned the word 'black' nor did they confirm or deny having a 'black' identity. Media portrayals of 'black' communities in Britain are dominated by images of peoples from the African and Indian subcontinents or of African descent from the West Indies. Although it is true that in Britain their populations are larger than other groups, these images exclude peoples of other ethnic origins. In this way, the notion 'black' renders many women, who are often unpoliticized and thus cannot visibly identify as 'black' (or 'white'), invisible. It would appear that as immigrants, the Chinese and Filipina women I interviewed failed to identify themselves as 'black' because they had not been socialized into thinking of themselves as a political category. Furthermore, in practice such women have at times been excluded from the category 'black' and 'black' groups have not always been welcoming because they do not see us as being 'black' enough. Being excluded from the category 'white' and its privileges and not accepted by other non-white women is a dilemma that exists for Chinese and Filipina women in the spaces of (un)location.

Whether or not a Chinese woman is 'black' enough, the category 'Chinese' is itself problematic. Benedict Anderson had previously asserted that through mechanisms of social control such as the Census, European colonization imposed and legitimated certain categories of identities: 'The fiction of the census is that everyone is in it, and that everyone has one – and only one – extremely clear place. No fractions' (1991: 166). He cites Mason Hoadley's (1982) account of the recording of a particular murder trial that was recorded in 1696 by both the Cirebonese Javanese court and the Dutch Company (VOC). Whilst the Javanese court classified the accused by rank and status, the VOC racialized the high official and identified him only as 'Chinese'. It did not matter that the man had achieved a title 'whose high status attested to his and his ancestors' long integration into Cirobonese society' (Anderson 1991: 167). In the course of history and the grip of Eurocentric imperialism, racialized categories such as those adopted by the VOC have remained in place. Anderson further commented that by 1870, colonial presence was so entrenched in Southeast Asia that Census-takers were kept busy:

> counting the objects of its feverish imagining and a 'Cochin-Chinese' woman could live out her life, happily or unhappily, in the Straits Settlements, without the slightest awareness that this was how she was being mapped from on high.
>
> (Anderson 1991: 169)

In contrast to the one Chinese woman in the example above who identified specifically as 'black', all the other women interviewed did not claim this identity. Although each woman addressed the problem of racism at the level to which she experienced it, there was no indication that they were even aware that such a category 'black' might be applied to them. It would appear that the 'black' identity that anti-racist discourse promotes is a British phenomenon that is in fact alien to many immigrant women who may not realize that they have been identified and categorized as such. In such ways, some immigrant women, e.g. Chinese, Filipina, Malay or Japanese, unfamiliar with British anti-racist language are denied spaces from which they can voice their own rights and concerns. Mindful of the aforementioned Cochin-Chinese woman in 1870, it strikes me as ironic that anti-racist discourse has adopted what was originally an imperialist enterprise, when colonial powers imposed identities on colonized peoples and refused them the power to name themselves.

Meanwhile in contemporary Britain, the processes of social control through ethnic monitoring continue to be perpetuated. In previous census counts, reliance was placed on birth place as an indicator of racial or ethnic origin but figures based on such reliance were not accurate because they included those white people born in former colonies and excluded 'black' and other ethnic minority people born in the Britain. However, in the 1991 Census, members of the public were explicitly asked to indicate their ethnic origin. After consultation with the Commission for Racial Equality among others, nine separate categories – White, Black Caribbean, Black African, Black Other, Indian, Pakistani, Bangladeshi, Chinese and Any Other Ethnic Group – were decided upon. Far from being a progressive step towards eliminating ethnic discrimination, or towards the recognition of difference within a multicultural Britain, this kind of structured racialization actually highlights the racist legacy of a neo-colonial society obsessed with categorizing those who are perceived to be immigrant outsiders.[14] Subsequent to the 1991 Census, several debates around the 'ethnic group' question have highlighted the shortcomings of current vocabulary when attempting to categorize people in this way.[15] Within the context of Marxist analysis, Louis Althusser (1969) previously proposed that ideology was not simply about ideas but that it was grounded in material systems of social practices. He asserted that social processes and ideological state apparatuses (ISA) serve to mask the mechanisms of these relations of dominance. More recently, Michel Foucault (1981) also drew attention to the ways in which the construction of social norms serve as a disciplinary strategy and that principles of exclusion determine what may or may not be permitted in terms of dominant discourse. In particular, the 'problem' of classifying peoples of mixed parentage betrays a hidden assumption about the desirability of racial purity. Once again, the creation of supposed identities based on an ambiguous mixture of racial, national and ethnic classifications demonstrate how administrative technologies of the state construct the categories they then proceed to regulate.

Additionally, 'immigrant' as a word is often wrongly linked only to 'black' people. The majority of immigrants are actually Caucasians – from Eire or the Old Commonwealth (Australia, New Zealand and Canada) or from other European countries. For example, the 1981 Census Country of Birth Tables revealed that nearly 3.4 million people in Britain were born overseas. The majority of these, 1.9 million, were Caucasians – 607,000 were born in Ireland, 153,000 in the Old Commonwealth and about 1.13 million in other countries including Western Europe. Surely if greater ethnic accuracy was intended in the 1991 Census, categories such as Australian, Canadian, Italian, French, Jewish, Spanish and so on should also have been included to reflect ethnic differences amongst Caucasians resident in Britain. Instead, in postcolonial times, it would appear that the same name game is still being played such that colonialists remain in control of how 'other' (meaning non-white) peoples are categorized.

IMAGINARY COMMUNITIES AND THE MYTH OF AUTHENTICITY

The term 'Chinese' is itself problematic. When it is used as a unifying category it forces a unilateral homogeneity on Chinese peoples and fosters the myth of 'authentic ethnicity'. Dominant racialized stereotypes whether manifested as 'typical immigrant' or 'true native', encourage an essentialist identity that ignores the materiality of other social factors such as class, ethnicity and sexuality – all negotiated historically and geographically. In my sample of Chinese women, when encouraged to speak about their friendships and personal support structures, only one woman admitted to having mainly Chinese friends. It was interesting that the others not only spoke warmly of their white friends but gave no indication that they had any close Chinese friendships in their locality. One woman in particular described how she depended heavily on her white friends when she suffered a family bereavement but received no emotional support from her own kind – her Chinese friends. In terms of community, she was clear that she belonged with her Chinese friends and spoke of her white friends as if they were outsiders – reflecting dominant modes of thinking. However, if we were to interpret her testimony in a non-racialized way and listen to her perspective as a woman who transgressed racial boundaries in her friendship circles, we can argue that she did receive support from her own kind – newly married women with young school-aged children. Apart from common Chinese descent, she had nothing in common with her Chinese friends whom she saw only once a week. The commonalities we share as women are not always overridden by 'race'. Other social attributes such as shared experience of childbearing, childrearing, mothering, marriage, political or religious beliefs and lifestyles are equally significant in the construction of social relationships and to our social location as women.

Only in choosing to privilege the racialization of myself and of my research participants, can I say that as a Chinese woman researching other Chinese women we share the same identity and belong to the same group. The moment we admit the possibility of other concurrent social categories, group membership becomes repeatedly re-negotiable. For example, as part of my research I tried to gain access to a particular group of Hong Kong Chinese women to interview them. When I made initial contact with the leader of the group on the telephone, I was dismayed to discover that she was reluctant to let me attend their meetings. However, when I realized that because she could not see me over the telephone line, she had assumed from my Anglicized first name and my local Scottish accent I was Caucasian, I specifically declared myself to be Chinese and her subsequent response to me changed dramatically. 'Oh! If you are Chinese, you are most welcome. I look forward to seeing you next Tuesday.' It was clear that while my status as a Chinese woman gave me an immediate right of access to that group, I was actually not allowed to belong until I colluded with the myth of authentic ethnicity and confessed my 'true' Chinese identity. In the absence of visible and conversational markers – my skin colour and features, my choice of language, accent and name – my perceived identity allowed me, unintentionally, to masquerade as 'white' and allowed her to decide that I did not belong. The other woman's separate construction of a different reality demonstrated afresh that there was a parallel subjectivity and our individual subjectivities were equally dependent on the two 'realities'. While I was otherizing her as a potential research subject, she was in turn otherizing me as a potential intruder to her group. Due to our specific positioning in British colonial history, this Hong Kong Chinese woman had a completely different ethnic makeup from mine and our Chineseness alone could not be automatically assumed to be a source of commonality. Still it was upon this premise that I gained access to a group that would otherwise have excluded me. In this case, the imaginary boundary that demarcated Chineseness was shifted by her to let me in. Since that time, more imaginary lines based on sexuality, class, religion, nationality, ethnicity and politics have indeed been drawn and I have been routinely excluded or included depending on the circumstances.[16]

BEING INVISIBLE IS NOT A NATURAL STATE

The failure to acknowledge diversity also hides the reality that lighter-than-black skin colour may give some ethnic minority women the option of assimilating and 'passing' as white.[17] In turn, this dubious privilege is at the expense of remaining 'invisible, ghost-like, identity-less, community-less, totally alienated . . . merging and yet remaining utterly alone and in the margins of our society' (Quintanales 1983: 153–4). All the Filipina women I interviewed are married to British Caucasians and have mixed-race children. It may not be co-incidental but in all these cases, the women concerned described themselves as Christian or practising Catholics. Although their skin colour marks them as non-white and 'passing' cannot be applied in the usual physical sense, as might in their children's case, I wonder if the combination of marriage into white society, the adoption of Anglicized names and their active identification with what is perceived to be a western religion allows them to assume token white status. I suspect that these factors rather than fluency in English or familiarity with British culture have had greater significance in the assimilation of these women into British life. Passing depends on a series of markers – visible and conversational – and when visible markers like skin colour, foreign names, ethnic costume are removed or hidden, the non-white person can pass into the 'currency of normative whiteness' (Butler 1993: 170).[18] In terms of conversation, it is what is withheld that permits her to pass and diasporic identity is centred on a complicated subjectivity that constantly negotiates its way to avoid exposure and possible rejection.

Some forms of Otherness are recognized as appropriate and tolerated because they support and perpetuate unequal relationships of power, e.g. when 'authenticity' is demarcated and controlled by a dominant western discourse. But when forms of Otherness that break out of the confines of dominant defined identity enclosures are articulated, these are perceived as subversive and rejected or repressed. Trinh refers to 'inappropriate Others' who resist definitions of their Otherness by Others and insist on defining difference from their own perspectives (1991: 74). To illustrate, Maxine Hong Kingston (1981) broke silences and started to dismantle the popular stereotypes of Chinese women when she addressed the experience of fractured identities and fragmented consciousness that were part of her own experiences as the American-born daughter of an immigrant woman. Her book became a bestseller several times over and yet although more and more Chinese women like Kingston have since begun to write of their own experiences of diaspora and about their specific location and negotiation in western society, the fact still remains that such pronouncements can only be tolerated in the form of fiction but not as part of everyday recognized realities. Unfortunately, although the notion of inappropriate Otherness is not just a fictional construct, and they are part of diasporic experience, these realities are mostly invisible.

Many of the immigrant women I interviewed spoke of their need to conform to societal norms – as mothers, wives, daughters – as a matter of 'survival' and that aspects of their identities that were previously freely expressed before immigration had to be silenced in order to fit in. For example, it is customary for Chinese women to retain their family names upon marriage but British society assumes that women – especially Chinese women who are perceived to be submissive types – adopt their husband's surnames. And some Chinese women who wish to avoid the 'stigma' of co-habitation that is implied by their having a different surname from their male partner, feel the need to conform to western custom and abandon their family names.[19] Adopting Anglicized names is another example. Like me, more than 90 per cent of the women I interviewed have Anglicized names, either given to them or self-adopted, and they did not use their Chinese names. Moreover, in the case of the women who have married Caucasian men and also adopted their surnames, this invisibility is even more insidious as they are hidden behind names such as Anne MacDonald, Julie MacNabb, Michelle Lawson.[20] Eurocentric naming practices render us invisible to each other, robbing us of pre-immigration identities, thus limiting opportunities for mutual recognition, affirmation and validation of our diasporic identities.

Assimilation on the basis of passing is not only a costly experience psychically but also an exhausting one for it depends on constant negotiation of what response is needed, working out what is appropriate and suppressing the inappropriate. Whether consciously practised or not, assimilation on the basis of passing is a diasporic experience that has yet to be explored from a feminist perspective. In the particular case of diasporic Chinese and Filipina women exiled from a 'home' culture, spiritual dimensions of psychic losses and separations become particularly cogent in the complexion of their social construction. The absence of local family support structures and her dependence on her spouse, not only financially but for her immigration status, are extremely strong factors in ensuring conformity. Yet, it is this physical (re)(dis)location, insider–outsider status and her polyphonic 'oppositional consciousness', that actually challenges the appropriateness and adequacy of current ways of conceptualizing diasporic identities and subjectivities (Cheva Sandoval, quoted in Kaplan 1987: 187). Spaces of silence need to be filled in. Or as Mitsuye Yamada (1983: 40) puts it, 'We need to raise our voices a little more, even as they say to us "This is so uncharacteristic of you".' To finally recognize our own invisibility is to finally be on the path towards visibility. Invisibility is not a natural state for anyone.

CONCLUDING THOUGHTS: MOVING BEYOND 'CORRECTNESS'

Sometimes the indiscriminate adoption of 'politically correct' language closes down ways of thinking rather than opening them up for the possibilities for understanding different women's experiences. Hence terms like 'black', Black or black are to be used with care not only for reasons of political correctness and political strategy, but to enable us to appreciate the complex, multi-dimensional aspects of women's identities. More importantly, in doing so we must not lose sight of our aim of working together towards social transformation – the meeting of women's needs. I would like to think that the ability to deal with difference is at the centre of feminism's survival as a movement for social change. In retaining the term 'women', we no longer insist on a universal homogeneity based on gender because we are learning to recognize differences and diversity along other social lines such as class, 'race', sexuality, nationality, abilities. Solidarity amongst all women is a utopian ideal and so long as it remains one, it would be strategic for us to continue to struggle together as 'women'. Yet this is no longer an unexamined strategy because the space is there to examine complexities and contradictions without losing sight of feminist ideals of sisterhood, social justice and freedom from oppression.

In the same way, I believe the time is here for 'black' identity to be similarly unmasked as only a useful strategy but no more. As a form of strategic essentialism that has the power to mobilize people, it is nevertheless a strategy not to be confused with substantive essentialism that stifles expressions of plurality (Spivak 1993). Too much effort has been wasted on ideological policing at the expense of neglecting feminist commitment to moving out of oppressive ways of living. In suggesting a way beyond IDPOL games, Judith Butler (1990) argued for an additional strategy of subversive repetition that interrupts the processes that define and endorse identity positioning again and again. Although Butler's remarks were made primarily within the context of gender identity and queer theory, they are applicable here; in establishing as political the very terms through which diasporic identity is articulated. In turn, bell hooks (1991: 29) argues for the practice and promotion of a 'postmodern blackness' which challenges colonial paradigms of 'black' identity – unidimensional identity that reinforces white supremacy – and opposes notions of 'authenticity'. However, this forces us to 'rearticulate the basis for collective bonding' and makes the recognition of multiple experiences of diaspora a possibility. Or as Sneja Gunew and Anna Yeatman (1993: xxiv) put it, 'The days of exclusionary solidarity as an unexamined strategy are long over . . . the dangers inherent in certain methods of accommodating difference need to be pointed out . . . we need to remain alert to their operations.'

Trinh (1991: 1) previously remarked, 'the new moon . . . cannot be seen at all.' Yet, the dark half that faces the earth is not an unnatural state for the moon to be in and the fact that it cannot be seen from the earth only reminds us that this is so only from the perspective of the earth. The uncharted territories of (un)location are like the 'new' moon. They are not new and they appear uncharted only because they cannot be seen from the perspective of dominant (feminist inclusive) discourse. The realities and immigration experiences of many diasporic Chinese and Filipina women have long been unmirrored because the inappropriate Otherness that they insist on illustrates the poverty of categorizations that are based on neo-colonialist definitions. What was interesting in Namjoshi's account of the blue donkey was that at the end of the story, those townfolk who used to think that white donkeys were preferable and who now supposedly accepted the blue donkey as she was, continued playing the colour game – they brought her blue flowers. Personally, I suspect the blue donkey would rather they brought her carrots – of any colour.

ACKNOWLEDGEMENTS

The author wishes to thank Shirley Geok-lin Lim and Stevi Jackson for their encouragement.

NOTES

1 A shorter version of this article was published as 'Shades of Meaning' in *Trouble and Strife*, no. 31, Summer 1995.

2 Although I recognize they carry an inherent danger of totalization, I have little choice but to use the terms 'west' and 'western' before other terms introduced can have more precise meanings.

3 This term, pronounced and sometimes spelt as 'nyonya', refers to a Chinese woman born in the Straits Settlements of Penang, Singapore and Malacca who belongs to an ethnic minority Chinese community called Straits Chinese or 'peranakan'. Whilst retaining most of its Chinese customs and traditions, this community is mainly assimilated into the dominant Malay culture.

4 The term 'race' is used with the understanding that this is a historical rather than a biological and scientific construct.

5 I use the term (re)location to represent the logistics and processes of emigration and (dis)location to represent the outsider–insider realities and experiences of immigrants (see Magdalene Ang-Lygate 1996c).

6 I prefer this term to 'migration' because the processes of arriving and settling in a new place not only encompass the present and the future but also the past narratives of immigrant realities.

7 Alice Walker (1984) coined the term 'womanist' to represent an identity that has been informed by issues of racism/sexism, to distinguish it from 'feminist', an identity she saw as mainly appropriated by 'white' women.

8 For a fuller discussion of 'black' as signifier and as sign, see F. Anthias and N. Yuval-Davis (1992).

9 See Tariq Modood (1994) for a critique of the political concept of 'blackness' and how, from his perspective, it harms Asians.

10 Kum-Kum Bhavnani and Ann Phoenix (1994) argue that when people of South Asian and African-Caribbean origin in Britain together embraced the term 'black', racist definitions of black meant to divide these populations became weakened. Nevertherless, in the context of this chapter, when charting unexamined territories of say 'black'–'black' racism, the point remains that current social vocabulary is limited and unhelpful.

11 One example of perceived internal 'conflict' amongst Chinese women I interviewed was in the way we chose to communicate. In identifying each other as Chinese, it often felt as if we should be speaking Chinese instead of English. However, in reality the variance in our fluency in the many Chinese dialects made this impractical.

12 As the story was based on Marc Chagall's *The Blue Donkey*, it is questionable whether the donkey might have, when pressed, further identified itself as Russian, Jewish, or French.

13 Some postcolonial theorists further suggest that western eyes are not always 'white' eyes. It is possible for 'black' peoples resident in the west to view immigrants with eurocentric eyes too. In her article 'Under Western Eyes', Chandra T. Mohanty (1988) claims that some western feminist scholarship categorize 'Third World' women as a singular monolithic subject, thus refusing to confront the differences and diversity which are part of these women's lives.

14 The Third Policy Studies Institute survey (Brown 1984) estimated that 40 per cent of Britain's 'black' population were British born; moreover it estimated that 50 per cent of those who came to Britain as immigrants had lived in Britain for over 15 years.

15 See for example, David Owen (1994) where he draws attention to the problematics of 4-way, 10-way classifications and the OPCS coding adopted

by various bodies and agencies in their attempt to reflect ethnic composition
of the population.

16 Issues related to standpoint methodology as raised within the context of being
a Chinese woman who researches other Chinese women are discussed in Ang-
Lygate (1996a). It is also interesting that my nonya identity, mainly signified
by an unfamiliarity with 'proper' Chinese language, has significantly contributed to my outsider status within the local Chinese community. I cannot
'pass' as 100 per cent ethnic – whatever this is.

17 The phenomena of colourism – ascribing greater value to same-race people
based on the lightness of their skin colour – is not discussed here but Virginia
Harris (1994) critiques this form of internalized racism.

18 See Frankenberg (1993) for a discussion on the social contruction of whiteness.

19 It is increasingly more acceptable in British society for women to keep their
own surnames even after marriage but in the absence of specific instructions,
educational, legal and financial institutions still assume a married woman will
abandon her own surname in favour of her husband's.

20 Due to confidentiality, these names are pseudonyms.

REFERENCES

Afshar, Haleh and Mary Maynard (eds) (1994) *The Dynamics of 'Race' and Gender:
Some Feminist Interventions*, London: Taylor & Francis.

Allen, Sheila (1994) 'Race, Ethnicity and Nationality' in H. Afshar and M.
Maynard (eds) (1994) *The Dynamics of 'Race' and Gender: Some Feminist Interventions*, London: Taylor & Francis, pp. 85–105.

Althusser, Louis (1969) 'Ideology and Ideological State Apparatuses' in L.
Althusser (1969) *Lenin and Philosophy and other Essays*, London: New Left Books,
pp. 121–73.

Anderson, Benedict (1991) *Imagined Communities: Reflections on the Origin and
Spread of Nationalism*, London: Verso.

Ang-Lygate, Magdalene (1995) 'Shades of Meaning', *Trouble and Strife*, no. 31
Summer, pp. 15–20.

Ang-Lygate, Magdalene (1996a) 'Waking from a dream of Chinese shadows',
Feminism and Psychology, vol. 6, no. 1: 56–60.

Ang-Lygate, Magdalene (1996b) 'Women Who Move: Experiences of Diaspora' in
M. Maynard and J. Purvis (eds) (1996) *New Frontiers in Women's Studies:
Knowledge, Identity and Nationalism*, London: Taylor & Francis.

Ang-Lygate, Magdalene (1996c) 'Everywhere to go but Home: On (re)(dis)(un)
location', *Journal of Gender Studies*, vol. 5, no. 3.

Anthias, Floya and Nira Yuval-Davis (1992) 'Racism and The Colour Black' in
F. Anthias and N. Yuval-Davis *Racialized Boundaries: Race, Nation, Gender, Colour
and Class and the Anti-Racist Struggle*, London: Routledge.

Barrett, Michele and Anne Phillips (eds) (1992) *Destabilizing Theory: Contemporary
Feminist Debates*, London: Polity Press.

Bhabha, Homi (ed.) (1990) *Nation and Narration*, London: Routledge.

Bhavnani, Kum-Kum and Ann Phoenix (eds) (1994) *Shifting Identities Shifting
Racisms*, London: Sage.

Brown, C. (1984) *Black and White Britain*, Third PSI survey, London: Policy Studies
Institute.

Butler, Judith (1990) *Gender Trouble: Feminism and the Subversion of Identity*, London:
Routledge.

Butler, Judith (1993) 'Passing, Queering: Nella Larsen's Psychoanalytic Challenge' in *Bodies That Matter: On the Discursive Limits of 'Sex'*, London: Routledge, pp. 167–85.

Donald, James and Ali Rattansi (eds) (1992) *'Race', Culture and Difference*, London: Sage.

Fanon, Frantz (1986, 1993) *Black Skin, White Masks*, London: Pluto Press.

Foucault, Michel (1981) 'The Order of Discourse' in R. Young (ed.) *Untying The Text*, Boston: Routledge & Kegan Paul, pp. 48–78.

Frankenberg, R. (1993) *The Social Construction of Whiteness*, London: Routledge, pp. 71–101.

Gunew, Sneja and Yeatman, Anna (eds) (1993) *Femininism and the Politics of Difference*, St Leonards, NSW: Allen and Unwin.

Hall, Stuart (1992) 'New Ethnicities' in J. Donald and A. Rattansi (eds) *'Race', Culture and Difference*, London: Sage, pp. 252–9.

Haraway, Donna (1991) 'A Cyborg Manifesto: Science, Technology and Socialist-Feminism in the Late Twentieth Century' in *Simians, Cyborgs, and Women: The Reinvention of Nature*, New York: Routledge, Chapman & Hall.

Harris, Virginia R. (1994) 'Prison of Color' in Elena Featherston (ed.) *Skin Deep: Women Writing on Color, Culture and Identity*, Freedom, CA: Crossing Press.

hooks, bell (1981) *Ain't I a Woman?*, Boston: South End Press.

hooks, bell (1991) 'Postmodern Blackness' in *Yearning: Race, Gender and Cultural Politics*, London: Turnaround.

Hoadley, Mason (1982) 'State vs Ki Aria Marta Ningrat (1696) and Tian Siangko (1720–21)' unpublished manuscript referred to in B. Anderson (1991) *Imagined Communities*, London: Verso.

Hull, Gloria T., Patricia Bell Scott and Barbara Smith (1981) *All The Women Are White, All The Blacks Are Men, But Some of Us Are Brave*, New York: The Feminist Press.

Jagger, Alison and Susan Bordo (eds) (1989) *Gender/Body/Knowledge*, New Brunswick: Rutgers University Press.

Kabbani, Rana (1988) *Europe's Myths of Orient: Devise And Rule*, London: Pandora Press.

Kaplan, Caren (1987) 'Deterritorializations: The Rewriting of Home and Exile in Western Feminist Discourse', *Cultural Critique*, no. 6, Spring.

Kingston, Maxine Hong (1981) *The Warrior Woman: Memoirs of a Girlhood Amongst Ghosts*, London: Pan Books.

Ling, Amy (1989) 'Chinamerican Women Writers: Four Forerunners of Maxine Hong Kingston' in A. Jagger and S. Bordo (eds) (1989) *Gender/Body/Knowledge*, New Brunswick: Rutgers University Press.

Lorde, Audre (1984) *Sister Outsider: Essays and Speeches*, Freedom, CA: The Crossing Press.

Maynard, Mary and June Purvis (eds) (1996) *New Frontiers in Women's Studies: Knowledge, Identity and Nationalism*, London: Taylor & Francis.

Modood, Tariq (1994) 'Political Blackness and British Asians', *Sociology*, vol. 28 no. 4, pp. 859–76.

Mohanty, Chandra T. (1988) 'Under Western Eyes: Feminist Scholarship and Colonial Discourses', *Feminist Review*, no. 30, Autumn, pp. 61–88.

Moraga, Cherrie and Gloria Anzaldúa (1983) *This Bridge Called My Back: Writings By Radical Women of Color*, Latham, NY: Kitchen Table, Women of Color Press.

Namjoshi, Suniti (1988) *The Blue Donkey Fables*, London: The Women's Press.

O'Grady, Lorraine (1992) 'Olympia's Maid: Reclaiming Black Female Subjectivity', *Afterimage*, Summer, pp. 14–23.

Owen, David (1994) *Ethnic Minority Women and The Labour Market: Analysis of the 1991 Census*, Manchester: Equal Opportunities Commission.

Patai, Daphne and Noretta Koertge (1994) *Professing Feminism: Cautionary Tales From the Strange World of Women's Studies*, New York: Basic Books.

Quintanales, Mirtha (1983) 'I Paid Very Hard For My Immigrant Ignorance' in C. Moraga and G. Anzaldua (eds) *This Bridge Called My Back: Writings By Radical Women of Color*, Latham, NY: Kitchen Table, Women of Color Press, pp. 150–6.

Said, Edward (1978) *Orientalism: Western Conceptions of the Orient*, London: Penguin Books.

Spelman, Elizabeth (1988) *Inessential Woman: Problems of Exclusion in Feminist Thought*, London: The Women's Press.

Spivak, Gayatri C. (1985) 'Three Women's Texts and a Critique of Imperialism', *Critical Inquiry*, vol. 12, Autumn, pp. 244–51.

Spivak, Gayatri C. (1988) *In Other Worlds: Essays in Cultural Politics*, NY: Routledge.

Spivak, Gayatri C. (1992) 'The Politics of Translation' in M. Barrett and A. Phillips (eds) *Destabilizing Theory: Contemporary Feminist Debates*, London: Polity Press, pp. 177–200.

Spivak, Gayatri C. (1993) 'In A Word: Interview' in *Outside in the Teaching Machine*, New York: Routledge.

Trinh T. Minh-Ha (1987) 'Difference: A Special Third World Women Issue', *Feminist Review*, no. 25, March, pp. 5–22.

Trinh T. Minh-Ha (1989) *Woman, Native, Other: Writing Postcoloniality and Feminism*, Bloomington: Indiana University Press.

Trinh T. Minh-Ha (1991) *When The Moon Waxes Red: Representation, Gender and Cultural Politics*, London: Routledge.

Walker, Alice (1984) *In Search of Our Mother's Gardens*, London: The Women's Press.

Yamada, Mitsuye (1983) 'Invisibility is an Unnatural Disaster: Reflections of an Asian American Woman' in C. Moraga and G. Anzaldúa (eds) *This Bridge Called My Back: Writings By Radical Women of Color*, Latham, NY: Kitchen Table, Women of Color Press, pp. 35–40.

Chapter 16

Fractured or flexible identities?

Life histories of 'black' diasporic women in Britain

Naz Rassool

INTRODUCTION

Used as a *racially* descriptive term 'blackness' has historically provided a universalizing, homogenizing category in which the concept of 'foreign Otherness' has been encapsulated *par excellence* in both colonial and post-colonial discourse. Emphasizing the need to understand the *'processes of subjectification'* (original emphasis) in colonial discourse, Bhabha (1994: 67) argues that:

> The construction of the colonial subject in discourse, and the exercise of colonial power through discourse, demands an articulation of forms of difference – racial and sexual . . . it is a discourse crucial to the binding of a range of differences and discriminations that inform the discursive and political practices of racial and cultural hierarchization.

Grounded in racist theories and encoded with meanings of 'foreign alienness', 'black pathology' and 'social and ethnic inferiority', blackness has historically provided the category *against* which the concept of the British 'nation' has been defined in popular consciousness. As such, black people conceived of as an amorphous, 'racially' and culturally homogenized 'outgroup' (captured in the all-encompassing term 'ethnic minorities') have served historically as a powerful hegemonic construct in shaping commonsense understandings of the British 'nation'. In the words of Hall (1993: 396) 'vis-à-vis the developed West, we are very much "the same". We belong to the marginal, the underdeveloped, the periphery, the "Other". We are at the outer edge, the "rim", of the metropolitan world.' However, this homogenized (dominant) view contrasts somewhat with the reality that the British 'black experience' comprises a complex tapestry of historical experiences grounded in different diasporas. The black British diasporas have their origins in the voluntary and involuntary migration of groups of people from different parts of the world. Scattered and dislocated from their countries of origin these colonial, and now post-colonial, peoples bring with them their own historical and cultural experiences within which both group and individual subjectivities have been shaped.

If we take account then of the range of cultures represented in the British 'black' experience it follows that the adoption of the term 'black' to describe different groups of people clearly needs to be appraised more critically. Aziz (1995: 162) exploring the contested nature of the concept of black-ness in Britain argues that:

> Black people do not comprise a hermetically sealed or homogeneous category: skin colour, history and culture all play a part in their definition. Black-ness is a product of self-conscious political practice: its meaning has been given by, and has in turn affected the struggles of people in Britain who have identified themselves (and have been identified) as black.

This chapter explores through the life histories of four women within the black diasporas the complex ways in which some 'black identities' have evolved in Britain. Underlying this is the view, first, that 'black' identities are not linear constructions but rather that they reflect a tapestry of interwoven life experiences having their origins within different socio-historical epochs. Second is the view that the socio-cultural, political and geographical displacement effected by political exile, as well as the racism in which slavery, colonial and neo-colonial relations were legitimated, indelibly mark the 'black experience' within metropolitan societies. The shaping of 'black' identities in British society therefore arises out of historically specific material conditions. Thirdly, and relatedly, human beings are not uni-dimensional; the ways in which they experience the world derive both directly and indirectly, consciously and unconsciously, from their socio-historical experiences. Although cultures perhaps in-evitably become transmuted across time and space, as memory 'traces' of past experiences, the cultural histories of peoples nevertheless and, however subliminally, continue to influence at different levels, the shaping of their subjectivities, needs and aspirations within everyday life. Mean-ings thus evolve dialogically in relation to society, culture and the individual. That is to say, although we recall past experiences individually we do so to the social world and it is ultimately in terms of that social world that we can understand and name our individual experiences. As is argued by Todorov (1984: x) 'culture consists in the discourses retained by collective memory (the commonplaces and stereotypes just as much as the exceptional words), discourses in relation to which every uttering subject must situate himself or herself'. This chapter explores the ways in which this organic and complex interweaving of 'past-present' (Bhabha 1994: 7) experience provides continuity, coherence and cohesion to what is, from the outside, often seen as a fragmented and alienated social experience.

CONCEPTUALIZING 'BLACK IDENTITIES'

'Black' identities therefore are not fixed states of 'being'; they are continually being shaped in their everyday interaction with the social world and thus they are flexible and engaged in a constant, reflexive, process of 'becoming'. The concept of reflexivity used here derives from Giddens' (1991) view of individuals' intentional use of knowledge of the social world in the re-ordering of the 'self' in relation to that reality. Cultural hybridity constitutes a key variable within this process of self-definition and, as is discussed below, it does not necessarily signify an unproblematic incorporation into the dominant culture. The notion of cultural hybridity is complex and can be viewed on different levels. At surface level, it refers to the reality that in an ongoing quest for rootedness within a society so fundamentally hostile to their presence, black people continually have to adapt, adjust and change their cultures, customs, behaviours, expectations, aspirations and cultural consciousness in order to 'belong' socially as well as to identify culturally and politically with the dominant culture. As will be seen later, this process takes place within a context of struggle, conflict, contradiction and ambiguity. At the same time, minority cultures by their very presence challenge the socially constructed 'homogeneity' of national cultures from within by changing expectations, behaviours and experiences of and within everyday life (Massey 1994). Moreover, within the context of the nation-state, minority cultures also create their own cultural space within which they can express their needs and suffuse society with a plurality of dissenting political voices articulating demands that often conflict with and/or challenge the hegemony of ethnic-nationalism. In this regard, their impact on the dominant culture can be viewed as being, intrinsically, counter-hegemonic.

However, analyses of different 'black' experiences and the shaping of 'black identities' in Britain cannot lose sight of the reality that racism is materially grounded. And, in terms of this, the notion of cultural pluralism as defined within the metropolitan nation-state, ultimately remains rooted in historically derived (unequal) power relations. Analyses of the social and self-construction of 'black identities' therefore cannot be examined within a de-historicized and de-politicized theory of cultural difference. Neither can the concept of cultural hybridization be addressed unproblematically in terms of the historical 'inevitability' of a globalized culture. To do so would be to ignore the materiality of historical forms of domination and control – and thus would run the risk not only of marginalizing black people's experiences but, indeed, to collude in the legitimation of their structured exclusion.

The notions of cultural hybridity and cultural differences then cannot be addressed in a politically meaningful way outside an analysis of societal racism and the impact of this on the everyday experiences of different generations of black people living in Britain.

REMEMBERING THE PAST: EXPLORING
INTERTEXTUAL MEANINGS

In South Africa, where I have my cultural and political roots, Apartheid oppressed black men and women, making them 'acquiescent' by silencing their voices – and thus sought to render them invisible. Part of that 'culture of silence' (Freire 1972) follows the exile across time and space as historical experiences become interlocked with other forms of oppression within a different society. It is in this sense that the 'past-present' (Bhabha 1994: 7) is inextricably woven into the text of everyday living. Finding a 'home' within the adoptive country then becomes a journey of learning to understand past experiences in order to clarify the present – and from that position of knowledge to find a voice – and, more importantly, to define a future. Learning to make sense of the complexity of my own socio-historical and cultural legacy led me to consider other subjugated histories and the complexity of other experiences. This, it was hoped, would allow me to identify common themes within our experiences and also to explore differences. Todorov (1984: x), in his exposition of Bakhtin's concept of dialogism or intertextuality, states that 'all discourse is in dialogue with prior discourses on the same subject, as well as with discourses yet to come, whose reactions it foresees and anticipates. A single voice can make itself heard only by blending into the complex choir of other voices already in place.' Listening to different voices articulating different experiences and exploring interconnections thus holds out the possibility of synthes-izing what may appear to be otherwise discrete experiences – and in the process perhaps yield a different, multi-faceted and mutli-layered under-standing of the construction of 'black identities' in Britain.

FRAMING THE SUBJECT

I locate my overall analysis within Giddens' view that although 'structures are produced by interactions that are constantly in the process of repro-ducing the overall characteristics of society; that such reproductions are not exact' (Giddens quoted in Ackroyd 1994: 291) – that they are subject to change through human action. Located within this context, the life histories of the women documented here will be presented in their own voices. That is to say, they will articulate their own understandings of how they have historically been constituted as subjects and of their social experiences. They will also describe the strategies that they have adopted consciously as agents of change within the context of their everyday living.

Adopting this framework should enable the participants' thoughts, experiences and actions to be placed at the centre of my analysis and thus allow their experiences to be articulated from a position of what Pecheux (1982) calls *dis-identification*. That is to say, rather than being regarded as passive recipients of racism, sexism and structural oppression, 'black' women are presented as engaging in an ongoing process of working 'on and against prevailing ideological practices in which black and gendered subjection are constructed' (Rassool 1995: 24). Such a position places emphasis on both personal and political agency as key elements within a politics of self-identification, self-definition and self-actualization which, in turn, are consciously linked to broader struggles and resistances against prevailing and historically oppressive practices.

Self-identification, in this instance, refers to the cognitive re-appropriation of the categories of racialized and genderized subjugation and the process of encoding these with empowering meanings as part of the struggle to gain control over their lives. Self-identity within this context then does not denote a fixed state of being but rather signifies a continuous process of 'becoming'. This refers to the discursive 'self' as is 'routinely created and sustained in the reflexive activities of the individual' (Giddens 1991: 52) and, in addition to this, the dialogical relationship in which the conscious self exists with the social and material world.

Self-definition, on the other hand, places emphasis on the affective and describes gendered and racialized subjects as they are engaged in an ongoing process of critique, negotiation, self-affirmation and validation of themselves in relation to their particular experience within society. As will become evident later, this process, by implication, involves social and cultural hybridization fundamentally as a survival strategy. Again, this is not to argue that hybridization is a neutral process since it also speaks of the conflict, contradictions and ambivalences in which the 'fractured self' exists within a society in which the concept of 'Britishness' has historically been defined in terms of an ethnic and cultural 'norm'.

In foregrounding 'experience' in this way I adhere to Probyn's (1993: 18) view that 'while experience describes the everyday, or "the way of life" it is also the key to analyzing the relations that construct that reality'. Speaking the 'self' in this way then is not to revert to forms of essentialism but effectively allows these women to explore the constitution of their life-experiences in relation to broader socio-political, historical and cultural processes.

USING ORAL HISTORY

Methodologically the study can be conceived of as a form of 'people's history' (Samuel 1981: xvi). In particular, it deals with the recovery of subjective experience which, in turn, is articulated within participants' maps of knowledge of the social world. Placing the 'remembered past' thus at the centre of analysis, the study draws experientially on the 'self-narratives' (Giddens 1991) of the focus group which comprises four women representing perspectives from different black diasporas. This includes an articulation of the Afro-Caribbean experience and contains a view of their history of slavery and social displacement; an Iraqi-Kurd speaks from the perspective of a refugee from political oppression whilst the South African 'black' experience in exile represents a view of neo-colonialist experience. The fourth participant provides the perspective of an Afro-Indian refugee following Kenya's expulsion policy during the 1960s.

The unifying factor amongst this apparently disparate group of women is the central role that colonialism/neo-colonialism, diaspora, ethnic 'Otherness' and the development of a cultural hybridity have played in the shaping of their subjectivities, hopes, dreams and aspirations – and how these have influenced their lived experiences within the host society. Their experiences, although not representative of the 'black' female experience as a whole in Britain, within the context of the study, serve primarily as a concrete referent around which the concept of a multi-facted British 'black' identity can be articulated. For the purpose of this exploratory study then the chosen focus group represents complexity of experience, a variety of subjugated histories whilst the limited number of participants featured in the study allows in-depth analysis to take place.

The voice of the individual speaking subject is central to this analysis which derives from oral historians who argue that 'people are not stamped into place by history and culture, but patch together a place for themselves . . . in personal statements, we see the power of the individual to compose the terms of [her] life' (Modell 1983: 11). In providing individuals with 'cultural space' from which to reflect upon and speak about how they perceive their identities – and why they have been constituted as gendered and racialized subjects – it is hoped to crystallize aspects of the multi-faceted and multi-levelled forms of oppression that constitute the 'black' British experience in the 1990s. Situating themselves in relation to the historical discourses that have structured their lives, their accounts, at meta-level, also serve as an attempt to understand the nature of post-colonial society. In order to do so, respondents needed to be able to articulate the complexity of their experiences within the wider context of socio-cultural and historical relations. I selected a group of professional black women who have a grounding in concepts used in the social sciences and also have a politicized view of the world. The inclusion of these criteria, it was hoped, would enable the discussion to take place within a context of shared understandings and, more importantly, to minimize the power disparities between interviewer and interviewee.

Harding (1987: 7) argues the importance for researchers to place themselves within the 'same critical plane' as those interviewed and that the assumptions, beliefs and frame of reference used in the research need to be clarified. In doing so, those studied are treated 'as subjects of their experiences rather than as objects of research' (quoted Chase and Bell

1994: 64). They argue further that 'when we treat those we study as subjects – as active knowers and agents – we transform the research relationship. We open ourselves to interaction, to intersubjectivity, to others under-standings of and relations to us as researchers' (ibid.). Respondents were contacted in person which allowed the nature and purpose of the study to be explained. They were then provided with a copy of a previous article written by me on a related subject plus a copy of the set questions prepared for the interviews. Respondents were thus given the opportunity to acquaint themselves with the nature of the issues to be raised in discussion – and presented with an example of how their views would be represented. It also provided them with an understanding of the frame of reference within which their views would be presented. Interviewees were informed that the interview would last for approximately two hours. On the basis of this, they could decide whether they wished to participate in the project.

Semi-structured interviews were chosen as these allow the interviewer to focus on issues of particular importance to the research question whilst also giving the participants freedom to explore those issues relevant to their experience – within a structured framework. This internal negoti-ation of what can be said and discussed at length removes a rigid adherence to the set questions and therefore 'what should be said'. Again, providing the participants with a sense of relative autonomy and control during the interview process helps to equalize power relations within the context of discussion. Moreover, whilst doing research into people's lived and personal experiences can often be cathartic to the interviewees, it can also become a traumatic experience in which painful, sublimated, emo-tions can be re-opened. Similarly, during the interview the interviewees may reveal more personal information than they had intended. These variables clearly highlight the importance of sensitivity, maturity and sensibility on the part of the researcher – who should listen to people and respect their subjects' interpretation of reality and history and not exploit deep-felt experiences in a voyeuristic manner. The questions were open-ended and structured along thematic lines focusing on the interviewees' perceptions of history, culture, experiences and self-defining strategies.

INTERNALIZED RACISM AND THE COLONIAL EXPERIENCE

The overall emphasis on British 'black' identity in the chapter derives from the fact that all the women interviewed expressed the opinion that societal oppression impacted on their lived reality first in racial terms. Indeed, it is within the historical discourse of 'race' that black family life has become pathologized and notions of black female 'passivity' and 'powerlessness' as well as the stereotype of black women's sexuality have been hegemon-ized in the metropolitan consciousness. In terms of this, they are excluded from power first because they are 'black'. However, racism is not a clear-cut and linear issue. Within both colonialism and neo-colonialism, group and individual subjectivities developed within relations of overt domination and subordination between oppressors and oppressed. These oppressions were multi-levelled and divided communities along 'race', class and ethnic lines – and in the case of Indian culture generally, also included divisions of caste, language and religion. Within these contexts, women existed as non-essential elements at the outer-periphery of society. These forms of separatism, subjugation and exclusion were reinforced by the divide-and-rule policies of colonialism. Moreover, according to Hall (1993: 396):

> The ways in which black people, black experiences, were positioned and subject-ed in the dominant regimes of representation were the effects of a critical exercise of cultural power and normalisation. Not only ... were we constructed as different and other within the categories of knowledge of the West by those regimes. They had the power to make us see and experience ourselves as 'Other'.

Indeed, the success of colonialist policy was the internalization of racialized identities which, in turn, contributed to the development of an inverted racism amongst oppressed social groups themselves. These social relations of colonialism have been perpetuated in post-colonial Britain where in different ways they have continued to shape the consciousness of black immigrant groups. Racisms operating at surface level are revealed in day-to-day encounters. One interviewee stated that:

> At school I remember my friend, Rana who is a British-born Pakistani calling her own friends 'Paki' and I laid into her for doing that. Also, my friend Sally whose father was a Ghanaian used to be called 'Kizzy' from the film 'Roots'- often also by her own black friends.

At a deeper level, one of the interviewees argued of the Caribbean experience:

> There is still a lot of resistance and hostility towards African people and there are many reasons for this: part of Western culture is about fostering divisions and hostilities amongst people from the diaspora ... so they do re-inforce this view that we don't have anything in common with each other ... and many of us are so desperate to belong, to be accepted, to have roots ... that we collude with these racist views. Also, being distanced from our African roots historically and having been socialized as colonial subjects have contributed to these negative attitudes towards African people. I think that much of this has been shaped around feelings of self-hate which – again is a left-over of the slave experience.

These forms of inverted racism, sexism and other forms of internalized oppressions highlight the fact that the 'black' British experience is fundamentally constituted in difference and, moreover, that it is riven with inner contradictions, 'racial' tensions and inter-ethnic group discrimination. Therefore, although white racism is structural and institutionalized we, nevertheless, cannot adopt a 'purist' view of racism because we are 'black'. hooks (1991: 31) stresses the importance of the need 'to confront the enemy within' which means a critical self-evaluation as well as working towards transforming female consciousness. She states that: 'Working together to expose, examine, and eliminate sexist socialization within ourselves, women would strengthen and affirm one another and build a solid foundation for developing political solidarity' (hooks 1991: 3). This, it can be argued, should also be extended to include a critical examination of racist socialization which needs to be grounded in an understanding of the complex ways in which our subjectivities have been shaped historically. One of the interviewees highlighted the need for a critical evaluation of disempowering and subjugating cultural practices within the community:

> I find the physical and emotional abuse that people within the community operate very distressing ... and my experience of that still lingers ... this business of authoritarianism ... beating children as opposed to negotiating with them, which to me is one of the most negative aspects of Caribbean life ... it still lingers as part of that whole slave experience ... an oppressive experience which we perpetuate rather than address critically. Then there is the male–female relationship ... although universal, it is also oppressive within Caribbean culture ... Our men carry with them their historical oppressions which they use to oppress women and children. I find that very difficult to understand, because Caribbean women are traditionally very strong ... we have tended to be mothers, fathers, providers yet we somehow seem to leave that aside and operate in victim-mode in our relationships with our men ... many Caribbean women still subscribe to that kind of behaviour.

This view highlights the fact that we need to acknowledge the subjugating practices within our own communities and to work actively against their reproduction; important are the ways in which we silence ourselves as well as the ways in which we undermine one another as women.

SKIN COLOUR, RACISM AND EXCLUSION

For a large section of black people in Britain, notably those who migrated from the Caribbean, India and countries in Africa, the diasporic experience originated within the 'master/mistress'–servant relations of colonialism.

As argued earlier, these relations are perpetuated within the metropolitan society where they form part of the nation's hegemonic consciousness. In their quest to belong many black people have tried different strategies in order to minimize their differences. The Afro-Caribbean interviewee stated that:

> I consciously changed my accent because I felt so traumatized by comments such as 'Nigger, Nigger, pull the trigger, Bang ! Bang! Bang!' Although in St Lucia I was regarded as a bright pupil, here they sent me to a remedial class because of my dialect ... after a long period of destructive rebellion I internalized my feelings and changed my speech register in order to belong.

The Kenyan interviewee arrived here later in life and had to change her accent because:

> I was teaching in an inner city school – and although the kids there all spoke non-standard varieties of English, they would nevertheless roar with laughter whenever I did not place the accents in the right places in words. I had to survive as a teacher and therefore learned to adapt my speech.

Having a middle-class accent and speaking Standard English did not help the third interviewee who stated that:

> My friends used to ask me 'Did you have elocution lessons, how come you speak like that?' They also used to say, 'You're just like a white person'. But although I was popular, well-liked, I was never invited to their homes ... I was never included in the group. As a result, I consciously developed a negative attitude towards belonging to groups ... still today, I don't have that sense of belonging. Speaking 'posh' did not prevent my fourth year History teacher from making racist remarks such as 'Oh, Selma doesn't need to worry, she won't get a black eye' ... But I wouldn't let them get away without challenging them ... maybe they saw me as this 'Paki' upstart ... I didn't care, I had to protect and assert myself. I've made my difference a strength but yet it was also a hurdle in terms of making friendships, building relationships ... two extremes to be reconciled.

These statements highlight conflict, ambiguity and compromise as intrinsic elements of the *process* of self-identification.

SELF-DEFINITION: DISPLACEMENT AND THE SEARCH FOR ROOTS

Experiences of marginalization thus for many create the need for a 'search for the self' which involves a critical examination of historical discourses of 'Otherness' and social exclusion – and within that process the subjects in a reflexive process of 'self-definition'. This integration of experience and social knowledge, according to the Popular Memory Group (1982: 240) can serve 'as a basis for larger understandings, for the deepening of progressive knowledge and for active political involvement' – a process which often requires a conscious re-assertion of previously sub-jugated histories as a form of cultural self-determination. As can be seen below, what emerges is a politicized identity. One of the respondents stated that although she locates her history within a Caribbean register she, nevertheless, regards herself as an African who was born in the Caribbean:

> I describe myself as African ... my name was Susan Jones and I never really liked that name. I changed my name by deed poll (to a Nigerian name) when I was about 30 after a lot of soul searching ... working on some rather painful issues around identity and alliances. I decided that I was very proud of being an African woman despite the fact that I was born within the diaspora. It took me a long time to come to terms with the fact that I was not culturally inferior to African people who were born on the Home Continent. I no longer wanted a European name tag.

Her conflict around cultural identity relates very directly to Caribbean emigres' search for 'rootedness'; a sense of historical 'belonging'. This, in turn, relates to their historical experience of social displacement and rootlessness grounded in the slave experience and colonization. For this interviewee, as is the case for many other Caribbeans and also African-Americans, 'Africa is the name of the missing term, the great aporia, which lies at the centre of (Caribbean) cultural identity and gives it a meaning which, until recently, it lacked' (Hall 1993: 394). In this particular instance, choosing to identify as a Caribbean rather than as a 'West Indian' or 'Black British' also constitutes a powerful means of dis-identifying with the host culture which is experienced fundamentally as being hostile. In response to this, the interviewee argued further that: 'You identify yourself as being different, being special from those around you because you need some-thing positive to hold onto.' Speaking from a different socio-historical experience, another expressed a similar view. She stated that:

> I've never really identified myself as British because you're always asked where you're from and they don't want to hear that you're from Plymouth or London, but your country of origin. Only in my adult years have I started to accept the role of Britain in my life. As a child I needed to hold on to being a black South African because I so desperately needed to belong somewhere. And I knew that they didn't want me to belong here because they always called me 'Paki' and I hated that. In

asserting that I was a black South African, I somehow felt morally superior and this provided me with tremendous strength.

Again, this self 'Othering' relates to her historical experience as an ethnicized 'Asian' in Apartheid South Africa where the concept of *eiesoortigheid* ('ethnic purity') had provided the basis of neo-colonialist divide-and-rule policy. Within that context, the disenfranchized identified very strongly as 'black' South Africans, as part of the struggle to fracture the racialized categories of hierarchized ethnicities. Faced with racism here in Britain, this interviewee's response was to revert to that self-defining concept of 'blackness'.

It could be argued that both these women responded to their situation in this particular way *because* of their particular historical experiences. And, rather than accept the disempowered social status accorded to them within the host society, they sought to displace and transform subjugated identities through a process of self-identification structured within dominant ideological discourses (Macdonell 1987) and thus they could, on an individual level, engage in praxis. Yet, whilst for the one, the change in name signifies her adoption of a permanent identity in relation to her African roots, for the other, the situation is more complex. Although she has retained her identity as a 'black' South African it has become less tangible because she argued that:

As I've grown older that identity has become more transparent because I came here when I was 4 years old – and my South African experience has largely been through others . . . through hearsay. All my formative years have been spent here in England and some aspects of that identity have been altered . . . . and I have to acknowledge and accommodate that.

She went on to argue that:

As Left Internationalists our family did not really belong to any specific community and I still retain that worldview . . . but it brings me into conflict with myself . . . people always want to define me as an 'Asian' and when I contradict them, they regard it as some form of self-denial . . . but it isn't. My life has been shaped by different cultural and political influences . . . I cannot now opt for cultural or ethnic labels that we have fought against so vigorously in the struggle against Apartheid. But I find that the world, including the 'British Asians', still want to classify you into neat ethnic categories and I cannot accept that. They also expect me to behave like an 'Asian' woman . . . I don't know what that really means. I am a Black South African and will always identify myself as that, but there are also other aspects of my life here that are important to me. I need to acknowledge that. I need to find my place within this society and I cannot do so as a victim.

POLITICIZED 'BLACK' IDENTITIES

In their quest to belong, others have tried to assimilate into British culture and, in the process, have lost their own cultural identity. One interviewee expressed the view that many of the first generation have:

> adopted not only British culture, but white British values and politics. I think that many of them have picked the worst of white working-class culture . . . and some very negative aspects of Black American culture . . . they have accepted the victim-like status. In this regard they have lost sense of their history and culture – and in the process, gained nothing but alienation . . . they still don't really belong. But there are others, those of my generation who have done well educationally and pro-fessionally because we set ourselves apart from the population – we identify as Afro-Caribbeans rather than to accept the 'West Indianism' bestowed on us by our colonial masters.

A similar understanding was reflected in another interviewee who argued that:

> My family's history of South Africa and especially their willingness to discuss it with me, to help me put things into perspective, fortified me as a child. It was also important to have that perspective of Left Internationalism . . . of having a world perspective and to define struggle in terms of humanity.

She added that:

> I always needed to know where I stood in terms of where I was living and identifying as a black South African helped me perhaps because I was different and couldn't be lumped in with the Indian stereotype . . . but maybe my denial of Indianness was a way of trying to be accepted on different terms by the whites. There was certainly a dual thing going on there. When my parents tried to integrate us with the Muslim community, I found that I had very little in common with them . . . I didn't understand, nor did I believe. Because my parents were secularist I didn't have any previous history of being a Muslim . . . as a result, I integrated more with British culture. . . . although I value the inclusiveness of my black South African heritage.

The Iraqi Kurd interviewee, when asked what she identifies as in Britain, stated that she does so strongly as a 'black' person:

> I do so because I'm excluded from British society because of my colour. Culturally I identify as a Kurd . . . a displaced person. I feel that I cannot identify with being an Iraqi because of what that regime is doing to my people.

The Kenyan, on the other hand, argued that:

When I think about my life now, I have lived it all as the 'Other' here and in Kenya. My life as a human being ... being able to live my life with dignity now means much more to me than being part of any particular ethnic group. I want power and control over my own life not an ethnic label. I belong to the world and if it so happens that a significant part of that world rejects me because I am black and undermines me as a woman then that is where the struggle lies. I'm not fighting with myself anymore ... I'm quite comfortable and happy about who I am. For many 'Asians', their identity is bound up very singularly with their religion rather than looking at themselves within a broader societal context, their relationship with this society, where they stand in relation to it, what their roles are ...

Again, these examples serve to illustrate that rather than constituting a unitary and linear variable the 'black' British experience is grounded in social and geographical discontinuities, cultural and social differences, diversity in terms of historical experience, cultural hybridity – and also, significantly, fractured identities existing in conflict with themselves within the context of a 'norm-oriented' society. Thus rather than representing ethnic or racial absolutism, British 'black' identity constitutes a discursive, polyvalent variable. That is to say, it does not represent a statically determined state of being; in its ongoing contact with British culture it is always in the process of becoming.

CULTURAL HYBRIDITY

Hall (1993: 394) argues that:

Cultural identities come from somewhere, have histories. But, like everything which is historical, they undergo constant transformation. Far from being eternally fixed in some essentialist past, they are subject to the continuous 'play' of history, culture and power ... identities are the names we give to the different ways we are positioned by, and position ourselves within, the narratives of the past.

The interviewee born in Kenya highlighted the complex dilemmas that this socially constructed identity has created for her:

Both my grandfathers came from India. The one married a German woman, the other a local African woman. Because mothers tended to be the main ones to rear their children, both my parents had strong influences from their mothers and therefore had no real 'Indian' identities. . . . We grew up as Kenyans ... and I identify very strongly with that. . . . when we were growing up in Kenya the Indians there did not really want to know us because we were not 'pure'. Here in Britain the assumption, (especially by the Asians) is that I am 'Asian' ... when

I challenge this it is assumed that I am willfully denying my cultural roots. The conflict for me lies in the fact that even if I were to accept their categorization, by colluding with what I call their 'ethnic essentialism', I am in fact denying the importance of my grandmothers and their struggles against so many different kinds of oppression – including that within the Indian community.

Although it highlights conflict, this example also illustrates the inter-connectedness of countries and continents reflected in the lives of peoples from the 'black' diaspora – carrying with it, the evolution of a trans-continental cultural identity; the globalization of cultural experience – not as a new phenomenon – but in generational terms across space and time. Similarly, Mama (1992: 154) argues that 'Black women's experiences and struggles, apart from being rooted in so many different contexts are further complicated by the varying penetrations by and relations with British society.' In Mama's terms, and as is evident in the interviews above, fragmentation, cultural hybridity and flexibility of the concept of self-identity – defined within a conscious and unconscious 'past-presentness' (Bhabha 1994: 7) – can be seen as being intrinsic to individual survival within the black diasporic experience. Cultural hybridity then can be seen as having been intrinsic to how life has been lived by ethnic minority groups within different societies during various historical periods and, as such, it constitutes a signifier of cultural change across time and space. However, its success in terms of political empowerment remains debatable as is highlighted here by one of the interviewees:

I don't deny British cultural influences that have been positive . . . for many years I felt very insecure about my identity so I rejected them . . . I no longer do so . . . they are very much part of what I am now. But I don't identify with British culture where it encourages dividing or separating ourselves from each other. Although they imply or state that we were born here and therefore need to identify as Britons, in reality that's not what we experience. On the one hand we are told to distance ourselves from our cultures and become British and on the other hand, we are not accepted . . . we are rejected. Very few of them have really worked through their racist values, practices and attitudes – and can value differences. After thirty one years I still regard myself as a foreigner, as a stranger, as a guest in this country . . . I'm certainly treated in that way . . . I'm still discriminated against. Depending on the political message of the times, sometimes we belong and other times we are foreigners.

Ultimately then it would seem that the dominant, homogenizing dis-courses of societal racism remain to exclude and marginalize the collective experience of black people in Britain.

CONCLUSION: INTERTEXTUALITY, REFLEXIVITY AND CULTURAL HYBRIDITY

The important point to emerge from the study overall is that the dominant framing of discourse does not quite succeed in constituting black people as static subjects; they are actively involved in questioning, challenging and fracturing hegemonic meanings and practices within the concrete experience of everyday life. The voices of black women could be heard narrating their different experiences and describing their social reality as well as their complex struggles to gain control over their lives. Although strategies varied, their experiences of being 'Othered' and 'self-Othering' shared many similarities. Most significant was the complexity of their experiences and, particularly, the collaging of their continuously evolving identities. At the same time, the determination of the interviewees to identify as 'black' women as a position from which to articulate and transform their social experiences within contemporary British society provided the basis of their process of self-definition. This analysis illustrates the ways in which focusing on individual and group action within particular arenas of struggle enables exploration of not only affective aspects of self-definition but also provides opportunity to examine the discursive ways in which these connect with systemic and hegemonic variables of racial, gender and class oppression. The processes of subjectification (Bhabha 1994) could thus be explored concretely through the lives of the women who participated in this study.

The accounts of these women have provided evidence also of the fact that in the process of defining themselves in relation to their social world, black women (and men) use history and engage in cultural dialogue and critique; that they are all part of a community of discourse (Grele 1985). The extent to which these women drew on their understandings of their histories, the 'memory traces' of past collective experiences, serves to illustrate the importance of intertextuality as a variable in understanding the shaping of the 'fractured self' historically. At the same time, it also highlights the inner coherence that the ability to draw meaningfully from the past provides to the reflexive process of political self-identification.

Their life histories also illustrate that the ongoing process of self-definition necessarily involves some measure of cultural hybridization as an integral part of survival within a society shaped around the notion of an ethnically homogeneous 'norm'. This organic process of change bears out the point made earlier that 'black identities' are not linear social constructions; they represent richly textured cultural and historical tapestries that continue to evolve within the concrete reality of everyday life. At the same time, their individual experiences also concretized the point that cultural hybridization often creates conflict and contains ambiguities and contradictions for the individual in terms of the racist realities of the social world. This multi-levelled and multi-faceted process of confrontation, compromise and self-empowerment highlights the complex and problematic inter-relationship between historical experience, socialization and individual struggles in the breaking down of historically derived racist and gendered structures within society. Nevertheless, in participating in this counter-hegemonic discourse, the self-defining strengths reflected in the lives of the women documented here have managed, at least to some extent, to fracture the 'power and pervasiveness of historical representations' (Popular Memory Group 1982: 207) of black women in contemporary Britain.

REFERENCES

Ackroyd, S. (1994) 'Recreating Common Ground: Elements for Post-paradigmatic Organisation Studies' in J. Hassard and M. Parker (eds) *Towards a New Theory of Organisation*, London: Routledge.

Appadurai, A. (1993) 'Disjuncture and Difference in the Global Cultural Economy' in P. Williams and L. Chrisman (eds.) *Colonial Discourse and Post-Colonial Theory: A Reader*, London: Harvester Wheatsheaf, pp. 324–39.

Aziz, R. (1995) 'Feminism and the Challenge of Racism: Deviance or Difference?' in H. Crowley and S. Himmelweit (eds) *Knowing Women: Feminism and Knowledge*, Cambridge: Polity Press in association with The Open University, pp. 291–305.

Berktay, F. (1993) 'Looking from the "Other" Side: Is Cultural Relativism a Way Out?' in J. De Groot and M. Maynard (eds) *Women's Studies in the 1990s: Doing Things Differently?* Basingstoke: Macmillan, pp. 110–31.

Bhabha, H. (1994) *The Location of Culture*, London: Routledge.

Chase, S.E. and Bell, S.L. (1994) 'Interpreting the Complexity of Women's Subjectivity' in E. M. McMahan and K. Lacy Rogers (eds) *Interactive Oral History Interviewing*, Hillsdale, New Jersey and Hove, UK: Lawrence Erlbaum Associates, pp. 63–82.

Freire, P. (1972) *Pedagogy of the Oppressed*, London: Penguin.

Giddens, A. (1991) *Modernity and Self-Identity: Self and Society in the Late Modern Age*, Cambridge: Polity Press.

Grele, R. (1985) 'Private Memories and Public Presentation: The Art of Oral History', *International Journal of Oral History*, vol. 6, no.1, pp. 243–83.

Hall, S. (1993) 'Cultural Identity and Diaspora' in P. Williams and L. Chrisman (eds) *Colonial Discourse and Post-Colonial Theory: A Reader*, London: Harvester Wheatsheaf, pp. 392–403.

Harding, S. (1987) 'Is there a Feminist Theory?' in S. Harding (ed.) *Feminism and Methodology*, Bloomington: Indiana University Press, pp. 1–14.

hooks, b. (1989) *Talking Back: Thinking Feminist – Thinking Black*, Boston, London: Sheba Feminist Publishers.

hooks, b. (1991) 'Sisterhood: Political Solidarity Between Women' in S. Gunew (ed.) *A Reader In Feminist Knowledge*, London: Routledge.

Macdonell, D. (1987) *Theories of Discourse: An Introduction*, Oxford: Basil Blackwell.

Mama, A. (1992) 'Black Women, The Economic Crisis and the British State' in M. Humm (ed.) *Feminisms: A Reader*, New York, London: Harvester Wheatsheaf, pp. 151–5.

Massey, D. (1994) *Space, Place and Gender*, Cambridge: Polity Press.

Modell, J. (1983) 'Stories and Strategies: The Use of Personal Statements', *International Journal of Oral History*, vol. 4, no. 1, pp. 4–11.

Pecheux, M. (1982) *Language, Semantics and Ideology*, translated by Harbans Nagpal, Basingstoke: Macmillan.

Popular Memory Group (1982) 'Popular Memory: Theory, Politics, Method' in *Making Histories*, London: Hutchinson University Library in association with Centre of Contemporary Cultural Studies, University of Birmingham.

Probyn, E. (1993) *Sexing the Self: Gendered Positions in Cultural Studies*, London: Routledge.

Rassool, N. (1995) 'Black Women as the "Other" in the Academy' in L. Morley and V. Walsh (eds) *Feminist Academics: Creative Agents for Change*, Basingstoke: Taylor and Francis, pp. 8–22.

Samuel, R. (1981) 'People's History' in R. Samuel (ed.) *People's History and Socialist Theory*, London: Routledge, pp. xvii–xviii.

Todorov, T. (1984) *Mikhail Bakhtin: The Dialogical Principle*, translated by Wlad Godzich, Manchester: Manchester University Press.

Chapter 17

In my father's house are many mansions

The nation and postcolonial desire[1]

Nalini Persram

> She is condemned to 'psychosis', or at best 'hysteria', for lack . . . of
> a valid signifier for her 'first' desire.
>
> (Irigaray 1991: 411)

> Autobiography is often a search for coherence and explanation [yet] we
> are strangers to ourselves.
>
> (Duncker 1992: 56)[2]

As far back as I can remember, I loved to watch old black and white war
movies with my dad, and still do. But the colours rubbed off on me, and
for a long time, I viewed the issues without shades. When I was 10 years
old, my dream was to feed the starving people of the world. It took
another two decades for me to realize that both black and white cultures
had been starved by empire. I remember the day when I became
coloured.[3] The image in the mirror at the age of 15 told me for the first
time that I was the product of a black[4] father and a white mother. At the
threshold of 20, the world was my oyster, but the stones were not pearls.

DISLOCATION

Place

We moved to Canada from Guyana because the political situation had
reached intolerable dimensions. Riots, burnings, lootings and threats
were beginning to take their toll on the Guyanese. Burnham had ruled
the country with a racist, dictatorial hand and we were part of the mass
exodus of people, particularly East Indians, who began leaving at the
end of the 1960s.

The usual plethora of questions – where was I from, what language
did I speak and was I a red Indian? (my two long black braids were
always cause for some concern) – were innocuous enough, coming from
children my own age, just simple curiosity. Race was not an issue. But
it was always there – to be exoticized, used abusively once in a while in

the form of 'Paki' or 'redskin', or to entertain through tales of the jungle, exotic animals, and, of course, my pet snake (a fabrication that none the less provoked the desired response).

Then my cousin showed up. She had accompanied her parents on a visit from Georgetown to see Guyanese relatives in Canada, but quickly found herself an unexpectedly permanent member of our family. Whilst my uncle and aunt were in Canada, Burnham had announced mandatory military service for all Guyanese schoolchildren. Spawned by years of racial tension, rumours had begun about the rape of Indian girls by members of the predominantly Afro-Guyanese military and my aunt and uncle were advised by a friend in Guyana to leave their daughter in Canada with relatives. So, at the tender age of 11, quite literally plucked from her home, she was left behind and bewildered in a place she would never learn to call home.

By 1992, there were approximately 19 million refugees in search of political asylum (*Guardian* 1993: 20). That is a lot of outsiders. Edward Said observes that one's self-consciousness as an outsider allows a comprehension of how the inside works, given that one's distance from it offers a better view of its contours (Said 1986: 49). But there is a price for this privilege.

If the nation represents the epitome of universal legitimacy in contemporary politics (Anderson 1991: 3), what Paul Gilroy describes as cultural insiderism is a series of rhetorical strategies in which the ideas of nation, nationality, national belonging, and nationalism are marked by a fundamental sense of ethnic difference.[5] Linked to some of the most powerful cultural kinship values, it assumes a sovereignty over all other forms of social and historical experience, cultures, and identities (Gilroy 1993: 8, 3). In this instance ethnicity, and all its associated indicators of identity – race, colour, culture – becomes intimately related to politico-territorial definitions of place, conceived both geographically and anthropologically. 'Nationalism, like patriarchy, favours singleness – one identity, one growth pattern, one birth and blood for all' (Boehmer 1991: 7). Thus, where one is from constitutes the determining factor in how far one's people have progressed.

RACE AND GENDER

Race did then become an issue. Being dark and with a 'funny' accent (and far ahead pubescently of everyone else), my cousin was subjected to horrendous mistreatment by her new classmates. Moreover, being extremely intelligent, but also from a British colonial education system, she was placed a year higher than her age would have suggested, which was nevertheless a year lower than suited her academically. Concerns about her social development had warranted a measured response to academic placement. Nevertheless, her obvious intelligence was exercised at the mercy of racism's forked tongue of jealousy and intimidation.

I watched what happened. We were good friends, but I was not about to go through the same ordeal. What had begun, in my case, as humorous speculations about how many cows my father had traded me for turned into something much more sinister. Gender, the most salient, available and subversive weapon at my disposal became the protection against racism. The simultaneous conformity to social stereotypes of femininity and the refusal to entertain the idea of femaleness as victimage resulted in a strategy designed to contain or limit abuse directed at my femininity, and by extension, my 'race'. I adopted a set of manoeuvres marked by an unconscious acceptance that the act of appeasing white males and gaining respect would only come by acknowledging that it was a (white) man's world; masculist roles and values would inhibit racial and sexist abuse and at the same time guarantee legitimacy and success. Black skin, white masks; female body, masculist armour.

Some would call this a feminist strategy. But feminism to me was mere hysterics, all about unstable or militant females. 'Women' itself was a dirty word. In my experience, female solidarity was about as meaningful as the forced intimacy of the girl's toilet. And why not? As far as I could see, the male gaze provoked female exhibitionism. Furthermore, my own attempts at conformity to the feminine ideal, which neutralized politics and turned insults into flattery, were what was allowing me to keep my head above water. Other strategies were much more painful, as the Jewish girl sitting next to me who refused to show deference to the enemy quickly found out. She was mercilessly persecuted. (But I have no doubts as to whose integrity remained more intact.)

The masculist subject is the author of meaning. More accurately, patriarchy has positioned the masculine subject as dominant within a globally consistent (culturally specific articulations notwithstanding) system of masculist social values. Gender, that specific system of values that hierarchically structures males and females into recognizable roles surrounding the economy of reproduction, informs nationalism. As Benedict Anderson, author of that highly seductive account of nationalism, *Imagined Communities*, asserts, modernity entails the imperative that 'everyone can, should, will "have" a nationality, as he or she "has" a gender' (Anderson 1991: 3).

With the rise of the bourgeoisie and the emergence of the middle-class family unit coincided a productive relationship between patriarchies in the domesticities of the nation-state, a development that characterized the emergence of nationalism. But if patriarchy was the ideological means of establishing the dominance of men over women, it nevertheless relied on the reification, as well as the subordination, of the concept of the feminine in order to sustain itself. One of the ironies of this historical social construction, notes Elleke Boehmer, is that nationalism in turn achieves legitimacy and coherence through various configurations of gender which, ideologically or politically, may bear 'a masculine identity [even] though national ideals may wear a feminine face' (Boehmer 1991: 7, 6).

Hence, England as metaphor and source of colonial paternalism was (and still is) considered 'motherland' to people from the West Indies. It is an ambivalence that has wreaked havoc with the identities of those same people who travelled from the Caribbean to the metropole, confident in their search for confirmation of who they were, as taught to them by a colonialism that boasted the success of its own civilizing mission.

DESIRE

The Nation

> Then identity. And the recognition that I had none. No secure origin, no opinion, no tangible cultural ontology. Only an unconsciously fractured individualist Self battling against a murky haze of desire.
>
> Visiting my Guyanese relatives in Toronto had always given me a feeling of belonging to something larger than myself or my immediate family. It was a community with a certain language, music, food and ritual that represented that part of my (colonized) ethnicity I remembered most. But even there I was aware that I was still half something else. Half ethnically illicit. Half colonial. I was only half home.
>
> Ireland for a semester witnessed, instead of the barrage of racist comments I had been expecting, a celebration of my colour. But it was there that the realization that I belonged to no nation, possessed no history, embodied no culture, hit me hard. When the time came to leave, it was with a great deal of kicking and screaming. Repatriated to Canada away from my vicarious existence as a European – as part of a people with a real history – I was left holding dual citizenship, but having no nation-ality.

The colonial legacy has left the imprint of history, or its absence, as the determining mark of cultural legitimacy. The experience of displacement, division and subordination within hegemonic ideologies of modernity, progress and civilization have created the conditions for counter-discourses of home, unity and self-determination based on the idea that temporal accumulation possesses the means to undermine the neo-colonial attempt at cultural imperialism through the consolidation of a collective, culturally specific consciousness. Whether it be movements in the name of the retrieval and expression of the 'native', pre- or uncolonized voice, or those claiming to achieve inter-national status in a liberal order of globalized capital, identity as an inherent quality, eternal possession or intrinsic self-worth is the weapon, sheathed or unsheathed, against alienation and delegitimization in this postcolonial era.

The political issues surrounding culture and imperialism in this century have shifted from confrontation and colonialism to independence and national integrity. The postcolonial nation has become the symbol of emancipation, sovereignty and resistance; the site of the retrieval of lost and suppressed histories, histories that have yet to be written. For Marcus Garvey, 'a nation without its past history [was] like a tree without roots' (quoted in Gilroy 1987: 207).

The dominant discourse of the nation as source of identity, destiny and liberation that prevailed during the time of decolonization struggles was one that accepted Fanon's pronouncement that

> it is national liberation which leads the nation to play its part on the stage of history. It is at the heart of national consciousness that international consciousness lives and grows. And this two-fold emerging is ultimately the source of all culture.
>
> (Fanon 1967: 199)

In Fanon's eyes, the nation expressed culture, and national consciousness was the most elaborate form of culture. The attempt by a colonized people to re-establish the sovereignty of their nation in a conscious and organized fashion constituted the most obvious and far-reaching cultural manifestation in existence. Culture depended on the support of the nation as well as the state for its existence and, in the colonial situation, culture collapsed and died. But it was not a simple matter of reviving it; retrieval involved an active struggle for freedom through which its creative potential could be unleashed (Fanon 1967: 198–9).

The narcissism of non-identity

Culture shifted from being a seduction to a commodity. Off to the south of France to try civilization. The Conservatoire kicked me out for being rude and untalented.

The existential lack of an identity, constructed through history, cultural heritage, or 'the nation' that could be expressed with others, and the absence of rituals in my life that could be identified with anything larger than the immediate family gradually became less the focal point of an on-going depression and more an issue of acceptance. Thus, the (non)being that was the longing slowly became resignation, and eventually simple reality.

Even the great narratives of human knowledge cannot answer the question why is the sky blue. The questions posed by the solitary 'I' must therefore not be the right ones. The order of things must be so if they have been so for so long. Resistance is therefore misapprehension. There are no square pegs, only round ones that haven't yet been carved. I made a decision to be content in the knowledge that, even though I would never have any direction in my life, there was indeed a 'there' there.

Simon Gikandi writes of exile that:

By distancing the subject from the idealized space of the nation, [it] also generates the desire for a compensatory national narrative – one in which the individual's longing for a unified image of the self is cast within the country's epic quest for its soul.[6]

(Gikandi 1992: 382)

Conceptualizing this in terms of migration and home, Carole Boyce Davies notes that the former creates the desire for the latter, which in turn produces its rearticulation. The displacement from one's home, resulting in either a rejection or longing for it, becomes a motivating factor in this rewriting; and home, like nationalism, can easily be conflated with a 'myth of unitary origin' (Davies 1994: 113).

DISILLUSIONMENT

Unmasking masculism

But it was in my reading of *Madame Bovary* (Flaubert 1857) that a new reality thrust itself before me. The way that Emma Bovary had curtailed her own life, and constructed a world of alienation and insanity for herself through the Romantic submission to desire in and for itself, profoundly disturbed my sense of (non)identity. And if Flaubert had cast doubt on the idea of fulfilment through desire, it would be Garcia Marquez who would manage to throw into complete crisis the still sustained secret (and not so secret) faith in the notion of linear time and cumulative progress: that is, the mutually constituted ideas of destiny and identity. If desire and destiny on the one hand putrefacted in the bourgeois bastion of European civility, in *Love in the Time of Cholera* (Garcia Marquez 1989) it proliferated in a magical hot southern landscape filled with bodies struck down by disease.

In such a world, the earth is not spherical; it does not allow for a meeting of realms on the horizon. I was now presented with the truly heretical idea that there may, in fact, not be a 'there' there. That the nation may not, after all, be the ultimate destination and source of fulfilment.

Nationalism, national consciousness, and the nation – discourses indebted to the powerful idea that the search for authenticity is fundamental to the experience of modern society as well as the modern state[7] – have ceased, for some time, to be unproblematic bases for the emancipation of the colonized. The African dilemma, for instance, was characterized by its ambivalent relationship to the actual colonial culture it attempted to resist. The most significant implication is that the achievement of decolonization was endowed with an inherently revolutionary epistemology that over-estimated the potential for emancipation offered by independence. Recent African writing has moved beyond the expression of disillusionment with the ineffectivities of independence. Recognizing that on the cultural level the new realities in many African countries necessitate a distancing from the deep oppositions – black/white, colonized/colonizer – structured by the colonial situation, this literature has begun to examine the com-plexities of neocolonialism and the inappropriateness of projecting the idea of decolonization onto the postcolonial world (Gikandi 1992: 382, 379). This move has been articulated as the problem of 'opposing a local model of essentialist culture and identity to the universalist essentialist model of cultural imperialism' (Griffiths 1992: 438).

In the case of Indian history, where there is a (legitimating) tradition extending back in time several centuries, Dipesh Chakrabarty (1992) notes that even with socialist dedication and nationalist sophistication, there remains an adherence to, or mimicry of, a certain 'modern' subject of 'European' history that is destined to dismally represent a degree of lack and failure. The construction of Europe as idealized subject ensures that other subject positions of similar dimensions never achieve comparable status. Nevertheless, if indeed Europe is a theoretical category, one that renders all other histories a matter of empirical realization that merely confirms the essentially 'European' nature of social existence (Chakrabarty 1992: 3), then the great failure of its civilization has been to not put its privileged historical position at the service of elevating humanity.[8]

These difficulties, however, do not imply that nationalism ceases to be a hegemonic discourse of identity in the postcolonial world. They indicate that its seemingly uncomplicated logic is now caught up in the forces of a global capitalism that conducts the fracturing of national populations along class and (neocolonialist) cultural lines, at the same time that national identity is a *cause célèbre* for the political project of ethno-cultural survival.

A passage to Identity

But how to know if the unmasking was not another seduction – an intellectual mantra chanted in the face of, in the place of, cultural alienation?

I had been warned that this place that was once and still remained a colony held more mystery and madness than I could ever have con-ceived. The mysticism of colour and shadow were not things I was yet ready to comprehend or master. For me, the crisis, the alienation, occurred through the practices of colour-coding and gender roles, and thus class positioning and sexual politics; those libidinal economies that structured the identities that constituted the nation.

This, moreover, not in the pallor of the great white north, but against the vivid background of my own place of birth. Desire for the nation, for a nation, blinded me and led me into the jungle. But it was not the primeval forest of origin, but a thicket of despair. Unlike Zora Neale Hurston, I felt most 'coloured' – that is, not white as well as white – when thrown against a sharp black background. Coloured skin, coloured masks. I do not understand them or their language, but, to my irritation, they seem to know me quite well.

Then Rushdie:

Outside the whale is the unceasing storm, the continual quarrel, the dialectic of history. . . . Outside the whale we see that we are all irradiated by history, we are radioactive with history and politics; we see that it can be as false to create a politics-free fictional universe as to create one in which nobody needs to work or eat or hate or love or sleep.
(Rushdie, in Said 1986: 51–2)

Gilroy (1993: 30–1) speaks of the intellectual heritage of Euro-American modernity determining the manner in which nationality is understood within black political discourse. This legacy fuels the need for acquiring an ostensibly authentic, natural, and stabilized identity, one that is almost always premised on a consciously 'racial' self whose continuity is derived from national identity. Goulbourne, on the other hand, notes that in Britain, the 'ethnicization' or 'racialization' of the West Indian has meant that the East Indian of the Caribbean is rarely perceived in terms of the former. 'He or she is slowly becoming an Asian – a category which has meaning for Britain and her empire in East and Central Africa where a milder system of apartheid than developed in South Africa existed and required there to be separate estates of Europeans, Asians and Africans as the three elements of humankind' (Goulbourne 1991: 212).

'HOME'

So on what estates, in which institutions, and through what kind of politics do we, the people with an ambiguous nationality, celebrate who we are, where we have come from, and how our origins are different but legitimate? But already the question is framed within a masculist discourse of lack. The desire for national identity is a powerful and hegemonic ideology (and thus a form of masculism) that posits the absence of a definitive nationality as a deficiency. In this way it operates as a means by which the hierarchies of power established by patriarchal Europe during the colonial era ensure their reproduction in a postcolonial space. Nevertheless, notes Homi Bhabha:

> the liminality of the western nation is the shadow of its own finitude: the colonial space [is being] played out in the imaginative geography of the metropolitan space; the repetition or return of the margin of the postcolonial migrant [serves] to alienate the holism of history.
>
> (1990: 318)

In his critique of the ontology of stasis, the Guyanese author, Wilson Harris, undermines the reduction of history to geography – that is, the nation(-state) – and its appropriation of the idea of 'home'. The process of change becomes the way in which the meaning of history and geography undergo rupture. Crumbling, a term Harris uses to describe this process,

> is affirmative. Here what crumbles is 'one's native land'. The impossibility of an origin or an original home introduces a 'process'. The continual recognition ... becomes the historical vision. The vision of history as a non-original process reveals that process itself to be the site of history.
>
> (Benjamin 1989: 83)

The authenticity of the past therefore does not produce the idea of a genuine and original past but a means by which to conceive the possibility of the past as the site of lost authenticity.[9] Like Gayatri Spivak, who articulates a feminist strategy of seizing the apparatus of value-coding and effecting changes in the meaning and thus power of language and social forms (Spivak 1990: 228), Harris attempts to subvert the ideology of the nation as home – the ultimate reservoir of identity by virtue of origin, and place – by shifting the limits of identity implied by the idea of home away from the concept of a specific place towards a notion of movement, or process.

Along a parallel path, Hélène Cixous encounters an orange in her fruit bowl and suddenly experiences a deep insight into what life is all about for her. 'The orange is a moment. Not forgetting the orange is one thing. Recalling the orange is another thing. Rejoining it is another' (Cixous 1994: 88). To live the orange is to engage with contingency so that the past is never statically familiar, the memorable never a reified icon. So that the final performance is itself always a privileged rehearsal (Harris 1989: 20).

It often takes a crisis of some sort to initiate the difficult but empowering feminist process of renegotiating the masculisms that dominate the discourses of origin, authenticity and belonging in a way that transforms margins into frontiers, lack into (ad)vantage. For home envisions a site of rest; somewhere that one does not have to try as hard, because one's identity works, speaks and constructs itself. A respite where there is being but no longing.

'The postcolonial space is now "supplementary" to the metropolitan centre; it stands in a subaltern, adjunct relation that doesn't aggrandise the presence of the west but redraws its frontiers' (Bhabha 1990: 318).

Homelessness on the other hand may be contingency, but contingency does not rely on myths of origin and geographies of belonging for its legitimation. The strangest irony of the imagination is that from a ground of loss one destabilizes assumed categories in such a way as to relocate them within a new capacity for self-judgment (Harris 1965). The idea of a 'there being there' is a masculist form of closure that in the contemporary world still finds its most seductive form in the discourse of national identity. It takes a re-knowing of one's identity to effect a shift in the contours of its constraints. The question that must therefore be asked, observes Sneja Gunew, is not about being a migrant but of speaking from a position of migrancy (Gunew 1992: 168). The risks associated with this strategy are redirected, accordingly, away from dangers of an imposed alienation towards those of an embraced marginalization.

I may live in my father's house, but it is a house of many mansions. If I am able neither to dismantle it nor leave its confines, there nevertheless exist unexplored areas and unrealized possibilities that are awaiting my discovery, if only I would choose to conceive (of) them.

It is a place of barefoot levitations, a womb of space.

NOTES

1 I would like to thank Dominic Marner and, in particular, Heidi Safia Mirza for their careful readings and insightful comments regarding previous versions of this essay.
2 I have brought together two of Duncker's phrases from different contexts to emphasize the complexities of writing about the self.
3 Zora Neale Hurston remembers this day for her as well (Hurston 1979: 152).
4 I use the term 'black' cautiously with regard to my own father. Being a Guyanese East Indian, the term for him historically and culturally refers to people of African descent. However, the discourse within which I operate is one that draws upon British conceptions of colour and race which, unlike those of the American discourse, include Asians, Arabs and people from Latin America, not merely Africans, in the category 'black' (Davies 1994: 9).
5 The 1988 Education Act illustrates Thatcherism's dual task of unifying the British (white, European) nation whilst marginalizing non-white minorities (Goulbourne 1991: 125).
6 Gikandi is speaking about Nuruddin Farah's *Maps* (Gikandi 1992: 382).
7 Marshall Berman observes that Rousseau and Montesquieu were the first to account for the reasons and provide illustrations of this project (Berman 1970: 87).
8 Goulbourne also notes that the main element of this civilization in the eyes of most non-Europeans was British (Goulbourne 1991: 104).
9 This is Benjamin's (1989: 91) interpretation of Harris. The idea of the relationship between an economy of reproduction and the potential of the imagination to effect radical change is evident in Wilson Harris' notion of the 'womb of space', a theme that recurs throughout his writings. The concept of the womb as a place of production is avoided in both Marx and Freud.

BIBLIOGRAPHY

Anderson, B. (1991) *Imagined Communities: Reflections on the Origin and Spread of*

Nationalism, 2nd edn, London: Verso.

Benjamin, A. (1989) 'The Crumbling Narrative: Time, Memory and the Overcoming of nihilism in *The Eye of the Scarecrow*', in M. Gilkes (ed.) *The Literate Imagination: Essays on the Novels of Wilson Harris*, London: Macmillan.

Berman, M. (1970) *The Politics of Authenticity: Radical Individualism and the Emergence of Modern Society*, London: George Allen and Unwin Ltd.

Bhabha, H.K. (ed.) (1990) *Nation and Narration*, London: Routledge.

Boehmer, E. (1991) 'Stories of women and mothers: gender and nationalism in the early fiction of Flora Nwapa', in S. Nasta (ed.) *Motherlands: Black Women's Writing from Africa, the Caribbean and South Asia*, London: The Women's Press.

Chakrabarty, D. (1992) 'Postcoloniality and the Artifice of History: Who speaks for "Indian" pasts?' *Representations* 37, Winter: 1–26.

Cixous, H. (1994) 'To Live the Orange', in S. Sellers (ed.) *The Hélène Cixous Reader*, New York: Routledge.

Davies, C.B. (1994) *Black Women, Writing and Identity: Migrations of the Subject*, London: Routledge.

Duncker, P. (1992) *Sisters and Strangers: An Introduction to Contemporary Feminist Fiction*, Oxford: Blackwell.

Fanon, F. (1967 [1963]) *The Wretched of the Earth*, Harmondsworth, Middlesex: Penguin.

Flaubert, G. (1930 [1857]) *Madame Bovary*, London: Jonathan Cape.

Garcia Marquez, G. (1989) *Love in the Time of Cholera*, London: Penguin.

Gikandi, S. (1992) 'The Politics and Poetics of National Formation: Recent African Writing', in A. Rutherford (ed.) *From Commonwealth to Post-Colonial*, Sydney: Dangaroo Press.

Gilroy, P. (1987) *There Ain't No Black in the Union Jack*, London: Hutchinson.

—— (1993) *The Black Atlantic: Modernity and Double Consciousness*, London: Verso.

Goulbourne, H. (1991) *Ethnicity and Nationalism in Post-imperial Britain*, Cambridge: Cambridge University Press.

Griffiths, G. (1992) 'Culture and Identity: Politics and Writing in Some Recent Postcolonial Texts' in A. Rutherford (ed.) *From Commonwealth to Post-Colonial*, Sydney: Dangaroo Press.

Guardian (1993) 'World refugee crisis "out of control"', 19 November, p. 20.

Gunew, S. (1992) 'Migrant Women Writers: Who's on whose margins?' in C. Ferrier (ed.) *Gender, Politics and Fiction: Twentieth Century Australian Women's Novels*, St. Lucia, Queensland: University of Queensland Press.

Harris, W. (1965) 'Author's note', *The Eye of the Scarecrow*, London: Faber.

Harris, W. (1989) 'Literacy and the Imagination: A Talk', in M. Gilkes (ed.) *The Literate Imagination: Essays on the Novels of Wilson Harris*, London: Macmillan.

Hurston, Z.N. (1979) 'How it Feels to be Colored Me' in A. Walker (ed.) *I Love Myself When I am Laughing . . . A Zora Neale Hurston Reader*, New York: The Feminist Press.

Irigaray, L. (1991) 'Another "Cause" – Castration', in R.R. Warhol and D.P. Herndl (eds) *Feminisms: An Anthology of Literary Theory and Criticism*, New Brunswick, New Jersey: Rutgers University Press. Originally published 1974.

Said, E. (1986) 'Intellectuals in the Post-colonial World', *Salmagundi* vol. 70–1: 44–64.

Spivak, G. (1988) *In Other Worlds: Essays in Cultural Politics*, New York: Routledge.

—— (1990) 'Poststructuralism, Marginality, Postcoloniality and Value' in P. Collier and H. Geyer-Ryan (eds) *Literary Theory Today*, London: Polity Press.

Chapter 18

Two stories, three lovers, and the creation of meaning in a Black Lesbian autobiography

A diary

Consuelo Rivera Fuentes

INTRODUCTION

Black Lesbians have herstories, feelings and intellects to share. In this chapter, I want to share mine with you. Firstly, I must tell you that I feel both excited and confused at the prospect of contributing to this 'unique attempt'[1] to put British Black feminist theoretical perspectives together in order to have Black women's voices *listened to*, not merely heard or added. My feelings of excitement spring from the certainty that the articles will undoubtedly stimulate other Black feminist scholars to be active in the transformation and undoing of dominant discourses of feminism in Britain. As for my confusion I have to confess that it started primarily in my not knowing whether my identity as a self-defined Black Chilean Lesbian[2] living and doing feminist research in Lancaster fitted within a British Black feminist tradition[3]. This was due to various friends (both Black and white) telling me that they did not see me as a Black woman. Typical comments, after I had asked them if they would describe me as a Black woman, were:

> 'I would only describe someone as a black person if they have an Afro-Caribbean origin'; 'your skin is lighter than black; you are Chilean to me'; and 'you are not obviously black but I would say that you are politically Black, with a capital B'.[4]

These comments do, in a way, reflect some of the current debates surrounding the meanings of 'race' which have changed notably over the last ten years (see, for example Spivak, 1990; Spelman, 1990; Skeggs, 1995). I was certain in my mind that I was a Black feminist Lesbian[5] but here there were all these friends telling me I was wrong and I began to panic! However, the confusion only lasted a day or two. I realized that the fact that people cannot (or do not want to) 'see' me as a Black person here in Britain is not going to change the fact that I am/feel/think as one.[6] At some point in my confusion, I stated that I was certainly 'not white' but that redefinition of my racial identity is one of opposition and essentialization, two 'sins' I have been trying to get away from – however, not always successfully. I realized that I was pushing myself in the marginalization that this dichotomy, i.e. white/not white, entails. This recognition and that part of my rebellious subjectivity which challenges oppressive structures, made me realize once more that my subversion has been/continues to be done *not* in opposition to dominant discourses but within the ones I choose; shifting in this way between my marginalizations (Lesbian, Black, working-class single mother, etc.) and my centres. In other words, I transform myself into a site of resistance and change.

The 'whiteness of theory' (Simmonds, 1992: 52) might question this shifting of mine with the argument that by putting my Black Lesbian self in the centre I am 'otherizing' white heterosexual women. However, I do not look for the implicit or explicit permission of dominant discourses (although I am willing to engage in dialogue with them) to transform myself; which leads me onto what this essay is about.

Briefly, this literary diary deals with the power of transformation and re-construction of my Lesbian identity that the reading of *Zami: A New Spelling of my Name* – from now on *Zami* – Audre Lorde's (1982) auto-biography[7] provides me with. This part of the paper is a brief example of the way I read/write Lesbian autobiographies and forms part of my current research on the construction of Lesbian identities in auto-biographies.

SIMULTANEOUS AND NOMADIC TRANSFORMATIONS

The reading I do of *Zami* in my diary is informed by the notion of 'simultaneity' (Braidotti, 1994; Pearce, 1994a) and Braidotti's 'nomadic epistemology' of female subjectivities (Braidotti, 1994). These concepts allow me to move away from a long period of dialectic logic of reading literary texts, which means, very often, detachment from my feelings and the taking of sides in an almost always binary opposition against my identification with either the narrator(s) or the writer(s) or both. The Bakhtinian concepts of *simultaneity* and *dialogics* in which 'differences can be reconciled' (Pearce, 1994a: 10) have helped me in the past to provide a context to a love–hate dialogue with myself and other women readers/writers out of and within our differences. However, in order for this dialogic logics to have meaning in the type of experiential reading stage I am in at the moment, I must remove the boundaries set by the splitting graphics of the slash in Clark and Holquist's dialogic *both/and* (quoted in Pearce, 1994a: 10) and add an *or* which provides me with a necessary and healthy possibility of living with different subjectivities within and out of myself. In other words, although I am always looking for new ways of being, I do not want to 'waste the person I am' as some anonymous person said.

This dialogic *bothandor* (sic) will allow me to argue that when reading *Zami* the simultaneous co-presence (Thompson, 1995) of my many selves, intermingle with the simultaneous speaking co-present selves of Zami and Lorde to create new layers of meanings and subjectivities and, at the same time, prevent a definite and definitive separation of 'speaking' subjects. I will be using the necessary grammatical *I* (Braidotti, 1994) as the blending raw egg which holds together these layers of meaning and subjectivities in order to present a more or less 'coherent' mix of feminist Lesbian reading of an autobiographical text, such as *Zami*.

Also, because the notion of *identity* is central to the type of research I am carrying out at the moment, I will briefly attempt to give an overview of what it means to me in the context of this paper. Braidotti's (1994) 'nomadic epistemology' of female subjectivity in which she suggests that identity is 'the living process of transformation of self and others' (ibid.: 157) proves useful for the purpose of this essay. This type of transformation results, she argues, in a 'multiple, open-ended, interconnected entity' (ibid.) which is what happens in my reading of *Zami*. The different simultaneous identities which form part of *my(reader)self*, move within and out of my relationship with the text, thus giving my different 'structures of subject-ivity' (Braidotti, 1994) a temporal and spatial shifting, as well as 'nomadic' signification.

However, this notion of identity is not enough, as it seems not to consider the *desire, decision* and *struggle* (not always located in an *I*) to engage in the process of transformation of self and others. I agree with Braidotti in that identity is nomadic, i.e., not a static, fixed and clearly conceptualized notion, yet I want to add to her definition that identity, as I understand it, has the power to defend itself and to form alliances in order to influence and exert social transformations through the 'daily deciding/risking' (Moraga and Anzaldúa, 1981) of our actions and re-actions. Teresa de Lauretis's feminist consideration of identity as 'a political-personal strategy of survival and resistance that is also, at the same time, a critical practice and a mode of knowledge' (1986: 9) can provide the missing link between Braidotti's and my own notion of identity. Although '[t]he place [I am} most likely to find [myself] is in [myself]' (Sparks, 1990: 136), the space and time that this self occupies in my life colludes with the time and space I look for (and find) in *Zami* and other Lesbian autobiographies and I use it to re-define my Lesbian identity. With this mode of reading/writing in mind I want to suggest that the separation of the *writer-self, the autobiographical-self* and the *reader-self* is yet another construction and that the more these selves engage in a passionate, almost obsessive, love affair with each other, the more a Lesbian autobiography has meaning for me. Such a relationship with a text provides me with endless possibilities of re-creation. I read, therefore

I construct myself; I write, therefore I construct myself; I interact, therefore I construct myself and so on.

Because of the emotional[8], moreover, *sensual-sexual* dimension of my reading process, I mix extracts from *Zami* with some of my auto-biographical Black Lesbian reader responses and identifications. Some-times, because my boundaries when reading tend to disappear, the voices, comments, feelings and silences will be uttered by *bothandor* (sic) Audre, Zami, Consuelo, Lorde, *Zami* (the text), *all of us with the power to give meaning to each other*. I am fully aware of the fact that this simultaneity of voices and identities does not mean harmony at all times. Moreover, I would say that it brings chaos and adds to my contradictions. However, I like this because it means that 'I am a Black woman warrior poet doing my work', in Lorde's words (quoted in Sparks, 1990: 131). Since my 'work' in this paper is to give you a glimpse of my relationship with *Zami*, let me dive into this loving love liaison which, because it is not over, will contain only five days in the shape of a diary.

LORDE, ZAMI AND I: *WE*

Sunday

Today I learned to talk:

> Perhaps learn isn't the right word to use for my beginning to talk, because to this day I don't know if I didn't talk earlier because I didn't know how, or if I didn't talk because I had nothing to say that I would be allowed to say without punishment. Self preservation starts very early in West Indian families.

> (Lorde, 1982: 21–2)

and in Chilean families too! Zami and I, once we started school, learned to 'talk' and recite the lesson that the institution of education was pushing down our throats. When Audre utters her first sentence by way of saying 'I want to read', her mother 'scooped [her] up from [a] low stool, and to [her] surprise, kissed [her] right in front of everybody in the library' (ibid.: 32). She had spoken, she had been a 'good' girl; she had 'for once done something right' (ibid.) and, in the same way my mother did so many times, hers also approved and rewarded the child for making her feel good in front of other people.

I have also learned today that

> *I am a reflection of my mother's secret poetry as well as of her hidden angers.*

> (ibid.: 32, emphasis in the original)

As Zami, I carry in me my mother's way of changing reality from *within*, a place inside myself which plays with language and makes love to poetry.

However, very often, because I also carry her anger, I define my reality through actions frowned upon, through physical and intellectual desire, through getting into the systems in order to upset them so that they work with me, for me. To be able to do this, I physically and voluntarily leave my mother's land framed by the Pacific Ocean, The Andes, The Atacama Desert, Antarctica and centuries of *machismo*, but I take her (colonized) and my (subversive) voice in my baggage. She comes with me, although she lets me go. She knows that I am leaving and staying, at the same time. I leave Chile, my mother and the rest of my familial ties but I bring Pachamama, the Andean goddess/mother of our land, with me.

In *Zami*, Carriacou is a metaphorical, mythical land (like Pachamama) where *women work together as friends and lovers* (ibid.: 225), some place where Zami's mother used to have a voice which had not been silenced - neither throttled nor bound up, some place where the name for women who worked together as friends and lovers was *Zami*. When Audre Lorde finally finds Carriacou in *The Atlas of the Encycloepaedia Britannica*, she has actually come to terms with the fact that her mother had never really had a free voice or self, as she had imagined. Her mother's voice had been 'colonized', it had never been her own. Consequently, the long journey in search of some originary identity had come to an abrupt halt. Zami, therefore, had to create her own voice because Carriacou was no longer in the imaginary; it was as real as her disconnection of familial ties. She had to find a new 'country', not mapped, not silenced, not throttled, a place where she was not punished for speaking differently, for having a subversive voice; so she decides to leave her mother, father and sisters. She creates herself in the process and while reading and writing her, I create myself too.

Monday

I have just read one of Lorde's essays entitled 'Uses of the Erotic: the erotic as power' in *Sister Outsider* in which she argues that the erotic is that female power of the unexpressed or unrecognized feeling. She says that: 'the erotic is a measure between the beginnings of our sense of self and the chaos of our strongest feelings' (1984: 54).

I was pleasantly surprised to realize that this is similar to what I said about the chaos of my selves. Somewhere in my other diary, the one *I* only read, and which I have decided to share with you in this space, I write:

> My mind, my body, my soul! My mind is not my soul, my mind is not my body, my body is not my soul yet I am mind, body and soul trapped in a name . . . Consuelo.

Once I realized that I cannot separate my mind, my body and my soul from whatever I do, I began to be aware of my sense of self and recognize that the erotic is something I refuse to resign, even if that gives me pain, sometimes. Moreover, I *lesbianize* my eroticism as I assert my Lesbian 'self' creating, recreating, reclaiming my own (as well as honouring the good things about my mother's, albeit 'colonized') voice – transforming, in the process, language as well . This erotic knowledge empowers me, at the same time that it gives me a 'lens through which [I] scrutinize all aspects of [my] existence' (Lorde, 1984: 57) and transforms me into the public Consuelo I am, the one who, I insist, *lesbianizes* all aspects of her existence. Furthermore, my eroticism emphasises the 'wild' woman, the *bad girl*, who asserts her right to be not only an object but also a verb, a noun, an adjective, an adverb, a subject.

Tuesday

I am full of questions today. Here is this Black Lesbian, growing up with me, loving her mother and hating her at the same time, having crushes on other women, rebelling, looking for a voice. This time the construction of my Lesbian self has merged with that of Lorde's and I've felt her desire and pain, I've made love to her and her lovers, and I've found my home in hers. Why is it that I feel like this with *Zami* and not with other 'lesbian-authored' texts (Pearce, 1994b)? Is it because I refuse to accept the 'death of the author' (Barthes, 1977) yet while reading and constructing my identity in and out of this text, I am Lorde giving meaning to our subjectivities? Is it because both Lorde and I belong by choice and geographical mapping to a part of the population which has been classified and neatly dumped/buried in a niche of 'exoticism' and wilderness? Or is it because Lorde's bodily and geographical journey towards self-construction of a Lesbian cast-out identity is my own? Was she exiled? Am I exiled in these two worlds I co-in-habit and which rip my voice? I am not sure but what I am certain about is that Lorde's literature 'lives on not just because her use of words is lovely, but because the words have meaning' as Jewelle Gómez asserts in her introduction to this year's reprint of *Zami* (1996: xi)

Thursday

I have just read chapter 10 of *Zami* and two things struck me and made me really angry to the point of weeping. First the fact that Audre, who at this point of my reading is already myself, had to 'squint' in an agonizing attempt to see the edges and shapes of things because her parents 'did not approve of sunglasses nor of their expense' (ibid. 70). Then everything turned red in my eyes and heart when she narrates the scene at the ice-cream and soda fountain.

There was I between my mother and father, and my two sisters on the other side of my mother. We settled ourselves along the white mottled marble counter, and when the waitress spoke at first no one understood what she was saying, and so the five of us just sat there.

(ibid.: 70)

until we heard it loud and clear: we were Black, we were not allowed to eat their white ice-cream, in their white heat. The waitress, the pavement, the counter, the stone monuments of Washington were all white. I had sat with Audre and her family, I wanted to eat that ice-cream, I had felt important sitting there, in that place for 'treats'. And suddenly the blow. You are Black, you don't belong here, in this all white atmosphere. A white country where neither Zami nor I belonged but which gave us, and here's the contradiction, yet another voice to express our anger. Back in 1995 I wrote:

There are so many noises in this ward . . . there is the breathing noise of an oxygen mask which leaves a very old woman dozing, dozing. . . . There are the steps of nurses who come and go; white, covered in white, white overalls, white plastic aprons, white plastic on my wrists with an identity tag reminding me of who I am, but I don't remember regardless . . . muffled noises, foreign conversations, white friends visiting me. On thinking about it I am the only Black being in the whole ward . . . well apart from a cockroach I captured this morning under a white plastic cup!

Without sunglasses, and in spite of the shadows and edges, both Audre and I finally saw what our mothers had been silencing: that Black is the exact opposite of white. But is it? Is it that simple/simplistic? I have to come back to this some other day.

Friday

I've read more articles in *Sister Outsider* (Lorde, 1984). The one that stayed with me all day is a conversation between Audre Lorde and Adrienne Rich (ibid.: 81–109). They spoke of poetry and how that type of language can express feelings, even if not everybody understands what we mean. I suppose that moisture and soap do not love each other but we draw them together. After that, I went on reading chapter 18 of *Zami*. Funny how I could make love to Zami and Lorde and Ginger on the bus and nobody seemed to notice . . . I 'dove[d] beneath [their] wetness, [their] fragrance, the silky insistence of [their] bodies' rhythms illuminat[ed] my own hungers. We rode each other's need' (Lorde, 1982: 139). *Is this eroticism? Does this mean that I am reducing all Lesbian relationships to an expression of sexual desire? Is this pornography?* Well, not for me. This is not only sexual love as people could imagine; this goes back to the way I construct my Lesbian identity; it is definitely not pornography because pornography does not speak in feelings; pornography leaves me cool, empty. The reading of this autobiography fills up my senses; Lorde's words blend in my blood and stay with me; they bring me tenderness and passion, and I be-come with her; I explode in the moist flesh of her poetry. I don't know how to explain this. Here's a poem for Audre, for my lover, and for Zami instead of explanations:

> This ardent body of mine/ under-mines the soft sound of silence/ echoes of whispers in the cold/ sheets of routine/ wake up my senses/ once again/ I taste her lips/ in each page of this book/ booked this table to slowly put her/ in my mouth/ no interruptions of is-this-table-busy? sort of speeches/ of passers-by/ pass by the dawn of edges/ stitched to my brown skin/ with white thread (I had written 'threat')/ that cuts/ splits, slits the fleshy mountains of my chest/ that part of me which fed her/ so many times/ the patchwork in this map of lust/ and agony/ rips me vertically, horizontally/ from north to south/ from east to west/ with my consent/ I lip the fresh lips/ of another name/ with no sha-me/ except for the revolutionary myth/ which carries blue deep waters/ to the bottom of my throat/ flooding feelings of thirst.

It seems that when I enter the world of *Zami* I be-come again and again but somehow always in a slightly different manner, depending on the way I approach the reading. If I'm thinking of the chapter I am supposed to produce for my research my brain denies the words I need and gives me poems instead. However, I force myself to read theory and I am keeping it there somewhere in that part of the brain which deals with philosophy. I suppose I will pick it up when I am ready to do so. In the meantime, I am enjoying this *trialogic* (both for trial and for love affair triangle) way of reading which stresses my own power and difference. This leads me to disagree in part with Lynne Pearce's idea that the reader-experience is 'located not in the reader's *life* but in her (dialogic) engage-ment with the text' (Pearce, 1994b: 163). My reading of *Zami* is located in my life because as I read I construct a Lesbian identity which will necessarily affect the way I live on earth. My reading is like twilight meeting dawn, kissing the waters in the horizon where I can see my home, my self. This hunger that *Zami* started has made me melt quotations and it is as if the *Osorno* volcano had erupted, burning layers and layers of acquired, received knowledge, leaving only the bare bones of my self . . . deep, healing fire and lava . . . all the rage unleashed, slowly calcinating the slopes of institutionalized love and wisdom, turning it into a refresh-ing 'ocean of brown warmth' (Lorde, 1982: 139). This explosion has mixed all the colours inside and outside of me changing me minute by minute, this bursting of shades and colours which gives me endless possibilities of transformation is simply wonderful . . .

> All the colors change and become each other, merge and separate, flow into rainbows and nooses. *I lie beside my sisters in the darkness, who pass me in the street, unacknowledged and unadmitted.*
>
> (ibid.: 58, Lorde's emphasis)

They say that white is all the colours together. If this is true, maybe some of my ghosts are white but I do not let them haunt me. They also say that black is the absence of colour, yet the black of the coal lit in a brazier by my mother in winter winks at me from some un-familiar corner, un-known but present in the blending of colours and the erotic I re-create in poetry. Black for me has never been the lack of colour. It has been my home, my Pachamama, as Lorde's once was her Carriacou.

Dear reader, I must come to the end of this sharing of uncertainties, desires, feelings, thoughts, contradictions and love affairs. This paper might seem unfinished to you, not academic enough, not theoretical enough but I am an ongoing process and *enoughness* does not fit me. This is why I have not attempted an academic conclusion because my feelings refuse to be concluded with the ending of this paper.

NOTES

1 Heidi Mirza used this expression in a letter to me and I quote it here because it shows how passionately and strongly she feels about this book she is editing.
2 I write the signs Black and Lesbian with a capital B and a capital L to mark not only how important they are for me as a way of life, but also to emphasize their political connotations.
3 The fact that the students and staff in the Centre for Women's Studies at Lancaster University are predominantly from a white Western background made me wonder about this 'tradition' in the Centre. However, the few Black women who chose to do their research there are not a 'mere' presence. Our ways of doing feminist politics within the dominant discourse, albeit from the margin in this case, show that we are *actively* and voluntarily engaged in the undoing of dominant ideologies.
4 My friend was probably referring to the definition of Black offered by the Black Lesbian and Gay Centre Project, quoted in (charles), Helen (1992: 35) which includes Latin American people as well.
5 My writing the word Lesbian after the word feminist means that I put my lesbianism before my feminism. For a more detailed explanation, see Rivera (1996).
6 It is here where my reconstruction of racial identity takes place. In Chile I would probably be considered 'mixed race' by peoples whose ancestors have a European (Spanish or other) origin only. However I would be considered 'Winka' (white) by native indigenous people.
7 Audre Lorde called her autobiography a 'biomythography'. In doing so she alerted Black women that all the things a Black woman must be are both ordinary and mythic (Gómez, 1996).

8 Lynne Pearce, who is doing something similar to me in this under-researched area of reception theory, defines her reading practices as 'emotional'. She has been doing this for a while now but her 'emotions' are clearer to me in her unpublished paper 'Feminism and the Emotional Politics of Reading' (from her forthcoming book *Feminism and the Politics of Reading*).

REFERENCES

Barthes, R. (1977) *Image, Music, Text*, selected and translated by Stephen Heath, London: Fontana.

Braidotti, R. (1994) *Nomadic Subjects: Embodiment and Sexual Difference in Contemporary Theory*, New York: Columbia University Press.

(charles) Helen (1992) 'Whiteness – The Relevance of Politically Colouring the "Non"' in H. Hinds *et al.* (eds) *Working Out: New Directions for Women's Studies*, London: The Falmer Press.

de Lauretis, T. (1986) 'Feminist Studies/Critical Studies: Issues, Terms and Contexts' in T. de Lauretis (ed.) *Feminist Studies/Critical Studies*, Bloomington: Indiana University Press.

Gómez, J. (1996) Introduction to *Zami: A New Spelling of my Name*, London: Pandora Press

Lorde, A. (1982) *Zami: A New Spelling of my Name*, London: Sheba.

—— (1984) *Sister Outsider: Essays and Speeches*, Freedom, CA: The Crossing Press.

—— (1996) *Zami: A New Spelling of my Name*, 2nd edn, London: Pandora.

Moraga, C. and Anzaldúa, G. (eds) (1981) *This Bridge Called my Back: Writings by Radical Women of Color*, Watertown, Mass.: Persephone Press.

Pearce, L. (1994a) *Reading Dialogics*. London: Edward Arnold.

—— (1994b) 'Reading as Autobiography' in G. Griffin (ed.) *Changing Our Lives: Doing Women's Studies*, London: Pluto Press.

—— (1995) 'Finding a Place from Which to Write: The Methodology of Feminist Textual Practice' in B. Skeggs (ed.) *Feminist Cultural Theory: Process and Production*, Manchester: Manchester University Press.

—— (1996) 'Feminism and the Emotional Politics of Reading', unpublished paper presented at Strathclyde University in February 1996, in L. Pearce (forthcoming) *Feminism and the Politics of Reading*, London: Edward Arnold.

Rivera, C. (1996) '*Todas Locas, Todas Vivas, Todas Libres*: Chilean Lesbians 1980–1995' in M. Reinfelder (ed.) *Amazon to Zami: Towards a Global Lesbian Feminism*, London: Cassell.

Simmonds, F. N. (1992) 'Difference, Power and Knowledge: Black Women in Academia' in H. Hinds *et al.* (eds) *Working Out: New Directions for Women Studies*, London: The Falmer Press.

Skeggs, B. (ed.) (1995) *Feminist Cultural Theory: Process and Production*, Manchester: Manchester University Press.

Sparks, D. (1990) 'The Poetry of Theory: Black Women Warrior Poets Doing Our Work: Audre Lorde as Guide' in M. Saulter (ed.) *Passion: Discourses on Blackwomen's Creativity*, Yorkshire: Urban Fox Press.

Spelman, E. (1990) *Inessential Woman: Problems of Exclusion in Feminist Thought*, London: The Women's Press.

Spivak, G.C. (1990) *The Post-Colonial Critic: Interviews, Strategies, Dialogues*, edited by S. Harasym, London: Routledge.

Thompson, J. (1995) 'The Rise of Mediated Communication' in J. Thompson *The Media and Modernity: A Social Theory of the Media*, Cambridge: Polity Press.

Chapter 19

My body, myself

How does a Black woman do sociology?

Felly Nkweto Simmonds

Social reality exists, so to speak, twice, in things and in minds, in fields and in habitus, outside and inside of agents. And when habitus encounters a social world of which it is the product, it is like a 'fish in water': it does not feel the weight of the water, and it takes the world about itself for granted.

(Bourdieu and Wacquant 1992: 127)

INTRODUCTION

I have a particular relationship with the subject of sociology because of who I am. I am a Black woman and a sociologist. At conferences, for example, I am asked to speak as a Black female academic. Black academics (and students) are expected to talk about issues of 'race' as personal experiences. White academics, even when they are 'race' experts, are not expected to. It's as if 'race', as an experience, is only of concern to those who are 'racialized' by social theory itself. But when I use autobiographical examples to illustrate the relationship between my embodied experience, and my sociological practice, to an audience which is almost always white, the impact is always dramatic. Reflecting on my experience as a Black woman challenges the silence of those who are privileged by whiteness (MacIntosh quoted in Minas 1993). It forces them to ask themselves the questions they take for granted, to locate their own 'racial' experience as I have to every day.

As a Black woman, I know myself inside and outside myself. My relation to this knowledge is conditioned by the social reality of my habitus.[1] But my socialized subjectivity is that of a Black woman and it is at odds with the social world of which I'm a product, for this social world is a white world. I cannot be, as Bourdieu suggests, a fish in water that 'does not feel the weight of the water, and takes the world about itself for granted'. The world that I inhabit as an academic, is a white world. This white world has a problematic relationship with blackness. Academic discourses of the social have constructed blackness as the inferior 'other', so that even when blackness is named, it contains a problem of relationality to whiteness. The British Sociological Association's guide to anti-racist language acknowledges 'white' and 'Black' (Caribbean/African/Other) as 'ethnic classifications', but fails to provide an actual definition of 'White' on its own. 'Black', however, has a detailed and problematized definition which begins with, 'This term is often used to refer to a variety of non-white ethnic groups'.[2]

Sociology gives me, even as a teacher of sociology, a 'non-white' existence, doomed to inhabit the margins of white theory. In this white world, the question becomes, How does a Black woman do sociology? As Fanon laments:

> The black man [sic] ... does not know at what moment his inferiority comes into being through the other. And then the occasion arose when I had to meet the white man's eyes. An unfamiliar weight burdened me. The real world challenged my claims. In the white world the man of color encounters difficulties in the development of his bodily schema. Consciousness of the body is solely a negating activity. It is a third-person consciousness. The body is surrounded by an atmosphere of certain uncertainty.... A slow composition of my self as a body in the middle of a spatial and temporal world – such seems to be the schema. It does not impose itself on me; it is, rather, a definitive structuring of the self and the world – definitive because it creates a real dialectic between my body and the world.
>
> (Fanon 1986: 111)

In this white world the question becomes: What relationship can a Black woman establish between being a sociologist and being a person? I want to argue that an intellectual understanding of social reality is not enough, and that such an understanding has to critically examine the relationship between individual/personal and collective/social realities. In this white world I am a fresh water fish that swims in sea water. I feel the weight of the water ... on my body.

'CERTAIN PRIVATE INFORMATION'

To talk about the body is to invite derision. We cannot invite bodies, ours and those of others, into sociological discourse without being accused of essentialism or narcissism. But I want to risk talking about the body, my body as a strategy, in the way that Gayatri Spivak suggests, as 'persistent (de) constructive critique of theory' (Spivak 1993: 3). In this sense talking about the body, my body, becomes both a strategy and a technique, to deconstruct my positioning as a woman, an African woman (a 'third world' woman) and an academic in a western institution. It is neither essentialist nor narcissistic. I want to explore the relationship between my body as a social construct and my experience of it. I want to examine the relationship I have with my body and how I negotiate, daily, with 'embodied social situations' (Scott and Morgan 1993: 112).

I live in Newcastle-upon-Tyne, which has a significantly smaller Black population that other British cities. I am the only Black person in my department, and in fact one of only a handful in the whole institution. Currently I only have two Black students out of the nearly two hundred I teach across the university. I cannot ignore the fact of my blackness, even if I wanted to. Neither can my colleagues or students,[3] even if they wanted to.

This makes me vulnerable.[4] In the final analysis, I might be an academic, but what I carry is an embodied self that is at odds with expectations of who an academic is. I can be invited and /or dismissed as the token (Black, woman, 'Third World'), and can be expected or presumed to be taking one or more of these positions in how I teach/what I teach. I can be invited to give conference papers as Black, woman, African or 'Third World' (but not British, which is what my passport says!). In her essay 'Marginality in the Teaching Machine', Spivak illustrates this position:

> At the conference on Cultural Value at Birkbeck College, the University of London, on July 16, 1988, where this paper was first presented, the speaker was obliged to speak of her cultural identity. From what space was she speaking, in what space was the representative member of the audience placing her? What does the audience expect to hear today, here? . . . To whom did they want to listen?
>
> (Spivak 1993: 54–5)

For some of us, it is impossible to escape the body and its constructions, even inside the 'teaching machine'. I am expected to not only carry my body, but to acknowledge it. I have a specific and clear relationship to the knowledge that I teach, through my body. The contradiction for me is that, whereas I can clearly be invited to speak about 'race' issues, it is only when I choose to speak about the experiences of the racialization of my body, that my authority to do this is questioned or dismissed as subjective and 'confessional'.[5] I'm expected to *be, but not to know about being*. This relationship between being and knowing exposes the fragility of theory's insistence that we can articulate truths only through a rational and objective epistemology of social reality. Ontological knowledge is suspect and at worst pathologized. This tradition is sanctioned, even by some whose practice is reflexive. For example, when Loic Wacquant asks Pierre Bourdieu the question, 'Can we do a Bourdieuan Sociology of Bourdieu? Can you explain yourself? If so, why this unwavering reticence to speak about the private person Pierre Bourdieu?' Bourdieu's response is defensive:

> It is true that I have a sort of professional vigilance which forbids me to adopt the kind of egomaniacal postures that are so approved of and even rewarded . . . this reluctance to talk about myself has another reason. By revealing certain private information, by making bovaristic confessions about myself, my lifestyle, my preferences, I may give ammunition

to the people who utilize against sociology the most elementary weapon there is – relativism. . . . The personal questions that are put to me are often inspired by what Kant would call 'pathological motives'.

(Bourdieu and Wacquant 1992: 202–3)

This, however, is a luxury. A white male academic has the privilege to opt for silence about 'private information'. As Scott and Morgan have observed, theory 'may admit the body', but demand that 'the theorist remains disembodied' (Scott and Morgan 1993: 112). Theory thus becomes only that knowledge which is created from outside ourselves, outside our bodies, out of our heads (as it were). It is as if 'facts' come out of our heads, and 'fictions' out of our bodies. As Anne Game observes:

> Sociological practice is conceived of as representation of the real, which for this discipline is conceived as the social. And there's nothing fictitious about the social and representations of it. Thus, the discipline is defined through oppositions, fact-fiction and theory-fiction. . . . Social reality is taken as determinant; theory as reflection. But, this reflection is privileged as adequate correspondence to social reality as opposed to fictional reflection.

> (Game 1991: 3)

Although in this case Game uses the sociology of literature as the example of 'fictional reflection', the same can be said of experience (which in any case can be presented as literature), which reveals 'certain private information'. Bourdieu also acknowledges that literature can teach sociologists more about the 'truth of temporal experience' such as those found in biographical writings, and warns us that although 'there are . . . significant differences between sociology and literature . . . we should be careful not to turn them into irreconcilable antagonism' (Bourdieu and Wacquant 1992: 206). But he also adds, 'It goes without saying that sociologists must not and cannot claim to compete with writers on their own turf' (ibid.).

As an African woman my 'certain private information' is not only inscribed in disciplines such as anthropology, but also in colonial narratives, literatures, photographs, paintings and so on. Here the 'facts' created by social theory and the 'fictions' created by literature can be difficult to separate. At times social theory itself becomes a fiction.[6] Anne Game concludes, 'the sociological fiction is that it is not fiction. . . . As an initial move in shifting the codes of sociology I will propose a reversal: that we think of sociological writing as fiction and fiction as social analysis' (Game 1991: 18).

One of the consequences, for a Black woman, of this insistence on the separation of the 'facts' of social reality, from the 'fictions' of experience and biographical knowledge is the creation of what Fanon has identified as 'the dialectic between my body and the world' (Fanon 1986: 111). The consequences are real enough. In academia, for example, I experience what Bourdieu himself has acknowledged; the 'feeling of being a stranger in the academic universe' (Bourdieu and Wacquant 1992: fn 208–9):

> In France, to come from a distant province, to be born south of the Loire, endows you with a number of properties that are not without parallel in the colonial situation. It gives you a sort of objective and subjective externality and puts you in a particular relation to the central institutions of French society and therefore the intellectual situation. There are subtle (and not so subtle) forms of racism that cannot but make you perceptive; being constantly reminded of your otherness stimulates a sort of permanent sociological vigilance. It helps you perceive things that others cannot see or feel.
>
> (Bourdieu and Wacquant 1992: 209)

But such an analysis can be a dangerous. It can glorify oppression in a way that can only be spoken by those who are privileged. 'Permanent sociological vigilance' is the consequence of oppression, a consequence of the subtle and not so subtle racism that permeates academic institutions in Britain. For a Black academic this is one of the burdens we carry, everyday. It is for this reason that we cannot and must not remain disembodied theorists. To put it simply, we cannot write a sociology of the Black experience without revealing certain private information.

As a woman, as a Black person, as an African, social theory has fed on my embodied experience. In anthropology, for example, one of the central tenets of 'defining the primitive' (Torgovnick 1990: 1–41) was the very basic idea that: 'primitives live life whole, without fear of the body' (Torgovnick 1990: 9). I have a body prescribed not only as primitive, but at the very 'heart of darkness'. In her re/interpretations of Conrad's *Heart of Darkness*, Marianna Torgovnick exposes the relationship Conrad, through Marlow, gives between the African woman and Africa itself.

> In my mind, I keep coming back to the African woman who stalks through the heart of darkness. . . . That African woman, is, for me the crux of *Heart of Darkness* . . . She is the representative 'native'. . . . She is, the text insists, the symbol of Africa. . . . Her death fulfils her role as emblem of the African landscape and makes . . . explicit the hidden reference of 'the feminine' and the 'primitive' to death. The African landscape is death in the novella. It is 'the white man's grave' . . . Europeans enter it but leave it either dead or ill or changed and marked for ever.
>
> (Torgovnick 1990: 154–5)

Both the nature and value of the 'primitive' body are prescribed. The Black body must remain 'voiceless' (Torgovnick 1990: 9). How then, are we to write a sociology of the Black experience in Britain, without taking on the body, and without revealing 'certain private information'?

FEAR AND DESIRE

When a young Black man is murdered by a group of young white men, we could write whole texts on the politics of race and racism, such as the collusion of the legal system in the killing of our sons.[7] But I fear such grand narratives ignore the very basic act of the killing of a Black body which is the final solution, the very logic of racism. History is littered with such bodies – Black bodies swinging from poplar trees in Alabama – Black bodies hanging from Mopane trees in Central Africa – Black bodies hanging from Flame trees in Kenya. Maybe, if we began by counting the bodies, we might arrive at a clearer picture of what the idea of race and racism as an ideology produces, socially and politically, and what the bodily experience can be.

In her essay, 'Myth of the Black Rapist', Angela Davis (Davis 1981) illustrates this with the example of the white institution of lynching (complemented by the rape of Black women). In the aftermath of the Civil War (and later, to a less extent), the lynching of Black men was used by white America as a valuable political weapon to guarantee the continued exploitation of Black labour 'and the political domination of Black people as a whole' (Davis 1981: 185) In this case, the history of the killing of Black bodies as a central political strategy cannot be separated from the social reality of how racism worked then, and continues to today, making a Black body always vulnerable to whiteness.

In this white world, the Black body, my body, is always on display. It has been documented by western disciplines such as anthropology. The essays in Elizabeth Edward's *Anthropology and Photography: 1860–1920*, chronicle how nineteenth century anthropologists used the authority of photography to construct and display knowledge of the 'other'. A particular fascination with the female body was quite explicit in the search for anatomical landmarks of different 'races'. For example, even Colonial Office records used Thomas Henry Huxley's standardized photometric methods to collect information on colonial subjects. As Frank Spencer notes in his essay, 'Some Notes on the Attempt to Apply Photography to Anthropometry during the Second Half of the Nineteenth Century':

> In an effort to produce a photographic document that would permit the subsequent recovery of reliable comparative and morphometric data, Huxley recommended that all subjects be photographed naked, according to established and anthropometric poses. . . . In particular Huxley noted the desirability that the arm in female subjects should be 'so disposed as not to interfere with the contour of the breast which is very characteristic in some races' (Huxley to Lord Granville, Dec. 8, 1869).
>
> (Spencer 1992: 100)

The spectacle of the colonized female subject in nineteenth century writings and readings of difference between the races was also symbolically captured in the public displays of African women as curiosities. The African woman named Saartjie Baartman, also called Sarah Bartmann or Saat-Jee and known as the 'Hottentot Venus', was on public display in London and in Paris in 1810. After her death in Paris in 1810, her sexual parts, her genitalia and her buttocks were preserved and continue, to this day, to be displayed in the *Musée de l'homme* in Paris (Gilman 1992: 180–1).

These public displays of images of 'other' societies were common forms of entertainment in the nineteenth century. In his essay 'British Popular Anthropology: Exhibiting And Photographing the Other', Brian Street illustrates how exhibitions of other societies 'with their underlying associations of race, hierarchy and evolution, were most vividly experienced through exhibitions, photographs and postcards . . . not simply as "entertainment" but as having educational value' (Street 1992: 122). In this case the 'facts' and the 'fictions' of 'others' were rendered one and the same thing.[8] As a Black woman, my body cannot escape this history.

It is particularly poignant for me that some of the photographs of the 'curiosities' documented in Street's chapter are of the Batwa, 'pygmies from the Ituri forest region of the Congo' (Street 1992: 128–9). The Batwa were some of the earliest settlers across most of Central Africa, including the islands of Lake Bangweulu in Zambia. My maternal ancestors are from those islands. Looking at the photographs of the Batwa (in which they are virtually naked, and includes one bare breasted woman) taken of them in London, by one Sir Benjamin Stone, in August 1905, I cannot help but take a second look to see if I can recognize myself.

Adorned and unadorned I cannot escape the fantasies of the western imagination. Robert Young illustrates this desire for colonized bodies as spectacle, as labour and so on, as essentially an extension the 'desiring machine' of capital. This has particular implications for the female body, and is highlighted by anthropology's particular fascination with female bodies and with sexual lives. In this sense, sexuality becomes part of the political economy of desire, for money, for products and for those who produce. It becomes part of:

> 'the libidinal unconscious' [which] opens up possibilities for the analysis of the dynamics of desire in the social field. Racism is perhaps the best example through which we can immediately grasp the form of desire and its antithesis, repulsion, as a social production: thus 'fantasy is never individual: it is a group fantasy'.
>
> (Young 1995: 168–9)

It is this politics of sex, race and desire which still affects 'racial' encounters in everyday life.[9]

As Brian Street concludes:

> as in written representations of non-European peoples, nineteenth-century European discourses on race and evolution continued to frame

visual portrayals, even at a time when anthropologists themselves were beginning to move, via field work methods, towards a more character- istically twentieth-century interest in how people might see themselves and towards a more relativist less physically based view of cultural difference. The interest in legends of little people, in little bodies as signs of little minds, in 'savage' customs as a justification and rationale for 'scientific' and business 'progress' . . . was firmly rooted in a common framework of race, evolution and hierarchy [and] served to construct and perpetuate this conceptual framework, beyond its academic life, for larger proportions of the public than could be influenced solely by the books and literature available on the subject at the time.

(Street 1992: 130)

MY BODY, MYSELF

'Racial' knowledge constructed about 'the other' is what provides the contradictory experience of 'race' as an everyday reality even at the end of the twentieth century. Here I want to unearth some of these bodily and embodied experiences of My Body, My Self and of how others see me and how I experience being a 'curiosity'.

First sketch

One day, I walked from the bus with an Italian waiter I knew a little, I'd been in the restaurant in which he works several times. Suddenly he said, 'I bet you have a beautiful body.'

In his imagination, in his fantasy, of course I have. He has seen Black female bodies. The Black female body is etched on his sexual un- conscious. As a white man he also has the weight of history behind him, which tells him Black women are available to him.

Suddenly conscious of my missing breast I say, 'No actually, no. I had a bad illness two years ago'. Illness? He vanished, didn't even wait for the end of the sentence, having conjured up in his imagination all the awful things I could be carrying. Blackness, dirt, disease . . . HIV AIDS, Ebola fever? He vanished.

I carry a contradictory body, so exotic and desirable, so threatening and deadly. Actually now, in my middle age, now that I've had to get in touch with my body, it feels OK. I think of my body quite often . . . pamper it with bath oils, take it to the gym twice or three times a week. . . . but still too much whiskey (Irish). My body never has hangovers from whiskey.

Second sketch

In Dublin a rather beautiful Irish man leans across the table, takes my hand and rubs the back of my hand: 'Do you know how exotic you are? Such beautiful ebony skin, so soft, so beautiful.'

Because he is so beautiful, and I suspect in love with me for the duration of the meal, I'm kind to him and remind him that I can only be exotic in Dublin, in my own space there are millions like me and we don't go round touching each other and telling ourselves how exotic our ebony skins are. . . .

And of course what he doesn't know, cannot know is that my skin is quite dry and I have to oil it everyday.

My skin, so soft, so black, so dry, the colour of my skin so exotic to a beautiful Irish man, such a deadly cloak to wear on a dark night on the streets of London, Liverpool, Birmingham, Leeds . . . Dublin.

Third sketch

Alice leans over and whispers; 'Barbara wants to touch your hair.' I take Barbara's hand and put it on my hair, on my dreadlocks, 'Ooh . . . Just like wool. I've always wondered what it feels like. Ooh.' She coos.

I try to remember Bourdieu's phrase 'permanent sociological vigilance'. Any Black person can tell you, hair is our special thing. It is as tanning is to white people, I suspect. We have special ways of torturing our hair, twisting, braiding, straightening, curling, colouring, extending . . . the perfect disguise. As this quote from the leading Black newspaper, the *Weekly Journal*, illustrates.

One . . . frivolous girl preferred white men for no other reason than that none of her white (and perhaps short sighted) lovers were ever sharp enough to work out that the cascading brown hair with blonde highlights reaching half way down her back was fake.

(*Weekly Journal*, 18 May 1995)

Fourth Sketch

Joe has his hands on my naked butt . . . kneading, 'I love this, I love this.'

With a Black man, I even like the idea that I have a big bum! But when I try to squeeze myself into a skirt from Warehouse, I realize that there's no life after size 10.

But I also think of Sarah Bartmann, The Hottentot Venus, whose image not only formed the 'central image of the black female throughout the nineteenth century' (Gilman 1992: 180), but has also fed countless white fantasies about the Black female form.

Fifth sketch

Steven says, 'You have the most beautiful eyes'. I worry. On my right eye I have a small growth which is slowly growing over my cornea. It's quite common in those who have lived in tropical climates. Ultra-violet rays damage our eyes. I have to keep watching it, if it suddenly starts to grow, or begins to affect my vision, I have to have it removed. The only problem is, once it's disturbed, as it were, it's likely to grow back faster than it's growing now.

What did he say? Beautiful eyes. I think they say beauty is in the eye of the beholder

Or is it? My experience of my body, inside and outside of myself, leaves me with more questions than answers. But I need to unearth this bodily experience for myself as an act of sorting through the fictions of theory, of realizing that for me there is a very fine line between the 'facts' and 'fictions' of my body as I experience it in the here and now, and the history of that body.

I have come to this realization through my experience of breast cancer and the 'fact' and 'fiction' of the body I live with everyday.

Sixth sketch

From my Cancer Diary (Moss, Tuesday 24.3.92)

I'm trying to remember my body. With two breasts. With no pain. What did it feel like to have two breasts? To touch them . . . together or one at a time. To cradle a man's head between my breasts. . . . It all feels so impossible now. Will I ever let a man see my lone (lonely) breast? I don't know if I can relate to a whole body again. . . . This is how the surgeon broke the news to me:

'We have found a cancer in your right breast . . . in its early stage . . . a ductile carcinoma in situ . . . still contained in the ducts . . . has not invaded the breast tissue or the lymph nodes . . . but the whole breast tissue is unstable. . . . My recommendation is that we remove the breast, thus ensuring that the whole cancer is removed.'

I think he was talking about my breast. I felt it then, and knew I hated it, wanted it off, there and then. Little did I know how much I'd miss it at first, and how much I'd forget it, in time.

It is the loss of my right breast that has made me take account of the embodied experience in the making of social reality. It's not very often we get the chance of a new body. I was 42 when I lost my breast. On the outside I carry the same body; a fact and a fiction. But I'm different, not just because the shape of my body is different, but because I have to relate to that different body. I am transformed, and the world around me is transformed also.[10] It is this new relationship with my body that has allowed me to re/think myself and my place in the social.

CONCLUSION

Being conscious of myself as a person, an embodied self, is what helps me perceive things that 'others cannot see or feel' as sociologists. This is what gives me a particular relationship with the subject of sociology. The relationship between my embodied reality and my sociological practice is at the very core of how I do sociology. I have to be equally as aware of the reality that my body imposes on my practice and of the reality that social theory imposes on that body. I cannot be silent about it. As Paulo Freire suggests:

> men [sic] are aware of their activity and the world in which they are situated. They act in function of the objectives which they propose, have the seat of their decisions located in themselves and in their relation with the world and with others, and infuse the world with their creative presence by means of the transformation they effect upon it. Unlike animals, they do not only live but exist; and their existence is historical. . . . For animals, 'here' is only a habitat with which they enter into contact; for men, 'here' signifies not merely a physical space, but an historical space.
>
> (Freire 1972: 71)

The 'here' of academia is also 'an historical space'. When I teach sociology, as a Black woman in an almost all-white institution, the social reality of academia and of academic discourse is transformed. My practice is reflexive in the way that Alvin Gouldner has argued, and that is:

> A Reflexive Sociology . . . is characterized not by what it studies. It is distinguished neither by the persons and the problems studied nor even by the techniques and instruments used in studying them. It is characterised, rather, by the relationship it establishes between being a sociologist and being a person, between the role and the man [sic] performing it.
>
> (Gouldner 1993: 470–1)

I have chosen to acknowledge this relationship between being a sociologist and being a person, openly, and to acknowledge the impact this has on my practice. A reflexive sociology allows me, as a person, to use embodied social realities, to do sociology and to inform theory. It is a process of uncovering embodied social reality through the practice of sociology. In this process *sociological theory has to admit the body*. The body cannot remain 'voiceless'. This is how I teach sociology.

Recently a young Black man doing a Ph.D. on sport and identity, wrote to me after a conference:

> you suggested that I keep a personal diary of my feelings about the research alongside the more 'serious' research notes. Anyway you'll be pleased to know that I did, grudgingly, start to do this and over time (and you'll no doubt be aware of this) I found it increasingly difficult to separate the two types of notes until my field notes became increasingly reflexive and 'personalised'. I am currently at the stage of writing up my notes and attempting to theorize them.[11]

I'm aware that he has embarked on a difficult journey – toward the discovery of (an embodied) self through the practice of sociology. It is an act of transforming theory, an act of admitting the body and embodied social experiences into theory.

As Black academics (and students), one of our tasks has to be to transform theory itself, if we are not to remain permanent 'curiosities' in academia. For us, the habitus of academia is as dangerous as society at large, because we are not 'fish in water' (Bourdieu and Wacquant 1992). Our work is often marginalized and dismissed as 'not theory', because we challenge the limits of theories that will not admit our embodied realities. To have our bodies, ourselves, admitted on our own terms, will be an act of naming ourselves on this journey through the 'heart of whiteness' (Gates, quoted in Mirza 1996).

NOTES

1 As Diane Reay (1995) explains: 'Bourdieu has developed the concept of habitus to demonstrate not only the ways in which the body is in the social world but also the ways in which the social world is in the body (Bourdieu 1981):

> The habitus as the feel for the game is the social game embodied and turned into second nature. (Bourdieu, 1990b: 63)

Thus, one of the crucial features of habitus is that it is embodied; it is not composed solely of mental attitudes and perceptions. Bourdieu writes that it is expressed through durable ways "of standing, speaking, walking, and thereby feeling and thinking" (Bourdieu, 1990a: 70).'

2 British Sociological Association, *Anti-Racist Language: Guidance For Good Practise* (undated, unacknowledged authorship), gives this definition:

> **Black** – This term is often used to refer to a variety of non-white ethnic groups. This term has taken on more political connotations with the rise of black activism in the USA since the 1960s and now its usage implies solidarity against racism. The idea of 'black' has thus been reclaimed as a source of pride and identity. To accept this means that we should be sensitive to the many negative connotations relating to the word 'black' in the English

language (black leg, black list, etc.). However, some Asians in Britain object to the use of the word 'black' being applied to them and some argue that it also confuses a number of ethnic groups which should be treated separately – Pakistanis, Bangladeshis, Indians and so on. One solution is to refer to 'black peoples' 'black communities', etc. in the plural to imply that there are a variety of such groups. It is also important to be aware of the fact that in some contexts – such as South Africa – 'black' can also be used in a racist sense.

3   In a seminar, I was asked by one of my white students if I had come to Britain 'to better myself'. I'm quite sure she wouldn't ask a white teacher on a lucrative 'Aid' contract in Africa the same question!

4   When, for example, I pointed out the racist nature of a policy document, the response of those in authority was to call into question the validity of my assertion.

5   I first aired some of the ideas in this chapter at a meeting of the Feminist Research Group at the University of Northumbria. A man (uninvited to the meeting!) asked if 'we all had to become confessional'. My reply was that he'd used the word 'confession' not me! I refused to be drawn into having to justify (to the white man) what I was saying and how I chose to say it.

6   See for example Adam Kuper (1988) and Mary Midgley (1985).

7   Since 1969 more than one hundred Black people have died in custody in Britain, (police, psychiatric and prison custody), nearly half of them in police custody (from a special report in the *Voice* 30 January 1996).

8   This practice continues today in television documentaries. For example, 'Watching Brief' (*Guardian* 7 January 1996) introduces the programme *Under The Sun: A Caterpillar Moon* (BBC2) thus: 'After the honey season, the caterpillar season is the favourite time of the year for the Aka pygmies of the central African rainforest. They get to gorge themselves on the juicy titbits which rain down from the tree canopy. . . . Julia Simmons' fascinating film focuses on the family of Bosseke, a warm and friendly Aka who tells his son to give the first caterpillar pickings to the film crew. At first you are just relieved for the crew that the hairy, squirmy grubs are in strangely short supply.' For myself, these 'hairy, squirmy grubs' are a delicacy.

9   See, for example, Kathryn Perry, 'The Heart of Whiteness: White Subjectivity and Interracial Relationships'; Inge Blackman, 'White Girls Are Easy, Black Girls Are Studs'; Helen (charles), '(Not) Compromising: Inter-skin Colour Relations'; Felly Nkweto Simmonds, 'Love in Black and White' all in Lynne Pearce and Jackie Stacey (1995) (eds) *Romance Revisited*, London: Lawrence Wishart 1995.

10   One way I observe this transformation is when I first tell someone that I have one breast. I can literally see the bodily reaction to it . . . sometimes of surprise, confusion, pity, and even fear. I've also noticed that they also 'hear' or 'read' me differently, whatever I'm talking about. In these instances I catch a glimpse of the reality of those whose embodied realities, such as disabled people, cannot be ignored.

11   Personal communication 26.10.95.

REFERENCES

Bourdieu, Pierre (1981) 'Men and Machines' in K. Knorr-Cetina and V. Cicourel (eds) *Advances in Social Theory and Methodology: Towards an Integration of Micro and Macro Sociologics*, London: Routledge & Kegan Paul.

Bourdieu, Pierre (1990a) *The Logic of Practice*, Cambridge: Polity Press.
Bourdieu, Pierre (1990b) *In Other Words: Essays Towards a Reflexive Sociology*, Cambridge: Polity Press.
Bourdieu, Pierre and Wacquant, Loic J. D. (1992) *An Invitation to Reflexive Sociology*, Cambridge and Oxford: Polity Press/Blackwell Publishers.
Davis, Angela (1981) *Women, Race and Class*, London: Women's Press.
Donald, James and Rattansi, Ali (eds) (1992) *'Race', Culture and Difference*, London: Sage Publications in association with the Open University.
Edwards, Elizabeth (ed.) (1992) *Anthropology and Photography 1860–1920*, New Haven and London: Yale University Press in association with The Royal Anthropological Institute, London.
Fanon, Frantz (1986) *Black Skin, White Masks*, London: Pluto Press.
Freire, Paulo (1972) *Pedagogy of The Oppressed*, London: Penguin.
Game, Anne (1991) *Undoing The Social*, Buckingham: Open University Press.
Gilman, Sander (1992) 'Black Bodies, White Bodies: Towards an Iconography of Female Sexuality in Late Nineteenth-Century Art, Medicine and Literature' in J. Donald and A Rattansi (eds) *Race, Culture and Difference*, London: Sage Publications in association with the Open University.
Gouldner, Alvin W. (1993) 'Towards a Reflexive Sociology' in C. Lemert (ed.) *Social Theory: The Multicultural and Classic Readings*, Boulder, CO: Westview Press.
Griffiths, Morwenna and Troyna, Barry (eds) (1995) *Antiracism, Culture and Social Justice in Education*, Stoke-on-Trent: Trentham Books Limited.
Kuper, Adam (1988) *The Invention of Primitive Society: Transformations of an Illusion*, London: Routledge.
Midgley, Mary (1985) *Evolution as Religion*, London: Methuen.
Minas, Anne (1993) *Gender Basics: Feminist Perspectives on Women and Men*, Belmont, CA: Wadsworth Publishing Company.
Mirza, Heidi Safia (1996) 'Black Educators: Transformative Agents for Social Change', *Adults Learning*, NIACE, vol. 7, no. 6, February.
Pearce, Lynne and Stacey, Jackie (eds) (1995) *Romance Revisited*, London: Lawrence and Wishart.
Reay, Diane (1995) 'Using "Habitus" to Look at "Race" and Class in Primary School Classrooms' in M. Griffiths and B. Troyna (eds) *Antiracism, Culture and Social Justice in Education*, Stoke-on-Trent: Trentham Books Limited.
Scott, Sue and Morgan, David (eds) (1993) *Body Matters: Essays on the Sociology of The Body*, London: The Falmer Press.
Spencer, Frank (1992) 'Some Notes on the Attempts to Apply Photography to Anthropology During the Second Half of the Nineteenth Century' in E. Edwards (ed.) *Anthropology and Photography 1860–1920*, New Haven and London: Yale University Press, in association with the Royal Anthropological Institute, London.
Spivak, Gayatri Chakravorty (1993) *Outside in The Teaching Machine*, New York and London: Routledge.
Street, Brian (1992) 'British Popular Anthropology: Exhibiting and Photographing the Other' in E. Edwards (ed.) *Anthropology and Photography 1860–1920*, New Haven and London: Yale University Press, in association with the Royal Anthropological Institute, London.
Torgovnick, Marianna (1990) *Gone Primitive: Savage Intellects, Modern Lives*, Chicago and London: University of Chicago Press.
Young, Robert J. C. (1995) *Colonial Desire: Hybridity in Theory, Culture and Race*, London: Routledge.

Chapter 20

The fabulous adventures of the mahogany princesses

Gargi Bhattacharyya

In recent years it has often seemed as if all attempts to make sense of the troubled meanings of skin and genitals have returned again and again to pictures and words. Getting to the magic word 'politics' depends on guessing the right thing to say, the best picture to draw. Spending so much time arguing about representation has drained everyone's resources – we have all forgotten other ways of thinking and fighting it seems. Instead of seeing words and pictures as malleable parts of other battles, resources and entertainments, dreams and warnings, the battles become about words and pictures. We see only in absolute terms of positive and negative, to be framed and to be silenced – and forget all the other things we can and must do. This is my answer to those troubled years of watching what I said.

For us, telling stories has become a way of life. Living is hard and confusing and narrative promises to guide us through. Of course, things get left out, misplaced, but the stories help us to keep on. Fictional tracks for unplanned journeys, that last memory of progress binds us still. Please don't shout white boy teleology. This isn't quite the linear track of western science – that has its uses, but it isn't the right story for our everyday. Nor is it the overview of their panopticon god. We aren't waiting for the jailer of destiny to serve up the final sentences – there is no one watcher who can fix the ending here.

These are stories to live by – open to adaptation by ordinary contexts and unexpected giggles. Slip your self into your role of choice. Try things out – see what fits, what helps you fly. If you find yourself in a story which doesn't help you to live, give it up. Stories with no chance of a happy ending aren't worth telling. Save your breath for the adventures to follow.

Before we go too far, it's important to believe that you know what I am talking about, maybe not in this form, but still the same thing. Think of the words of our favourite brothers:

> The early eighties ... saw the gathering of critical mass through collectivist activities whose emergent agendas began to impact upon

public institutions during the mid-eighties around the key theme of *black representation*. But to call it a 'renaissance,' while capturing the atmosphere of optimism and renewal, implies an authenticating myth of origins which Black Britain did not really have at its disposal: which is to say, if such myths did not exist they would have to be reinvented, using whatever materials came to hand.

Having come to voice, what and whose language do you speak? What or whose language speaks you?

(Mercer 1994: 14)

This is the same will to enter the story, to be seen, to make sense – even if the bargain costs us dear, ties us to forms which can never be ours. It's too late to turn back, the plot is already in motion. Not being in the story isn't an option.

Think about representation, our bane and our obsession – why is this a good way to think about how 'race' and 'gender' work? Why isn't it? Where did class go? Here are some thoughts:

1 This kind of social analysis seems to be inevitably about pictures for us – place this kind of body in this kind of landscape and try to judge the effects. We think you can understand 'race' and gender by looking – you can see the different sorts there are and gauge what happens around them. How we make sense of what we see has an effect on our response – and our response feeds back into the scary real world of events.
2 The drawback is that we get fixated on looking. Looking becomes the main social relation, the one that counts, the activity which shapes the world. All our energy goes on looking different and looking differently. The things we can't see we have no hope of understanding.
3 Some dangers aren't about how things look. There is no picture to show how this works, what it looks like, where it lives. It makes a difference to what we see, but we can't see how, where, when. Even looking at the most ugly pictures is easier than this not knowing. As the shiver of the world hits our shoulders, the distracting activity of tampering with pictures comes as a welcome relief.

It is too late to give up on representation now – too many of our hurts are refracted through this frame. Better to push the logic until the contract snaps. Better to leap into adventure, changing stories like party outfits.

FIRST THINGS FIRST

Fabulous – the stuff of fable, folklore at its most heart-warming and educational. The kind of story which tells it like it is, but also shows you how it could be. A story where none of the characters are real, but you know them all. Remember Aesop ... 'his complexion so swarthy, that he took his very name from it; for Aesop is the same as Aethiop ... such an impediment in his speech, that people could hardly understand what he said' (Richardson, 1975). Named by our skin, we inherit his form. Garble our best truths through fantasy, telling stories which seem at once too obvious and too obscure. Not founded on fact, we mix supernatural characters and legendary tales, idle talk and false statements – halfway between possibility and deception, the special visionary lies of the undervalued. Instead of certainty, here morals are about confounding expectation – the things worth knowing are not straightforward to tell.

Adventures – what every life should hold. Experience as thrill not threat. Battles of the good against evil, quests for lost treasures, a twisting plot which stays surprising. There is risk and danger, of course, the inevitable gambles of the still living. Daringly speculative, hazardously active, adventure turns away from past pain to what is about to happen.

Mahogany – dark brown polish with the time running out. Cut down, chopped up, from tropical forest to draughty dining rooms, only the shiny surface is left. No amount of benefit socials can make things how they were before. Better instead to love the colour, texture, smooth hardness, slippery feel.

Princesses – fantasy creatures fallen out of fairy tales, waiting to be discovered, appreciated, swept off their feet out of drudgery into luxury. Built to be adored, we have fallen on hard times. No calls to let down our hair, climb the mountain of mattresses. When we shout 'Rumplestiltskin', no one respects our ingenuity.

YESTERYEARS

Long ago, in the land of fairy tales, the mahogany princesses lived their lives of wild adventure with no fear but nature, no enemy but death. Their bodies were not yet the imagery of lascivious fantasy. The light bounced off the burnish of their skins, and they savoured the sensation of warmth. Not yet somebody else's picture, their bodies were still a source of non-scopic pleasures. In this world flesh is about touch, smell, taste. Looking isn't the main thing to do and skin is for stroking.

Across the seas the white men dream of what the world might hold. Standing quite still and turning their heads, they imagine the reach of their territory. Looking makes them the centre of the world. They are the vantage spot, the place from which order emanates. Puffed up with this suggestion they crane their necks further, and imagine all the things which they could have.

It was easiest of all to believe that what was good for Europe must be even better for the 'natives'. By now the white man had worked himself into a high state of self-conceit.

(Kiernan 1986: 26)

Sold on the new range of narcissistic fantasy, the white men stretch out to print their mark on the world. The endless repetition of blockprint stamped on the delicate sari length covering all our bodies.

Adventure no. 1

This is a story for times of despair and exhaustion. A dream of that magical time before history – the idyll broken by destructive events and charted occurrence.

Here the princesses are still invisible to their enemies – subject to no one, not yet conquered. The story mixes up all these freedoms, from military occupation, economic impossibility, identity formation. As if that whole other world of pre-colonial civilization was blighted by the first white-man's glance.

In this other time, when some other logic prevailed, the mahogany princesses were happy and doubt-free. They achieved easily, collecting success as their due. From our jumpy shell-shocked world, this looks like a time of innocence. Unaware of the colonial complexes to follow, the princesses bounce around the world charged with expectation.

This is the story we whisper to our children at bedtime. Taking off the battles of the day, heads hitting the pillow, that moment when we sense their connection to what we all used to be. Soft words into nearly sleeping ears, breathing the hope that we could be those things again.

To work this story has to link certain key themes – these are the plot points which must be remembered.

1 There are ways of being beyond the ugliness of colonial relations. In this story we assume a before – the state of grace from which we have sadly fallen – but it is as much about possibility as nostalgia.
2 The time before – the place outside the damaging relations which form our consciousness – offered untold possibilities and achievements. We don't have to be constituted through a paralysed face-off in which we always lose. Beyond Hegel, Fanon, circular determination. The endless face-off of master/slave, colonizer/colonized, us only in relation to them, is a sickness of our time not all time.
3 For the mahogany princesses, this is importantly about a time before the regime of the scopic. We were not always constituted through some-one's glance – maybe looking doesn't have to be the point.

THE COLONIZING GAZE IS TAUT WITH ENVY

Frozen in the white gaze, the mahogany princesses shiver. Suddenly surface is what matters. They still touch – fill their mouths with flavour, breathe deeply the smells of experience – but they are caught in the nets of representation. Looking becomes the route to knowledge. Information is what you can see. Increasingly the mahogany princesses imagine themselves as the two-dimensional mirage of someone else's look. Self as picture sucks away the pleasures of self as flesh. The things which can't be shown lose their power to the demonstrable.

The scopic pressures distort the lovely bodies of the princesses. Their skins take over their beings. They are engulfed by surface. Colour becomes a sensation so intense it hurts. What is visible is all there is – nothing else seems so stark, so conspicuous. Texture is the way light is reflected, warmth is the promise from a pleasing curve. Sight sucks out the essence of other ways of being. What used to seem thick and solid becomes less substantial than a picture – sensations float away without the shared currency of visible proof.

Adventure no. 2

This is more painful altogether – much too close to our everyday ambivalence for any comfort. This is the story we sing to each other – a hen night special to boost our broken self-esteem. In those moments aside, over chopping boards and bubbling pots, the chorus comes back. Helping each other dress, coiling the heavy hair slicked with coconut, smoothing dusty skin back into its shine – we remind each other how this trap works.

When we look for knowledge, we find a thousand stories of how we have lost. The pain comes not from being written out of their histories, but from being written in so insistently. Endless pictures, lascivious anecdotes, the background character in all their life-stories. Their most important stories are told through us. We are the shapes of their best dreams and worst fears. They look at pictures of us to recognize themselves, to see inside, to balance the thrill between feeling bad and feeling good. What we see doesn't come into it at all.

Looking at their pictures makes us feel like monsters – our sense of self shifts to fit what we see, all around, everywhere, from way back when to next week, month, year. They are the scopic masters, squashing everything jealously into two-dimensions. The weight of invasion flattens our volume out, the heavy breath of subjugation. Nothing left but the limp skins of their fantasy.

This story smarts with its telling – that moment of loss, the beginning of the end, the long descent to today. The plot needs these interludes of suffering. All superheroes endure ordeals on their journeys to victory. Dwelling on these downsides serves a variety of purpose.

1 We see more clearly how the past haunts our lives.
2 The reminder that we are living diminished lives prompts us to regain size, shape, weight, form. To imagine ourselves as something more than someone else's picture.
3 Most importantly, things are not what they seem. This is the lesson which could change the future. The mahogany princesses are demeaned by a culture which secretly loves them better than itself. The centuries of ugliness are rooted in fear, the destruction comes from a child's half-formed jealousy at sensing things beyond their reach. The worst things in the world spring from weakness masquerading as strength, a terror of what others have. This story reminds us that even our persecutors are awed by our gifts, stunned by our beauty, desperate to climb inside our bodies (Young 1995).

HALF DEVIL – HALF CHILD

The children of the sun feed the hungry white gaze – all the flavours of their previous lives offered up in one delectable image. Children's drawings, family heirlooms, holiday gifts – guzzled in to the visitors' appetite. And still more – today's breakfast, dinner, tea, favourite clothes, tomorrow's hopes – all fallen in to the void. Even before birth future generations became pledged to keeping the picture show going. So much work and so little to show. Whatever they shovelled in seemed to get lost, leaving no traces of the offered comforts but that one same image. No fat, no warmth, no love, nothing saved. Just a picture of fear and desire.

Adventure no. 3

This is a story about physical endurance – giving beyond reason, careless of scarcity. We tell this story to recall the mixture of innocence and largesse which we once were. Excess was possible, we thought, more than enough to go around.

Whole worlds of resources were sucked into the West's hunger. Nothing held back, no extra tucked away for later. These gifts are registered nowhere, subsumed in achievements which show no acknowledgement. Instead, all that shows is that same old fantasy – the one which registers psychic fear and vengeful desire, but no economic relation, no one-way traffic in goods and services. We tell this story to remind ourselves of what the pictures don't show. At those dangerous moments when we almost believe what we see, when only images seem true, this story asks 'Who is the child in this game of manipulation?' We are used up feeding an infantile fury which is never appeased. This story acknowledges this relation of care as a way of managing bitterness.

1 The pictures of ourselves hide our efforts, talents, resources.
2 Cutting close ties always leaves pain. Remembering how intertangled our lives have been explains the confusion that follows.
3 Now it is time to reclaim that pre-betrayal generosity as strength and possibility, not a foolish mistake to be put right by experience. So concerned not to be suckered again, we forget to live at all.

A daydream of alternative subject formation – THE EXOTIC WHITE MAN[1].

Not my object, my thing, my fantasy. I'm looking – but I can't fix him in my sights.

More and less human than us, he reddens easily. The scuffs of living come up tender on his skin. Not a story of the past, but still some map of pain. His surface cracks under pressure, grabs destruction from heat, weeps mucous tears. No lubricant to ease this brittleness – being wet just means being more sore.

Even as he flakes away and falls apart, the white man can't see himself. The world's audience can't recognize another's glance. Unaware, he lets it all hang out. Flaunts his paunch, scratches his crotch, wipes body ooze on his surroundings, convinced the marks don't show. Settling down for the performance, sinking into smugness, slumping as if the body belongs to someone else. Certainly no picture. Who'd look at that?

This weakness is touching. A clumsy child, finger in nose. So vulnerably oblivious. My job is to soak up the mess without accusing the source. Endless care and no more tears. My charge is too innocent for account-ability, too pre-responsible for blame. The piss-stains on the carpet are nobody's fault. People with no sense of self deserve protection. I meet the bargain and hold the trust. The fiction of the one-way look, a master lie to live by.

I'm laying out the pieces – one by one, side by side. I touch, sniff, lick each fragment, curating carefully. The contract has come back round and I'm paying what I owe, the care that I have received. Who knows you better than me, recorder of your delicate places, vessel of your wounds. I hold what your life could never be. In me your fears are carried back as trophies, what hurts belongs to someone else. Trust me because I remember what you have been.

Looming in out of vision, she felt that she had won. Impossible to focus at this range – no barriers until, too late, they were broken. She knew that in his mind's eye he held a picture-reminder of her, a prompt for the frightening moments when looking didn't work. She knew that he remembered those other spaces where she was his object – that it was this memory of mastery which got him hard, guided him across her warmth. To him touch meant colour, form, responses filtered back through the thing he knew. Sensation as picture.

This was his weakness. She held his expectation, stroked and petted. Touched carefully, knowing he thought in pictures and stories, that her special skills were lost in his translations.

> The artist is somewhat prone to see the foreigner as a comic creature. Our features were odd, our pinkish colour somewhat revolting, our kinder moments endearing. And this was how we were seen, odd creatures from far away who were sometimes quite charming, and sometimes hatefully cruel. In this book we shall have to take ourselves as others found us.
>
> (Burland 1969: 11)

Boy flesh – unfamiliar meat. Less pliant, less movement. The polite words flick by – wiry, gaunt, artistic, sensitive androgyne, gawky manchild. Of course, that wasn't it. Nothing like the thrill of the new. She wanted to remake him as an image of herself. Her mirror, her object – vessel to her dreams, mould to her body. In him she saw a slip, a twist, an inside-out version of the world she knew. The same, the same, the same. Same picture, same story. A confirmation of her hopes and fears screening out the possibility of anything different. What he lacked was proof of what she had. Against him she puffed up, splayed out, shone.

Sometimes he turned his head as if pulled by recollection. Some other place from before or to come. A home elsewhere. She dried up in the breeze from that movement, the thought that she didn't centre the world. The idea of a place beyond their two cracked her heart wide open, and out flew the safety of her name.

TERRITORIAL BATTLES

In the struggles over land, people forgot to look. Flesh ripped and no one remembered the lures of warm brownness. The princesses waited for darkness, regained powers which had been lost to pictures – found their teeth had bite, their nails could claw.

The violence snapped the brittle contract of desire. Better not to look at that tantalizing flesh. Better to give up those favourite pin-ups. Sometimes it is too noisy for titillation. Delectation needs a moment's peace, a sense of leisure. Now you can't be sure it costs nothing to look. The edges are blurring, things you can't quite see creep up from behind, beyond, underneath. The lookers are scared to stand still in case they are eaten. No time for head-swivelling. Nothing in view to recentre that eye.

Adventure no. 4

This most heroic moment, fought just yesterday, seems the most distantly mythic. Such a well-known narrative, good against evil, the weak kicking back, ultimate victory. A countless collection of individual sacrifices – everybody's uncle, cousin, village beauty, school sportstar – each told as proof of the master narrative of 'We whipped their arses, they didn't think we could, after so long, so long, but we did and now we are home.'

All over the world the mahogany princesses lap up the flavour of that victory, a nourishing supplement to spice up more everyday battles. This becomes our most formative story – an oedipalized break from inter-dependency to . . . interdependency? These are the stories of holidays and public events. Big crowd pleasers, sure to get them dancing. We know how to deal with the proud and defiant heritage of our homelands.[2]

But this story conceals other lessons to be saved.

1 That violence – the wrench that makes you, but from which you never recover. The desolation you wake up to. A story helps us encounter that unsettling rupture and move on.
2 Only victory songs which recall the costs of victory can help in what follows.
3 All wounds need mourning – maybe most of all the ones you don't know you suffer.

> Disremembered and unaccounted for, she cannot be lost because no one is looking for her, and even if they were, how can they call her if they don't know her name?
>
> (Morrison 1987: 274)[3]

JOURNEYS WEST

After the battle dusts settled, there was no moment of longed-for calm, no well-deserved relief. The princesses lifted their heads slowly and looked around, as the white men had taught them. What was left to survey? Smashed up, ripped out, cracked open. Shattered, splintered, torn, trashed. Not much to look at. Bits and pieces which didn't quite make a whole, injuries from no particular source. Plenty of pain.

The princesses scrunched up their lovely eyes and tried to imagine a better future. Spinning out, stretching into possibility – nostrils flared, fingers spread, reaching for all the things that might be. For a moment they float, on the edge of a new deal, a fresh space, the old contracts are almost broken. Eyes shut, we're almost there, sugar sweet, cotton soft. The hum of life takes over. Bodies feel like luxury items. The princesses throw back their heads and laugh.

Wallop. History smashes back. Dead weights on your back, rubble in the streets. The journey to this point, the ways things make sense. Yesterday's traces fill our todays. Cut out the past and there's nothing left. Of course, we follow where we can, what we know. Shifting our dreams to whatever seems likely.

Adventure no. 5

This story is about troubled journeys and permanent exile, about packing our bags and starting afresh. Like all women who love too much, we are addicted to destructive relationships. Run half-way around the globe to be close to those we've worked so hard to leave. In days wracked with homesickness, heads turned back to dreams we have left, being here is the punishment we choose, no one but ourselves to blame. This is the story of our journey to this place, pulled by history, not addicted to pain.

1 We are here for a reason, living out a logic of pathology set in motion long ago.
2 The ripples of past relationships always shake up the present. Nothing is ever completely over. Smart is learning to live with the repercussions.
3 The sense of travel makes us what we are – nostalgic for back homes which some have never seen, living with our bags packed, always ready to up and leave, holding on to nothing too heavy or bulky or breakable.

CONTEMPORARY ADVENTURES

Stepping out into unpredictable streets, it's hard to tell how people react to princess-skin. The old possibilities are there somewhere. The promise of warmth, the spread of colour – bodies smooth as appleskin, solid as hardwood. Pebble beach women who bruise their playmates, pushing hard to get back to touch.

Are all those things still true?

As time goes on, the princesses lose their burnish. Not so shiny happy. The past sinks away into water ghost hauntings – no sense of distance only a fear of depth. Princesses become everyday, hardly worth an objectifying turn of the head.

The millennium approaches and the exotic resides in the heartlands of the metropolis. There is no fantastic distance through which to imagine mammoth appetites, monstrous bodies. The edge of humanity folds in and suddenly these people are pushed right up against the white gaze.

At bus-stops and supermarkets, in the cities and suburbs of rundown cold old Britain, the daughters of the sun are here. The dark bodies which peopled the excesses of the orientalist imagination scatter the landscape of contemporary Britain. Fulfilling the fearful expectations of human imagination, things change, and keep right on changing.

The earth shifts and new monsters appear out of the cracks in its surface. Some mate with the horrors of yesterday and their mutant offspring emerge as fresh terrors for an unsuspecting humanity. The mahogany princesses glance backwards towards the mythic homelands of their mothers, then take a breath and prepare to fight.

Their battles straddle the worlds of yesterday and today – at once colonial fantasy and scourge of the white nation. The eyes that watch are hungry for contact – closer, closer, touch, taste. The dark women move through this network of scrutiny as best they can, alert or numb, slipping between impossible options.

Choosing our routes is an endless adventure – an exercise in balancing risk and possibility. The mahogany princesses, mixed up children of a changing world, weigh up their choices and jump right in.

BEING A GIRL

Girl is the opposite to boy – this story splits the world in two, endlessly, seemingly for all time. Either one or not-one, presence or absence, subject or object. If you're not one then you must be the other.

Boy is central, pivotal, tall, strong and hardly ever visible. Far too good for everyday. Girl is everything else, background, container, water, nature, earth and home. The most taken for granted and the least seen. Here gender is the zero-sum game filling up the world, assigning roles, determining response. The first name we learn, our entry into language, the social, human living. All other relations happen after this first one – echoes of this two of non-communication. Apparently.

In the arena of skin the white boys win again. Central, pivotal, tall, strong and hardly ever visible. So far so familiar. The powerful hog the privilege of the norm and the rest of us squeeze in behind, around, wherever there is room. Boys stride and girls cower, light skin preens while dark skin waits. In the economy of two there are only winners and losers, tops and bottoms bonded in a hermetic contract with no outside. The mahogany princesses fall out of both contracts – too much skin to be simply girl, too feminine to be just dark. If the world is full of ones and their others then white/black is an echo of man/woman is an echo of master/slave is an echo of culture/nature is an echo of coherence/confusion. We recognize the winning team again and again – the couplets must be true. But where are the mahogany princesses in this map of the world? Doubly marked, unspeakable in two, more than the other of white or boy – how do we choose what to be? Do we frock up? Primp our way into girlhood? Or swagger our way alongside gender and live in the names of skin? Of course, the answer is both and neither, whatever will work for right now. It is still impossible to tell which comes first, which hurts most, which is most precious, formative, scratched deep on the inside.

Try to picture a mahogany princess – what do you see first, her colour or her shape?

The picture may not be important to you, but it is to her. The pictures you have of yourself structure what you can do, tell you how to go about getting some of the things you want.

PASSING

Some pictures are pre-make-over – the before of the process of becoming a new and miraculous after. The point is to identify the weak points and conspicuous features which need toning down.

You might choose to be a girl – wear a dress, curl your hair, talk sexuality, domestic violence, personal politics. You might paint your face and go for ultrafemininity, dangerous dagger heels or sweet-enough-to eat prettiness. You might collect the stories of international sisterhood, link up all those details about petty slights and major mutilations which punish girls and run straight to the women's caucus. You don't lose your skin, but you tone down its colours to fit in and get things done.

You might choose to let skin take over – wear ethnicity, authenticity, tradition, talk colonialism, racist violence, pride and heritage. You might wear clothes as extensions of your skin, back-home outfits cut to please grandmothers or those looks which white girls never wear. You might collect all those histories of slavery and colonialism, the scary disregard for the value of human life in a dark skin, then and now, and put your energies into black self-organization. You are still a girl, but you put that to one side for a while and concentrate on defending your community.

We learn these stories as dangerous cop-outs to be avoided at all costs – lose sight of the complexities of identity and things will never get better. We don't value disguise these days. We've forgotten the ballerina skills of those deceptions, the disciplines which played with perception and changed possibilities.

The most risky disguise is taking the centre – by yourself, on the enemy's terms. The least elegant passing, the walking-on-daggers bargain which never stops cutting. Desperate measures for desperate times, wiping out everything we used to be. This story is a cautionary tale.[4]

DIFFERENCE

We pretend that we have learnt better than to try and pass. No point trying to be what you are not, so instead we work hard at being ourselves. Everyone is looking for their own spaces, and ours is the tapestry fun palace, the sunken-bath land of exotic mysteries. Instead of camouflaging our most conspicuous features, we are building them up, showing them off. Flaunting what we have to those who don't. Preening for each other in mutual appreciation. We can't escape the world of pictures. Memory no longer extends to the time before. Now skin really is the main thing we are, the way we imagine ourselves. Feeling better depends on altering the picture, the criteria of visual values. It's too hard to see beyond that scopic contract any more. Other ways of being are forgotten – they don't feel real to us.

The only option is to rework the pictures to show off our best sides.

IMAGINATION

Eager to learn, heads in books, scrabbling up the schooling of our parents' sacrifice – too many of the lessons stop us dead in despair. Bolted down by circumstance and held tight by the knowledge of how things are. The kind of education which wears you out, grinds you down, makes you lie down, give up, hide. Knowing hurts so much that living seems impossible – and anyway, not worth the effort.

All the stories so far serve a purpose, but trap us where we are. Forgetting the exuberant pleasures of narrative, we play over and over the unhappy endings which it is too late to change. I want to stop – to take the lessons and move on, up, out, away.

The stories worth telling join the unbearable past to the exuberant future just a breath away. Everything is not yet lost. Now, in the middle of the film, battered by the events of yesterday and just now, the plot twists ahead seem unimaginable. Take a breath and jump right in.

NOTES

1 Worlds away from Luce Irigaray and *Speculum of the Other Woman* (1985).
2 See Partha Chatterjee (1986) for a warning against these celebrations.
3 Toni Morrison (1987), *Beloved*, a book which was a big event for mahogany princesses everywhere.
4 See sad and familiar stories in bell hooks (1993), *Sisters of the Yam, Black Women and Self-Recovery*, particularly chapter 7, 'Facing and Feeling Loss'.

REFERENCES

Burland, C. A. (1969) *The Exotic White Man*, London, Weidenfeld and Nicolson.
Chatterjee, P. (1986) *Nationalist Thought and the Colonial World*, Minneapolis, University of Minnesota Press
hooks, b. (1993) *Sisters of the Yam: Black Women and Self-Recovery*, London, Turnaround.
Irigaray, L. (1985) *Speculum of the Other Woman*, New York, Cornell University Press.
Kiernan, V.G. (1986) *Lords of Human Kind, Blackman, Yellow Man and White Man in an Age of Empire*, New York, Columbia University Press.
Mercer, K. (1994) *Welcome to the Jungle*, London, Routledge.
Morrison, T. (1987) *Beloved*, London, Chatto and Windus.
Richardson, S. (1975) (ed.) *Aesop's Fables 1740*, New York and London, Garland Publishing.
Young, R. (1995) *Colonial Desire, Hybridity in Theory, Culture and Race*, London, Routledge.

Part III

Changing our place

The chapters in this final section of the book look forward to the future and explore new directions and opportunities for change that a black feminist perspective can engender. Black British feminism has from its inception been underpinned and informed by political and social activism. Black British feminism had its genesis over 50 years ago in the activism and political struggles of black women migrants from the postcolonial Caribbean, African and Asian continents. In this section, the chapters demonstrate the link black feminism maintains to this tradition of activism. Here the black women writers challenge official definitions, institutional marginalization and the limits of a dominant language that cannot speak of their experience. Through articulating black women's activity and agency, black British feminism remains a critical force for social change in the postmodern terrain that is postcolonial Britain at the end of the twentieth century.

Chapter 21

Third wave feminism and black women's activism

Pragna Patel

The time has come, the Walrus said, to talk of many things . . .
>   (L. Carroll, *Alice's Adventures in Wonderland*)

I was born in Kenya and came to Britain at the age of 4. I have known no other landscape, but I never felt that I belonged here. With no other choice but to make my life here, I grew into a politics of resistance; against the racism that I experienced outside my home because I was the wrong colour, and against the injustices I experienced because I was the wrong gender. In this way I fashioned for myself a strong political identity, in struggle with other black men and women. Despite hovering on the margins of British society, this identity is a source of tremendous power and strength, and even, dare I say it, moral righteousness.

It was precisely this sense of belonging, this black identity, which fell apart in December 1992. When militant right-wing Hindu nationalists destroyed the sixteenth century Babri-Masjid mosque in India, I was forced to confront the elements of the 'Hindu' identity within me which I had supposed had all but withered away. By virtue of being a member of that diaspora of Indian-Hindu origin, I was, whether I liked it or not, also part of a Hindu collectivity. This collectivity contained elements which, as part of a majority in India, was embarking in the name of God and religion on a course of annihilation of minorities and dissenters, and attacking the very foundations of democracy in that country. Yet this very same collectivity, as a minority elsewhere in the world, knows what it is like to experience discrimination and hatred. These painful contradictions compelled me critically to re-examine my own Hindu background in order to be able to understand, and crucially to oppose those who, in the name of Hinduism, were acting in a way which was deeply inhuman and shameful to witness.

The recognition that I may belong at one and the same time to an oppressed minority and to an oppressive majority, with all the contradictions that entails, has found an echo in my experiences in Britain. Many of the struggles we have waged as black people here have rested, sometimes uncritically, upon a white majority/black minority dichotomy.

This has been useful in creating the sense of solidarity necessary to mobilize against racist attacks from the state and thugs on our streets, uniformed or otherwise, but in asserting a singular and absolute identity – as 'victims' of racism – we have evaded the need to look critically at the inner dynamics of our communities. This has resulted in a tendency to deny uncomfortable realities and has tended to give us a distorted and partial view of ourselves and the world around us. This tendency has been particularly difficult for black women to deal with, as our struggles often arise out of our experiences *within* our communities, and in fighting to force these onto the wider political agenda we have also often had to fight against the imposition of a singular identity either on ourselves or on our communities.

What follows is an attempt to locate these struggles by retracing some of the campaigns of Southall Black Sisters (SBS) and our sister organization, Brent Asian Women's Refuge. Our struggles have, out of necessity, arisen from the routine experiences of many Asian, African, Caribbean and other women who come to these centres with stories of violence, persecution, imprisonment, poverty and homelessness experienced at the hands of their husbands, families and/or the state. In attempting to meet the challenges they pose in their demands for justice for themselves and for women generally, we have had to organize autonomously. But we have always endeavoured to situate our practice within wider anti-racist and socialist movements, involving alliances and coalitions within and across the minority and majority divides. This has not always been easy, but it is the only way we know in which a new and empowering politics can be forged.

By organizing in women's groups and refuges, many of us have fought for autonomous spaces and for the right for our own voices to be heard in order to break free from the patriarchal stranglehold of the family. In the process we have also had to challenge the attitudes of the wider society, as well as the theory and practice of social policy and legislation which seeks to restrict our freedom to make informed choices about our lives. Our organizations and our practice are critical in unmasking the failures, not only of our communities and the state and wider society, but perhaps more tellingly, of so-called multi-culturalist and anti-racist policies.

Throughout our campaigns on domestic violence, whilst countering racist stereotypes about the 'problematic' nature of South Asian families, SBS has sought to highlight not only the familiar economic and legal obstacles faced by all women struggling to live free of abuse, but also the particular plight of Asian women; language barriers, racism, and the specific role of culture and religion which can be used to sanction their subordinate role and to circumscribe their responses. Culture and religion in all societies act to confer legitimacy upon gender inequalities, but these cultural constraints affect some women more than others in communities where 'culture' carries the burden of protecting minority identities in the face of external hostility. We have had to formulate demands and strategies which recognize the plurality of our experiences, without suppressing anything for the sake of political expediency. Alliances have been crucial in this, not only in gaining wider support, but also in breaking down mutual suspicion and stereotypes, and to ensure that some rights are not gained at the expense of others.

We began our protests in the early 1980s over the murder of Mrs Dhillon and her three daughters by her husband who burnt them to death. In 1984 we took to the streets in response to the death of Krishna Sharma, who committed suicide as a result of her husband's assaults. Organizing with other women in very public ways, through demonstrations and pickets, we broke the silence of the community. Until that point there had been not a single voice of protest from either progressive or conservative elements within the community. The women who led the demonstrations had themselves fled their own families in Southall, but returned to join us with scarves wrapped around their faces so that they might escape recognition. We demanded and won the support of many white women in the wider feminist movement, although initially they were hesitant in offering support for fear of being labelled 'racist'! One of our slogans – 'self-defence is no offence' – was appropriated from the anti-racist 'street-fighting' traditions, but ironically it has now become the much quoted slogan of the wider women's movement against male violence in Britain. The form of our protests drew directly from the varied and positive feminist traditions of the Indian sub-continent. We picketed directly outside Krishna Sharma's house, turning accepted notions of honour and shame on their heads. It is the perpetrators of violence, we shouted, who should be shamed and disrobed of their honour by the rest of the community, not the women who are forced to submit. Another slogan – 'black women's tradition, struggle not submission' – was first coined on this demonstration, and that, too, has been adapted to become the rallying cry of feminists against male violence in this country.

The lessons of those early years have ensured that we have understood the importance of campaigns and direct action as an essential means of articulating the needs of the women who turn to us daily. From the murder of Balwant Kaur by her husband at the Brent refuge in 1985, to the life imprisonment of Kiranjit Ahluwalia for killing her violent husband in 1989, our response has been driven by a recognition that those tragedies reflected, albeit in extreme forms, the day-to-day experiences of many Asian women facing violence on the home. Over the years we have managed to retain a campaigning edge to our work, while also providing day-to-day services.

THE KIRANJIT AHLUWALIA CAMPAIGN

The campaign to free Kiranjit Ahluwalia following her murder conviction in December 1989 illustrated the need for, and the potential impact of, alliances as a form of political action. We had to raise the specificity of her experiences as an Asian woman, drawing on her own depiction of her life, but we also had to draw out the connections with the experiences of other women in order to make demands relevant to all women in this society. Black and white, young and old, activists and non-activists, we found ourselves involved in one of the main empowering mobilizations of women against injustice seen for a long time. The women who use our centre and refuge wept and laughed with joy at Kiranjit's eventual release. Many from across the religious, caste and class divisions claimed her personal triumph as their own personal and collective victory.

In July 1991, Sara Thornton lost her appeal to overturn her murder conviction because the legal system was not then ready to accept a feminist critique of the homicide laws. Her hunger strike and the consequent publicity, against the background of the case of Joseph McGrail who was freed after kicking his alcoholic wife to death, struck a chord with the public which was to change the course of the Kiranjit Ahluwalia campaign. In the face of government intransigence, there was growing support for our critique of the legal system's untenable position on 'battered women'. Every day yielded more voices of support, ranging from almost all sections of the media and lawyers, civil servants, members of Parliament across the political divides, academics, activists and the general public. On our part, we were able to mobilize women in SBS and at the refuge; women who had experienced violence and who understood Kiranjit's tragic act.

Our main allies were radical feminists, with their long and rich history in campaigning around violence against women, and Asian women, particularly those working in refuges and women's centres. The unity we forged had two main aims: to ensure the release of battered women who kill their tormentors and who are unjustly incarcerated, and to demand a reform of the homicide legislation responsible for their imprisonment. There were many points of contention within the alliance as to the nature of the demands we ought to make of the state. Should we agitate for a reform of the existing laws as a tactical demand, or should we campaign for entirely new homicide laws that more accurately reflect women's daily experience of violence? Should we aim for new laws which are specific to women, or should they subsume areas such as racial violence and harassment? These tensions were never entirely resolved, nor could they have been, but despite divergent and sometimes irreconcilable views, we have been able to sustain the alliance.

Recently our campaign for the reform of homicide legislation, and more generally for changes in the criminal justice system have led us into a new temporary alliance with more long-established women's organizations with a far from radical image, such as the Townswomen's Guild and the Women's Institute. Although we have only been able to come together on the narrow issue of changing the law of provocation, it is, nevertheless, a tactically important alliance of wider political significance. Conservative and liberal women from these groups have joined us in mutual recognition of the fact that the law fails women. The outcome in this instance is less important than the process by which consciousness around domestic violence can continue to grow. The established women's groups are extremely nervous about the radical elements within the alliance, but they are still soldiering on with us to organize a mass lobby at the Houses of Parliament, and a letter-writing campaign to the Home Secretary. The alliance has already led to the right-wing Home Secretary, Michael Howard, developing a defensive posture when responding to letters by members of the Women's Institute and the Townswomen's Guild. A few years ago we would not have dared participate in such a forum, fearing that our politics or terms of reference might be compromised by such co-operation. We are now much more confident about the nature and boundaries of our participation in political alliances with other women's groups.

Since the Kiranjit Ahluwalia campaign we have witnessed a resurgence in campaigns around violence against women in the South Asian and other minority communities, often in consultation with one another. These campaigns seek to redefine the relationship of women to the criminal justice system and to change the language of wider movements. So, the term 'miscarriage of justice', which initially meant the wrongful conviction and punishment of those who are innocent, has been extended to include those who are routinely failed by the criminal justice system in other ways, through the failure of the police and the prosecuting authorities to protect women from abusive partners, to the transgressions of women which the law is unable to comprehend in its wider context. Internationally, too, the debates around domestic violence and other forms of male violence are defining women's rights as human rights, and issues like rape as crimes against humanity. These developments open up the potential for creating women's alliances which transcend artificial national boundaries.

By virtue of campaigns like ours, the law has been forced to take into account the social conditions and pressures which push women into contact or conflict with the criminal justice system. The years of hard campaigning by feminists against male violence are beginning to bear some fruit within the legal system, although contradictions remain. Gains in some areas of the law are offset by losses in others, and there is no room for complacency. In the Kiranjit Ahluwalia case, the legal definition of provocation has shifted to reflect the inability of some women to retaliate immediately after an assault or threat, and expert evidence to show the psychological impact of cumulative provocation was admitted for the first time. However, the attempt to fit complex realities into neat legal definitions can construct women in ways which deny their anger and agency, rendering them less threatening to the status quo. Thus the 'battered women syndrome' has been used to explain women's inaction in the face of repeated violence, but in the process the experience of women is medicalized and relegated to the realms of mental disorder. In other words, women are not 'permitted' to be angry or to locate their actions in a socio-economic context or in the failures of the institution of the family.

As feminists we have to be careful about the uncritical acceptance of superficially attractive solutions offered by the state in response to our campaigns and demands. For example, recent shifts in police attitudes and practices on domestic violence may appear to have 'solved' the problem of previous police indifference. The domestic violence units and multi-agency forums which are the practical outcome of these shifts in police strategy have done nothing to bring the issue of police accountability any closer to being addressed. In our experience the police still continue to fail women in their response to women's calls for help, and this should not inspire any confidence in the view that the police are now 'on our side'.

Similarly, as feminists we have to be careful not to separate ourselves off from other human and civil rights demands that at first sight may not appear to be a feminist concern. For instance, the abolition of the right to silence will have a profound effect on the rights of many: blacks, lesbians and gays, new age travellers and women. Kiranjit Ahluwalia exercised her right to silence at her original criminal trial, but had she been forced into the witness box in the vulnerable, confused and frightened state she was then in, the outcome of her appeal might have been very different. The legal system is not like an onion which, if peeled, might reveal an egalitarian core. The institutions of the state represent and articulate vested interests, constantly shifting ground the better to maintain the status quo. Any gains we make can be reversed or diluted in the face of power and privilege.

THE STATE AND THE FAMILY

The state for us has never been an abstract concept. It has a real existence which defines our roles and position in society; it negotiates our existence as women within our families. Our understanding of a family as an institution governing our relationship with the outside world is therefore vital. It has been shaped by the women who came to us questioning their roles and their lack of rights within and outside the family. Their experiences of domestic violence, sexual abuse, forced arranged marriages and racism are reflected in their demands to assert their rights as individuals. Yet within dominant anti-racist discourse, the black family is often constructed solely as a 'haven', a bulwark against the worst excesses of state harassment and racism. Whilst not denying that the family can perform this role, the construction of the homogeneous Asian family hides other realities, power relations and power struggles between different caste, class and ethnic groups, and especially between men and women.

There are different ways in which the state constructs families, whether in the majority or minority community. The law and social policy take as 'natural' or given certain power relations between different groups and between men and women. These power relations reproduce and perpetuate inequalities between different sections of society. One good example is the construction of minority families in current immigration law, which operate largely to limit immigration from 'Third World' countries, and to restrict freedom of movement and speech, by curtailing rights of appeal against unfair and blatantly discriminatory decisions.

Anti-racist politics has effectively illuminated the racist assumptions which lie behind the immigration laws. Black families are routinely denied the right to privacy and unity in contravention of internationally recognized definitions of human rights. Intimate and intrusive questioning is commonplace in immigration cases, and the relations between partners and their dependants is probed for the slightest hint of inconsistency. In these ways black families are denied the rights taken for granted by families in the majority community. Anti-racism, however, pays little attention to the complex interplay between racist laws and patriarchal control which acts to place women in the most vulnerable position in the operation of immigration law.

It has been left to women to highlight the manner in which immigration law can combine with the institution of the family to construct the women as an appendage to her husband, economically and socially dependant upon him, and a potential prisoner of violence and abuse within the home. When a woman has come from abroad to marry here, should the marriage break down within a year her immigration status is rendered illegitimate should she leave her husband (this is known as the 'one year rule'). In the absence of an immigration status in her own right, a women's option to leave a violent or abusive home becomes virtually non-existent. In such a situation if a women does leave her husband, not only is she ineligible for any form of state assistance in the form of housing or welfare benefits, which are a prerequisite for giving women a real choice about leaving a violent home, but she also risks deportation. As there is no right of appeal in such cases, her fate is then entirely dependent upon political decisions taken by the Home Office. The arbitrary and discriminatory nature of such decisions, underpinned by notions of Third World peoples as 'aliens' or 'undesirables', means that the majority of women in such cases are forcibly deported to countries where their futures may be at risk. Persecution based on gender is not recognized as grounds for asylum in this, as in many other western countries.[1]

In this way, as in many others, we see the state applying double standards to the treatment of families from different communities. The premise of social services intervention, for example, is to preserve the unity of the family as far as possible, whilst the police and immigration services end up dividing and separating many black families. Women in the majority community have, through women's own action, managed to extend their choices to enable women to leave unhappy marriages, but for women from minority communities, particularly those with immigration difficulties, that choice is absent. Our demand is for the right of black and minority families to live undivided when they choose, but for women to have a real option of leaving an unhappy marriage without the state and the community colluding to deny that choice. If all women are to be empowered, it is essential to understand how the intersection of race, class and gender has the effect of locking different groups of men and women into varying subordinate and dominant positions within the family, community and the wider society. It is at the point of these intersections that women's access to power and resources are differentially structured, as is their level of participation in decision-making within the family and the community.

The family has always been an important battleground for resistance. In a contribution written for a public meeting organized in 1990 to launch her campaign, Kiranjit Ahluwalia delivered a devastating critique of her circumstances, unpicking the intertwining threads of religion, culture and tradition to show how her family life had become a prison. She argues, as do many of the women who come to see us, that she tried to be a 'good' wife and mother, to live by the rules of her religion and culture.

> My culture is like my blood – coursing through every vein of my body. It is the culture into which I was born and where I grew up which sees the women as the honour of the house. In order to uphold this false honour and glory, she is taught to endure many kinds of oppression and pain, in silence. In addition religion also teaches her that her husband is her God and fulfilling his every desire is her religious duty. A women who does not follow this part in our society has no respect or place in it. She suffers from all kinds of slanders against her character. And she has to face all sorts of attacks and much hurt entirely alone. She is responsible not only for her husband but also for his entire family's happiness. . . . This is the essence of my culture, society, religion. Where a women is a toy, a plaything – she can be stuck together at will, broken at will. . . . Today I have come out of the jail of my husband and entered the jail of the law.

The challenge to religion and culture is not easy. The choice for women who dare break out of the very narrow confines of the roles prescribed by religion and culture is stark; either they remain within the parameters of permissible behaviour, or they transgress and risk becoming pariahs within their own community. Many women cannot even conceive of a life of isolation and loneliness, preferring instead to risk their health, sanity and even their lives. Suicide rates among Asian women between the ages of 16 and 35 in Britain are up to three times the national average. Others, like Kiranjit Ahluwalia, refuse to internalize their anger and rage, and transgress into the unchartered 'male' territory of outward expression through homicide, and by doing so they defy social constructs of women as nurturers and carers.

MULTICULTURALISM AND RELIGIOUS FUNDAMENTALISM

Religion and culture is the terrain on which the politics of multi-culturalism and variants of anti-racism are built, often amounting to nothing more than a preservation and celebration of minority culture and religion. Multiculturalism has its roots in past British colonial practices in such countries as India (Sahgal 1992). In Britain it allows the state to mediate between itself and minority communities, using so-called 'com-munity leaders' as power-brokers and middle-men. Needless to say, such leaders are male, from religious, business and other socially conservative backgrounds who, historically, have had little or no interest in promoting an agenda for social justice and equality, least of all the rights of Asian women (Ali 1992). In return for information and votes, the state concedes some measure of autonomy to the 'community leaders' to govern their communities. In reality, this means control over the family – women and children. Together the state and community leaders define the needs of minority communities, to limit their influence and to separate off the more radical elements by labelling them extremists.

In the name of tolerance of 'cultural differences', the rights of women are dismissed, and many Asian women seeking support to escape from violence are often told by state agencies that such a breach is not an acceptable method of resolving their problems in 'their cultures'. They are denied protection and delivered back to their families and communities. In 1991 an Asian man was charged with grievously assaulting his wife, an assault which nearly killed her. He was given a very lenient (non-custodial) sentence by the judge on the grounds that he was an 'immig-rant'. On passing sentence the judge commented that had he been white, he would have dealt with him more severely. The judge's remarks and sanctions are shot through with multiculturalist perceptions. He acknowl-edged the criminal offence that had been committed, but offered effec-tively to 'tolerate' it as it occurred in a different cultural context. Such views not only help to shape notions of Asian cultures as backward, monolithic and static, with no internal contesting struggles, they also help to reinforce patriarchal control of women in Asian communities.[2]

Multiculturalism has provided the ideological framework for fundamentalist and conservative leaders within the Asian communities to emphasize the primacy of religious identities. In this country the rise of religious fundamentalism is in part a response to the upsurge in European nationalism and racism, and the failure of progressive left politics, coupled with the fallout from the Rushdie affair and the Gulf War. These developments have contributed greatly to the current state of race and gender politics. Unlike multiculturalism, religious fundamentalism privileges religion as the main mark of identity, and constructs itself in total opposition to secularism. It seeks to reaffirm and harness religious identity in the quest for power and resources at the local and national level.

The resurgence of religious fundamentalism feeds off parallel developments within the majority community. The reassertion of Christianity as the main signifier of 'British' identity in schools, or the 'Back to Basics' campaign, underlined by a Christian morality aimed at preserving the nuclear and heterosexual family unit, are developments that have fuelled reactionary demands for formal recognition of minority religious lifestyles. Fundamentalist movements may differ in detail, but they have two major objectives in common: recognition as distinctive (to legitimate the claim for access to resources); and the reclamation of family values, with particular emphasis on control over the sexuality and fertility of women.

Increasingly the received wisdom in the formulation and implementation of social policy is that minority communities are identified according to their religious backgrounds. Other social divisions of class, caste and gender are hidden beneath this monolithic characterization. Increasingly references are made not to Asian culture, but to Sikh, Muslim or Hindu culture. Such multicultural norms are also permeating popular perceptions of Asian communities.

Women's minds and bodies are the battleground for the preservation of the 'purity' of religious and communal identities. So the role of women as signifiers and transmitters of identity within the family becomes crucial. There is a growing phenomenon of organized gangs and networks of Asian men who hunt down runaway Asian girls and women who are perceived to have transgressed the mores of their culture and religion, and to have defiled their honour and identity. The family has therefore become a site of struggle for feminists and fundamentalists alike.

In Huddersfield in 1992 we saw the emergence of the so-called 'bounty hunter'. This man had set himself up as custodian of the morality of the local Asian communities. Offering his services to local Asian families, he claimed to be able to locate and return to their families young women and girls who had chosen to leave to make their own lives elsewhere. Some of these women had left to escape from violence, abuse, restrictions on their freedom of movement, and forced arranged marriages. Many of the women possessed court orders to restrain their husbands and families from pursuing them. When challenged about his activities, the former taxi-driver maintained the sacrosanct nature of the Asian family. Like many others within the community, he was personally angry at the idea that Asian women could protest and demand assistance from the state in response to domestic violence and other abuses. So with the blessing of the 'community' he engaged in what were clearly illegal activities, utilizing a network of informers within the Labour-controlled local author-ity, social welfare systems and Asian mini-cab and business services to trace the whereabouts of 'missing' women. He even boasted that knew the secret addresses of every women's refuge and hostel in northern England. In such circumstances, success in 'reuniting' families may rest upon threats of violence and harassment.

The response of society at large to this 'bounty hunter' was salutary for its indifference to his victims. Like the Channel Four television docu-mentary which brought him to wider public attention, the rest of the media, including the 'quality' newspapers, referred to him as a 'mediator' who was 'salvaging' Asian marriages from the crisis of modernity.

We refused to turn the clocks back. In December 1992 SBS, Women Against Fundamentalism (WAF), other Asian women from around the country and some white women who had worked with us on the Kiranjit Ahluwalia campaign, joined women in Huddersfield for a loud and visible demonstration. Armed with anger and songs set to the seasonal tunes of Christmas carols, we marched around the city centre to the bemusement of Christmas shoppers. The 'anti-racist' director of the Channel Four documentary turned up at the demonstration to lend his support to the 'beleaguered' and 'misunderstood' bounty hunter. He suggested that the underlying theme of his film was to explore the question of 'whether Asian women take freedom if given the opportunity'. His film, he claimed, suggested that they did not want freedom, as they eventually returned home! What was missing from his simple argument was any under-standing of the oppressive context in which Asian women can make 'choices' about freedom. We demanded instead the right for women to speak for themselves and to tell their own stories, we would not be forced into our homes again. Instead we sang out:

Jingle bells, jingle bells, jingle all the way / We have come to Hudderfield to chase the thugs away! / We are not afraid, we will not retreat, we will struggle for our rights in victory and defeat / This is our tradition, struggle not submission, courage is our faith, and dissent is our religion.

The following year in Bradford, a committee consisting of conservative and religious men was formed to ensure that Bradford police and social services refer to them for guidance and advice regarding every single case of a runaway Asian woman.

In the wake of the destruction of the Babri-Masjid and the burning of Hindu temples in this country, SBS and the Brent refuge became centrally involved in a loose coalition of predominately Asian men and women from a range of campaigning backgrounds – anti-racist, feminist, anti-caste (Ambedkarite), activist, academic, secularist and humanist. We came together to form an anti-communal organization, the Alliance Against Communalism and for Democracy in South Asia. The aim was to support anti-communalist forces in India who were facing an uphill struggle in turning the tide of sweeping Hindu nationalism, and to prevent communalism from breaking out in our communities in Britain. For many of us this was not only a way in which we could voice our horror and opposition to developments in India, it was also an opportunity for feminists active in the fight against religious fundamentalism to seek support from other constituencies in resisting movements which placed the control of women as central to their agenda. The Alliance was effective in unsettling the confidence of those who were galvanizing financial and other support for communalist forces in India, as they liked to pretend that their support from Hindus was absolute. Our campaigning was nevertheless difficult. We found that in the larger Hindu communities of London, Leicester and elsewhere, there was widespread cross-class support for the main right-wing Hindu groupings such as the Vishwa Hindu Parishad (VHP), the Bharatiya Janata Party (BJP) and the Bombay-based Shiv Sena. The response to us at many meetings and social gatherings was to adopt aggressive and disruptive tactics to suppress us. The vociferous presence of women was felt to be particularly provocative, and they labelled us as Muslim-loving prostitutes, outcastes, women in the pay of Muslim fundamentalists or the Congress Party of India.

Within the Alliance, despite its name, many of the left, anti-racist activists could not come to a decision to oppose all religious fundamentalist movements operating here and in the Indian sub-continent. Whilst willing to compare the rise of the BJP to the rise of the British National Party (BNP), to some extent a valid comparison, they failed to go further and to look critically at all our communities from within. The demonization of Islam by the West has led to a marked reluctance by progressive and left forces within our communities to confront Islamic fundamentalism here, for fear of alienating Muslims and weakening unity against racism and class exploitation. A good example of this reluctance is shown in the way many anti-racist activists have argued that in the current wave of anti-Muslim racism, all blacks should regard themselves as Muslims. Even as a political stance expressing solidarity, this is an extremely problematic position for women in our struggle for personal freedom and alliances with progressive social forces.

As feminists and anti-fundamentalists we were determined to maintain the unity of the Alliance, but its failure to make women's rights a central component of the wider struggle has enormous implications for its future development. Abandoning the women's question for short-term political gain, or making alliances with right-wing movements, offers us nothing. We must oppose all religious fundamentalism, and recognize that the strength of Asian women's struggle has been in its ability to mobilize across religious, caste and class divisions. To go further, in the feminist, secular political spaces we have created lies hope for the defeat of religious fundamentalism. This is an insight which, unfortunately, has not been appreciated by our male allies in left and anti-racist movements.

The task of confronting these fundamentalist and other reactionary developments within our communities has been left to women. The result is that we have had to develop a new politics and culture of resistance to oppose these undemocratic and misogynistic developments. Women Against Fundamentalism, with its heterogeneous composition of women from a variety of religious backgrounds, is an example of the new direction in which coalition feminist politics is developing. In WAF recognizing our differences gives us strength, and a better understanding of the complexities involved in resisting racism, sexism and fundamentalism.

CONCLUSION

With the collapse of the Babri-Masjid in India, I found that a wall surrounding some of my own guarded orthodoxies had crumbled. At the conclusion of a highly successful public meeting organized by some of us in the Alliance Against Communalism in the Hindu stronghold of Wembley in Brent in 1993, a friend and colleague of Muslim origin broke down and wept. Many of those who had attended the meeting had been mobilized by local and national Hindu organizations, and their virulent anti-Muslim sentiments and abuse, devoid of any rationality, had left my friend feeling as if she had been stripped of her own humanity. I understood then the full significance of the struggles we have been engaged in, and we pledged together to fight for the right to occupy and defend the secular space we had created for ourselves as feminists, even if we needed to rethink what to put in that space.

The third wave of feminism has a lot to contend with. The rise of new forms of racism, fascism, nationalism and religious fundamentalism world-wide demands from us a new and visionary politics. We must avoid the pitfalls of the identity politics of the 1970s and 1980s which made it so difficult to share experiences, and we must move beyond the limitations of anti-racism and multiculturalism which equally limit our perspectives and our ability to act. We must reject the vicious and blinkered vision of nationalism and fundamentalism. Our task is to find new ways of resisting, and new ways of truly democratic thinking which give us the optimism to go beyond all of these failed forms of politics. Our alliances must cross our different identities, and help us to reconceptualize notions of democracy, human rights and citizenship. Whatever the dividing lines drawn by priests, mullahs, gurus and politicians, we will then be able to reach out to our each other, to support one another in our transgressions and defiance. Above all, we must leave room for doubt and uncertainty in our own orthodoxies. The time has come, in the words of the Walrus in Lewis Carroll's poem, to talk of many things. . . .

ACKNOWLEDGEMENTS

I would like to thank Yazmin Ali, at whose instigation this piece was written in 1994. Thanks are also due to Rahilla Gupta and Raju Bhatt for their comments and support.

NOTES

1 See Southall Black Sisters submission to the Home Affairs Select Committee, *Immigration and Domestic Violence*, HMSO, 1992.
2 For a more detailed account of the devastating effects of multiculturalism in practice, see Patel (1991).

REFERENCES

Ali, Y. (1992) 'Muslim Women and the Politics of Ethnicity and Culture in Northern England' in Sahgal, G. and Yuval-Davis, N. (eds) *Refusing Holy Orders*, London, Virago Press.
Patel, P. (1991) 'Multi-culturalism: Myth and Reality', *Women, A Cultural Review*, vol. 2, no. 3, winter.
Sahgal, G. (1992) 'Secular Spaces: The Experience of Asian Women Organising' in Sahgal, G and Yuval-Davis, N. (eds) *Refusing Holy Orders*, London, Virago Press.

Chapter 22

Black women in education

A collective movement for social change

Heidi Safia Mirza

This chapter is concerned with the issue of how to theorize the paradox of inclusive acts by excluded groups. Research on young black (African-Caribbean) women's strategies to succeed at school and into further and higher education raises the question, 'How can such conservative and instrumental actions be deemed subversive?' On the surface, it appears that they are conforming, identifying with the ideology of meritocracy, climbing the conventional career ladder, wanting to succeed on society's terms – buying into the system. The problem is simply this, how can I claim (as I do) that black women's desire or motivation to succeed within the educational system is radical? How can what appears on the surface to be compliance and willingness to conform to systems and structures of educational meritocracy, be redefined as strategic or as evidence of a covert social movement for change?

What we need is a complex analysis of what is going on among the majority of black women who are not, as we have come to expect from the popular presumptions, 'failing'. We need to move toward a coherent understanding of black female educational orientation that begins to reveal the subversive and transformative possibilities of their actions. From school through to university and into the community black women access educational resources and subvert expected patterns of educational mobility. This active engagement challenges our expectations. Black women who have been, after all, theorized in our dominant academic discourse as 'the most oppressed', deemed the least 'visible', the least empowered, the most marginal of groups, do relatively well. They appear to strive for inclusivity.

However, no one wants to look at their success, their desire for inclusivity. They are out of place, disrupting, untidy. They do not fit. The notion of their agency and difference is problematic for the limited essentialist and mechanical social reproduction theories that dominate our explanations of black female inequality (Moore 1996). Traditionally, and in common-sense accounts that rely on such theories, black women's contradictory actions are analysed in terms of subcultural resistance.

However, because young black women's subcultures of resistance are deemed conformist, the idea is cleverly reworked and presented instead as 'resistance through accommodation' (Mac an Ghaill 1988). Black women, we are told, employ this particular strategy of resistance, because they are motivated by their identification with the role model of the 'strong black mother'. Such essentialist constructions presumes that the role model of the black mother provides young black women with special powers of endurance and transgenerational cultural understandings that especially equip them in their struggles against racism and sexism (Mirza 1992).

But in this chapter I want to suggest that black female educational urgency cannot be understood simply as 'resistance through accommodation'. Their desire for inclusion is strategic, subversive and ultimately far more transformative than subcultural reproduction theory suggests. The irony is that black women are both succeeding and conforming in order to transform and change. By mapping black women's covert educational urgency I hope to move toward a radical interpretation of black female educational motivation. Valorizing their agency as subversive and transformative rather than as a manifestation of resistance, it becomes clear that black women do not just resist racism, they live 'other' worlds.

EVIDENCE OF COLLECTIVE EDUCATIONAL URGENCY

Black women do buy into the educational system. They do relatively well at school, relative that is to their male and female working-class peers as measured in terms of *average* exam performance at GCSE level. This phenomenon was first documented over ten years ago in 1985 in the Swann Report and confirmed by the ILEA in 1987 (Mirza 1992). More recently the findings of the 1992 National Youth Cohort Study appear to confirm this (Drew *et al.* 1992).

In my own research for *Young, Female and Black* (Mirza 1992), which was a small local study of two inner city working-class schools, I also found black girls do as well as, if not better than, their peers in average exam performance. I found young black women collectively identified with the notion of credentialism. They subscribed to the meritocratic ideal, which within the parameters of their circumstances meant 'getting on'. In difficult and disruptive conditions the majority of young black women would sit in the back of the class getting on with their own work. However, whatever the young black women's achievements they were always within the constraints of the class conditions of inner city schooling.

What is clear from all the studies on race and education is that black girls have to stay on longer at school to achieve their long-term educational aspirations. In order to overcome obstacles of racism and sexism in school large numbers stay on in order to get the opportunities that enable them to take a 'backdoor' route into further and higher education. Young women do this by strategically rationalizing their educational opportunities. They opt for accessible careers (gendered and racialized jobs) which give them the opportunity to get onto a college course. Their career aspirations were tied to their educational motivation and by the prospect of upward mobility. A job was an expression of their desire to move ahead within the educational process. The young black women chose 'realistic careers' that they knew to be accessible and (historically) available to them. For example, social work and other caring jobs such as nursing or office work. The occupations they chose always required a course or several courses of rigorous professional training, and is why they choose them. Thus while it may appear young black women are reproducing stereotypes of black women's work, they are in effect expressing their meritocratic values within the limits of opportunities allowed to them in a racially and sexually-divisive educational and economic system. They are in effect subversively and collectively employing a 'backdoor' entry to further and higher education.

This picture of collective educational urgency among young black women to enter colleges of further and higher education is confirmed by national statistics. The 1993 Labour Force survey shows 61 per cent of all black women (aged 16–59) to have higher and other qualifications (*Employment Gazette* 1993). Figures for 1995 show that 52 per cent of all black women (aged 16–24) are in full-time education, compared to 28 per cent of white women, 36 per cent of black men, and 31 per cent of white men (*Employment Gazette* 1995). Similarly a recent study for the Policy Studies Institute shows that in relation to their respective population sizes, ethnic minority groups, overall, are over-represented in higher education (Modood and Shiner 1994). This over-representation was especially apparent in the new universities. Here people of Caribbean origin were over-represented by 43 per cent, Asians by 162 per cent and Africans by 223 per cent! This compared to the white population which was under-represented by 7 per cent.

But educational urgency does not stop there. As mothers black women strategically negotiate the educational advantage of their children within the constraints offered by the decaying urban education system and limited access to cultural capital (Reay, forthcoming 1997). Black women are disproportionately involved in the setting up and running of black supplementary schools. They invest in the education of the next generation. In ongoing research on black supplementary schools, Diane Reay and myself have done a preliminary survey of black schools in London (Reay and Mirza forthcoming). So far we found sixty officially documented black schools within four London boroughs, but we believe we only scratched the surface. Through networks and word of mouth we hear of more and more everyday. Sometimes there would be several on one council estate.

They appear to spring up 'unoffically' in houses, community centres, and unused school rooms. Of those we found, 65 per cent were run by women; and of those run by men, women's involvement as teachers and mentors was the overwhelming majority input.

IS BLACK FEMALE EDUCATIONAL URGENCY A NEW SOCIAL MOVEMENT?

It could be argued, as indeed I wish to suggest here, that the extent, direction and intensity of the black female positive orientation to education is significant enough to qualify their collective action as a transformative social movement. However, Paul Gilroy does not think so. He describes the black struggles for educational opportunities as constituting 'fragile collectivities'. He argues such movements are symptoms of 'resistance to domination', defensive organizations, with their roots in a radical sense of powerlessness. As they cannot make the transition to 'stable forms of politics' they are not agents for social change (Gilroy 1987: 230–1).

However, I believe an analysis of female collective action offers a new direction in the investigation of black social movements. As Gilroy's argument demonstrates, black female agency has remained invisible in the masculinist discourse of 'race' and social change. There has clearly been a black and male monopoly of the 'black subject' (West 1990). In the masculinist discourse on race and social change the assumption is that 'race' is contested and fought over in the masculine arena of the streets – among the (male) youth in the city (e.g. Solomos 1988; Keith 1993, 1995; Solomos and Back 1995). Urban social movements, we are told, mobilize in protest, riots, local politics, and community organizations. We are told it is their action, and not the subversive and covert action of women that gives rise to so called 'neo-populist liberatory authentic politics' (Gilroy 1987: 245). This is the masculinist version of radical social change; visible, radical, confrontational, collective action, powerfully expressed in the politics of the inner city, where class consciousness evolves in response to urban struggle.

Thus notions of resistance which are employed in this male discourse of social change to signify and celebrate black struggle, remain entrenched in ideology that privileges dominance. The black feminist theorist Patricia Hill Collins tells us black women writers have rejected notions of power based on domination in favour of a notion of power based on a vision of self-actualization, self-definition and self-determination (Collins 1991). However, the political language of 'community' around which black social movements are traditionally articulated in the masculinist discourse remains a relational idea. It suggests the notion of antagonism and oppositionality – of domination and subordination – between one community and another (Young 1990). But what if, for black women, community identity is not relational and antagonistic but inclusive with regard to the mainstream? This could be a possibility; there must be another way of understanding our lives other than always in relation to the 'other'. There is after all more to life than opposition to racism (Mirza 1995).

BLACK WOMEN'S ACTIVISM: STRATEGIES FOR TRANSFORMATION

Mapping the hidden histories, subjugated knowledges, the counter memories of black women educators in black supplementary schools, reveals the possibilities for covert social movements to achieve social change. Black supplementary schools, as organic grassroots organizations, are not simply a response to mainstream educational exclusion and poor practice, as they are so often described. They are far more radical and subversive than their quiet conformist exterior suggests. It is little wonder they are viewed suspiciously by uninformed observers as 'black power places'!

Such schools provide an alternative world with different meanings and shared 'ways of knowing'. As one mother said, 'There is white bias everywhere except at Saturday school.' It is a place where whiteness is displaced and blackness becomes the unspoken norm. It is a place of refusal and difference; a place of belonging.

In the four supplementary schools in our research black children discovered 'really useful knowledge' (Johnson 1988) which allowed them 'to step outside the white hermeneutic circle and into the black' (Gates quoted in Casey 1993: 110). Each of the four schools in our study was distinct, but they were underpinned by two main pedagogies. Some focused more on black images, black history and black role models. Others focused more on back to basics, the formal teaching of the 3 Rs. Some did both.

In the same way as the schools were paradoxically radical and conservative in their aims, so too were the teachers both radical and conservative in their praxis. On the one hand, the women, who were for the most part voluntary unpaid teachers, talked of their 'joy' of what they do, the 'gift of giving back', of their work to 'raise the race'. Many had been giving up their weekends for twenty years. Others had become ill from overwork and dedication.

On the other hand, the same teachers saw themselves as complimenting mainstream education. They were concerned about 'fitting in', assisting parents with home–school relations and getting the children to do better. On the surface these schools appeared conformist and conservative, with their focus on formality and buying into the liberal democratic ideal of meritocracy.

But as Casey writes in her excellent book, *I Answer with My Life* (1993) in a racist society a black person is located very differently than a white person.

> In a racist society for a black child to become educated is to contradict the whole system of racist signification. . . . to succeed in studying white knowledge is to undo the system itself . . . to refute its reproduction of black inferiority materially and symbolically.
>
> (Casey 1993: 123)

Thus it could be argued, as I am doing here, that in certain circumstances, *doing well can become a radical strategy.* An act of social transformation.

The black women educators did not accept the dominant discourse. In their space on the margin they have evolved a system of strategic rationalization of the dominant discourse. They operate within, between, under, and alongside the mainstream educational and labour market structures, subverting, renaming and reclaiming opportunities for their children through their transformative pedagogy of 'raising the race' – a radical pedagogy, that ironically appears conservative on the surface with its focus on inclusion and dialogue with the mainstream.

Patricia Hill Collins (1991) calls our attention to the dual nature of black women's activist traditions in their attempt to bring about social change. She suggests black women engage in activism that is both conservative and radical. Black women create culture and provide for their families. Fostering self-evaluation and self-reliance, patterns of consciousness and self-expression shape their cultures of difference. This struggle for group survival may appear conservative with its emphasis on preserving customs and cultural maintenance. Collins argues this struggle for group survival is in contrast to the radical tradition of black women's engaged activism. Because black communities and families are so profoundly affected by the political, economic and social institutions they are situated in, black women also find themselves working for radical institutional transformation through legal and civil action in terms of the traditional and valorized (masculine) form of visible social action.

However, it is in the uncharted struggle for group survival that black women in supplementary schools are located. Rose, a mother in one of the schools, tells us:

> We always have a session which is about giving children a voice. We teach them to speak, to develop a voice that can be heard. We tell them to be proud of what they are, to be strong about speaking out. I think perhaps that is the most important thing we do, helping them develop a voice that gets heard because it is easy for black children not to be listened to in school, to be thought of as a nuisance when they say something. I think in Saturday school it is quite clear that they are expected, entitled to speak out.
>
> (Rose in Reay and Mirza forthcoming)

Charity's narrative on how Colibri was started includes similar themes of activism, community and commitment that characterize the struggle for group survival and the desire for social change:

> There was a group of about six parents who like myself, as a black teacher, were dissatisfied with what was happening to black pupils. They felt if they had been in the Caribbean their children would be much further on academically and they decided something had to be done, schools weren't doing anything, so it had to be them. I really wish someone had the time to chart the enormous amount of work they put in those first few years. It was immense. The school started off in someone's front room on Saturday mornings. The parents doing all the teaching themselves to start with and it was very much focused on what was their main concern; their children not being able to read and write properly. Then these parents found the group of children grew from 10 to 15 and soon it was 20 and at this point it was unmanageable running a Saturday school in someone's front room so they petitioned the council for accommodation and finally got one of the council's derelict properties. They spent their spare time shovelling rubbish out of the room, tramps had been living there. Also doing building, repair work, getting groups of parents together to decorate. They pulled together and did all this work themselves, used the expertise they had to get the school on its feet.

> (Charity in Reay and Mirza, forthcoming)

What the black women appeared to have learnt is an awareness of the need for social support and collaborative action through their experience of marginality in a white racist society. From this awakening of consciousness and socio-analysis (Bourdieu 1990: 116) the women created their own cultural capital. Their habitus embodied 'real intelligence' in their ways of knowing and understanding (Luttrell 1992). As their words show, this ultimately led to collective action and social change.

CONCLUSION

In conclusion the question we must return to is this: Is the coherent educational urgency uncovered among black women a radical social movement with transformative possibilities from the margin or, as some suggest, no more than a conservative act?

Research on black women in education shows there is much evidence to suggest black women do not accept the dominant discourse, nor do they construct their identities in opposition to the dominant discourse. They redefine the world, have their own values, codes and understandings, *refuse* (not resist) the gaze of the other. As Spivak says: 'Marginal groups do not wish to claim centrality but redefine the big word human in terms of the marginal' (Spivak quoted in hooks 1991: 22). Black women live in counter hegemonic marginal spaces where, as hooks describes: 'Radical black subjectivity is seen not overseen by any authoritative other claiming to know us better than we know ourselves' (hooks 1991: 22).

For black women strategies for everyday survival consist of trying to create spheres of influence that are separate from but engaged with existing structures of oppression. Being successful and gaining authority and power within institutions that have traditionally not allowed black women formal authority or real power enables them to indirectly subvert oppressive structures by changing them. By saying this I do not wish to argue that black women are simply empowered through their educational achievement. Empowerment assumes a notion of power that is relational. It suggests the positive power of a collectivity or individual to challenge basic power relations in society (Yuval-Davis 1994). The assumption here is that black women's actions empower them, but any gains are always oppositional and in relation to the hegemonic culture (Steady 1993). What I have tried to show instead is that black women are not simply resisting, but have evolved a system of strategic rationalization which has its own logic, values and codes. Black women struggle for educational inclusion in order to transform their opportunities and so in the process subvert racist expectations and beliefs. By entering into dialogue with others they are not conservative or colluding with the mainstream. They are collectively opening up transformative possibilities for their community through their pragmatic recognition of the power of education to transform and change the hegemonic discourse (McLaren 1994; hooks 1994).

So, finally, can I claim black women's educational urgency and desire to do well within the system is radical and subversive? To answer the question I leave you with the words of a black woman university student:

> When not given success we need to be successful . . . that is the most radical thing you can do.
>
> (Alisha in Mirza 1994)

REFERENCES

Bourdieu, P. (1990) *In Other Words: Essays Towards a Reflexive Sociology,* Cambridge, Polity Press.

Casey, K. (1993) *I Answer with My Life: Life Histories of Women Teachers Working for Social Change*, New York, Routledge.

Collins, P.H. (1991) *Black Feminist Thought: Knowledge Consciousness and the Politics of Empowerment*, London, Routledge.

Drew, D. Gray, J. and Sime, N. (1992) *Against the Odds: The Education and Labour Market Experiences of Young Black People*, Employment Department, Youth Cohort Series Report, no. 19, June, London, HMSO.

Employment Gazette (1993) 'Ethnic Origins and the Labour Market' Employment Department, February, London, HMSO.

Employment Gazette (1995) 'Ethnic Minorities' Employment Department, June London, HMSO.

Gilroy, P. (1987) *There Ain't No Black in the Union Jack*, London, Hutchinson.

hooks, b. (1991) *Yearning: Race, gender and Cultural Politics*, London, Turnaround.

hooks, b. (1994) *Teaching to Transgress: Education and the Practice of Freedom*, London, Routledge.

Johnson, R. (1988) 'Really Useful Knowledge 1790–1850: Memories for Education in the 1980s' in T. Lovett (ed.) *Radical Approaches to Education: A Reader*, New York, Routledge.

Keith, M. (1993) *Race, Riots and Policing: Lore and Disorder in a Multiracist Society*, London, UCL Press.

Keith, M. (1995) 'Shouts of the Street: Identity and Spaces of Authenticity' *Social Identities*, vol. 1, no. 2, August, pp. 297–315.

Luttrell, W. (1992) 'Working Class Women's Ways of Knowing: Effects of Gender, Race and Class' in J. Wrigley (ed.) *Education and Gender Equality* London, Falmer Press.

Mac an Ghaill, M. (1988) *Young Gifted and Black: Student Teacher Relations in the Schooling of Black Youth*, Milton Keynes, Open University Press.

McLaren, P. (1994) 'Multiculturalism and the Postmodern Critique: Towards a Pedagogy of Resistance and Transformation' in H. Giroux and P. McLaren (eds) *Between the Borders: Pedagogy and the Politics of Cultural Change*, London: Routledge.

Mirza, H.S. (1992) *Young, Female and Black*, London, Routledge.

Mirza, H.S. (1994) 'Making Sense of the Black Female Student Experience in Higher Education' paper given at the Society for Research in Higher Education (SRHE) Conference, The Student Experience, University of York, December.

Mirza, H.S. (1995) 'Black Women in Higher Education: Defining a Space/Finding a Place' in L. Morley and V. Walsh (eds) *Feminist Academics: Creative Agents For Change*, London, Taylor and Francis.

Modood, T. and Shiner, M. (1994) *Ethnic Minorities and Higher Education: Why are there Differential Rates of Entry?* London PSI Publishing.

Moore, R. (1996) 'Back To the Future: the Problem of Change and the Possibilities for Advance in the Sociology of Education' *British Journal of Sociology of Education*, vol. 17, no. 2 June, pp. 145–61.

Reay, D. (forthcoming, 1997) *Class Work: Mothers' Involvement in their Children's Primary Schooling*, London, Taylor and Francis.

Reay D. and Mirza, H.S. (forthcoming) 'Uncovering Genealogies of the Margin: Black Supplementary Schooling', *British Journal of Sociology of Education*.

Solomos, J. (1988) *Black Youth, Racism and the State*, Cambridge, Cambridge University Press.

Solomos, J. and Back, L. (1995) *Race, Politics and Social Change*, London, Routledge.

Steady, F.C. (1993) 'Women and Collective Action: Female Models in Transition' in S.M. James and A.P. Busia (eds) *Theorizing Black Feminisms: The Visionary Pragmatism of Black Women*, London, Routledge.

West, C. (1990) 'The New Cultural Politics of Difference' in R. Ferguson, M. Gever, T. Minh-ha and C. West (eds) *Out There: Marginalisation and Contemporary Cultures*, New York, New Museum of Contemporary Art.

Young, I.M. (1990) 'The Ideal of Community and the Politics of Difference' in L. Nicholson (ed.) *Feminism/Postmodernism*, London, Routledge.

Yuval-Davis, N. (1994) 'Women, Ethnicity and Empowerment' in K. Bhavnani and A. Phoenix (eds) *Shifting Identities Shifting Racisms*, London, Sage.

Chapter 23

The language of womanism
Re-thinking difference[1]

Helen (charles)

BLANKET TERMINOLOGY AND GENERALIZING WOMEN

The politicization of the western black woman germinates at the moment of recognizable resistance to outside forces which deem her subordinate to others. The potential to understand herself is as justified within the context of a feminist ideology as it is within a non-feminist ideology. This chapter questions the viability of womanism as a doctrine for (black) women activists[2] who have been visibly ignored by the white women's movement. It is an attempt to think further towards an understanding of the notion of difference within the feminist arena and examines the terminology used by women who are conscious of feminism but resistant to taking on the white western labelling that goes with it.

As the focus of this chapter is directed to language, an understanding of feminist nomenclature provides a means to tackle areas of black women's invisibility that have long been ignored. I want to consider placing the black woman activist within mainstream feminist terminology. Using the notions of womanism and difference to illustrate, I argue for an examination of the necessity of a viable language from which the black woman activist can speak and, more importantly, is listened to.

Terminology: why is it needed? In what ways is it used and for what purposes? In terms of progression and development, how does it manifest itself? Terming the activities of the Self – political or otherwise – makes it easier to identify the causes and circumvents the assumption that feminism is essentially white feminism. It takes us to a place where we can question what feminism is *qua* feminism. The possibility within women's activism to overcome racial imbalances opens up greater political autonomy within such a feminism. Before exploring the main themes in detail I will examine briefly some aspects of political activism through an analysis of terminology.

Most would agree that given the worlds that we live in, to hope that a perfect term could exist to encompass all identities (class-wise, gender-wise, colour-wise, race-wise, sexuality-wise, and so on) is a fantasy. A term that does not pay lip-service to, but encompasses black women's activism would recognize the viability and equality of all political women in the main body of the women's movement. The split or the branching away of 'black' and 'other' women from this main body would be a sign that these women are not being recognized for what they are worth by a dominant core. After the split three options are available to a black woman. First, she can join another organization. Second, she can give up the cause altogether and get on with her life, creating her own individual (feminist) framework which is perhaps shared with friends. Third, she can create her own movement, academic or otherwise, to which she attracts others like herself. With this third option, appropriate language is fashioned and created by her and her followers.

The evolution of the term feminist perhaps initially came about in an attempt to address all the issue-wise aspects of class, colour, race and sexuality. As we move through progressive waves which indicate that the majority view is changing, the etymology of feminism *per se* also changes. For example, in the early 1980s cultural difference made its debut on the feminist agenda, as some white women in North America collaborated with some black women to address issues of exclusion. Joseph and Lewis write in *Common Differences: Conflicts in Black and White Feminist Perspectives* (1981) that, 'From the early generalizations about "all women," feminists are recognizing the need to understand the specific nature and conditions of women's oppression in differing cultures, societies, and economies.' (1981: 67). Significantly, as a consequence of the development of feminism, the term has become not only arguably passé but also one of generalization and exclusion. Feminism now is often linked to the theory that it is not reaching a potential activist populace outside the academe. A manifestation of this was the question which was beginning to be asked at the end of the 1980s. Has feminism gone out of fashion and is it out of date? Maybe, maybe not, but the language of feminism has definitely left newer generations and others who feel like they have seen it, done it, been brought up by it and read all the books, searching for alternative lifestyle politics.

There is no single woman who encompasses all the said issues, and fights for rights to be equated to all of them. Where limitations abide, you will always find the need for acknowledgement. This acknowledgement often arrives via term-creation, adding to already existing terminology. To place the word black, for example, or disabled before the term feminist, does not solve the problem. Instead, it makes it explicit that the term is exclusive of the previously ignored or acknowledged group. This instantly valorizes the situation of non-acknowledgement. The idea of a black, disabled or feminist utopia for instance, is useless as an idea on which to base a reality because its premise is not set up to encompass *all* of the so-called black, disabled or feminist people's realities at once. The view that there are as many definitions of feminism as there are feminists runs counter to what a main definition of feminism ought to be striving for – eliminating the possibility of splits from the main body. While feminism should be the stem from which differences can branch out, instead there is a reluctance to put efforts into maintaining the growth of such a stem. Indeed, it could well be said that it was because of the laxity of a feminism which relied on whiteness, that feminism began to dissipate underground.

WOMANISM AS AN (IN)SUFFICIENT STRATEGY FOR BLACK WOMEN

The instance of womanism is interesting to examine at this stage, as it seeks to offer a universal means to a black women-based end. When Alice Walker came up with the idea of a special name for black women, her term 'womanist' provided an equivalent to 'feminist'. Composed and placed at the very start of her book, *In Search of Our Mother's Gardens* (1984a), the definition presents itself as introductory to the book's subheading, *Womanist Prose*. This book begins with the very kernel of its concept: 'Womanist. From *womanish* . . . A black feminist or feminist of color' (Walker, 1984a: xi). The specificity of the black woman's experience becomes a viable basis for feminist interpretation right from the beginning. Although the term 'womanist' has not made headline news, there was a possibility of it becoming more than just a notion, if only because its germination became possible through Alice Walker. However, this was not to be – at least not in this century – as womanism's seedling struggled from the very beginning when it was placed at diametrically opposed ends with feminism. It has been discussed from some positions in North America. bell hooks argues that womanism is not to be confused as an opposing doctrine to feminism: 'I hear black women academics laying claim to the term "womanist" while rejecting "feminist". I do not think Alice Walker intended this term to deflect from feminist commitment, yet this is often how it is evoked' (hooks, 1989: 181). Here in Britain, the term womanism is barely recognized or used. Nevertheless, the notion was taken up in the late 1980s by West African writer Buchi Emecheta (in Granqvist and Stotesbury, 1989: 19) and on a more local level by the London-based group, Camden Black Sisters (CBS). Valentina Alexander, formally of CBS, viewed activism for black and white women as the 'twin revolutions of Black Womanism and White Feminism'. Under 'Some Statements of Fact', she explains: 'Womanism for the Black Woman/Woman of Colour came about as a direct response to the oppression she experienced, through the exploitation of her gender, race and class' (Alexander, 1989a: 29).

It is not always necessary to look for the origins of terms and concepts but if the etymology exists as womanism did, as a potential twentieth-century phenomenon, then it presents a good opportunity to examine the roots[3] and reasons for invention. The term 'womanist', whatever its intention, is essentially for black feminists (Walker, 1984a). The black woman activist could not fail to respond to what seems like an answer for the need to re-evaluate an ignored, forgotten, marginalized section of society. The excitement, no doubt, reached many who, like myself, find it difficult not only in terms of what appendage (if any) to attach to themselves but also in terms of what is behind the difficulties of nomenclature: why the need for labels anyhow? If the majority of black women are unhappy about being called feminists then the advent of a new term that has a potential for black women in particular would have inevitable allure on a socio-political platform. But somehow womanism did not make the grade despite Walker's belief that she is, 'offering society a new word when the old word it is using fails to describe behaviour and change that only a new word can help it more fully see' (1984b: 25). The crucial question is not whether womanist as a new word can satisfy a new feminist vision, but whether womanist as a new and viable doctrine can make our ever-changing, traditional white feminism adapt to it. Additionally, it is important to consider at which point womanism as a North American experience departs from the experience of black feminists globally.

I want to now turn to looking closely at four sections of Walker's definition of womanism. In the first section of her definition she states womanism is: 'From the black folk expression of mothers to female 'children', "You acting womanish," ... interchangeable with another black folk expression: "You trying to be grown"' (1984a: xi). Walker shows here that womanish as a term comes from the experience of the language and folk culture which is central to a certain group of people with roots in the southern states of North America. Because black languages differ from place to place, the word womanish from a southern US context is not necessarily linked directly to the same experience of girls and women elsewhere. To adopt language in one culture from another is not unusual, but there must exist some initial identification of whatever the term is or is seen to substitute. Looking closely at Walker's dictionary-style definition of womanism reveals an ambitious attempt to cater for a stylized, individual, all-encompassing woman.

In the second part of Walker's definition, there is evidence of her preference to expand the definition womanism in order to escape the problem of exclusion, which is so much a part of white-dominated women's movements. Here she states that a womanish woman is:

Also, a woman who loves other women, sexually and/or non-sexually. Appreciates and prefers women's culture, women's emotional flexibility ... and women's strength. Sometimes loves individual men, sexually and/or non-sexually. Committed to survival and wholeness of entire people, male and female. Not separatist, except periodically for health. Traditionally universalist.

(Walker 1984a: xi)

It is punchy and humourous, a very important ingredient for anything new on the market. It is also clear in this definition that Walker, in offering a new concept for black women in particular, does not wish to ignore or not acknowledge 'non-black' women. Interestingly, black as a prefix to woman is not included in this second part of Walker's definition of womanist. While its absence magnifies a feminist need (Walker's?) to accept all women of all skin colours it can also be seen as slightly confusing. If the intention is to make 'womanist' follow a poly-textual mode of definition, then it would be safe to assume the utilization of womanist by white women too; used in preference to, or in conjunction with feminist to illustrate *white women's* development in changing society. However, in acknowledging the viability of black women who are as much women as white women are, the celebration of the possible change from exclusive white feminism to inclusive feminism has potential if we introduce the 'white womanist'. In so doing, the promise of a truly inclusive womanism would be eliminated in favour of a compromisory change, because as black feminists have suggested, 'In many cases the attitudes of white women researchers towards their Third World women subjects appears to be one of pity and distance' (Kazi, 1986: 87–8; Mohanty, 1988).

On the sexuality front, there is an assumption in Walker's second definition that womanist substitutes for lesbian as well as terms like transgendered, bisexual, heterosexual, celibate and so on. Does this term really have the power to account for all these issues, or would it give rise to exhaustive appendages? Having said this, issues such as class and race are strangely unrecorded in this second definition. If Walker presumes their inclusion, it is regretful to misinterpret the reading as equal to their explicit exclusion. Walker's 'universality' in this sense exposes a blanket terminology; a blanketing which attempts to cover up exclusion and is as such questionable in its generalization.

Diana Fuss, having written extensively on the subject of essentialism versus constructionism, attempts to throw up old notions that have been criticized for lacking theoretical substance. In her writings she talks about the work of Luce Irigaray (a scholar who has been labelled 'essentialist' by many in the western academe) who makes an interesting comparison to Walker, here. In *Essentially Speaking* (1989), Fuss talks about Irigaray's 'language of essence' in the search, 'not to create a theory of woman, but to secure a place for the "feminine" within sexual difference' (1989: 72). If the invention of essentialist terminology arrives because of the need to fit in somewhere on a macro level, then linguistically and politically, writers like Irigaray and Walker, as Fuss has said, are opting out of the 'P.C.' rat-race and choosing a path of strategic essentialism. Walker in inventing womanism is, perhaps, not trying to create an essentialist theory of black feminism *per se*, but seeks to secure a home for the black feminine or essence embodied within racial or skin-colour difference which is strategic.

Walker's use of womanism, in raising the question of an essentialist universality, throws up more than the issue of theorizing. It also offers the chance to tackle the question of politics. The phrase which begins, 'Committed to survival . . .' spotlights Walker's emphasis on the value of collective commitment as part of this womanist make-up. By referring to this commitment to 'survival and wholeness of entire people' it is difficult to understand the exactitude through which this proposed method ought to be practised. The implications of a politics of 'entire people' and 'wholeness' are at once evaded through a suggestion of global simplicity.[4] Conglomerated into one body, like her view that there can exist a 'woman's culture', it is reminiscent of the notion of an all-encompassing 'single black super-woman'. If 'womanists' were meant to be ubiquitous humanists, committed not merely to international affairs but also to the whole notion and existence of universal affairs, a problem surfaces: if to be womanist means to be black, then the issue of western racism must affect and duly concern the would-be 'womanist', notwithstanding the fact that racism ought not to be a black problem.[5]

Given the triple subordination of the black-identified woman, her experience could be used to gauge the overall development towards attainment for freedom and recognition among all people. As Kwame Nkrumah once said: 'The degree of a country's revolutionary awareness may be measured by the political maturity of its women' (Francis, 1983: 36). Similarly, Staples heroically contends that 'Black women cannot be free *qua* women until all blacks attain their liberation' (Staples, 1985: 348). What is recognized here is a project of universal humanism that black feminism represents. However, this political germination has been prevented. And prevention is no cure as the Combahee River Collective well understand: 'If Black women were free, it would mean that everyone else would have to be free, since our freedom would necessitate the destruction of all the systems of oppression' (1983: 278). How is the commitment to universal humanism fostered and developed and in what ways is its development equally beneficial to all black and non-black thinking peoples? Given these problems would it then be safer to accept that womanism can be a viable concept only within the realms and parameters of a Walker-based theory? To foster the womanist thesis may only serve to encourage an essentialist notion based solely on instinct, and in 'nature', rather than in combination with activism or socio-political consciousness:

> I don't choose womanism because it is 'better' than feminism . . . I choose it because I prefer the sound, the feel, the fit of it; because I cherish

the spirit of the woman (like Sojourner) the word calls to mind and because I share the old ethnic-American *habit* of offering society a new word.

(Walker 1984b; my italics)

If term-proposal is 'habitual' to black people then all the more reason to take a serious look at the terminology.

Walker's third definition of 'womanist' shows further, its apolitical nature. She states: 'Loves music. Loves dance. Loves the moon. Loves the Spirit. Loves love and food and roundness. Loves struggle. Loves the folk. Loves herself. Regardless' (Walker, 1984a: xii). Now, some might say that in being black, one is already political and as Meridy Harris has rightly said, being black is certainly turning the English dictionary definition of woman 'upside down' making it 'an *immediately* satisfying subversion of "the weaker sex" ideology which appears to be contested by far too few to effect any radical change from within white culture' (1991: 4). But suppose I am looking for terminology which will give something more in the way of impact. A terminology that would make not only black women sit up, but will make white women listen. Instead of taking an ambiguous or excluded role, such a terminology would enable black women to be heard. The emphasis of Walker is not on political activism, as many, including bell hooks would like, and because of this, it could be said that Walker does not subscribe to a specific woman-activism. Here is what bell hooks has to say:

For me, the term 'womanist' is not sufficiently linked to a tradition of radical political commitment to struggle and change. What would a 'womanist' politic look like? If it is a term for black feminism, then why do those who embrace it reject the other?

(hooks 1989: 182)

Coming to Walker's fourth definition, 'Womanist is to feminist as purple to lavender', I would say that it speaks for itself in that Walker places both states of being into a kind of extended family situation, a brave gesture of inclusion. My only difficulty with this is that purple and lavender, being traditional white feminist hues (recall 1970s British sartorial politics), are insinuative of a *plea* for inclusion. This attitude is not very symbolic of the western black woman's *amour propre* and as such, indicates an inevitable death of pride in the family.

For one person to 'offer' society a new term appears somehow un-collective in the decision-making process, though creative. But perhaps because of what appears to be an apolitical gloss on Walker's offer of womanism, this is uncollectively intentional. Her womanist ideology can be seen to describe more the spirit of black women, which also has a place, as opposed to a fiercely political identity. However, having said this, it is quite common for language to evolve naturally alongside political change. Think, for example, of the term 'queer', which has in some circles been appropriated from 'odd' with perjorative connotations, to an umbrella term of (political) pride for those who do not consider themselves heterosexual.

WHAT'S THE DIFFERENCE? IGNORING BLACK WOMEN'S VISIBILITY

What can be assumed is the general feeling that black women activists in Britain and in North America do not wish to remain on a perpetual feminist agenda as marginalized contributors to a political, woman-based cause. To be listened to is the *raison d'être*. Moreover, 'Black women *resist* being grafted onto feminism in a tokenistic manner [and] argue that feminism has to be transformed if it is to address them' (Ramdin, 1987: 469; my emphasis). Wanting 'our issues to be on the agendas in a wide range of political organizations [struggling] to raise racism as a central issue within the women's movement' (Amos and Parmar, 1984: 7) was paramount to the black woman activist at a time that seems long ago now. And black women have been re-stating the problem over and over again as they recognize the difference in approach, form, content and attitude within feminism. What that difference is exactly and how it can be attributed to useful and developing practical analysis, is now so important that it must be viewed from as many different angles as possible so as to provide maximum visibility. That this vision produces realization and also sets one up for exposure is inevitable and integral to moving obstinate and lazy ideology. What I have referred to as 'guilt-awareness'[6] among white women activists, goes a long way to localizing very sore points in the activist's consciousness and it is a crucial part of her self-awareness and developing or evolving political clout. But there must be a place at which she surpasses the former condition where practical activism takes over to intercept the potential paralysis that can emanate from guilt-awareness.

THE DIFFERENCE WITHIN DIFFERENCE: DIVERSITY AND BINARY OPPOSITIONS

What follows is a short dialogue in identity politics which necessarily cuts across any discussion about language, terminology and women. A black woman announces a separate identity in adopting womanism as a doctrine viable to her own experience as a black feminist, she could adopt 'black feminism' as an appellation appropriate to her situation as 'black activist', or even place a safe bet and identify with an 'intra-ethnic feminism'.[7] The very existence of all these terms is proof that even in the all-embracing universal world that Walker and her followers espouse, there is (and always will be) difference in black feminist identity. There is difference on two obvious counts. First, within the parameters of blackness, not all black women are the same. They are diverse politically, culturally, sexually; colour, caste and class-wise. Second, within the parameters of whiteness, black women are seen as different and identified as 'other'. The difference here is understood as a binary opposition. So, if a woman is black in, for instance, South Africa she is aware of her blackness as something other than 'coloured-ness'. White South African women are more aware of their whiteness than those in, for example, Britain (Harris, 1991). A woman only knows she is black or white because the woman next to her is non-black or non-white. Walker's view would incorporate elements of the latter notion of binary difference to acknowledge the difference between, for example, women who are 'capable' or have reached the point of understanding and those who are not (yet) 'womanist'. I recall Walker: 'Tradition *assumes*, because of our experiences during slavery, that black women already *are* capable' (1984b: 25). An example of the binary opposition is for the already capable woman calling herself 'capable' to be placed next to the white woman (against which she must define herself) who is not already 'capable'.

Explanatory of the first point, that not all black women are the same, is the philosophy of bell hooks who tells us that difference can emanate also from a historical praxis: 'Often professional black women with academic degrees are quite conservative politically. Their perspectives differ greatly from our foremothers, who were politically astute, assertive, and radical in their work for social change' (hooks, 1989: 181). Ladner has a similar and perhaps more concise approach: 'In discussing the black woman from a historical perspective, it is important to know that there is no monolithic concept of the black woman, but there are many models of black womanhood' (1985: 271). The diversity among black women can also be seen as integral to the structure of Filomina Chioma Steady's work. She writes,

> From the available literature it is already apparent that the black woman, within a cross-cultural perspective, represents much diversity in terms of nationality, class affiliation, generational differences, and particularly historical experience. The aim of this book is not to present a uniform profile or elicit a monolithic image.
>
> (Steady 1985: 7)

In a pioneering presentation, *The Black Woman Cross-Culturally* (1985), from which the previous extract is taken, the anthology as a whole explores the different experiences of black women cross-culturally. Steady provides food for thought on what she considers to be 'true feminism'.[8] She says:

> True feminism springs from an actual experience of oppression, a lack of the socially prescribed means of ensuring one's well-being, and a true lack of access to resources for survival. True feminism is the reaction

which leads to the development of greater resourcefulness for survival and greater self-reliance.

Above all, true feminism is impossible without intensive involvement in production. All over the African Diaspora, but particularly on the Continent, the black woman's role in this regard is paramount. It can, therefore, be stated with much justification that the black woman is to a large extent the original feminist.

(Steady 1985: 36)

True feminism does imply an essentialism and exclusivity here: placing one kind of woman over and above another or others. This can propagate negative divisions and visibility within a woman-based, cross-cultural experience.[9] Conversely, Walker takes another angle on true feminism. For her feminism is true as in applicable to *all* women. She states: 'Feminism (all colors) definitely teaches women they are capable, one reason for its universal appeal' (1984b: 25). If this is the case, it is with some concern to discover that in the early 1980s some women of colour right here in Britain were not aligning themselves to feminism, but were instead opting for a separate black women's movement. This is explained in *The Heart of the Race* (Bryan *et al.*, 1985) and warrants a full citation:

We began to discuss our common experiences of racial and sexist oppression, and as we forge the links we were unknowingly laying the foundation of the Black Women's Movement which would emerge in the years to follow.

(Bryan *et al.* 1985: 148)

Following on from this is a statement from a member of the Brixton Black Women's Group:

A lot of people think black women began to challenge what was happening in mixed organisations because we were influenced by what was going on in the white women's movement. But I think we were influenced far more ... by what was happening in the liberation movements on the African continent ... although we had begun to form women's caucuses and women's study groups, what Samora Machel had to say about women's emancipation made a lot more sense to us than what Germaine Greer and other middle-class white feminists were saying. It just didn't make sense for us to be talking about changing life-styles and attitudes, when we were dealing with issues of survival, like housing, education and police brutality.

(Bryan *et al.* 1985: 148)

Does this view make imperative the western (as opposed to universal) need to re-term? What of the non-western black woman activist resident in the west? In an interview Buchi Emecheta states firmly,

I will not be called a feminist here, [England] because it is European, it is as simple as that, I just resent that. Otherwise, if you look at everything I do, it is what the feminists do, too; but it is just that it comes from Europe, or European women, and I don't like being defined by them.
(Emecheta in Granqvist and Stotesbury 1989: 19)

The views by black women are numerous. However the distinct differences within black feminist ideology remain distinct and, as such, perpetuate the divisions between different kinds of women, black and non-black.

The general fragmentation of the women's movement into splinter groups that focus on specific oppression (racism, anti-Semitism, homophobia, and so on) on the one hand, and concentrate on theoretical analyses of women's issues on the other, has had a knock-on effect within black women's movements. Here too, recognition and acknowledgement of difference in black women's cultures announce a stalemate: Giving voice to differences of opinion (an aspect that can disrupt or gel), exposes women activists as people who are different from one another. Their difference is, of course, not just because of their genders, their classes, their mobilities, or their nationalities,[10] but also because of the unsameness of their opinions: 'It is not only that there are differences between different groups of women, but that these differences are often also conflicts of interest' (Bhavnani and Coulson, 1986: 84).

In Britain, the fragmentation of OWAAD[11] and the struggles of pioneering black women's organizations, like the acclaimed Southall Black Sisters and the now defunct Brixton Black Women's Group in London, suggest that enthusiasm for a black woman-based politics has waned to a non-public presence. It would appear that a woman-based politics only exists within smaller groups who practise activism mainly on a local level. Pratibha Parmar looks back in retrospect to the mid-1980s. She writes:

It seems difficult to fathom where the optimism and stridency which many of us had who were active in the black women's movement has gone, and why. Where are the diverse black feminist perspectives which we felt were in the process of growth? And where, indeed, is the movement itself? In moments of despair, one wonders if those years were merely imagined.
(Parmar 1989: 55)

On the second point of the binary difference between black and white women there are two examples which elucidate the notion of 'otherness'. First, more than two decades ago, Toni Cade questioned the emerging white women's analysis of the black women's experience. She asked whether, as another experience, difference ought to be treated as equivalent:

How relevant are the truths, the experience, the findings of white women to black women? Are women, after all, simply women? I do not know that our priorities are the same, that our concerns and methods are the same, or even similar enough so that we can afford to deal with this new field of experts [white, female].

(Cade 1970: 9)

Second, Rosalyn Terborg-Penn has explored the outcome of recognizing difference between black and white women. In her article, 'Discrimination Against Afro-American Women in the Woman's Movement, 1830–1920' (1985), she suggests the difference between women in the early women's movement was compounded by the fact of race-consciousness: 'Not all Afro-American women sought to join racially integrated organisations. Some organised separate racial groups in response to common problems and to a common sense of identity' (1985: 302). It must be accepted then, that if all feminists are to be regarded as different though they travel similar paths, the theory of difference ought to connect with the experience of difference within a women-based movement. It could be said that the theory and the experience of difference are separate entities:

The dialogues that have been attempted have been concentrated more upon viable empirical differences that affect black and white women's lives than upon developing a feminist theoretical approach that would enable a feminist understanding of the basis of these differences.

(Carby 1982: 221)

All too often there is a preoccupation with the assertion of difference within the black (and white) woman activist's text. Once asserted, the recognition of difference leaves no space for a 'come back' to a position where a total reckoning of black and non-black women's work against oppression might begin. It sets the ball rolling toward negating sameness. So, in terms of theory, it can be claimed that acknowledging difference in theory begins with the realization of a political motive. That seed – the one that germinates in the black woman activist, grows, but in its roots there is a (feminist) theory based on recognizing difference which is particular but not necessarily exclusive to black women. This can be seen in early black British feminist theory.

Hazel Carby's then-controversial article, 'White Woman Listen!' (1982), was the beginning of a response to a 'theoretical development of a critique of white feminist theories' (Parmar, 1989: 31). Theories specific to challenging white feminism were present long before and are evident in the many letters and statements produced in nineteenth-century abolitionist literature. Black women fighting to be heard refused the offers by white women abolitionists (Harriet Beecher Stowe, for example) to shadow-write their misfortunes as the slave under-class. Instead black women wrote themselves a place in history. Harriet Jacobs' *Life as a Slave Girl – Written by Herself* (1987) testifies to their determination to be heard.

THE LANGUAGE OF DIFFERENCE: RECOGNIZING THE SELF

Taking the analysis of difference into the comparative subject area of language develops the theory of difference. It enables us to enhance and draw in interrelated themes without which a substantial and binding case for recognizing diversity could not be found. Language as a medium of communication finds itself as exigent and imperative when a belief is transcended into a movement. It would not be conducive to the development of a theory of difference for views which suggest a hierarchy of difference, such as the following, to be nurtured – 'The very language and style of the women's movement of the west is an admission of the women's belief that they are inferior to men' (John, quoted in Steady, 1985: 34). It would be essential that views on relative difference and the possibility of their existence be anticipated along with any other rash conclusions. For it is precisely the publicized views held by people that will dictate the continuance of the ideology that shapes the belief or movement. It is crucial to get the message across, enlighten potential followers and participants, work on manifestos and policies. These are the basic means for fostering whatever belief there is. These aspects need language as a vehicle. In the case of womanism, development of the term in language can only arise if it, as a doctrine, is successful in the transportation of its own meaning and is, therefore, meaningful (and viable) to its prospective supporters.

While difference exists between the black woman and the non-black woman, it also exists between a black woman and her *individual* black woman counterparts. The following linguistic interpretation given by Harland (1987) demonstrates the difficulty in finding a term within feminist language to suit all black and non-black women.

Harland[12] suggests that our ordinary methods of thinking are eventually taken over by the desire to think differently. A change from A to B in our understanding takes place in what Harland calls a 'superstructuralist' way, that is to say, the memory of a particular way of thinking is replaced and becomes more important than the memory of what *used* to be a particular way of thinking. Without entering into the complexities of linguistic analysis, what I want to pinpoint is the need to locate the purveyors of language within political frameworks particular to their set of beliefs. Change, which frames the construction of meaning, can be seen to alter language and thus perception. It is this need or desire felt by Walker and others toward a new politicized meaning which prompts the feeling of a 'habitual offering' of terminology. Words such as womanist show that meaning evolves from the experience of difference. There is nothing inherent or fixed in language. If the meaning of womanism came from the experience of exclusion from feminism then its identity as a term would depend on its difference *from feminism*. This is precisely how bell hooks has treated womanist as distinct from feminist: 'When I hear black women using the term "womanist", it is in opposition to the term feminist; it is viewed as constituting something separate from feminist politics shaped by white women' (hooks, 1989: 181). The existence of difference in whatever form, makes for enquiries into the need for homogeneous terminology which labels representative groups of people in society. Ironically the most obvious reason is for the purposes of differentiation, for example, so that one group can be differentiated from another.

The persistence of reductionist terminology cannot be linked to the pro-woman movement as it changes from suffragette to feminist to potential womanist. These defining terms exist in contemporary obscurity insofar as splits within the movement produce a hazy understanding of what the aims of each phase of the women's movement actually is or was. That labelling gives rise to a form of cohesion, and is used to stabilize and bind together a newly forming group or movement, suggests that the process of naming is integral and imperative to a society that dreams of development. To invent or adopt terminology to suit a proposed development is to trigger a development *per se*. The remaining question is then, to what extent can the development be sustained?

As a visibilizing process, terming becomes a metalanguage to be used for the voicing of ideas, the standing of ground and the assertion of potentially viable doctrines. In the black feminist or womanist case, it is used as a specifying tool for politicization. It spotlights the seeming desire to call oneself a name which has been chosen by a core of like-minded people. As the black woman's voice is created, be it on a plantation or in a palace, a distinct and recognizable term from which a belief can emanate becomes more important. It stands to reason that if the Self, the Black Self as it is termed, is not given voice within the conglomerating body-term of woman, then the force with which the Self is asserted becomes far more exigent. Consequently, the black woman's Self is shaped by an encounter with the languages of western patriarchal white discourses. The black woman is seen in terms of non-Self. That is, she is untermed, invisible – but not absent.[13]

Being defined in terms of the non-Self never remains a static position. For the condition of being untermed triggers a response among those who are deemed to have no power, a *demand* to be recognized by those in power; a demand that those with power recognize that they have it. It is, therefore, important to foster positive self-recognition in (and outside) the sphere of black feminisms.[14] However, Steady speaks of the black woman's predicament of how to valorize her many 'Selves'. It is neither uncommon nor an arbitrary claim to acknowledge multiple identities:

Several factors set the black woman apart as having a different order of priorities. She is oppressed not simply because of her sex, but ostensibly because of her race and, for the majority, essentially because of their [sic] class. Women belong to different socio-economic groups and do not represent a universal category.

(Steady 1985: 23–4)

FROM WOMANISM TO POST-BLACK FEMINISM

If I reject the notion of womanism the idea of a black feminism still remains. Black feminism remains current to the ideology of many black women in groups, organizations, and individually. Whether this is because womanism has not (yet?) been fully taken up, or whether it is perhaps used simultaneously with 'black feminism', I do not know. What I do know is that despite its relative demise, feminism has met with appreciation for a long time now. Feminism must change with the tide. Whether this is successful or not remains to be seen. Black feminism describes overall black women's activism within a socio-political structuring of black women's thinking. If a black woman wants to call herself 'Black-lesbian-feminist-warrior-poet' as Audre Lorde did, it is because of a desire to voice that which is personally and politically important as well as the almost desperate need to be recognized. In the Combahee River Collective, black women activists expand: 'A political contribution which we feel we [as black women] have already made is the expansion of the feminist principle that the personal is the political' (Combahee River Collective, 1983: 276).

If I embrace womanism and perhaps look to creating further terms to describe essentially black women's activism, the *sine qua non* of new terminology must be approached carefully. It is essential to ascertain the degree of cruciality and what particular *differences* the making of new terms warrant. Some might say that a change in terminology would be prophylactic to the progress of a core idea and struggle. In seeking to clarify the terms under which we struggle and succeed in the west, I have to say that the constant changing of terms can also impede the growth and development of the main aims and ideological development of a movement as well as of a people, never mind the erosion of fundamental racism.

If the focus for too long is on the terminology instead of what I call the inherent 'race-sexism' of feminism, the consequences point to serious circumvention of real change. Localizing the lesion where the black and white women's movements fail to adhere to their own principles of inclusion is to address the problem of adapting to a changing society directly and effectively. Understanding the 'problem' of circumvention can precipitate success. Perhaps the most valuable thing that came out of the birth of womanism was its direct challenge to white feminist racism.

It provided an instantaneous critique which some white feminists would find hard to ignore. But what worries me is that the term womanism could be used to further the distance between black and non-black women activists. How easy it would be to assume that the advent of womanism had absolutely nothing to do with anyone but black women, so that within a presumed homogeneous group of women it should stay.

The different and new ways that black women are organizing themselves (more focus on gaining higher education, fighting for better employment, better business opportunities and more improved domestic situations) seems to lead to a much needed expression and acknowledgement of an up-to-date feminism. The possibility of a post-black feminist ideology surfaces to co-join an era of post-modern ethics and theorizing. If feminism exists as 'post', then it could be said that it is still carved out of the present definition. However, there seems to be little point in term-proposal if there is no real demand. To ascertain a term's usefulness, questions must be asked. For example, if a term such as 'post' is agreed, what use, if any, will it have for the development of the movement? Does it make important moves, structurally, towards a specific and positive goal for black feminism? Does it advocate total rejection of prejudice – in a way that Walker's womanism does not clarify? Has the term been agreed collectively? Finally and crucially, does the goal of (black) feminism ultimately embrace a universal unity?

With white feminism's track record, it is not really surprising that younger generations are rejecting what they know older generations have been struggling with for decades. In an article in *The Chronicle of Higher Education* (1994), bell hooks talks about how 'most young black females learn to be suspicious and critical of feminist thinking long before they have any clear understanding of its theory and politics' (1994: A44). She goes on to say that,

> Even though feminist scholars like me have worked to create an inclusive feminist movement, one that acknowledges the importance of race and embraces black perspectives, many of today's black students seem to reject the entire idea of feminism ... Just as some black males hold on to macho stereotypes about maleness as a way of one-upping white men, whom they characterise as wimpy, some young black females feel that they finally can one-up white girls by insisting that they are already 'real' women, taking care of business, with no need of feminism.
>
> (hooks 1994: A44)

As someone who has 'followed' feminism for two decades, and as a victim of habit I, myself, cannot reject it. But I would favour more the idea of the inclusive feminist movement. I acknowledge the importance of discussing the adoption of more appropriate terminology, but alert the reader to the inevitable and eventual situation of a *fait accompli* in doing so. The preservation of the terminology 'feminism', like the preservation of homogeneous grouping such as 'Asian', 'Black' or 'African-Caribbean' ensures a strategic identity. Within black women's activism it ensures kudos and sets up a legitimate basis for organized action. Feminism is thus constructed not as a strict and impenetrable concept but as one which is pervious to change. If it embraces our differences it can also give rise to our strengths.

My proposal now is for a halt to further umbrella terms until there is more cohesion within especially British black women's networks. Womanist creativity and spirit as an appendage to black feminist activism does provide a much fuller text for feminists to work with. In conclusion, despite Walker having been 'hailed as a developer of the "womanist process"' (Pinckney, 1987: 18), an upsurge of womanist power and politics, and even spirituality, has yet to come to Britain.

Womanism might be to feminism what purple is to lavender, but it must be remembered that when lavender wanes annually from mid- to late summer, the first task of the western gardener is to lop off its purple flowers so as to benefit the lavender as a plant.

ACKNOWLEDGEMENTS

Along with Tina Papoulias, I also thank Tiz Cartwright and Heidi Safia Mirza for persuading me to revive this essay.

NOTES

1 This paper has been edited from the first time it was published as Occasional Paper no. 21, 1990, University of Kent.
2 The use of the term '(black) woman activist' is deliberate. It is not intended to replace or reject other terms such as 'black feminist'. It is a phrase to describe and convey (black) women's political involvement. The use in this paper of the words 'black' and 'non-black' is also deliberate. It is my preference for clarifying the issue of difference without adding confusion to an already complex debate. 'Black' for me means anyone who wishes to publicly call themselves black for reasons that are political or otherwise. And 'non-black' can mean white, or be appropriated to those who do not feel appropriated as 'black'. This is also a strategy (perhaps not the most effective) of resistance to the continual reading of "non-white" – as if most of the world operated on a white 'control' basis.
3 I am not using 'roots' in the usual sense as an originating source as I believe that there is no 'origin' as such. Roots, for myself, are the sources that extend *as far back as possible*. But it should be noted that seeds are subsumed as roots come into existence.
4 A dedication in Walker's *The Temple of My Familiar* (1989) displays a projection of the Self which is in juxtaposition with the environment, in a way that is politically suggestive, but evasive all the same. The last sentence under the

acknowledgments in *Temple* says, 'I thank the Universe for my participation in Existence' (1989: 405).

5 To illustrate what I mean here, I use the following which is taken from Audre Lorde's presentation on 'The Uses of Anger: Women Responding to Racism' at the National Women's Studies Association Conference, Connecticut, 1981:

> After fifteen years of a women's movement which professes to address the life concerns and possible future of all women, I still hear in campus after campus, 'How can we address the issues of racism? No women of Color attended.' Or, the other side of that statement, 'We have no-one in our department equipped to teach their work.' In other words, racism is a Black woman's problem, a problem of women of Color, and only we can discuss it.
>
> (Lorde 1984: 125)

6 See (charles), H. (1992) 'Whiteness – The Relevance of Politically Colouring the "Non"', in H. Hinds, A. Phoenix and J. Stacey (eds) *Working Out: New Directions for Women's Studies*, London: Falmer.

7 Steady explains,

> since sexism exists in the black community as well, sexism is relevant to the black woman, although some aspects of its analysis can best be conducted within a framework of what I term 'intraethnic feminism' – that is, within the black group's experience.
>
> (Steady 1985: 3)

8 This is also taken up by Alexander (1989a).

9 The diversity of Steady's excellent essay-collection defies the unity promised in the title.

10 The pluralization of these issues is in recognition of the multiplicities of cultural make-up in the west today.

11 Organization of Women of Asian and African Descent. For a short historiography see Bryan *et al.* (1985: 164–81).

12 Because Harland's 'superstructuralist' thesis is taken from specific male-oriented sources it must be understood that his language pertains to something which does not include the feminist theorist. It is to be regarded differently and for illustrative purposes in conjunction with what I am arguing.

13 See Toni Morrison's *Playing in the Dark* (1992). She refers to this issue of the absence of blackness. She agues the narrative of whiteness is shaped by a fear of blackness – which is untermed but ever-present.

14 I pluralize this to illustrate that there are many varied possibilities of black women's activisms, whilst also pinpointing the necessity of a viable political option for black women.

REFERENCES

Alexander, V. (1989a) 'White Feminism/Black Womanism', *Camden Black Sisters Bulletin*, September, London.

Alexander, V. (1989b) 'Black Woman, Black Womanism: Repainting the Rainbow', *Camden Black Sisters Bulletin*, October, London.

Amos, V. and Parmar, P. (1984) 'Challenging Imperial Feminism', *Feminist Review*, Autumn, 17: 3–19.

Bhavnani, K. and Coulson, M. (1986) 'Transforming Socialist Feminism: The Challenge of Racism', *Feminist Review*, Spring, 22: 81–92.

Bryan, B., Dadzie., S. and Scafe, S. (1985) *The Heart of the Race*, London: Virago Press.

Cade, T. (ed.) (1970) *The Black Woman: an anthology*, New York: New American Library.

Carby, H. (1982) 'White Woman Listen! Black Feminism and the Boundaries of Sisterhood', in The Centre for Contemporary Studies *The Empire Strikes Back: Race and Realism in 70s Britain*, London: Hutchinson.

Carmen, Gail, Neena and Tamara (1984) 'Becoming Visible: Black Lesbian Discussions', *Feminist Review*, Autumn, 17: 53–72.

Combahee River Collective (1983) 'Combahee River Collective Statement', in B. Smith (ed.) *Home Girls*, New York: Kitchen Table, Women of Color Press.

Feminist Review (1987) *Sexuality*, London: Virago Press.

Francis, A. (1983) *The Black Triangle*, London: Seed Publications.

Fuss, D. (1989) *Essentially Speaking: Feminism, Nature and Difference*, London: Routledge.

Granqvist, R. and Stotesbury, J. (1989) *African Voices: Interviews with Thirteen African Writers*, Sydney: Dangaroo Press.

Harland, R. (1987) *Superstructuralism: The Philosophy of Structuralism and Post Structuralism*, London: Methuen.

Harris, M. (1991) '"Colour Me Purple": the white "would-be womanist" in search of community', unpublished paper, Women's Studies MA, University of Kent.

Higginbotham, E. B. (1992) 'African-American Women's History and the Meta-language of Race', *Signs: Journal of Women in Culture and Society*, vol. 17, no. 2: 251–74.

hooks, b. (1984) *Feminist Theory: From Margin to Center*, Boston: South End Press.

hooks, b. (1986) 'Political Solidarity Between Women', *Feminist Review*, Summer, 23: 125–38.

hooks, b. (1989) *Talking Back: Thinking Feminist Thinking Black*, London: Sheba Feminist Publishers.

hooks, b. (1994) 'Black Students Who Reject Feminism', *The Chronicle of Higher Education*, July 13.

Hull, G. T., Scott, P. B. and Smith, B. (1982) *But Some of Us Are Brave*, New York: The Feminist Press.

Jacobs, H. (1987) *Incidents in the Life of a Slave Girl: written by herself*, London: Harvard University Press.

Joseph, G. and Lewis, J. (1981) *Common Differences: Conflicts in Black and White Feminist Perspectives*, New York: Anchor/Doubleday.

Kazi, H. (1986) 'The Beginning of a Debate Long Due: Some Observations on Ethnocentrism and Socialist-feminist Theory', *Feminist Review*, spring, 22: 87–91.

Kramarae, C. and Treichler, P. A. (1985) *A Feminist Dictionary*, London: Pandora Press.

Ladner, J. A. (1985) 'Racism and Tradition: Black Womanhood in Historical Perspective', in F.C. Steady (ed.) *The Black Woman Cross-Culturally*, USA: Schenkman Books.

Lorde, A. (1984) *Sister Outsider*, New York: Crossing Press.

Mabey, R. *et al.* (eds) (1988) *The Complete Herbal*, London: Guild Publishing.

Mohanty, T. C. (1988) 'Under Western Eyes: Feminist Scholarship and Colonial Discourses', *Feminist Review*, Autumn, 30: 65–88.

Morrison, T. (1992) *Playing in the Dark: Whiteness and the Literary Imagination*, London: Harvard University Press.

Ngcobo, L. (1987) *Let It Be Told*, London: Virago Press.

Parmar, P. (1989) 'Other kinds of Dreams', *Feminist Review*, spring, 31: 55–65.

Piercy, M. (1976) *Woman on the Edge of Time*, London: Women's Press.

Pinckney, D. (1987) 'Black Victims, Black Villains', *New York Review*, 29 January: 17–20.

Ramdin, R. (1987) *The Making of the Black Working Class in Britain*, Hampshire: Wildwood House Ltd.

Segal, L. (1987) *Is the Future Female?*, London: Virago Press.

Smith, B. (ed.) *Home Girls: A Black Feminist Anthology*, New York: Kitchen Table: Women of Color Press.

Staples, R. (1985) 'Myth of the Black Matriarchy' in F.C. Steady (ed.) *The Black Woman Cross-Culturally*, USA: Schenkman Books.

Steady F.C. (1985) 'The Black Woman Cross-Culturally: An Overview' in F. C. Steady (ed.) *The Black Woman Cross-Culturally*, USA: Schenkman Books.

Terborg-Penn, R. (1985) 'Discrimination Against Afro-American Women in the Women's Movement, 1830–1920' in F.C. Steady (ed.) *The Black Woman Cross-Culturally*, USA: Schenkman Books.

Walker, A. (1984a) *In Search of Our Mothers' Gardens*, London: The Women's Press.

Walker, A. (1984b) *New York Times Magazine*, (interview) January 8: 25.

Walker, A. (1989) *The Temple of My Familiar*, London: The Women's Press.

Weedon, C. (1987) *Feminist Practice and Poststructuralist Theory*, London: Basil Blackwell.

Williams, F. (1996) 'Postmodernism, Feminism and the Question of Difference' in N. Parton (ed.) *Social Theory, Social Change and Social Work*, London: Routledge.

Index